D0212325

# Chinese Link

中 文 天 地
Zhōng　Wén　Tiān　Dì

## *Intermediate Chinese*

### Second Edition

| Level 2 | Part 1 |

吴 素 美
Sue-mei Wu

于 月 明
Yueming Yu

**Prentice Hall**

Boston　Columbus　Indianapolis　New York　San Francisco　Upper Saddle River
Amsterdam　Cape Town　Dubai　London　Madrid　Milan　Munich　Paris　Montréal　Toronto
Delhi　Mexico City　São Paulo　Sydney　Hong Kong　Seoul　Singapore　Taipei　Tokyo

*Executive Acquisitions Editor:* Rachel McCoy
*Editorial Assistant:* Noha Amer Mahmoud
*Executive Marketing Manager:* Kris Ellis-Levy
*Marketing Coordinator:* William J. Bliss
*Executive Editor, MyLanguageLabs:* Bob Hemmer
*Senior Media Editor:* Samantha Alducin
*Development Editor:* Judy Wyman Kelly
*Development Editor for Assessment:* Melissa Marolla Brown
*Media Editor:* Meriel Martinez
*Senior Managing Editor:* Mary Rottino
*Associate Managing Editor:* Janice Stangel
*Production Project Manager:* Manuel Echevarria
*Senior Manufacturing and Operations Manager, Arts and Sciences:* Nick Sklitsis
*Operations Specialist:* Brian Mackey
*Senior Art Director:* Pat Smythe
*Art Director:* Miguel Ortiz
*Text and Cover Designer:* Wanda España, Wee Design Group
*Cover Image:* Jochen Helle
*Full-Service Project Management:* Margaret Chan, Graphicraft Limited
*Printer/Binder:* LSC Communications
*Cover Printer:* LSC Communications
*Publisher:* Phil Miller

Credits and acknowledgments borrowed from other sources and reproduced, with permission, in this textbook appear on page xxiv.

Copyright © 2008, 2012 Pearson Education, Inc., publishing as Prentice Hall, 1 Lake St., Upper Saddle River, NJ 07458. All rights reserved. Manufactured in the United States of America. This publication is protected by Copyright, and permission should be obtained from the publisher prior to any prohibited reproduction, storage in a retrieval system, or transmission in any form or by any means, electronic, mechanical, photocopying, recording, or likewise. To obtain permission(s) to use material from this work, please submit a written request to Pearson Education, Inc., Permissions Department, 1 Lake St., Upper Saddle River, NJ 07458.

This book was set in 12/15 Sabon by Graphicraft Ltd., Hong Kong, and was printed and bound by Courier/Kendallville. The cover was printed by Courier/Kendallville.

Library of Congress Cataloging-in-Publication Data

Wu, Sue-mei, 1968–
   Chinese link : intermediate Chinese, level 2 / Sue-mei Wu, Yueming Yu = [Zhong wén tian dì / Wu Sumei, Yu Yueming]—2nd ed.
      p. cm.
   Includes index.
   Parallel title also in Chinese characters.
   ISBN 978-0-205-78280-2 (Level 2 : pt. 1)
   1. Chinese language—Textbooks for foreign speakers—English. I. Yu, Yueming, 1944– II. Title. III. Title: Intermediate Chinese. IV. Title: Zhong wén tian dì.
   PL1129.E5C4196 2012
   495.1'82421—dc22

                                                                              2010038322

Printed in the United States of America
6

**Prentice Hall**
is an imprint of

www.pearsonhighered.com

ISBN 10: 0-205-78280-9
ISBN 13: 978-0-205-78280-2

# 目錄 (目录)  CONTENTS

# 範圍和順序 (范围和顺序)
# SCOPE AND SEQUENCE

| Lessons & Topics 課程 & 主題 (课程 & 主题) | Objectives & Communications 教學目標 & 交際活動 (教学目标 & 交际活动) | Grammar 語法要點 (语法要点) | Idiom Story 成語故事 (成语故事) | Culture Link 文化知識 (文化知识) |
|---|---|---|---|---|
| **1**<br><br>**Moving to a New Place**<br>搬家(搬家)<br>*p. 1* | ■ Describe how to move to a new place<br>■ Describe the result of an action | I. The resultative complement (RC) 結果補語 (结果补语)<br>II. The resultative complement and 把 | The fox makes use of the tiger's majesty 狐假虎威 (狐假虎威) | **Culture Notes:** When you move: celebrations and taboos 中國人的搬家誌慶和禁忌 (中国人的搬家志庆和禁忌)<br><br>**Fun with Chinese:** Saying: 喬遷之喜 (乔迁之喜)<br><br>**Let's Go:** Residential area 住宅區 (住宅区) |
| **2**<br><br>**Experiencing Culture and the Arts**<br>文藝經驗 (文艺经验)<br>*p. 27* | ■ Describe an ongoing or past event<br>■ Describe a continuous state<br>■ Talk about different experiences | I. When two 了 co-occur, and review of the single 了<br>II. The aspect 著(着)<br>III. The experiential aspect 過(过) | Dongshi frowns to imitate Xishi 東施效顰 (东施效颦) | **Culture Notes:** The four Chinese classics 中國四大古典小說(中国四大古典小说)<br><br>**Fun with Chinese:** Saying: 隔牆有耳 (隔墙有耳)<br><br>**Let's Go:** Signs in the airport 機場入境/出境的告示 (机场入境/出境的告示) |

| Lessons & Topics 課程 & 主題 (课程 & 主题) | Objectives & Communications 教學目標 & 交際活動 (教学目标 & 交际活动) | Grammar 語法要點 (语法要点) | Idiom Story 成語故事 (成语故事) | Culture Link 文化知識 (文化知识) |
|---|---|---|---|---|
| **3** **Asking for Directions** 問路(问路) *p. 59* | ▪ Describe a measurement of length, distance, or weight ▪ Ask for and give directions ▪ Describe an unexpected or gradual change ▪ Hail a cab, pay your fare, and receive change | I. (有)多 + Adj. (How + Adj.?) II. Ask for and give directions: 往/向 + direction/ location + V. III. V. + 起來(起来) | Yugong (the foolish old man) moves the mountain 愚公移山 (愚公移山) | **Culture Notes:** China's new economic development zones 中國的新經濟開發區(中国的新经济开发区) **Fun with Chinese:** Saying: 拐彎抹角 (拐弯抹角) **Let's Go:** Airport arrival guidelines and procedures 機場入境須知及流程(机场入境须知及流程) |
| **4** **Hospitality** 請客和做客 (请客和做客) *p. 95* | ▪ Offering gifts properly and being a polite guest ▪ Receiving guests properly and being a good host ▪ Mealtime manners and proper etiquette ▪ Describing similarities and making comparisons | I. 比較(比较) Comparison (1): simple comparison sentences 簡單的比較句(简单的比较句) II. Comparison (2): relative, superlative, and emphatic degree 比較(比较), 最, 更 III. Comparison (3): gradual change 一天比一天 IV. Comparison (4): with emphasis 比 + ... 多了 | Inconsistent; self-contradictory 自相矛盾 (自相矛盾) | **Culture Notes:** Chinese hospitality: being a good host and a polite guest 中國人的好客, 請客和做客 (中国人的好客, 请客和做客) **Fun with Chinese:** Saying: 人逢喜事精神爽(人逢喜事精神爽) **Let's Go:** Airport departure guidelines and procedures 機場出境須知及流程(机场出境须知及流程) |

| Lessons & Topics<br>課程 & 主題<br>(课程 & 主题) | Objectives & Communications<br>教學目標 &<br>交際活動<br>(教学目标 &<br>交际活动) | Grammar<br>語法要點<br>(语法要点) | Idiom Story<br>成語故事<br>(成语故事) | Culture Link<br>文化知識<br>(文化知识) |
|---|---|---|---|---|
| **5**<br><br>**My Trip to China – Review**<br>我的中國行–<br>復習(我的中<br>国行–复习)<br><br>*p. 135* | ■ Make a report<br>■ Recall memories and past experiences | Grammar Review:<br>語法復習(语法复习)<br>I. Resultative complement (RC)<br>II. 把 sentences and the resultative complement<br>III. The aspects 了, 著(着), and 過(过)<br>IV. (有)多 + Adj. (How + Adj.?)<br>V. Ask for and give directions<br>VI. Comparison (1): simple comparison sentences<br>VII. Comparison (2): relative, superlative, and emphatic degree | Waiting for hares by the tree<br>守株待兔<br>(守株待兔) | **Culture Notes:**<br>Traveling in China<br>在中國旅行<br>(在中国旅行)<br>**Fun with Chinese:**<br>Saying: 趕鴨子上架(赶鸭子上架)<br>**Let's Go:** Hotel guest satisfaction survey<br>旅館賓客調查表(旅馆宾客调查表) |
| **6**<br><br>**Opening a Bank Account**<br>開銀行帳戶<br>(开银行账户)<br><br>*p. 165* | ■ Open a bank account<br>■ Describe interest and exchange rates | I. Various kinds of phrases<br>  A. Juxtaposed phrase<br>  B. Endocentric phrase<br>  C. Subject + V. phrase<br>  D. V. + Object phrase<br>II. Ways to express percentages and proportion<br>III. Decimals<br>IV. N./Pron. + 這兒/那兒(这儿/那儿) | A frog in a well<br>井底之蛙<br>(井底之蛙) | **Culture Notes:**<br>China's banking industry<br>中國的銀行業<br>(中国的银行业)<br>**Fun with Chinese:**<br>Saying: 三百六十行，行行出狀元。(三百六十行，行行出状元。)<br>**Let's Go:**<br>Bank deposit slip<br>銀行存款單<br>(银行存款单) |

| Lessons & Topics 課程 & 主題 (课程 & 主题) | Objectives & Communications 教學目標 & 交際活動 (教学目标 & 交际活动) | Grammar 語法要點 (语法要点) | Idiom Story 成語故事 (成语故事) | Culture Link 文化知識 (文化知识) |
|---|---|---|---|---|
| **7** **Traveling and Visas** 旅遊與簽證 (旅游与签证) *p. 201* | ■ Talk about possibility and feasibility ■ Describe how to get plane tickets and travel visas | I. Potential complement (PC) 可能補語 (可能补语) II. Questions with structural particles 嗎/呢(吗/呢) | Covering one's ears while stealing a bell 掩耳盜鈴 (掩耳盗铃) | **Culture Notes:** China: a multi-ethnic country 中國：一個多民族的國家 (中国：一个多民族的国家) **Fun with Chinese:** Saying: 四海之內皆兄弟(四海之内皆兄弟) **Let's Go:** Visa application form 簽證申請表 (签证申请表) |
| **8** **Chinese Movies** 中國電影 (中国电影) *p. 231* | ■ Talk about movies ■ Describe contrasts ■ Express personal opinions | I. Comparison (2) A. A 比 B + V. + degree of complement B. 比 + quantifier II. Emphatic pattern: 連……都/也…… (连……都/也……) III. Preposition 對(对) | Feeling complacent or extremely proud 得意洋洋 (得意洋洋) | **Culture Notes:** The movie industry in China 中國的電影事業(中国的电影事业) **Fun with Chinese:** Saying: 比上不足，比下有餘 (比上不足，比下有余) **Let's Go:** A movie ticket 電影票 (电影票) |

| Lessons & Topics 課程 & 主題 (课程 & 主题) | Objectives & Communications 教學目標 & 交際活動 (教学目标 & 交际活动) | Grammar 語法要點 (语法要点) | Idiom Story 成語故事 (成语故事) | Culture Link 文化知識 (文化知识) |
|---|---|---|---|---|
| **9** **Fitness and Health** 健身與健康 (健身与健康) *p. 267* | ■ Talk about fitness and health<br>■ Make comparisons | I. Comparison (3): 比 and the emphatic degree 更(要), 還(要) [更(要), 还(要)]<br>II. Progressive change 越來越…… (越来越……)<br>III. 越……越…… pattern | To add feet to a snake while drawing it 畫蛇添足 (画蛇添足) | **Culture Notes:** The culture of slimness and beauty in China 中國的瘦身美容業(中国的瘦身美容业)<br>**Fun with Chinese:** Saying: 人不可貌相(人不可貌相)<br>**Let's Go:** Weight-loss advertisement 瘦身廣告 (瘦身广告) |
| **10** **A Vacation in China – Review** 假期在中國–復習(假期在中國–复习) *p. 289* | ■ Make an oral report<br>■ Discuss plans | Grammar Review: 語法復習(语法复习)<br>I. Phrases<br>II. Percentages and proportions<br>III. Complements<br>IV. Comparison<br>V. Progressive change 越來越…… (越来越……)<br>VI. 越……越…… pattern | The arrogance of Yelang 夜郎自大 (夜郎自大) | **Culture Notes:** The Great Wall of China 中國的長城(中国的长城)<br>**Fun with Chinese:** Saying: 滿載而歸 (满载而归)<br>**Let's Go:** Bus guide 大巴指南 (大巴指南) |

## Appendices

## 前言 (前言)  PREFACE

**CHINESE LINK: Zhongwen Tiandi 中文天地** (Intermediate Chinese) serves as the intermediate level in the *Chinese Link*: 中文天地 program. This series systematically emphasizes and integrates the "5Cs" principles of the National Standards for Foreign Language Education—Communication, Cultures, Comparisons, Connections, and Communities—throughout the program.

The intermediate curriculum encompasses 20 lessons. It is designed to be completed in an academic year of college-level study. This intermediate level program is designed to be well linked to the introductory level program by continuing to provide a practical, learner-centered, and enjoyable language and culture learning experience for intermediate level Chinese learners, as well as an efficient and comprehensive teaching resource for instructors.

While learners of Chinese at the intermediate level need to continue to build their mastery of commonly used vocabulary and grammatical structures, they also need to begin to train for advanced level language usage. Thus, there are two main goals for the intermediate level program:

1. The first goal is to continue to systematically build learners' abilities in the four skills of listening, speaking, reading, and writing so that they can reach the intermediate level of competence. The content and exercises in the intermediate level program build upon what has been studied in the introductory level program, gradually adding more sophisticated vocabulary and grammatical structures. Frequent consolidation and review exercises are included.

2. The second goal is to help the learners to get ready for advanced Chinese study by introducing formal and written expressions and increasing students' "media literacy." This is accomplished by providing exposure to common Chinese idioms and the stories behind them, and by including texts written in the style of newspaper, magazines, and Internet news articles.

### What's New to this Edition

Thanks to the many instructors and students who provided valuable feedback on the first edition, the second edition incorporates several new features that we believe will make the materials more effective and easier to use. These new features are highlighted below:

### 1. In General

- Lessons have been revisited to provide greater balance among lessons, add more review and recycling of materials, enhance consistency, and emphasize student outcomes. More engaging and communicative exercises for learners have been added, and several of the Culture Notes have been updated.

## 2. Full-Color Design

- The use of a full-color design makes the text more appealing to today's learners by providing them with realistic images of China today and provides a clear delineation between various items within the chapter.

## 3. Lesson Opener

- Opening photos have been updated to show students more contemporary photos of China that also highlight the theme of the chapter.
- A new "Connections and Communities Preview" section has been added to help learners make connections to their daily life and build links among their communities. Questions focus on the lesson and Culture Link themes.

## 4. Sentence Patterns

- Key grammar points in the Sentence Pattern section are now highlighted to show the grammar in context and make it more explicit for the students.

## 5. Language Notes

- "Language Notes" are now in the margin next to the "Language in Use" dialogues, rather than in a separate section, to make them easier for students to reference while reading the dialogue.

## 6. Grammar

- Grammar explanations have been simplified to help learners more easily understand concepts.
- A new "Try it!" section has been added to provide guided communicative practice and reinforcement immediately following grammar presentation.

## 7. Supplementary Practice

- New questions have been added to aid students' reading comprehension of the supplementary texts.

## 8. Activities

- Activities have been updated and additional communicative activities have been added to the end of each chapter to support the aim of the text to help develop students' communicative competence.

## 9. Culture Notes

- Culture Notes, thematically linked to the content of the lesson, have been updated with new information and some new topics to ensure they will be of interest to today's students.
- A "Do You Know . . ." section of introductory questions has been added before the reading to engage student motivation, attention, and interest before reading the Culture Notes.
- Comparison questions following the reading help learners compare their own culture to Chinese culture and discuss the differences or similarities. Questions also encourage discussion on issues related to the readings and lesson's theme.

- Photos have been updated to present scenes related to the reading. Captions encourage students to reflect upon the information learned in the reading.

### 10. Fun with Chinese

- New activity questions have been added to highlight familiar words in the sayings and to help students to connect real-life situations with the sayings.

### 11. Let's Go!

- Information and activities have been updated to further the connection to the lesson's theme.

### 12. Student Activities Manual

- The *Student Activities Manual* incorporates listening, character, grammar, and comprehensive exercises into each lesson's homework.
- Situational dialogues have been created for each lesson to incorporate themes, expressions, and pragmatic settings of the lesson. Dialogues also contain some vocabulary and expressions that students have not yet studied.
- More challenging and authentic materials have been added to the listening exercises. The situational dialogues will challenge students from the very beginning and help them develop the skill of picking out useful information, even if they don't fully understand everything they hear. This helps develop an important survival skill for students who will encounter real life settings in Chinese societies through study abroad, travel, or interaction with Chinese communities in their own countries.
- A new "Progress Checklist" has been added to the end of each SAM chapter so that students can monitor their progress and the accomplishment of lesson goals and language competencies in each lesson.

### 13. Character Book

- The character exercises have been put into a separate volume to make it more convenient and efficient for students to work with characters.
- The *Character Book* provides the Chinese characters for the core vocabulary in every lesson to help student practice writing chinese characters.
- Both traditional and simplified characters are included, thus making the learning of both forms easy for the students.
- Blank boxes are also included for students to practice writing the character.
- As a handy reference, four **types of glossaries** are provided in the Character Book: (1) By number of strokes; (2) By Lesson number; (3) Alphabetical by Pinyin; (4) Common Radicals.

### 14. MyChineseLab™

- My **MyChineseLab™**, part of the award-winning Pearson's MyLanguageLabs™ suite, is a nationally hosted online learning system created for students and instructors of language courses. It brings together, in one convenient, easily navigable site, a wide array of language-learning tools and resources, including an electronic interactive version of the *Chinese Link* student text, *Student Activities Manual*, downloadable PDFs of the

*Character Book,* a file of the artwork in the text, and all materials from the audio programs. Readiness checks, chapter tests, and grammar tutorials personalize instruction to meet the unique needs of individual students. Instructors can use the system to make assignments, set grading parameters, listen to student-created audio recordings, and provide feedback on student work. Instructor access codes to MyChineseLab™ are available for purchase. Take a tour! Visit www.mylanguagelabs.com.

## Features of CHINESE LINK: 中文天地 (Intermediate Chinese)

- The **5Cs** (**National Standards**) are addressed consistently throughout the content, exercises, and homework in the intermediate level program.
- **Clearly and systematically linked** to the introductory level program. This helps Chinese learners reuse and review what they have learned, as well as continue to develop their skills in listening, speaking, reading, and writing for daily communication.
- **Topics** are selected to be **interesting and practical** from the students' point of view. Topics in the intermediate level program are expanded to **more abstract** and **more societal phenomena** to help learners better understand current Chinese society and be able to discuss, compare, and analyze cultural differences. Learners will also be exposed to various communicative situations that require them to develop and use skills such as basic summary, description, discussion, debate, and report.
- While equal emphasis is still given to both vocabulary and grammatical structures, students are guided to write **longer and more cohesive essays** in Chinese.
- Students learn to build from words and phrases, to sentences and cohesive passages, and then to application in **communicative tasks**.
- The **grammar points** and **core vocabulary** are presented naturally in the main texts. The main texts, in turn, provide model situations in which the grammar and vocabulary for each lesson are integrated into **realistic** communicative situations.
- Care has been taken to indicate regional differences in Chinese societies in expressions, pronunciation, and culture notes.

## Highlights of the Differences between the Introductory and Intermediate Level Programs

Much of the lesson structure and pedagogical strategy of the introductory program has been incorporated in the intermediate level program. Key differences between these programs are summarized below:

- In the intermediate level the texts and examples are provided in both traditional and simplified characters in order to accommodate different users' needs and preferences.
- In order to help the learners become accustomed to reading Chinese characters without phonetic transliteration, in the intermediate level the Pinyin has been removed from under the characters in the core lesson texts. However, a Pinyin version of Language In Use section has been placed in an appendix for reference.

- An *Idiom Story* passage is provided as an interesting way to introduce Chinese history and traditions and expose learners to important formal and written expressions. Exercises are provided and are designed to link the learner's comprehension of the text to his/her personal experiences and opinions.
- *Media Literacy* is promoted in the intermediate level textbook through various channels such as idiom stories and articles written in the style of newspapers, magazines, and the internet.
- Review lessons follow every two lessons. These are specifically designed as grammar summary, review, and consolidation lessons. They require learners to apply what they have learned to interesting and practical communicative situations.

## Organization of the Textbook

The intermediate level program is divided into two volumes: Level 2, Part 1 (Lesson 1 to Lesson 10) and Level 2, Part 2 (Lesson 11 to Lesson 20). Both volumes contain the **Core lessons** and **Appendices**.

### Core Lessons

- Lesson Opening: Lesson objectives, related photo, and *Connections and Communities Preview* section.

The major sections of each lesson are described below:

- Core Vocabulary: Core vocabulary terms, which appear in the **Language Link** section, are introduced here. For each vocabulary item, traditional and simplified character forms are presented along with Pinyin pronunciation, grammatical function, and English meaning. This section also points out differences between Mainland China and Taiwan usage.
- Language Link: This section contains situations that incorporate the lesson's core vocabulary and grammar points. It is accompanied by an art program that adds context and makes the lesson more interesting. **Language Link** serves as a model of the correct usage of the vocabulary and grammar points introduced in the lesson. Notes are provided to further explain the text. For most of the lessons, **Language Link** includes dialogues; for some selections it includes essays, diaries, e-mail, and letters. The length of **Language Link** is carefully controlled, and gradually increases to provide pedagogical sufficiency and challenge.
- Grammar: Core Grammar points from **Language Link** are explained in this section. A broad variety of more advanced grammar points and expressions is introduced in order to strengthen students' ability to express themselves in Chinese. The **Grammar** section contains many examples and summary tables to organize the information for students. The intermediate level program also emphasizes frequent and systematic **review**, **summarization**, and **consolidation** of grammatical structures throughout the content and exercises.
- Supplementary Practice: Each lesson has a **Supplementary Practice** section with themes, vocabulary, and grammar similar to those found in **Language Link**. This allows students to practice immediately what they have learned from their study of the main text. Care has

been taken to use a different format from that found in **Language Link**. For example, if **Language Link** contains a dialogue, **Supplementary Practice** will include a prose format, and vice versa. The pedagogical purpose is to help students learn to use vocabulary and grammar structures in varying forms of communication.

- **Idiom Story** is carefully chosen and written to consolidate the core grammar points of that lesson. Its purpose is to introduce students to the rich Chinese cultural and literary tradition while reviewing what they have learned in yet another interesting way.

- **Media Literacy** texts, which are incorporated into Lessons 11–20, are short texts written in the style of newspapers, magazines, and Internet news articles. These texts introduce students to the formal grammatical structures common in these written genres. **Exercises** in this section include text skimming, comparing written and spoken expressions, translation, and finding examples of the lesson's grammar points in the article. This section will not only promote students' media literacy skills, but will also give them motivation and confidence toward becoming life-long independent readers of Chinese.

- **Activities:** This section is designed primarily for classroom use. Listening, character, grammar, and communicative exercises are included throughout the text. Care has been taken to provide balance between structural drills and real-life communicative tasks. The exercises integrate with the grammar points to provide a systematic extension of usage skills from vocabulary-item level to sentence level and on to discourse-level narration and description. Since these exercises are for class meeting time, they are designed to be dynamic and interactive. Most involve interaction between instructor and students, student and student, or group and group. Communicative activities are based on situations designed to elicit the grammar points and vocabulary students have learned in the lesson and in prior lessons. Visual aids are provided to help set the context for the communicative activities. Our goal in providing classroom exercises is to help save instructor time, which makes the text convenient and efficient for instructors to use.

- **Culture Link:** This section contains three components:
  - **Culture Notes:** The topics of the **Culture Notes** are carefully chosen to relate to those of the core lessons. It is hoped that the **Culture Notes** will help students to better understand Chinese societies, as well as how language reflects culture. Authentic photos are provided to create a vivid and interesting learning experience. The discussion questions are designed to encourage students to discuss and compare cultural differences by helping them to be aware of the features of their own culture while gaining understanding of other cultures.
  - **Fun with Chinese:** This section introduces a common slang expression, an idiom, or a motto that either utilizes new vocabulary presented in the lesson or is closely related to the theme of the lesson. Drawings are included to help students better understand the content in an eye-catching way. Discussion questions are provided to offer another fun way to relate the common Chinese expressions to the theme of the lesson.
  - **Let's Go!:** This section gives students an opportunity to interact with Chinese in an authentic context. It assists the students to connect themselves to authentic Chinese societies and communities. This section promotes students' motivation and helps them develop survival skills for life in authentic Chinese societies.

### *Appendices*

The appendices serve as a learning resource for both students and teachers. They can also be used for review exercises in class or for self-study. The Appendices include the following:

- Traditional/Simplified Character Table
- English Translations of Language in Use
- Language in Use with Pinyin
- Glossaries (Pinyin and English)
- Characters in the Character Book

## Program Components

### *Instructor Resources*

### Instructor's Resource Manual

The **Instructor's Resource Manual** provides sample syllabi, daily schedules, and the answer keys for in-class and homework exercises. This manual is available for download on the Instructor Resource Center (IRC) and MyChineseLab to qualified adopters. Upon adoption or to preview the online resources, please go to PearsonSchool.com/Access_Request and select "Online Teacher Supplements." You will be required to complete a one-time registration subject to verification. Upon verification of educator status, access information and instructions will be sent via e-mail.

### Testing Program

A highly flexible testing program allows instructors to customize tests by selecting the modules they wish to use or by changing individual items. This complete testing program, available in electronic format via the IRC and MyChineseLab includes quizzes, chapter tests, and comprehensive examinations that tests speaking, reading, and writing skills as well as grammar, vocabulary, and cultural knowledge. For all elements in the testing program, detailed grading guidelines are provided.

### *Student Resources*

### Student Activities Manual

The **Student Activities Manual** contains homework assignments for each lesson in the main textbook. Homework activities are divided among listening, character recognition and writing, grammar exercises, and communicative tasks.

### Character Book

The **Character Book** provides the Chinese characters for the core vocabulary in every lesson. It shows the following for each character:

1. Character with its stroke order indicated by numbers.
2. Traditional form of the character.
3. Simplified form of the character.
4. Pinyin pronunciation, grammatical usage, and sample sentences or phrases.

5. Stroke order illustrated by writing the character progressively.
6. Radical of the character with its Pinyin pronunciation and meaning.
7. Dotted graph lines to aid students' practice.

Blank boxes are also included for students to practice writing the character. As a handy reference, four types of glossaries are provided in the Character Book: (1) By number of strokes; (2) By Lesson number; (3) Alphabetical by Pinyin; (4) Common Radicals.

## Audio Materials

The audio recording for all the lesson's texts, vocabulary, listening exercises, as well as listening exercises in the Student Activities Manual are provided in audio program either via the CW, CD's, or MyChineseLab.

## Online Resources

### Companion Web site, <www.pearsonhighered.com/chineselink>

This open-access robust site offers the resources to accompany the text, including parts of the audio program.

### MyChineseLab™

Over 200,000 students use the award-winning MyLanguageLabs online learning and assessment system to succeed in their basic language courses. If your instructor has required use of MyChineseLab, you will have online access to an eText, an interactive Student Activities Manual, audio and video materials, and many more resources to help you succeed. For more information or to purchase access, visit www.mylanguagelabs.com.

## 致謝 (致谢)　ACKNOWLEDGMENTS

We are very happy to complete the *Chinese Link*: 中文天地 (Intermediate Chinese), second edition. We would like to take this opportunity to thank many individuals who offered us support, suggestions, and encouragement, all of which led to the improvement and development of this edition.

We are especially grateful to the folks at Pearson Education's World Languages team for bringing their talent and professional publishing experience to the *Chinese Link* project. Many thanks to: Rachel McCoy, Executive Acquisitions Editor, for her commitment and confidence to the Chinese Link program; Phil Miller, Publisher, for his support of Chinese Link; and Noha Amer Mahmoud, Editorial Assistant, for helping with every aspect of preparing the revision and ensuring the manuscripts were ready for production. Mary Rottino, Senior Managing Editor, Janice Stangel, Associate Managing Editor, and Manuel Echevarria, Production Project Manager, have been wonderful conduits for channeling the vision of the second edition through development and into the final phase of production. Thanks also to Meriel Martinez, Media Editor, for carefully overseeing the production of the Audio program and Companion Web Site; Melissa Marolla Brown, Development Editor for Assessment, for providing guidance in preparing various manuscripts for MyChineseLab™; Samantha Alducin, Senior Media Editor, and Bob Hemmer, Executive Editor for MyLanguageLabs, for their skillful management of the excellent media products in MyChineseLab™; and Judy Wyman Kelly, Development Editor, who provided some suggestions that enabled this second edition to be more outstanding than the first. And a big thanks to our marketing team for their wonderful promotion of the second edition, Kris Ellis-Levy, Executive Marketing Manager, and William J. Bliss, Marketing Coordinator.

Our sincere appreciation goes to Margaret Chan, Project Manager, and her Graphicraft team members. Their hard work and dedication helped this project to reach final production. Thanks to Mark Haney for his assistance with English proofreading of the manuscript during the many different stages of preparation. With Mark's devotion and patience, the *Chinese Link* project moved along smoothly.

We wish to thank our families, without whose love and support this project would not have been possible. Many thanks to our husbands, Mark and Denny, for their patience and support. Thanks also to the *Chinese Link* Program lead author, Dr. Sue-mei Wu's children, Carrie, Marion, and baby Kevin, for their love and for giving up a lot of time with their mom so that this project could be completed.

We extend our sincere thanks and appreciation to the colleagues who reviewed the manuscript and provided valuable input. Their detailed comments and insightful suggestions helped us to further refine our manuscript.

Hsiu-hsien Chan – Yale University
Pei-Chia Chen – University of California, San Diego
Matthew B. Christensen – Brigham Young University

Doris Chun – City College of San Francisco

I-Ping Fu – Radford University & Virginia Tech

Wayne Wenchao He – The University of Rhode Island

Michael Gibbs Hill – University of South Carolina

Wenze Hu – US Naval Academy, MD

Alexander C. Y. Huang – Pennsylvania State University

Dela Xiao Jiao – New York University

Julia Hongwei Kessel – New Trier High School, IL

Wen-Chao Li – San Francisco State University

Hua-Fu Liu – San Jose City College

Weihsun Mao – Ohlone College

Kitty Shek – San Joaquin Delta College

Chao-mei Shen – Rice University, TX

Cindy Lee Shih – University of Arizona, Tucson

Mary-Ann Stadtler-Chester – Framingham State College, MA

Hongyin Tao – University of California, Los Angeles

Jean Wu – University of Oregon

Yun Xiao – Bryant University

John Yu – The City University of New York, Baruch College

Zheng-sheng Zhang – San Diego State University

Sue-mei Wu 吳素美, Ph.D.
Lead author of *Chinese Link*
Teaching Professor of Chinese Studies
Carnegie Mellon University

| | | | |
|---|---|---|---|
| Adj. | = adjective | 形容詞(形容词) [xíngróngcí] | e.g., 好 [hǎo] (good)<br>美 [měi] (beautiful) |
| Adv. | = adverb | 副詞(副词) [fùcí] | e.g., 很 [hěn] (very)<br>也 [yě] (also) |
| Aux. | = auxiliary verb (helping verb) | 助動詞(助动词) [zhùdòngcí] | e.g., 會(会) [hui] (can) |
| Conj. | = conjunction | 連詞(连词) [liáncí] | e.g., 可是 [kěshì] (but) |
| Int. | = interjection | 嘆詞(叹词) [tàncí] | e.g., 啊 [a] (Ah?) |
| M.W. | = measure word (or classifier) | 量詞(量词) [liàngcí] | e.g., 本 [běn] (used when counting books) |
| N. | = noun | 名詞(名词) [míngcí] | e.g., 老師(老师) [laoshī] (teacher)<br>書(书) [shū] (book) |
| Num. | = numeral | 數詞(数词) [shùcí] | e.g., 二 [èr] (two)<br>十 [shí] (ten) |
| Part. | = particle (word with grammatical function) | 助詞(助词) [zhùcí] | e.g., 嗎(吗) [ma] (a word that turns a sentence into a question) |
| Prep. | = preposition | 介詞(介词) [jiècí] | e.g., 在 [zài] (in; at)<br>從(从) [cóng] (from) |
| Pron. | = pronoun | 代詞(代词) [dàicí] | e.g., 你 [nǐ] (you)<br>他 [tā] (he) |
| V. | = verb | 動詞(动词) [dòngcí] | e.g., 學(学) [xué] (to study)<br>說(说) [shuō] (to speak)<br>跑 [pǎo] (to run) |
| V.O. | = verb + object | 動賓(动宾) [dòng bīn] | e.g., 說中文(说中文) [shuō Zhōngwén] (to speak Chinese) |
| V.C. | = verb + complement | 動補(动补) [dòng bǔ] | e.g., 搬過來(搬过来) [bān guò lái] (to move over)<br>打破 [dǎ pò] (to hit, broken) |

## 圖片供應者 (图片供应者) PHOTO CREDITS

**Cover photo:** David Mager\Pearson Learning Photo Studio; **page 1:** Mira.com/Artist Name; **page 24 (left):** Justin Guariglia/National Geographic Image Collection; **page 24 (right):** © Dorling Kindersley; **page 27:** Chen Chao © Dorling Kindersley; **page 51 (left):** Richard Nowitz/National Geographic Image Collection; **page 51 (right):** HARVEY LLOYD\Getty Images, Inc.—Taxi; **page 59:** Justin Guariglia/National Geographic Image Collection; **page 90 (left):** argus / Schwarzbach\Photolibrary/Peter Arnold, Inc.; **page 90 (right):** © Michael Yamashita/CORBIS; **page 95:** Justin Guariglia/National Geographic Image Collection; **page 124 (left):** Richard Nowitz/National Geographic Image Collection; **page 124 (right):** Chen Chao © Dorling Kindersley; **page 135:** Justin Guariglia/National Geographic Image Collection; **page 161 (top):** ? KEREN SU / DanitaDelimont.com; **page 161 (bottom):** ? KEREN SU / DanitaDelimont.com; **page 165:** Frans Lemmens\Photolibrary/Peter Arnold, Inc.; **page 194 (left):** Rob Crandall; **page 194 (right):** Jason Lee\CORBIS—NY; **page 201:** Chen Chao © Dorling Kindersley; **page 227 (left):** Keren Su / PacificStock.com; **page 227 (right):** © Walter Bibikow/Taxi/Getty Images, Inc.; **page 231:** TEH ENG KOON\Getty Images, Inc. AFP; **page 259 (top):** Reuters NewMedia Inc.\CORBIS—NY; **page 259 (bottom):** Mark Ralston\Getty Images, Inc. AFP; **page 267:** John Coletti\Creative Eye/MIRA.com; **page 286 (left):** Dominis, John\Photolibrary.com; **page 286 (right):** Getty Images; **page 289:** Colin Sinclair © Dorling Kindersley; **page 313 (top):** D E Cox\Getty Images Inc.—Stone Allstock; **page 313 (bottom):** Tony Waltham\Robert Harding World Imagery

# 搬家 (搬家)
# Moving to a New Place

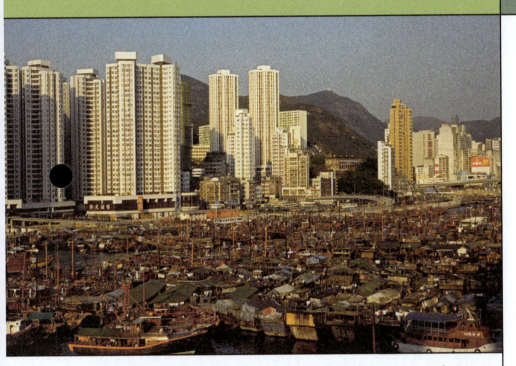

*There are many luxury high-rise apartments on the Hong Kong waterfront.*

## 教學目標 (教学目标) OBJECTIVES

- Describe how to move to a new place
- Describe the result of an action

### CONNECTIONS AND COMMUNITIES PREVIEW

Discuss the following questions with a partner or your class. What similarities and differences do you think there might be between Chinese culture and your own culture?

1. In your culture or community, what are the common customs associated with moving to a new place?

2. What are some specific ways that people celebrate moving in your culture or community?

# 生詞 (生词) VOCABULARY

## 核心詞 (核心词) Core Vocabulary

| TRADITIONAL | SIMPLIFIED | PINYIN | | |
|---|---|---|---|---|
| 1. 倒 | 倒 | dào | V. | to move backwards, to reverse |
| 2. 別 | 别 | bié | Aux. | don't |
| 3. 房東 | 房东 | fángdōng | N. | landlord |
| 4. 樹 | 树 | shù | N. | tree |
| 5. 撞 | 撞 | zhuàng | V. | to collide with, hit, strike |
| 6. 壞 | 坏 | huài | Adj. | bad |
| 7. 呀 | 呀 | ya | Part. | (used at the sentence end to soften the tone) |
| 8. 小心 | 小心 | xiǎoxīn | Adj. V. | careful, cautious to be careful |
| 9. 鏡子 | 镜子 | jìngzi | N. | mirror |
| 10. 破 | 破 | pò | Adj. | broken |
| 11. 分工合作 | 分工合作 | fēngōnghézuò | | to collaborate by dividing up the work |
| 12. 主意 | 主意 | zhǔyi | N. | idea |
| 13. 負責 | 负责 | fùzé | V. | to be responsible for |
| 14. 行李 | 行李 | xíngli | N. | luggage, baggage |
| 15. 放 | 放 | fàng | V. | to put, place |
| 16. 裝 | 装 | zhuāng | V. | to install, assemble; to load, pack |

| TRADITIONAL | SIMPLIFIED | PINYIN | | |
|---|---|---|---|---|
| 17. 掃 | 扫 | sǎo | V. | to clean, sweep |
| 18. 整理 | 整理 | zhěnglǐ | V. | to arrange, sort out |
| 19. 箱子 | 箱子 | xiāngzi | N. | box, case |
| 20. 衣服 | 衣服 | yīfu | N. | clothes |
| 21. 掛 | 挂 | guà | V. | to hang |
| 22. 累 | 累 | lèi | Adj. | tired, get tired of |
| 23. 請客 | 请客 | qǐngkè | V. | to act as the host, to treat |
| 24. 死 | 死 | sǐ | Adj.<br>V. | dead<br>to die |
| 25. 附近 | 附近 | fùjìn | N. | nearby |
| 26. 忘 | 忘 | wàng | V. | to forget |
| 27. 門 | 门 | mén | N. | door |
| 28. 窗 | 窗 | chuāng | N. | window |
| 29. 關上 | 关上 | guānshàng | V.C. | to close (door/window) |
| 30. 外套 | 外套 | wàitào | N. | coat |
| 31. 咱們 | 咱们 | zánmen | N. | we, us (when used by the speaker to include him/herself and the person(s) being spoken to) |

## 語文知識 (语文知识) LANGUAGE LINK

Read and listen to the following sentence patterns. These patterns use vocabulary, expressions, and grammar that you will study in more detail in this lesson. After reading the sentence patterns, read and listen to the Language in Use section that follows.

### 句型 (句型) Sentence Patterns

A: 讓我把車停在旁邊。
让我把车停在旁边。
Ràng wǒ bǎ chē tíng zài pángbiān.

B: 我先把我的車開走，你再把車
我先把我的车开走，你再把车
Wǒ xiān bǎ wǒde chē kāizǒu, nǐ zài bǎ chē

開過來。
开过来。
kāi guòlái.

A: 我負責把行李搬下來、放好。
我负责把行李搬下来、放好。
Wǒ fùzé bǎ xínglǐ bān xiàlái, fànghǎo.

B: 我來掃地、整理客廳，再把書放好。
我来扫地、整理客厅，再把书放好。
Wǒ lái sǎodì, zhěnglǐ kètīng, zài bǎ shū fànghǎo.

A: 這次搬家把你們累壞了。你們一定餓了！
这次搬家把你们累坏了。你们一定饿了！
Zhècì bānjiā bǎ nǐmen lèihuài le. Nǐmen yídìng è le!

B: 對呀！我快餓死了！
对呀！我快饿死了！
Duì ya! Wǒ kuài èsǐ le!

## 課文 Language in Use: My Friend Helps Me Move
## (繁體字 Traditional Character Version)

謝進學：　我們到了，讓我把車停在旁邊。

常天：　　等一會兒[1]，我先把我的車開走，你再把車開過來。

夏中明：　你在倒車的時候，我幫你看看，別把房東的樹撞壞了。

常天：　　對呀[2]！上次我們搬進來的時候，不小心把房東的鏡子打破了，真不好意思[3]。

謝進學：　我們先把床和書桌搬到樓上去，然後再分工合作，怎麼樣？

夏中明：　好主意，我負責把行李搬下來、放好，我也會把電腦裝好。

謝進學：　好，我來掃地、整理客廳，再把書放好。

常天：　　我來洗碗，把箱子打開，再把衣服掛好。

謝進學：　謝謝你們幫我的忙，這次搬家把你們累壞了。今天晚上想吃什麼？我請客！

常天：　　好極了！我快餓死了。

夏中明：　這附近有一家很不錯的中國飯館，可是我把地址忘了。

常天：　　沒關係，我有。你們看，我找到了。

謝進學：　太好了，讓我把門窗關上。

夏中明：　別忘了把外套穿上，咱們[4]走吧！

---

**1. 等一會兒(等一会儿)**

一會兒(一会儿) means "a moment."
等一會兒(等一会儿) means "Wait a moment." It means the same as "等一下兒(等一下儿)."

**2. 對呀!(对呀!)**

"Right!": a colloquial expression used to show agreement.

**3. 不好意思(不好意思)**

不好意思(不好意思) means "embarrassing" or "embarrassed." The phrase is used to comment on an occasion or behavior which makes people feel embarrassed. It is also commonly used to be polite when someone has done something for the speaker or the speaker has inconvenienced someone in some way.

**4. 咱們(咱们)**

咱們(咱们) is a very colloquial way to express "we," used by the speaker to include him/herself and the person(s) being spoken to.

## 课文 Language in Use: My Friend Helps Me Move
### (简体字 Simplified Character Version)

谢进学： 我们到了，让我把车停在旁边。

常天：　 等一会儿[1]，我先把我的车开走，你再把车开过来。

夏中明： 你在倒车的时候，我帮你看看，别把房东的树撞坏了。

常天：　 对呀[2]！上次我们搬进来的时候，不小心把房东的镜子打破了，真不好意思[3]。

谢进学： 我们先把床和书桌搬到楼上去，然后再分工合作，怎么样?

夏中明： 好主意，我负责把行李搬下来、放好，我也会把电脑装好。

谢进学： 好，我来扫地、整理客厅，再把书放好。

常天：　 我来洗碗，把箱子打开，再把衣服挂好。

谢进学： 谢谢你们帮我的忙，这次搬家把你们累坏了。今天晚上想吃什么? 我请客!

常天：　 好极了! 我快饿死了。

夏中明： 这附近有一家很不错的中国饭馆，可是我把地址忘了。

常天：　 没关系，我有。你们看，我找到了。

谢进学： 太好了，让我把门窗关上。

夏中明： 别忘了把外套穿上，咱们[4]走吧!

## 語法 (语法) GRAMMAR

### I. 結果補語 (结果补语) The Resultative Complement (RC)

The resultative complement (RC) indicates the result, extent, or goal of an action. It is formed by attaching an adjective or a verb directly to another verb. The RC should be regarded as a unit, and usually does not allow the insertion of another element.

| V. + Adj./V. | → | RC |
|---|---|---|
| 看　錯 (wrong) | → | 看錯 (wrong seeing) |
| 看　错 (wrong) | → | 看错 (wrong seeing) |
| 完 [wán] (finish) | → | 看完 (finish seeing) |
| 完 [wán] (finish) | → | 看完 (finish seeing) |
| 見 (perceive) | → | 看見 (see) |
| 见 (perceive) | → | 看见 (see) |

- The first verb 看 indicates the meaning. The following adjective (or verb) tells the result or goal of the first verb.
- The object and the aspect particle 了 usually occur after the complement. 沒(有)[没(有)] is used for its negation.

| Subject + RC + (Object) + (了) |
|---|

**Positive**

我看錯了。
我看错了。
I saw it wrong.

我看完書了。
我看完书了。
I finished reading the book.

我看見他了。
我看见他了。
I saw him.

**Negative**

我沒(有)看錯。
我没(有)看错。
I didn't see it wrong.

我沒(有)看完書。
我没(有)看完书。
I didn't finish reading the book.

我沒(有)看見他。
我没(有)看见他。
I didn't see him.

The following adjectives (or words) are commonly used as the complement in the RC structure.

| Adj./V. | Features | Examples |
|---|---|---|
| 完<br>完 | Indicates some work is finished by some action. | 看完　做完　寫完<br>看完　做完　写完 |
| 好<br>好 | Indicates the desired state of an action or completion of an action. | 坐好　拿好　放好<br>坐好　拿好　放好<br><br>收好　搬好　做好<br>收好　搬好　做好 |
| 到<br>到 | Indicates the continuation of an action to a certain point or a certain time. | 找到　看到　回到<br>找到　看到　回到 |
| 在<br>在 | Indicates that a person or thing ends up at a place as the result of an action. The 在 RC is followed by a place. | 放在　坐在　站在　住在<br>放在　坐在　站在　住在 |
| 上<br>上 | Indicates the completion of an action has brought about a certain result, such as coming together or being closed up. | 接 ([jiē]: to connect) 上　穿上<br>接上　　　　　　　穿上<br><br>關上　蓋 ([gài]: to cover) 上<br>关上　盖上 |
| 開<br>开 | Indicates the result of an action that moves an object away from its original position. | 打開　拿開　拉 ([lā]: to pull) 開　跑開<br>打开　拿开　拉开　　　　　　跑开 |
| 成<br>成 | Indicates that the items have become, become treated as, or become regarded in a certain way. | 換 ([huàn]: to exchange) 成　看成<br>换成　　　　　　　　　　看成<br><br>當 ([dàng]: to treat as) 成<br>当成<br><br>翻譯 ([fānyì]: to translate into) 成<br>翻译成 |
| **Aspect**<br>了<br>了 | Usually indicates a change of state, but is also commonly associated with the 把 structure. | 開了　看了　寫了　吃了<br>开了　看了　写了　吃了 |

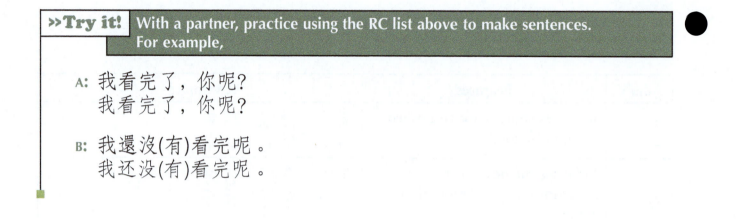

**≫Try it!**    With a partner, practice using the RC list above to make sentences. For example,

A: 我看完了，你呢?
我看完了，你呢?

B: 我還沒(有)看完呢。
我还没(有)看完呢。

## II. 把字句和結果補語的搭配 (把字句和结果补语的搭配)
### The Resultative Complement and 把

Since the RC indicates the result or influence of an action, it is often used with the 把 structure. Note that when the object is definite, the 把 structure is preferred. For example,

| Group A | Group B (with a definite object) |
|---|---|
| 我找到孩子了。<br>我找到孩子了。 | 我把你的孩子找到了。<br>我把你的孩子找到了。<br>I found your child(ren). |
| 孩子都搬到北京去了。<br>孩子都搬到北京去了。 | 我把我的孩子都搬到北京去了。<br>我把我的孩子都搬到北京去了。<br>I moved my children to Beijing. |
| 我打破了杯子。<br>我打破了杯子。 | 我把你的杯子打破了。<br>我把你的杯子打破了。<br>I broke your cup. |
| 我洗完衣服了。<br>我洗完衣服了。 | 我把你的衣服洗完了。<br>我把你的衣服洗完了。<br>I washed your clothes. |
| 我寫錯地址了。<br>我写错地址了。 | 我把他家的地址寫錯了。<br>我把他家的地址写错了。<br>I wrote the wrong address for his house. |
| 我裝好電腦了。<br>我装好电脑了。 | 我把弟弟的電腦裝好了。<br>我把弟弟的电脑装好了。<br>I set up my younger brother's computer. |

• The 把 structure is usually compulsory in the following situations:

| 把 Object ＋ V. 在/到 Place |
| --- |

*Examples:*

我把床搬到樓下。
我把床搬到楼下。
I moved the bed downstairs.

我把車停在河 ([hé]: river) 邊。
我把车停在河边。
I parked my car by the river.

我把他們送到機場了。
我把他们送到机场了。
I took them to the airport.

**≫Try it!**　With a partner, use 把 and the RC to ask and answer questions. For example,

A: 誰把我的杯子打破了?
　　谁把我的杯子打破了?

B: 我把你的杯子打破了。
　　我把你的杯子打破了。

## 補充課文 (补充课文) SUPPLEMENTARY PRACTICE

*Read the following passage. Then listen and repeat.*

### I Love My New Home! (繁體字 Traditional Character Version)

小文:

　　你好，忙嗎? 上星期我們搬到了一個新的地方，我們三個人分工合作，已經把家搬好了。我們還把室內重新安排了一下。本來一進門是一個大沙發，小謝說這樣不方便，有點兒窄，風水也不太好，所以我們就把那個大沙發搬到裡邊，還買了幾個盆栽放在窗戶的旁邊。

　　我們也把臥室裡邊的音響和電視都搬到客廳了。小謝說他還有幾張畫，明天要把那些畫掛上去，那麼，我們的客廳看起來就會寬敞舒服多了。

　　雖然搬家把我們累壞了，可是看到我們的新家，又整齊、又乾淨，心裡就覺得很高興。我們想來一個新居誌慶，想邀請你來參加，希望你能來。

祝

　　好

中明
九月三日

*Notes:*

室內(室内) [shìnèi]: indoor
重新(重新) [chóngxīn]: anew, afresh
安排(安排) [ānpái]: to arrange; arrangement
沙發(沙发) [shāfā]: sofa
不方便(不方便) [bùfāngbiàn]: inconvenient
窄(窄) [zhǎi]: narrow
風水(风水) [fēngshuǐ]: geomancy, fengshui
盆栽(盆栽) [pénzāi]: potted plant
音響(音响) [yīnxiǎng]: music system
寬敞(宽敞) [kuānchǎng]: spacious
整齊(整齐) [zhěngqí]: tidy
乾淨(干净) [gānjìng]: clean
新居誌慶(新居志庆) [xīnjū zhìqìng]: celebrations for moving to a new home
邀請(邀请) [yāoqǐng]: to invite; invitation

## 補充課文 (补充课文) SUPPLEMENTARY PRACTICE

*Read the following passage. Then listen and repeat.*

### I Love My New Home! (简体字 Simplified Character Version)

小文：

　　你好，忙吗？上星期我们搬到了一个新的地方，我们三个人分工合作，已经把家搬好了。我们还把室内重新安排了一下。本来一进门是一个大沙发，小谢说这样不方便，有点儿窄，风水也不太好，所以我们就把那个大沙发搬到里边，还买了几个盆栽放在窗户的旁边。

　　我们也把卧室里边的音响和电视都搬到客厅了。小谢说他还有几张画，明天要把那些画挂上去，那么，我们的客厅看起来就会宽敞舒服多了。

　　虽然搬家把我们累坏了，可是看到我们的新家，又整齐、又干净，心里就觉得很高兴。我们想来一个新居志庆，想邀请你来参加，希望你能来。

祝

　　好

中明<br>九月三日

### Exercises: work with a partner or in small groups

1. 他們是怎麼把室內重新安排一下的呢？
   他们是怎么把室内重新安排一下的呢？

2. 找出有下面語法的句子：the directional complement (DC), RC, and the 把 structure.
   找出有下面语法的句子：the DC, RC, and the 把 structure.

3. 用你自己的話再把這封信說一遍。
   用你自己的话再把这封信说一遍。

## 成語故事 (成语故事) IDIOM STORY

### 狐假虎威 (狐假虎威) [hú jiǎ hǔ wēi]

*Meaning:* The fox makes use of the tiger's majesty.

*Usage:* This is used to describe somebody who bullies the weak by flaunting his/her powerful connections.

*Example:* 他 "狐假虎威"，以為他爸爸是校長，搬新家的時候，
就叫老師們去幫忙。

他 "狐假虎威"，以为他爸爸是校长，搬新家的时候，
就叫老师们去帮忙。

Pay special attention to the DC, RC, and the 把 structure.

(繁體字 Traditional Character Version)

有一隻老虎餓了，牠走過來走過去，
要找東西吃，可是都找不到。後來牠看到
有一隻狐狸走過來了，就很快地跳上去，
把狐狸抓住了，牠要把狐狸吃了。

狐狸：你不可以吃我。
老虎：我為什麼不能吃你?
狐狸：天帝叫我下來管理所有的動
　　　物，你要是把我吃了，那就是
　　　不聽天帝的命令，天帝是會
　　　把你殺死的。
老虎：我才不相信你說的話呢!
狐狸：要是你不相信，你讓我起來，然後走在我的後面，你會看
　　　到很多動物都很怕我。

老虎聽了就把狐狸放開，走在狐狸的後面。牠們走進森林裡面，
狐狸很威風地走在老虎的前面，所有的動物一看到老虎都嚇壞了，
就很快地跑開了。老虎以為那些動物是真的怕狐狸，所以都跑開了。
狐狸就對老虎說：「現在你應該相信了吧!」老虎就把狐狸放了，自己
走開了。

(简体字 Simplified Character Version)

　　有一只老虎饿了，它走过来走过去，要找东西吃，可是都找不到。后来它看到有一只狐狸走过来了，就很快地跳上去，把狐狸抓住了，它要把狐狸吃了。

　　狐狸：你不可以吃我。

　　老虎：我为什么不能吃你？

　　狐狸：天帝叫我下来管理所有的动物，你要是把我吃了，那就是不听天帝的命令，天帝是会把你杀死的。

　　老虎：我才不相信你说的话呢！

　　狐狸：要是你不相信，你让我起来，然后走在我的后面，你会看到很多动物都很怕我。

　　老虎听了就把狐狸放开，走在狐狸的后面。它们走进森林里面，狐狸很威风地走在老虎的前面，所有的动物一看到老虎都吓坏了，就很快地跑开了。老虎以为那些动物是真的怕狐狸，所以都跑开了。狐狸就对老虎说：「现在你应该相信了吧！」老虎就把狐狸放了，自己走开了。

*Notes:*

成語故事(成语故事) [chéngyǔ gùshi]: idiom story

假(假) [jiǎ]: to make use of

威(威) [wēi]: prestige, majesty; 威(威) is an abbreviation for 威風(威风)

老虎(老虎) [lǎohǔ]: tiger

牠(它) [tā]: it (third person pronoun for an animal)

後來(后来) [hòulái]: later

狐狸(狐狸) [húli]: fox

抓住(抓住) [zhuāzhù]: to catch

天帝(天帝) [Tiāndì]: the Lord of the Heavens

管理(管理) [guǎnlǐ]: to rule, manage

所有的(所有的) [suǒyǒude]: all of . . .

動物(动物) [dòngwù]: animal

命令(命令) [mìnglìng]: order

殺死(杀死) [shāsǐ]: to kill

相信(相信) [xiāngxìn]: to believe

怕(怕) [pà]: to be afraid of, fear

森林(森林) [sēnlín]: forest

嚇壞(吓坏) [xiàhuài]: scared

以為(以为) [yǐwéi]: to think, to regard . . . as

那些(那些) [nàxiē]: those

對⋯⋯說(对⋯⋯说) [duì . . . shuō]: to tell, to talk to

放(放) [fàng]: to let go, to release

## Exercises: work with a partner or in small groups

1. 找出有下面語法的句子：the DC, RC, and the 把 structure.
   找出有下面语法的句子：the DC, RC, and the 把 structure.

2. 用你自己的話說說 "狐假虎威" 的故事。
   用你自己的话说说 "狐假虎威" 的故事。

3. 請用 "狐假虎威" 造一個句子或者說一個 "狐假虎威" 的例子。
   请用 "狐假虎威" 造一个句子或者说一个 "狐假虎威" 的例子。

4. "狐假虎威" 的故事，告訴了我們什麼？
   "狐假虎威" 的故事，告诉了我们什么？

# 練習（练习）ACTIVITIES

## I. Listening Exercises

**1-1**  In the blanks provided, write the Pinyin with tones for the words you hear, then check them with your partner.

1. 我們 _____ _____ _____ _____，把房子 _____ _____ _____ _____。
   我们 _____ _____ _____ _____，把房子 _____ _____ _____ _____。

2. 好 _____ _____，我 _____ _____ 把 _____ _____ _____ 好，
   也把 _____ _____ _____ 乾淨。
   好 _____ _____，我 _____ _____ 把 _____ _____ _____ 好，
   也把 _____ _____ _____ 干净。

3. 我 _____ 他家的 _____ _____ _____ 了。
   我 _____ 他家的 _____ _____ _____ 了。

4. 天氣 _____ 了，_____ 把外 _____ _____ _____。
   天气 _____ 了，_____ 把外 _____ _____ _____。

**1-2** Listen to the following passages and answer the questions. Then check them with your partner.

**第一段(第一段) [dìyī duàn] Passage 1:**

*Notes:*
其它(其它) [qítā]: other
家具(家具) [jiājù]: furniture
方便(方便) [fāngbiàn]: convenient
碰(碰) [pèng]: to hit, strike
花瓶(花瓶) [huāpíng]: vase
生氣(生气) [shēngqì]: to be angry

**第一段問題(第一段问题):**

1. 他們前天做什麼了？
   他们前天做什么了？

2. 他們先搬什麼？然後再搬什麼？
   他们先搬什么？然后再搬什么？

3. 小謝的房間在哪兒？搬東西的時候方便嗎？
   小谢的房间在哪儿？搬东西的时候方便吗？

4. 小謝的床大嗎？發生 ([fāshēng]: to happen) 了什麼事？
   小谢的床大吗？发生了什么事？

5. 房東太太生氣了嗎？
   房东太太生气了吗？

**第二段(第二段) [dì'èr duàn] Passage 2:**

*Notes:*
地毯(地毯) [dìtǎn]: carpet
乾淨(干净) [gānjìng]: clean
外賣(外卖) [wàimài]: (food) delivery
匹薩(匹萨) [pǐsà]: pizza
雞翅膀(鸡翅膀) [jīchìbǎng]: chicken wings
開始(开始) [kāishǐ]: to start
直到(直到) [zhídào]: until
半夜(半夜) [bànyè]: midnight

第二段問題(第二段问题):

1. 他們這次幫小謝搬家，累不累？餓不餓？
   他们这次帮小谢搬家，累不累？饿不饿？

2. 他負責做什麼？
   他负责做什么？

3. 小謝請他們吃飯了嗎？吃什麼？
   小谢请他们吃饭了吗？吃什么？

4. 他們整理到什麼時候才回家？
   他们整理到什么时候才回家？

## II. Character Exercises

**1-3** Work with a partner. Read the following words, phrases, and sentences.

| | |
|---|---|
| 壞 | 關 |
| 坏 | 关 |
| | |
| 撞壞了 | 關上 |
| 撞坏了 | 关上 |
| | |
| 把房東的樹撞壞了 | 把門窗關上 |
| 把房东的树撞坏了 | 把门窗关上 |
| | |
| 別把房東的樹撞壞了 | 讓我把門窗關上 |
| 别把房东的树撞坏了 | 让我把门窗关上 |

Now with your partner, try to use the following characters to make words, phrases, and then sentences.

1. 撞    2. 鏡    3. 破    4. 餓    5. 掛    6. 責    7. 裝    8. 掃
   撞       镜       破       饿       挂       责       装       扫

**1-4** Write down the traditional forms for the following simplified characters, then check your answers with a partner.

1. 房东 _____ _____          2. 树木 _____ _____

3. 镜子 _____ _____          4. 挂好 _____ _____

5. 饿死 _____ _____          6. 装坏 _____ _____

7. 负责扫地 _____ _____ _____ _____

**1-5**  With a partner or a group, create phrases with the following words (pay attention to the various usages of each word).

> *Example:*　塊：十五塊　　　一塊鏡子，一塊麵包，一塊蛋糕
> 　　　　　　块：十五块　　　一块镜子，一块面包，一块蛋糕

1. 開：_____　_____
   开：_____　_____

2. 客：_____　_____
   客：_____　_____

3. 近：_____　_____
   近：_____　_____

4. 停：_____　_____
   停：_____　_____

5. 分：_____　_____
   分：_____　_____

6. 床：_____　_____
   床：_____　_____

7. 意：_____　_____
   意：_____　_____

8. 地：_____　_____
   地：_____　_____

## III. Grammar Exercises

**1-6**  With a partner, rewrite the following sentences using 把.

1. 他寫完第三課的作業了。
   他写完第三课的作业了。

2. 他送一件襯衫給他女朋友。
   他送一件衬衫给他女朋友。

3. 媽媽洗了衣服。
   妈妈洗了衣服。

4. 弟弟打破鏡子了。
   弟弟打破镜子了。

5. 我的中文書忘在宿舍了。
   我的中文书忘在宿舍了。

6. 妹妹吃了藥了。
   妹妹吃了药了。

7. 姐姐穿上新裙子。
   姐姐穿上新裙子。

8. 哥哥幫我裝好電腦了。
   哥哥帮我装好电脑了。

9. 弟弟吃了我的蛋糕。
   弟弟吃了我的蛋糕。

10. 我室友洗好我的碗了。
    我室友洗好我的碗了。

11. 他打開那個箱子了。
    他打开那个箱子了。

12. 他餓死小狗了。
    他饿死小狗了。

**1-7**  In pairs or a group, role-play the following situation.

Picture talk: 去公園烤肉(去公园烤肉)

With the help of the clues provided, use DCs, RCs, and the 把 structure to describe the picture below.

*Notes:*
烤肉(烤肉) [kǎoròu]: to grill, barbecue
烤肉醬(烤肉酱) [kǎoròu jiàng]: barbecue sauce
烤爐(烤炉) [kǎolú]: barbecue grill
夾(夹) [jiā]: to pick up (with clips/tongs)
盤子(盘子) [pánzi]: plate
吃完(吃完) [chīwán]: to eat up
端(端) [duān]: to hold something level with both hands
收拾(收拾) [shōushi]: to tidy up

乾淨(干净) [gānjìng]: clean
垃圾(垃圾) [lājī]: trash (pronounced as [lèsè] in Taiwan)
垃圾桶(垃圾桶) [lājītǒng]: trash can (pronounced as [lèsètǒng] in Taiwan)

上個星期天，我們去烤肉，爸爸把車停在河邊……
上个星期天，我们去烤肉，爸爸把车停在河边……

_____

_____

_____

_____

_____

_____

_____

(1)     (2)     (3)

(4)     (5)

## IV. Communicative Activities

Situational dialogue:

**1-8    Situation 1:**

One of your friends is concerned about you. She/he tends to use a demanding tone to tell you what to do. (Perform this situation in groups of two or four. Each person should try to say at least five sentences.)

Use 把 sentences and DCs and RCs to form commands, such as:

整理房間，收拾好廚房，洗衣服，
別看電視，穿上大衣，洗碗，書放好，
搬好桌子，吃了午飯，吃飯，吃藥……

整理房间，收拾好厨房，洗衣服，
别看电视，穿上大衣，洗碗，书放好，
搬好桌子，吃了午饭，吃饭，吃药……

**1-9    Situation 2:**

You live with your younger brother in an apartment. Tomorrow the parents of your girlfriend/boyfriend are coming to see her/him. She/he will bring them over to meet you. You want your younger brother to help clean up the apartment so that they will have a better impression of you. Use 把 sentences and the resultative and directional complements.

**Scene 1:**    You and your younger brother are discussing the assigned tasks.

**Scene 2:**    You are talking while cleaning up.

**Scene 3:**    Two hours later, you and your younger brother are checking the apartment.

**Scene 4:**    The next day, the visitors arrive.

# 文化知識 (文化知识) Culture Link

## 文化點滴 (文化点滴) CULTURE NOTES

### 中國人的搬家誌慶和禁忌 (中国人的搬家志庆和禁忌)
### When You Move: Celebrations and Taboos

There are many traditional Chinese customs and practices related to moving. The purpose is to avoid bad luck and to bring good fortune to the new home.

First of all, it is very important to choose an auspicious date on which to move. People planning a move usually consult the lunar calendar, which indicates the dates that are good for performing certain activities such as weddings, funerals, moves, and travel. In general, moving and other auspicious events are not recommended during the lunar month of July, which is known as the "ghost month." It is believed that during this month ghosts are released and wander about. To appease them, people offer food and other sacrificial items.

A pregnant woman should avoid moving into a new home or moving/repairing any furniture in her bedroom, if possible, because the Chinese believe that the spirit of a fetus is not yet settled and might be scared by the move. In the event that a pregnant woman has to move or repair furniture, the area around the furniture should be swept with a broom before the move or the repair in order to avoid scaring the spirit.

> **Do you know...**
>
> - the Chinese cultural customs and practices related to moving?
> - why Chinese people generally avoid the lunar month of July for auspicious events?
> - how Chinese people celebrate a move?
>
> **Read and find out!**

Another important belief is that the first person to enter the new home should be the head of the household. Also, the home should always be entered from the front, not the back. When first entering the home, a broom should be carried inside not only to help sweep out dirt, but also to sweep out bad luck and anything old to make room for the new things that will be placed inside. Moreover, each time a person enters the new home they should carry something in with them. Stoves are another important item for a move. Often, small clay stoves will be lit and carried around the home in order to ward off evil spirits. The stove should be kept burning for a while to symbolize growth. The sparkle given off by the stove also represents wealth increasing. Finally, before everything is arranged in the new home, the owner may sometimes consult a fengshui expert to help determine the ideal arrangement of furniture in the home to maximize good fortune.

The owner of the new home will also pick a lucky day to host a celebration banquet. They will invite friends and family over to help celebrate the move. These celebrations are similar to holiday celebrations. Lots of food is prepared for the guests and tables are covered with red cloth, as red represents happiness, fortune, and prosperity. The guests generally bring cash in red envelopes or other gifts. Incense is often lit and firecrackers are set off to celebrate the move and to scare away any bad spirits that may be around the house.

A banquet held in a restaurant to celebrate a move. What do guests generally bring as gifts?

Firecrackers are set off to celebrate the move. Why?

**問題討論 (问题讨论)** *Discuss the following with a partner or in small groups.*

1. 在你們的文化或者其他文化中有沒有一些搬家誌慶和禁忌?
   請舉出一些例子。

   在你们的文化或者其他文化中有没有一些搬家志庆和禁忌?
   请举出一些例子。

   Are you familiar with any celebrations or taboos to do with moving in your culture or other cultures? Provide some comparative examples.

2. 你會想送你朋友什麼樣的搬家誌慶禮物 ([lǐwù]: gift)? 你想收到什麼樣的搬家誌慶禮物? 為什麼?

   你会想送你朋友什么样的搬家志庆礼物? 你想收到什么样的搬家志庆礼物? 为什么?

   What kinds of gifts would you like to give to, or receive from, your friends to celebrate a move? Why?

# 趣味中文 (趣味中文) FUN WITH CHINESE

喬遷之喜
乔迁之喜
Best wishes for your move to a new home.

| qiáo | qiān | zhī | xǐ |
|------|------|-----|-----|
| 喬 | 遷 | 之 | 喜 |
| 乔 | 迁 | 之 | 喜 |
| tall | move | (Particle) | happy event |

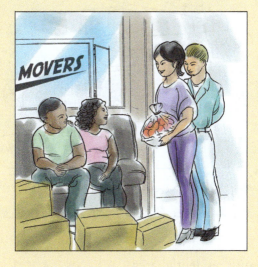

**問題討論 (问题讨论) *Discuss the following with a partner or in small groups.***

Do you know similar sayings in English or other languages that are used to congratulate people who have moved to a new home?

## 行動吧! (行动吧!) LET'S GO!

### 住宅區 (住宅区) Residential Area

常天 is visiting his friend's house in Shenzhen, Guangdong Province. This is a signpost at the entrance of the residential community where his friend lives.

*Notes:*

住宅區(住宅区) [zhùzhái qū]: residential area

蔚藍(蔚蓝) [wèilán]: sky blue

海岸(海岸) [hǎi'àn]: seashore

棕櫚(棕榈) [zōnglǚ]: palm

棟(栋) [dòng]: ridgepole (here it is used as a measure word for buildings)

社區(社区) [shèqū]: community

中心(中心) [zhōngxīn]: center

會所(会所) [huìsuǒ]: room, chamber

社康(社康) [shèkāng]: an abbreviation of 社區康樂(社区康乐) [shèqū kānglè] community entertainment

幼兒園(幼儿园) [yòu'ér yuán]: kindergarten

### 問題討論 (问题讨论) *Discuss the following with a partner or in small groups.*

1. Translate the following signs into English:

    (1) 2號會所 社康中心 (2号会所 社康中心)

    (2) 社區服務中心 (社区服务中心)

    (3) 棕櫚園1–3棟 (棕榈园1–3栋)

2. What is this residential community called? What facilities are provided for the community?

第二課 (第二课)
**LESSON**

**2**

文藝經驗 (文艺经验)

# Experiencing Culture and the Arts

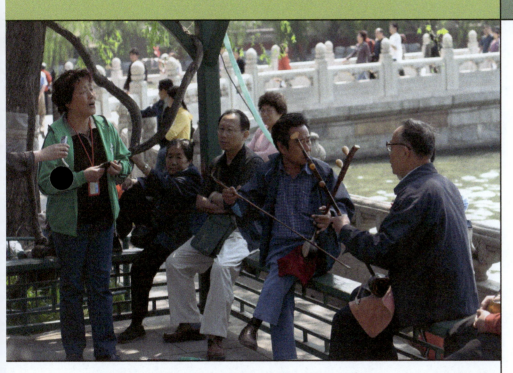

*Accompanied by some musicians, a woman sings Chinese opera in a Beijing park.*

## 教學目標 (教学目标) OBJECTIVES

- Describe an ongoing or past event
- Describe a continuous state
- Talk about different experiences

**CONNECTIONS AND COMMUNITIES PREVIEW**

Discuss the following questions with a partner or your class. What similarities and differences do you think there might be between Chinese culture and your own culture?

1. What are some typical cultural and arts events in your culture or community?

2. Describe how people participate in these events.

# 生詞 (生词) VOCABULARY

## 核心詞 (核心词) Core Vocabulary

| TRADITIONAL | SIMPLIFIED | PINYIN | | |
|---|---|---|---|---|
| 1. 牆 | 墙 | qiáng | N. | wall |
| 2. 著 | 着 | zhe | Part. | (indicates continuous or stationary status) |
| 3. 照片 | 照片 | zhàopiàn | N. | photograph, picture |
| 4. 服裝 | 服装 | fúzhuāng | N. | clothes |
| 5. 舞台 | 舞台 | wǔtái | N. | (performance) stage |
| 6. 擺 | 摆 | bǎi | V. | to place, put |
| 7. 各種 | 各种 | gèzhǒng | Adj. | various, all kinds of |
| 8. 樂器 | 乐器 | yuèqì | N. | musical instrument |
| 9. 演員 | 演员 | yǎnyuán | N. | actor or actress, performer |
| 10. 表演 | 表演 | biǎoyǎn | N.<br>V. | performance<br>to perform |
| 11. 樂師 | 乐师 | yuèshī | N. | musician |
| 12. 打 | 打 | dǎ | V. | to play (the drum); to hit |
| 13. 鼓 | 鼓 | gǔ | N. | drum |
| 14. 拉 | 拉 | lā | V. | to play (a stringed musical instrument); to pull |
| 15. 胡琴 | 胡琴 | húqín | N. | two-stringed bowed instruments |
| 16. 彈奏 | 弹奏 | tánzòu | V. | to play, pluck, strike |
| 17. 自己 | 自己 | zìjǐ | N. | oneself |

| TRADITIONAL | SIMPLIFIED | PINYIN | | |
|---|---|---|---|---|
| 18. 齣 | 出 | chū | M.W. | measure word (classifier) for Chinese theater performances |
| 19. 戲 | 戏 | xì | N. | play, drama |
| 20. 畫 | 画 | huà | V. N. | to paint, draw a painting |
| 21. 臉 | 脸 | liǎn | N. | face |
| 22. 拿 | 拿 | ná | V. | to hold, take |
| 23. 把 | 把 | bǎ | M.W. | measure word (classifier) for a utensil with a handle |
| 24. 刀 | 刀 | dāo | N. | knife |
| 25. 神氣 | 神气 | shénqì | Adj. | energetic, high-spirited, proud |
| 26. 座位 | 座位 | zuòwèi | N. | seat |
| 27. 滿 | 满 | mǎn | Adj. | full |
| 28. 觀眾 | 观众 | guānzhòng | N. | audience |
| 29. 站 | 站 | zhàn | V. | to stand |
| 30. 一言為定 | 一言为定 | yì yán wéi dìng | | it's a deal |

## 專名 (专名) Proper Nouns

| TRADITIONAL | SIMPLIFIED | PINYIN | | |
|---|---|---|---|---|
| 1. 李訪 | 李访 | Lǐ Fǎng | N. | (name) Fang Li |
| 2. 關明遠 | 关明远 | Guān Míngyuǎn | N. | (name) Mingyuan Guan |
| 3. 關公 | 关公 | Guān Gōng | N. | (name of a famous general in *The Romance of the Three Kingdoms*) |
| 4. 北京 | 北京 | Běijīng | N. | Beijing, the capital of China |
| 5. 長城 | 长城 | Chángchéng | N. | the Great Wall |

# 語文知識 (语文知识) LANGUAGE LINK

Read and listen to the following sentence patterns. These patterns use vocabulary, expressions, and grammar that you will study in more detail in this lesson. After reading the sentence patterns, read and listen to the Language in Use section that follows.

## 句型 (句型) Sentence Patterns

A: 你學中文學了多久了? (or 你學中文學了多長時間了?)
你学中文学了多久了? (or 你学中文学了多长时间了?)
Nǐ xué Zhōngwén xuéle duō jiǔ le? (or Nǐ xué Zhōngwén xuéle duō cháng shíjiān le?)

B: 我學中文學了兩年了。
我学中文学了两年了。
Wǒ xué Zhōngwén xuéle liǎngnián le.

*Notes:*
多久(多久) [duō jiǔ]: How long (duration of time)?
多長時間(多长时间) [duō cháng shíjiān]: How long (duration of time)?

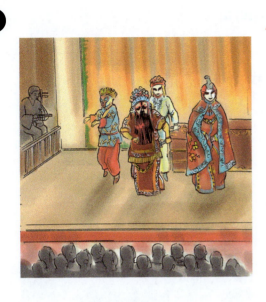

A: 演員正忙著表演，旁邊還
演员正忙着表演，旁边还
Yǎnyuán zhèng mángzhe biǎoyǎn, pángbiān hái

坐著幾個樂師。
坐着几个乐师。
zuòzhe jǐge yuèshī.

B: 人真不少啊！有的觀眾還得
人真不少啊！有的观众还得
Rén zhēn bùshǎo a! Yǒude guānzhòng hái děi

站著。
站着。
zhànzhe.

A: 你在中國的時候去過哪兒？
你在中国的时候去过哪儿？
Nǐ zài Zhōngguó de shíhòu qù guo nǎr?

B: 我只去過上海，可是沒去過北京
我只去过上海，可是没去过北京
Wǒ zhǐ qù guo Shànghǎi, kěshì méi qù guo Běijīng

和長城。
和长城。
hé Chángchéng.

🔊 **課文 Language in Use: My Sister Enjoys Beijing Opera!**
**(繁體字 Traditional Character Version)**

李訪：　那邊牆上掛著一張照片。那是誰？我好像沒見過。

關明遠：那是我姐姐照的照片。

李訪：　她現在在哪兒？

關明遠：她現在正在北京留學，她在那兒學中文，已經在那兒住了一年多了。

李訪：　她學中文學了多久了？

關明遠：她學了三年了。

李訪：　那是京劇的服裝吧！

關明遠：是的。這是她上個月去看京劇的時候照的照片。以前她沒看過京劇，現在看到了，她很高興。

李訪：　舞台上面擺著什麼？好像是中國的各種樂器。

關明遠：沒錯[1]！你看台上京劇演員，正忙著表演呢。旁邊還坐著幾個樂[2]師，有的[3]在打鼓，有的在拉胡琴，他們都忙著彈奏自己的樂器。

李訪：　這齣戲說的是什麼？好像很不錯。

關明遠：這齣戲說的是關公[4]。你看關公他畫著紅臉，手上拿著一把大刀，真神氣！

| 1. 沒錯(没错) |
| --- |
| 沒錯(没错) means "Correct!" or "What you said was correct." It is commonly used in a conversation to express agreement with what someone else has just said. |

| 2. 樂(乐) [lè, yuè] |
| --- |
| 樂(乐) has two pronunciations which have two different meanings:<br>快樂(快乐) [kuàilè]: happy, happiness<br>音樂(音乐) [yīnyuè]: music |

*Continued on page 34*

## 课文 Language in Use: My Sister Enjoys Beijing Opera!
## (简体字 Simplified Character Version)

李访：　那边墙上挂着一张照片。那是谁？我好像没见过。

关明远：那是我姐姐照的照片。

李访：　她现在在哪儿？

关明远：她现在正在北京留学，她在那儿学中文，已经在那儿住了一年多了。

李访：　她学中文学了多久了？

关明远：她学了三年了。

李访：　那是京剧的服装吧！

关明远：是的。这是她上个月去看京剧的时候照的照片。以前她没看过京剧，现在看到了，她很高兴。

李访：　舞台上面摆着什么？好像是中国的各种乐器。

关明远：没错1！你看台上京剧演员，正忙着表演呢。旁边还坐着几个乐2师，有的3在打鼓，有的在拉胡琴，他们都忙着弹奏自己的乐器。

李访：　这出戏说的是什么？好像很不错。

关明远：这出戏说的是关公4。你看关公他画着红脸，手上拿着一把大刀，真神气！

---

**3. 有的(有的)**

有的(有的) means "some part (of a group)."

e.g.: 中文課的學生都得學漢字。
中文课的学生都得学汉字。
All the students in the Chinese class have to learn Chinese characters.

有的(人)喜歡學繁體字，有的(人)喜歡學簡體字。
有的(人)喜欢学繁体字，有的(人)喜欢学简体字。
Some like learning traditional characters, others like learning simplified characters.

---

**4. 關公(关公)**

關公(关公) is one of the main characters in the well-known ancient Chinese historical novel 三國演義(三国演义) [*Sānguó Yǎnyì* (*The Romance of the Three Kingdoms*). 關公(关公) is known for his bravery, loyalty, and righteousness. He is also referred to as 關羽(关羽) [Guān Yǔ] or 關雲長(关云长) [Guān Yúncháng].

*Continued on page 35*

## 課文 Language in Use: My Sister Enjoys Beijing Opera!
## (繁體字 Traditional Character Version) —— 接第三十二頁

李訪： 人真不少啊！你看，座位都坐滿了，有的觀眾還得站著。
對了，你看過[5]京劇嗎？

關明遠： 我看過兩次，都是在上海看的。

李訪： 你在中國的時候去過上海，還去過哪兒？

關明遠： 我只去過上海。那時候，我每天都忙著上課，所以沒有機會去北京和長城[6]。

李訪： 我聽說上海的小籠包很好吃，你吃過嗎？

關明遠： 吃過，我還學過做小籠包呢！

李訪： 真有意思！我也想去中國看看。

關明遠： 我下個月要去中國，你跟我去吧！我們可以一起去看京劇，怎麼樣？

李訪： 好，一言為定！

---

**5. 過(过)**

過(过) has the following different usages:

1. As a verb, it means "to pass,"
   e.g.: 現在是三點過五分。
   现在是三点过五分。
   It is now 3:05.

2. As a verb, it means "to celebrate,"
   e.g.: 我昨天過生日。
   我昨天过生日。
   I celebrated my birthday yesterday.

3. As an aspect, it indicates past experience,
   e.g.: 我去過長城。
   我去过长城。
   I have been to the Great Wall.

## 课文 Language in Use: My Sister Enjoys Beijing Opera! (简体字 Simplified Character Version) —— 接第三十三页

李访：　人真不少啊！你看，座位都坐满了，有的观众还得站着。对了，你看过<sup>5</sup>京剧吗？

关明远：我看过两次，都是在上海看的。

李访：　你在中国的时候去过上海，还去过哪儿？

关明远：我只去过上海。那时候，我每天都忙着上课，所以没有机会去北京和长城<sup>6</sup>。

李访：　我听说上海的小笼包很好吃，你吃过吗？

关明远：吃过，我还学过做小笼包呢！

李访：　真有意思！我也想去中国看看。

> **6. 長城(长城)**
>
> 長城(长城) is the Great Wall, one of the greatest projects in world history. It was started during the Qin Dynasty (221–206 **B.C.**) and completed in the Ming Dynasty (1368–1644) to defend China from invasions by the Mongolians. It is said to be the only man-made structure on earth that can be seen from the moon.

关明远：我下个月要去中国，你跟我去吧！我们可以一起去看京剧，怎么样？

李访：　好，一言为定！

## 語法 (语法) GRAMMAR

### I. When Two 了 Co-occur, and Review of the Single 了

• A single 了 indicates a completed action. It is placed after a verb or at the end of the sentence.

|  | **Structure** | **Examples** |
|---|---|---|
| Question | 了嗎/了沒有<br>了吗/了没有 | 你吃飯了嗎? /你吃飯了沒有?<br>你吃饭了吗? /你吃饭了没有? |
| Affirmative Answer | V. + 了/sentence-end + 了 | 我吃了。<br>我吃了。 |
| Negative Answer | (還)沒有......呢<br>(还)沒有......呢 | 我還沒有吃呢。<br>我还没有吃呢。 |

• When two 了 co-occur, it usually indicates that the action is still ongoing at the moment of speaking.

*Examples:*

她學中文學了三年了。
她学中文学了三年了。
She has been studying Chinese for three years. (*Note:* She is still studying Chinese at the moment of speaking.)

他已經在這兒住了一年多了。
他已经在这儿住了一年多了。
He has lived here for over a year. (*Note:* He still lives here.)

我看了三本書了。
我看了三本书了。
I have read three books. (*Note:* It implies that I have read three books and there are more books for me to read.)

---

**»Try it!** | **With a partner, ask and answer the following questions.**

1. 你喜歡學什麼? 你學了多久了?
   你喜欢学什么? 你学了多久了?

2. 中文你學了幾年了?
   中文你学了几年了?

## II. The Aspect 著 (着)

著(着) is an aspect particle that is added to a verb to describe a state which is continuous or stationary.

*Examples:*

他穿著一件外套。
他穿着一件外套。
He is wearing a jacket. (*Note:* He has a jacket on.)

牆上掛著一張照片。
墙上挂着一张照片。
There is a picture hanging on the wall.

台上坐著幾個樂師。
台上坐着几个乐师。
There are a few musicians sitting on the stage.

V. + 著(着) is also used to provide the background to which an action is carried out.

*Examples:*

媽媽忙著做飯。
妈妈忙着做饭。
Mother is busy cooking.

觀眾站著看戲。
观众站着看戏。
The audience is watching the play while standing.

他們都忙著彈奏自己的樂器。
他们都忙着弹奏自己的乐器。
They are all busy playing their own instruments.

*Note:* The difference between 在 + V. and V. + 著(着) is that 在 indicates a dynamic action while 著(着) is stative. See the following examples:

他在穿外套。
他在穿外套。
He is putting a coat on.

他穿著外套。
他穿着外套。
He has a coat on.

**»Try it!** With a partner, take turns describing the settings, people, and so on, in the classroom. For example,

1. 老師穿著一件黑色外套。
   老师穿着一件黑色外套。

2. 老師站著上課。
   老师站着上课。

## III. The Experiential Aspect 過 (过)

The aspect 過(过) is added to a verb to indicate past experience (ever . . . before).

| Pattern | V. + 過(过) |
|---|---|
| Negation | 沒(有)[没(有)] + V. + 過(过) |
| Question | V. + 過(过)......沒有(没有)?<br>V. + 過(过)......嗎(吗)? |

*Examples:*

A: 你看過京劇沒有?
   你看过京剧没有?
   Have you (ever) seen Beijing Opera?

B: 我看過京劇。
   我看过京剧。
   I have seen it.

A: 你去過長城嗎?
   你去过长城吗?
   Have you (ever) been to the Great Wall?

B: 我沒(有)去過長城。
   我没(有)去过长城。
   I have never been to the Great Wall.

Since V. + 過(过) indicates past experience, it often co-occurs with time phrases that indicate the past, such as 以前, 去年, 上個星期(上个星期), etc.

我以前看過那本小説。
我以前看过那本小说。
I have read that novel before.

他兩年以前去過中國。
他两年以前去过中国。
He went to China two years ago.

我上個星期吃過他做的菜。
我上个星期吃过他做的菜。
I ate what he cooked last week.

**»Try it!** With a partner, take turns asking and answering questions about your experiences using 過 (过). For example,

1. A: 你去過中國嗎?
   你去过中国吗?

   B: 我沒去過中國，你呢?
   我没去过中国，你呢?

2. A: 你包過餃子嗎?
   你包过饺子吗?

   B: 我包過，你呢?
   我包过，你呢?

# 補充課文 (补充课文) SUPPLEMENTARY PRACTICE

*Read the following passage. Then listen and repeat.*

## My Sister's Letter (繁體字 Traditional Character Version)

親愛的明遠:

　　最近好嗎? 我已經在北京住了一年多了, 一切都很好, 請放心。

　　以前我沒有看過京劇, 上個月我和我的中國朋友去看了一齣, 很棒! 我們看的戲叫 "關公", 這些照片是在戲院照的。你看, 台上京劇演員穿著戲服忙著表演; 上面坐著幾個樂師, 他們都忙著彈奏自己的樂器。因為這齣戲特別有名, 所以來了很多觀眾, 座位都坐滿了, 有的觀眾還得站著看戲呢!

　　你聽說過關公嗎? 你可以在《三國演義》的小說裡找到很多他的故事。其中有一個很有名的故事叫 "桃園三結義", 書中寫著關公、劉備和張飛他們三個人結拜成為兄弟的故事。他們本來不認識, 後來遇見了, 談得非常高興, 決定要成為結拜兄弟。他們一起來到桃花園中, 手上拿著香, 一起發誓說 "不能同年同月同日生, 但願同年同月同日死"。然後他們三個人就一起打天下。這個故事非常好, 有機會你應該看看。爸爸媽媽好嗎? 請代我向他們問好。

祝

　　好

　　　　　　　　　　　　　　　　　　　　　姐 明華
　　　　　　　　　　　　　　　　　　　　　九月六日

Notes:

一切(一切) [yíqiè]: everything

放心(放心) [fàngxīn]: to feel relieved

有名(有名) [yǒumíng]: famous

小說(小说) [xiǎoshuō]: fiction

故事(故事) [gùshi]: story

桃園三結義(桃园三结义) [táoyuán sān jiéyì]: three men, Liu Bei, Guan Yu, and Zhang Fei have sworn in a peach orchard to be brothers.

劉備(刘备) [Liú Bèi]: Liu Bei, who later became ruler of the 蜀 [Shǔ] State (221–263 A.D.)

結拜(结拜) [jiébài]: to pledge to a sworn brotherhood

成為(成为) [chéngwéi]: to become

兄弟(兄弟) [xiōngdì]: brothers

本來(本来) [běnlái]: originally, initially

遇見(遇见) [yùjiàn]: to run into

結拜兄弟(结拜兄弟) [jiébài xiōngdì]: sworn brothers

桃花園(桃花园) [táohuā yuán]: peach orchard

香(香) [xiāng]: incense

發誓(发誓) [fāshì]: to swear

但願(但愿) [dànyuàn]: to wish

天下(天下) [tiānxià]: the world, on earth (literally, "under heaven")

代我向……問好(代我向……问好) [dài wǒ xiàng . . . wènhǎo]: send my regards to . . . , say hello to . . . for me

## 補充課文 (补充课文) SUPPLEMENTARY PRACTICE

*Read the following passage. Then listen and repeat.*

### My Sister's Letter (简体字 Simplified Character Version)

亲爱的明远:

　　最近好吗? 我已经在北京住了一年多了, 一切都很好, 请放心。

　　以前我没有看过京剧, 上个月我和我的中国朋友去看了一出, 很棒! 我们看的戏叫 "关公", 这些照片是在戏院照的。你看, 台上京剧演员穿着戏服忙着表演; 上面坐着几个乐师, 他们都忙着弹奏自己的乐器。因为这出戏特别有名, 所以来了很多观众, 座位都坐满了, 有的观众还得站着看戏呢!

　　你听说过关公吗? 你可以在《三国演义》的小说里找到很多他的故事。其中有一个很有名的故事叫 "桃园三结义", 书中写着关公、刘备和张飞他们三个人结拜成为兄弟的故事。他们本来不认识, 后来遇见了, 谈得非常高兴, 决定要成为结拜兄弟。他们一起来到桃花园中, 手上拿着香, 一起发誓说 "不能同年同月同日生, 但愿同年同月同日死"。然后他们三个人就一起打天下。这个故事非常好, 有机会你应该看看。爸爸妈妈好吗? 请代我向他们问好。

祝

　　好

　　　　　　　　　　　　　　　　　　　　姐 明华
　　　　　　　　　　　　　　　　　　　　九月六日

### Exercises: work with a partner or in small groups

1. 這封信是誰寫給誰的? 信上分成幾段 ([duàn]: passage, paragraph)?
   每一段的大意 ([dàyì]: outline) 是什麼?
   这封信是谁写给谁的? 信上分成几段? 每一段的大意是什么?

2. 照片上有什麼?
   照片上有什么?

3. 用你自己的話, 說說桃園三結義的故事。
   用你自己的话, 说说桃园三结义的故事。

## 成語故事 (成语故事) IDIOM STORY

### 東施效顰 (东施效颦) [Dōngshī xiào pín]

*Meaning:* Dongshi frowns to imitate Xishi.

*Usage:* It is used to describe somebody who imitates poorly, making the imitator appear even more awkward and unpleasant.

*Example:* 很多人喜歡小王的室友，小王想只要他室友做什麼，他就做什麼，他以為這樣，大家就會喜歡他了。結果 "東施效顰"，沒有一個人喜歡小王。

很多人喜欢小王的室友，小王想只要他室友做什么，他就做什么，他以为这样，大家就会喜欢他了。结果 "东施效颦"，没有一个人喜欢小王。

Pay attention to the aspects of the two 了，著(着), and 過(过).

### (繁體字 Traditional Character Version)

中國古代有一個美女叫西施。人人都喜歡看她，都說她很美。她有一個鄰居叫東施，東施長得很醜，沒有人說過東施漂亮。她們倆都在同一個村莊住了十幾年了。東施很羨慕西施，常常看著西施，模仿她。她以為這樣她就能跟西施一樣漂亮了。她常模仿西施，模仿了三年了，可是還是沒有人說過她漂亮。

西施以前得過心病。有一天，她的心很痛，她穿著一件很普通的衣服，摸著胸口，皺著眉頭，走出去看大夫。東施沒看過西施這樣做過，她覺得西施今天皺著眉頭的樣子特別好看，就想到一個好主意。她快快地跑回家去，換了一件跟西施一樣普通的衣服，然後她也學著西施摸著胸口，皺著眉頭，裝著心痛的樣子走在路上。可是，東施本來就不好看，她再皺著眉頭，裝著心痛的樣子就更醜了。別人看到她都嚇壞了，也都快快地躲開她。

(简体字 Simplified Character Version)

　　中国古代有一个美女叫西施。人人都喜欢看她，都说她很美。她有一个邻居叫东施，东施长得很丑，没有人说过东施漂亮。她们俩都在同一个村庄住了十几年了。东施很羡慕西施，常常看着西施，模仿她。她以为这样她就能跟西施一样漂亮了。她常模仿西施，模仿了三年了，可是还是没有人说过她漂亮。

　　西施以前得过心病。有一天，她的心很痛，她穿着一件很普通的衣服，摸着胸口，皱着眉头，走出去看大夫。东施没看过西施这样做过，她觉得西施今天皱着眉头的样子特别好看，就想到一个好主意。她快快地跑回家去，换了一件跟西施一样普通的衣服，然后她也学着西施摸着胸口，皱着眉头，装着心痛的样子走在路上。可是，东施本来就不好看，她再皱着眉头，装着心痛的样子就更丑了。别人看到她都吓坏了，也都快快地躲开她。

*Notes:*
東施(东施) [Dōngshī]: name of an ugly woman in ancient China
效(效) [xiào]: to imitate
矉(矉) [pín]: to frown (used in Classical Chinese); its counterpart in modern Chinese is 皺眉頭
　(皱眉头) [zhòu méitóu]: to frown
古代(古代) [gǔdài]: ancient times
西施(西施) [Xīshī]: name of a famous beauty in the Spring and Autumn period (around
　722–484 B.C.)
鄰居(邻居) [línjū]: neighbor
醜(丑) [chǒu]: ugly
村莊(村庄) [cūnzhuāng]: village
羨慕(羡慕) [xiànmù]: to envy
模仿(模仿) [mófǎng]: to imitate
心(心) [xīn]: heart (note: a heart as an organ is called 心臟(心脏) [xīnzàng])
普通(普通) [pǔtōng]: common
摸著胸口(摸着胸口) [mōzhe xiōngkǒu]: (a state of) to touch the chest
皺著眉頭(皱着眉头) [zhòuzhe méitóu]: (a state of) to frown
大夫(大夫) [dàifu]: doctor
裝著(装着) [zhuāngzhe]: (a state of) to pretend
嚇(吓) [xià]: frighten, scare
躲開(躲开) [duǒkāi]: to dodge, avoid

## Exercises: work with a partner or in small groups

1. 找出有下面語法的句子：the aspects of two 了，著，and 過。
   找出有下面语法的句子：the aspects of two 了，着，and 过。

2. 用你自己的話說說 "東施效顰" 的故事。
   用你自己的话说说 "东施效颦" 的故事。

3. 請用 "東施效顰" 造一個句子或者說一個東施效顰的例子。
   请用 "东施效颦" 造一个句子或者说一个东施效颦的例子。

4. "東施效顰" 的故事，告訴了我們什麼？
   "东施效颦" 的故事，告诉了我们什么？

# 練習 (练习) ACTIVITIES

## I.  Listening Exercises

2-1   In the blanks provided, write the Pinyin with tones for the words you hear, then check them with your partner.

1. 他在 ＿＿＿＿ ＿＿＿＿ 住了一年 ＿＿＿＿ 了。
   他在 ＿＿＿＿ ＿＿＿＿ 住了一年 ＿＿＿＿ 了。

2. ＿＿＿ 上 ＿＿＿＿ ＿＿＿ 一張 ＿＿＿ 片。
   ＿＿＿ 上 ＿＿＿＿ ＿＿＿ 一张 ＿＿＿ 片。

3. ＿＿＿ 台上面 ＿＿＿ 著各 ＿＿＿ 樂 ＿＿＿。
   ＿＿＿ 台上面 ＿＿＿ 着各 ＿＿＿ 乐 ＿＿＿。

4. 我沒去 ＿＿＿ 北 ＿＿＿ 和 ＿＿＿ ＿＿＿。
   我没去 ＿＿＿ 北 ＿＿＿ 和 ＿＿＿ ＿＿＿。

**2-2**　Listen to the following passages and answer the questions. Then check them with your partner.

*Notes:*
四川(四川) [Sìchuān]: Sichuan Province (in southwest China)
推薦(推荐) [tuījiàn]: to recommend
麻辣(麻辣) [málà]: numbing and spicy
擺(摆) [bǎi]: to put, place
魚缸(鱼缸) [yúgāng]: fish tank
麻婆豆腐(麻婆豆腐) [mápó dòufu]: hot and spicy tofu

問題(问题):

1. 他要介紹什麼?
   他要介绍什么?

2. 那個飯館的門上寫著什麼?
   那个饭馆的门上写着什么?

3. 牆上掛著什麼?
   墙上挂着什么?

4. 他什麼時候去? 他和誰去吃飯了?
   他什么时候去? 他和谁去吃饭了?

5. 麻婆豆腐怎麼樣? 好吃嗎?
   麻婆豆腐怎么样? 好吃吗?

## II. Character Exercises

**2-3**   Work with a partner. Read the following words, phrases, and sentences.

| | |
|---|---|
| 擺<br>摆 | 齣<br>出 |
| 擺著<br>摆着 | 一齣戲<br>一出戏 |
| 上面擺著樂器<br>上面摆着乐器 | 一齣關公的戲<br>一出关公的戏 |
| 舞台上面擺著各種樂器<br>舞台上面摆着各种乐器 | 這是一齣說關公的戲<br>这是一出说关公的戏 |

Now with your partner, try to use the following characters to make words, phrases, and then sentences.

1. 牆      2. 眾      3. 滿      4. 鼓      5. 拉      6. 畫      7. 彈      8. 臉
   墙          众          满          鼓          拉          画          弹          脸

**2-4**   Write down the traditional forms for the following simplified characters, then check your answers with a partner.

1. 摆各种乐器 _____ _____ _____ _____ _____

2. 观众 _____ _____

3. 看过 _____ _____

4. 神气 _____ _____

**2-5** With a partner or a group, create phrases with the following words (pay attention to the various usages of each word).

*Example:*　塊：十五塊　　　一塊鏡子，一塊麵包，一塊蛋糕
　　　　　　块：十五块　　　一块镜子，一块面包，一块蛋糕

1. 過：_____　　_____
　　过：_____　　_____

2. 裝：_____　　_____
　　装：_____　　_____

3. 公：_____　　_____
　　公：_____　　_____

4. 自：_____　　_____
　　自：_____　　_____

## III. Grammar Exercises

**2-6** Form pairs to ask/answer the following questions (remember to switch roles).

1. 你在這兒住了多久了？(or 你在這兒住了多長時間了？)
　 你在这儿住了多久了？(or 你在这儿住了多长时间了？)

2. 你學了多久的中文了？(or 你學了多長時間的中文了？)
　 你学了多久的中文了？(or 你学了多长时间的中文了？)

3. 你今天上了多久的課了？(or 你今天上了多長時間的課了？)
　 你今天上了多久的课了？(or 你今天上了多长时间的课了？)

4. 你已經學了多少漢字 ([hànzì]: Chinese character) 了？
　 你已经学了多少汉字了？

**2-7**   Picture talk:

With the help of the clues provided, use V. + 著(着) to describe 小李's love story. (Work in groups. Try to make at least eight sentences. Be creative!)

*Notes:*
聊(聊) [liáo]: to chat
躺(躺) [tǎng]: to lie down
情書(情书) [qíngshū]: love letter

(1)　　　　　　(2)　　　　　　(3)　　　　　　(4)

**2-8**   With a partner, use V. + 過(过) to conduct a conversation.

Pattern:　　V. + 過(过)
Negation:　沒(有)[没(有)] + V. + 過(过)
Question:　V. + 過(过)......沒有(没有)?
　　　　　　V. + 過(过)......嗎(吗)?

*Examples:*

A: 你看過京劇沒有?
　　你看过京剧没有?

B: 我看過，我已經看過三次京劇了。你呢?
　　我看过，我已经看过三次京剧了。你呢?

A: 我沒有看過京劇......
　　我没有看过京剧......

(去過中國、上海、北京、長城; 做過中國菜; 包過小籠包; 看過中國小說、電影......)

(去过中国、上海、北京、长城; 做过中国菜; 包过小笼包; 看过中国小说、电影......)

**2-9**   Talk about your experiences.

Ask your friends about their previous experiences. Form groups to discuss the following questions.

*Notes:*
漂亮(漂亮) [piàoliang]: pretty, beautiful
帥(帅) [shuài]: handsome
報告(报告) [bàogào]: report

你吃過的最好吃的菜是什麼菜? (你看過的最好的電影；你見過的最漂亮的女人/最帥的男人；你去過的最好玩的地方；寫過的最難的報告；上過的最有意思的課, etc.)

你吃过的最好吃的菜是什么菜? (你看过的最好的电影；你见过的最漂亮的女人/最帅的男人；你去过的最好玩的地方；写过的最难的报告；上过的最有意思的课, etc.)

## IV.  Communicative Activities

**2-10**  Work in groups. Use two 了, V. + 過(过), and V. + 著(着) to create a story.

(1)          (2)          (3)          (4)

**2-11**  報告(报告) [bàogào]: report:

Use two 了, V. + 過(过), and V. + 著(着) to report on your previous experiences (such as the most delicious dish you have ever had, the most interesting novel you have ever read, the most unforgettable person/event, etc.) (Each person should come up with at least 12 sentences.)

*Example:*
吃過的最好吃的菜，這是我看過的最有意思的小說，
見過的最好的人

吃过的最好吃的菜，这是我看过的最有意思的小说，
见过的最好的人

# 文化知識 (文化知识) Culture Link

## 文化點滴 (文化点滴) CULTURE NOTES

### 中國四大古典小説 (中国四大古典小说) The Four Chinese Classics

1. 三國演義(三国演义) [Sānguó Yǎnyì]: *The Romance of the Three Kingdoms*

2. 水滸傳(水浒传) [Shuǐhǔ Zhuàn]: *The Water Margin*

3. 西遊記(西游记) [Xīyóujì]: *Journey to the West*

4. 紅樓夢(红楼梦) [Hónglóu Mèng]: *The Dream of the Red Chamber*

**Do you know...**
- the four Chinese classics?
- the famous three characters who form a brotherhood in *The Romance of the Three Kingdoms* and what they promise?
- which novel features the Monkey King and what is his main task?

**Read and find out!**

China has a long and rich literary tradition. The four classic novels, 三國演義(三国演义) [Sānguó Yǎnyì], 水滸傳(水浒传) [Shuǐhǔ Zhuàn], 西遊記(西游记) [Xīyóujì], and 紅樓夢(红楼梦) [Hónglóu Mèng], are written in vernacular Chinese and are well known to most Chinese. They have had a great influence on Chinese literature and society, with their plots told over and over again through Chinese drama, theater, storytelling, folk performances, television series, and movies.

三國演義(三国演义) [Sānguó Yǎnyì] was written by 羅貫中(罗贯中) [Luó Guànzhōng] (1330–1440) during the 明 [Míng] Dynasty, and is based on actual events that happened near the end of the 漢(汉) [Hàn] Dynasty (220–280 A.D.). During this period, three kingdoms, 魏 [Wèi], 蜀 [Shǔ] and 吳(吴) [Wú], and their respective leaders, 曹操 [Cáo Cāo], 劉備(刘备) [Liú Bèi], and 孫權(孙权) [Sūn Quán], fought for the throne of the Han, each claiming direct lineage from the last Han emperor. The novel begins with 劉備(刘备), 關羽(关羽) [Guān Yǔ], and 張飛(张飞) [Zhāng Fēi] forming a brotherhood and swearing to endure the good and the bad together. The novel includes many well-known stories, including accounts of the strategic brilliance of 劉備(刘备)'s minister 諸葛亮(诸葛亮) [Zhūgě Liàng], and tales of 關羽(关羽)'s loyalty, courage, and bravery.

水滸傳(水浒传) [Shuǐhǔ Zhuàn] is generally believed to be written by 施耐庵 [Shī Nài'ān] (*ca.* 1296–1370). Set at the end of the Northern Song period (around the 13th century A.D.), it tells the stories of a group of heroes, 105 men and 3 women, who dare to struggle against evil. The heroes, who are thought to stand for the different classes of people, rise up against the oppression of corrupt and unjust officials. Although they do many good deeds helping the poor and fighting evil, they later surrender to the officials and work with them to fight invaders. In the end, most die or are badly hurt.

西遊記(西游记) [Xīyóujì] was written by 吳承恩(吴承恩) [Wú Chéngēn] (around 1500–1582 A.D.) during the Ming Dynasty. It tells the story of 唐三藏 [Táng Sānzàng], a monk who undertakes a journey to India to retrieve Buddhist holy texts. He is joined by three disciples along the way, 孫悟空(孙悟空) [Sūn Wùkōng] (the Monkey King), 豬八戒(猪八戒)[Zhū Bājiè] (a pig-headed fellow), and 沙悟淨(沙悟净) [Shā Wùjìng] (a reincarnated water creature). They encounter many adventures and together overcome 81 hardships. 孫悟空(孙悟空) uses his talents and skills to protect his master. In the end, all four companions are honored and become gods.

紅樓夢(红楼梦) [Hónglóu Mèng], an outstanding classic of the 清 [Qīng] Dynasty, was written by 曹雪芹 [Cáo Xuěqín] (1715–1763). It is generally assumed that the author drew on his own experiences and that his hero, 賈寶玉 (贾宝玉) [Jiǎ Bǎoyù], is a self-portrait. The novel chronicles the fall of the wealthy 賈(贾) clan, and the relationship of the clan's heir, 賈寶玉(贾宝玉), with two women, 薛寶釵(薛宝钗) [Xuē Bǎochāi] and 林黛玉 [Lín Dàiyù]. 賈寶玉 (贾宝玉)'s family believes that his marriage with 薛寶釵(薛宝钗) has been predetermined. 賈寶玉(贾宝玉) and 薛寶釵(薛宝钗) both wore the same jade pendant at birth, and 薛寶釵 (薛宝钗) has great social poise and would make a very good traditional Chinese wife. 賈寶玉(贾宝玉), however, is actually in love with 林黛玉, who is temperamental, sickly, and generally the opposite of 薛寶釵 (薛宝钗). After much pressure from his family, 賈寶玉(贾宝玉) enters into a very unhappy arranged marriage with 薛寶釵(薛宝钗). 林黛玉, hearing the bad news, falls ill and dies soon after. 賈寶玉(贾宝玉) is so distraught by this event that he runs away and becomes a monk.

A fighting scene from *The Water Margin*. The heroes are helping the poor by fighting corruption. Do you know any stories with similar themes?

"Ladies Portrait" is one of the major scenes in *The Dream of the Red Chamber*. Which love stories are most famous in your culture?

**問題討論 (问题讨论)** *Discuss the following with a partner or in small groups.*

1. 在西方小說中有沒有和四大中國小說相似的故事？
   在西方小说中有没有和四大中国小说相似的故事？
   Are there any Western novels which have stories similar to these four Chinese classics?

2. 在這四大古典小說中，哪一個故事是你最感興趣的？為什麼？
   在这四大古典小说中，哪一个故事是你最感兴趣的？为什么？
   Which story sounds most interesting to you? Why?

# 趣味中文 (趣味中文) FUN WITH CHINESE

隔牆有耳
隔墙有耳

(Literally) There are ears on the other sides of the wall –
it's difficult to keep a secret.

| gé | qiáng | yǒu | ěr |
|----|-------|-----|-----|
| 隔 | 牆 | 有 | 耳 |
| 隔 | 墙 | 有 | 耳 |
| partition | wall | have | ear |

**問題討論 (问题讨论)** *Discuss the following with a partner or in small groups.*

Are there similar sayings in English or in other languages? Provide some examples.

# ● 行動吧! (行动吧!) LET'S GO!

## 機場入境/出境的告示 (机场入境/出境的告示) Signs in the Airport

The following are common signs in airports. Let's study them together.

(1)

(2)

(3)

(4)

(5)                                                    (6)

(7)

*Notes:*
1.  入境(入境) [rùjìng]: arrival
    轉機(转机) [zhuǎnjī]: switch flights
2.  證照查驗(证照查验) [zhèngzhào cháyàn]: document check
    提領行李(提领行李) [tílǐng xíngli]: baggage claim
3.  等待線(等待线) [děngdài xiàn]: waiting line
4.  育嬰室(育婴室) [yùyīng shì]: nursery room
    淋浴室(淋浴室) [línyù shì]: shower room
    盥洗室(盥洗室) [guànxǐ shì]: toilet, restroom
5.  外幣兌換(外币兑换) [wàibì duìhuàn]: foreign-currency exchange
6.  登機門(登机门) [dēngjī mén]: boarding gate
7.  小客車(小客车) [xiǎokèchē]: van
    上車處(上车处) [shàngchēchù]: automobile boarding area
    計程車(计程车) [jìchéngchē]: taxi

# 復習 (复习) Review

## LESSON 1 TO LESSON 2

### I. Grammar

With a partner, use 把 and the following RCs to make sentences.

*Example:* 看完 → 我昨天把你借給我的那本英文小說看完了。
看完 → 我昨天把你借给我的那本英文小说看完了。

| Adj./V. | Features | Examples | | | |
|---|---|---|---|---|---|
| 完<br>完 | Indicates some work is finished by some action | 看完<br>看完 | 做完<br>做完 | 寫完<br>写完 | |
| 好<br>好 | Indicates the desired state of an action or completion of an action | 坐好<br>坐好<br><br>收好<br>收好 | 拿好<br>拿好<br><br>搬好<br>搬好 | 放好<br>放好<br><br>做好<br>做好 | |
| 到<br>到 | Indicates the continuation of an action to a certain point or a certain time | 找到<br>找到 | 看到<br>看到 | 回到<br>回到 | |
| 在<br>在 | Indicates that a person or thing ends up at a place as the result of an action. The 在 RC is followed by a place. | 放在<br>放在 | 坐在<br>坐在 | 站在<br>站在 | 住在<br>住在 |
| 上<br>上 | Indicates that the completion of an action has brought about a certain result, such as coming together or being closed up. | 接上<br>接上 | 穿上<br>穿上 | 關上<br>关上 | 蓋上<br>盖上 |
| 開<br>开 | Indicates the result of an action that moves an object away from its original position. | 打開<br>打开 | 拿開<br>拿开 | 拉開<br>拉开 | 跑開<br>跑开 |
| 成<br>成 | Indicates that the items have become, become treated, or become regarded in a certain way. | 換成<br>换成 | 看成<br>看成 | 當成<br>当成 | 翻譯成<br>翻译成 |
| 了<br>了 | Usually indicates a change of state, but is also commonly associated with the 把 structure. | 開了<br>开了 | 看了<br>看了 | 寫了<br>写了 | 吃了<br>吃了 |

## II. Activities

Form groups to conduct the following dialogue.

Topic: How did you clean up your apartment (with your roommate(s), or by yourself) last night? Use at least six sentences and remember to switch roles!

*Notes:*

拿走，搬過來，搬進去，搬到，負責，裝好，掃地，
整理，洗碗，打開，衣服，公寓，放好，門窗，關上，
分工合作，自己，乾淨，亂，髒

拿走，搬过来，搬进去，搬到，负责，装好，扫地，
整理，洗碗，打开，衣服，公寓，放好，门窗，关上，
分工合作，自己，干净，乱，脏

**A:** 昨天晚上你做什麼了？
昨天晚上你做什么了？

**B:** 昨天晚上我和我的室友把我們的公寓
整理乾淨了。
昨天晚上我和我的室友把我们的公寓
整理干净了。

**A:** 你們是怎麼整理你的房間的？
你们是怎么整理你的房间的？

**B:** 我們把……
我们把……

## III. Conversation

Form groups to ask/reply to the questions below.

*Examples:*

**A:** 你看過京劇沒有？
你看过京剧没有？

**B:** 我沒看過。你呢？
我没看过。你呢？

**A:** 我看過，很不錯。
我看过，很不错。

1. 你在這兒住了多久了?
   你在这儿住了多久了?

2. 你學了多久的中文了?
   你学了多久的中文了?

3. 你今天上了多久的課了?
   你今天上了多久的课了?

4. 你已經學了多少漢字了?
   你已经学了多少汉字了?

5. 你們吃過餃子嗎? 怎麼樣? 你包過餃子沒有?
   你们吃过饺子吗? 怎么样? 你包过饺子没有?

6. 你吃過最好吃的中國菜是什麼?
   你吃过最好吃的中国菜是什么?

7. 你上過最有意思的課是哪一門?
   你上过最有意思的课是哪一门?

8. 你去過最好玩的地方是哪兒?
   你去过最好玩的地方是哪儿?

9. 誰是你見過最難忘 ([nánwàng]: unforgettable) 的人? 為什麼 ([wèishénme]: why)?
   谁是你见过最难忘的人? 为什么?

10. 什麼是你碰到 ([pèngdào]: encounter) 過最難處理 ([chǔlǐ]: to deal with) 的一件事?
    什么是你碰到过最难处理的一件事?

## IV.  Picture Description

With your group apply 了, 著(着), and 過(过) to create a story.

## V.  Traditional and Simplified Characters

With a partner, read each character aloud. Write its traditional form and then make a phrase and a sentence using the character.

*Example:* 学 → 學 → 學生 → 我是學生

树 (　)　　坏 (　)　　挂 (　)　　墙 (　)　　着 (　)

摆 (　)　　种 (　)　　戏 (　)　　长 (　)

# 3

# 問路 (问路)
# Asking for Directions

The Peace Hotel 和平飯店(和平饭店) [Hépíng Fàndiàn], a historic landmark in Shanghai, is also a famous tourist attraction.

## CONNECTIONS AND COMMUNITIES PREVIEW

Discuss the following questions with a partner or your class. What similarities and differences do you think there might be between Chinese culture and your own culture?

1. What useful phrases are there in your language for asking for and/or providing directions?

2. Do you know of any economic development or historic preservation areas in your culture or community?

## 教學目標 (教学目标) OBJECTIVES

- Describe a measurement of length, distance, or weight
- Ask for and give directions
- Describe an unexpected or gradual change
- Hail a cab, pay your fare, and receive change

# 生詞 (生词) VOCABULARY

## 核心詞 (核心词) Core Vocabulary

| TRADITIONAL | SIMPLIFIED | PINYIN | | |
|---|---|---|---|---|
| 1. 往 | 往 | wǎng/wàng | Prep. | toward |
| 2. 各位 | 各位 | gèwèi | Pron. | everyone (a term used to address people) |
| 3. 旅客 | 旅客 | lǚkè | N. | traveler, passenger |
| 4. 降落 | 降落 | jiàngluò | V. | to land, descend |
| 5. 安全帶 | 安全带 | ānquándài | N. | seat belt, safety belt |
| 6. 繫上 | 系上 | jìshàng | V.C. | to tie, fasten, buckle up |
| 7. 計算機 | 计算机 | jìsuànjī | N. | computer |
| 8. 電子 | 电子 | diànzǐ | N. | electronics |
| 9. 用品 | 用品 | yòngpǐn | N. | product |
| 10. 搭乘 | 搭乘 | dāchéng | V. | to take (a means of transportation) |
| 11. 航空 | 航空 | hángkōng | N. | aviation, airline |
| 12. 出租 | 出租 | chūzū | V. | to rent |
| 13. 旅館 | 旅馆 | lǚguǎn | N. | hotel, hostel |
| 14. 路人 | 路人 | lùrén | N. | passerby |
| 15. 棟 | 栋 | dòng | M.W. | (measure word for buildings) |
| 16. 交叉口 | 交叉口 | jiāochākǒu | N. | intersection |
| 17. 左 | 左 | zuǒ | N. | left side |
| 18. 拐 | 拐 | guǎi | V. | to turn |
| 19. 一直 | 一直 | yìzhí | | straight |

| TRADITIONAL | SIMPLIFIED | PINYIN | | |
|---|---|---|---|---|
| 20. 路口 | 路口 | lùkǒu | N. | block, intersection, or a fork in a road |
| 21. 司機 | 司机 | sījī | N. | driver |
| 22. 假日 | 假日 | jiàrì | N. | holiday |
| 23. 公里 | 公里 | gōnglǐ | N. | kilometer |
| 24. 後車箱 | 后车箱 | hòuchēxiāng | N. | trunk (of a car) |
| 25. 發展 | 发展 | fāzhǎn | V.<br>N. | to develop<br>development |
| 26. 變化 | 变化 | biànhuà | V.<br>N. | to change<br>change |
| 27. 本來 | 本来 | běnlái | Adv. | originally |
| 28. 農田 | 农田 | nóngtián | N. | farmland; cropland |
| 29. 變成 | 变成 | biànchéng | V.C. | to become |
| 30. 馬路 | 马路 | mǎlù | N. | road, avenue, street |
| 31. 喔 | 喔 | ō | Int. | (used to indicate realization) |
| 32. 公尺 | 公尺 | gōngchǐ | N. | meter (measurement of length) |
| 33. 紅綠燈 | 红绿灯 | hónglùdēng | N. | traffic light |
| 34. 向 | 向 | xiàng | Prep. | toward |
| 35. 右 | 右 | yòu | N. | right side |
| 36. 轉 | 转 | zhuǎn | V. | to turn |
| 37. 小吃店 | 小吃店 | xiǎochīdiàn | N. | snack bar |
| 38. 彎兒 | 弯儿 | wār | N. | turn, detour |
| 39. 車費 | 车费 | chēfèi | N. | cab fare |
| 40. 找 | 找 | zhǎo | V. | to seek, look for; to give (change) |

## 專名 (专名) Proper Nouns

| | TRADITIONAL | SIMPLIFIED | PINYIN | | |
|---|---|---|---|---|---|
| 1. | 浦東 | 浦东 | Pǔdōng | N. | a place in Shanghai |
| 2. | 中山路 | 中山路 | Zhōngshānlù | N. | Zhongshan Road |
| 3. | 人民幣 | 人民币 | Rénmínbì | N. | RMB (name of currency used in mainland China) |

## 語文知識 (语文知识) LANGUAGE LINK

Read and listen to the following sentence patterns. These patterns use vocabulary, expressions, and grammar that you will study in more detail in this lesson. After reading the sentence patterns, read and listen to the Language in Use section that follows.

### 句型 (句型) Sentence Patterns

**A:** 坐出租汽車去有多快?
坐出租汽车去有多快?
Zuò chūzū qìchē qù yǒu duō kuài?

**B:** 很快,不到十分鐘就可以到了。
很快,不到十分钟就可以到了。
Hěnkuài, búdào shí fēnzhōng jiù kěyǐ dào le.

A: 請問，到出租汽車站怎麼走？
请问，到出租汽车站怎么走？
Qǐngwèn, dào chūzū qìchē zhàn zěnme zǒu?

B: 你從這兒往前走，走到前面
你从这儿往前走，走到前面
Nǐ cóng zhèr wǎng qián zǒu, zǒu dào qiánmiàn

的交叉口，往左拐。
的交叉口，往左拐。
de jiāochākǒu, wǎng zuǒ guǎi.

A: 中國看起來發展得很快。
中国看起来发展得很快。
Zhōngguó kàn qǐlái fāzhǎn de hěnkuài.

B: 是呀！這兒變得太快了！
是呀！这儿变得太快了！
Shì ya! Zhèr biàn de tài kuài le!

A: 車費多少錢？
车费多少钱？
Chēfèi duōshǎo qián?

B: 司機：一共是二十八塊人民幣。
司机：一共是二十八块人民币。
Sījī: Yígòng shì èrshíbā kuài Rénmínbì.

A: 給你三十塊。
给你三十块。
Gěi nǐ sānshí kuài.

B: 司機：找你兩塊，謝謝。
司机：找你两块，谢谢。
Sījī: Zhǎo nǐ liǎngkuài, xièxie.

## 課文 Language in Use: Visiting Shanghai
## (繁體字 Traditional Character Version)

**Scene 1:** 在飛機上

各位旅客，飛機再過二十分鐘就要降落了，我們就要到上海的浦東機場了。請您回到您的座位坐好，把安全帶繫上。請您也把計算機等電子用品關上。謝謝您的合作。再次感謝您搭乘中國航空。

**Scene 2:** 在機場

關明遠：  我們到了[1]，我們搭[2]出租汽車去旅館吧！搭出租汽車去快多了。

李訪：  搭出租汽車去有多快？

關明遠：  我想，不到十分鐘就可以到了。

李訪：  好的。我們來問路吧！

關明遠：  先生，對不起，請問，出租汽車站在哪兒？

路人：  出租汽車站在那棟[3]樓的後邊。你從這兒往前走，走到前面的交叉口，往左拐。從那兒再往前一直走，過兩個路口，你就能看到出租汽車站了。

關明遠：  謝謝。

路人：  不客氣。

| 1. 我們到了(我们到了) |
| --- |
| 我們到了(我们到了): literally means "We've arrived!" It can also be used colloquially to mean "Here we go!" |

| 2. 搭，乘，坐(車) [搭，乘，坐(车)] |
| --- |
| 搭(搭), 乘(乘), and 坐(坐) are verbs meaning "to take (a means of transportation)." 搭(搭) and 坐(坐) are commonly used in spoken Chinese, while 乘(乘) and 搭乘(搭乘) are more formal and used in writing. |

| 3. 棟(幢) [栋(幢)] |
| --- |
| 棟(栋) as a noun means "the main beam of a house." It is also used as a measure word (classifier) for buildings. For buildings, the measure word 幢(幢) [zhuàng] can also be used, meaning "a large beam used in a building of more than one story." |

**Scene 3:** 在出租汽車站

司機：  請問，兩位先生要搭車，是嗎？

關明遠：  是的，我們要去假日旅館，離這兒有多遠？

司機：  有三公里，不太遠，請上車。來，我先把行李放到後車箱去。

……

*Continued on page 66*

### 课文 Language in Use: Visiting Shanghai
### (简体字 Simplified Character Version)

**Scene 1:** 在飞机上

各位旅客，飞机再过二十分钟就要降落了，我们就要到上海的浦东机场了。请您回到您的座位坐好，把安全带系上。请您也把计算机等电子用品关上。谢谢您的合作。再次感谢您搭乘中国航空。

**Scene 2:** 在机场

关明远： 我们到了[1]，我们搭[2]出租汽车去旅 馆吧！搭出租汽车去快多了。

李访： 搭出租汽车去有多快？

关明远： 我想，不到十分钟就可以到了。

李访： 好的。我们来问路吧！

关明远： 先生，对不起，请问，出租汽车站 在哪儿？

Shanghai

路人： 出租汽车站在那栋[3]楼的后边。你 从这儿往前走，走到前面的交叉 口，往左拐。从那儿再往前一直 走，过两个路口，你就能看到出 租汽车站了。

关明远： 谢谢。

路人： 不客气。

**Scene 3:** 在出租汽车站

司机： 请问，两位先生要搭车，是吗？

关明远： 是的，我们要去假日旅馆，离这儿有多远？

司机： 有三公里，不太远，请上车。来，我先把行李放到后车箱去。

……

*Continued on page 67*

## 課文 Language in Use: Visiting Shanghai
## (繁體字 Traditional Character Version) —— 接第六十四頁

李訪： 中國看起來發展得很快。

關明遠： 是呀！這兒變得太快了！

司機： 聽起來你好像來過上海。

關明遠： 是的。我兩年前來過，可是現在有很多路我都想不起來了。

司機： 沒錯！上海變化得非常快，你看，本來這兒還都是農田，現在都變成大樓和大馬路了。

李訪： 你看，那棟樓真高，不知道有多高？

司機： 喔！那棟樓是新的，聽說有九十公尺高。

關明遠： 對了，我想起來了，那條是中山路。以前我常在那個紅綠燈等著過馬路，過了馬路以後我就向右轉，再走兩三分鐘，就到了上海小吃⁴店。那兒的東西好吃極了！

| 4. 小吃(小吃) |
|---|
| 小吃(小吃) refers to snacks, including noodles, wontons, dumplings, scallion pancakes, etc., all of which are readily available at small restaurants or from street vendors. |

司機： 假日旅館就在前面，可是我不能在這兒往左轉，我得多拐幾個彎兒。

李訪： 行，沒問題。

……

司機： 好，我們到了。

李訪： 車費多少錢？

司機： 一共是二十八塊人民幣。

關明遠： 給你三十塊。

司機： 找⁵你兩塊，謝謝！

| 5. 找(錢) [找(钱)] |
|---|
| 找(找) as a verb has two meanings: "to seek, to look for" and "to give (change) to." "找你兩塊錢(找你两块钱)" means "I'm giving you two dollars change." |

## 课文 Language in Use: Visiting Shanghai
(简体字 Simplified Character Version）—— 接第六十五页

李访：　中国看起来发展得很快。

关明远：是呀！这儿变得太快了！

司机：　听起来你好像来过上海。

关明远：是的。我两年前来过，可是现在有很多路我都想不起来了。

司机：　没错！上海变化得非常快，你看，本来这儿还都是农田，现在
　　　　都变成大楼和大马路了。

李访：　你看，那栋楼真高，不知道有多高？

司机：　喔！那栋楼是新的，听说有九十公尺高。

关明远：对了，我想起来了，那条是中山路。以前我常在那个红绿灯等
　　　　着过马路，过了马路以后我就向右转，再走两三分钟，就到了
　　　　上海小吃4店。那儿的东西好吃极了！

司机：　假日旅馆就在前面，可是我不能在这儿往左转，我得多拐几
　　　　个弯儿。

李访：　行，没问题。

　　　　……

司机：　好，我们到了。

李访：　车费多少钱？

司机：　一共是二十八块人民币。

关明远：给你三十块。

司机：　找5你两块，谢谢！

# 語法 (语法) GRAMMAR

## I. (有) 多 + Adj. (How + Adj.?)

(有) 多 + Adj. is a pattern used to ask about the degree of distance, length, speed, size, etc. It is similar to the English pattern "How + Adj." (for example "How far?" or "How fast?"). 有 is optional.

• Common adjectives for length, height, distance, speed, weight, and size.

| Length | 長(长) [cháng] (long) | 短(短) [duǎn] (short) |
|---|---|---|
| Height | 高(高) [gāo] (tall) | 矮(矮) [ǎi] (short) |
| Distance | 遠(远) [yuǎn] (far) | 近(近) [jìn] (close) |
| Speed | 快(快) [kuài] (fast) | 慢(慢) [màn] (slow) |
| Weight | 輕(轻) [qīng] (light) | 重(重) [zhòng] (heavy) |
| Size | 大(大) [dà] (big) | 小(小) [xiǎo] (small) |

• Common standard measures.

| | | |
|---|---|---|
| 公里(公里) [gōnglǐ] (kilometer) | 公尺(公尺) [gōngchǐ] 米(米) [mǐ] (meter) | 公分(公分) [gōngfēn] 厘米(厘米) [límǐ] (centimeter) |
| 英哩(英里) [yīnglǐ] (mile) | 英呎(英尺) [yīngchǐ] (foot) | 英吋(英寸) [yīngcùn] (inch) |
| 公斤(公斤) [gōngjīn] (kilogram) | 磅(磅) [bàng] (pound) | |

| How + Adj.? | (有)多 + Adj. | Example | English |
|---|---|---|---|
| How long? (length) | (有)多長? <br> (有)多长? | 長城(有)多長? <br> 长城(有)多长? <br><br> 長城有五千公里。 <br> 长城有五千公里。 | How long is the Great Wall? <br><br> The Great Wall is 5,000 kilometers long. |
| How long? (duration of time) | (有)多久? <br> (有)多久? | 你來這兒有多久了? <br> 你来这儿有多久了? <br><br> 我來這兒有兩年了。 <br> 我来这儿有两年了。 | How long have you been here? <br><br> I have been here for two years. |
| How tall? | (有)多高? <br> (有)多高? | 這棟大樓(有)多高? <br> 这栋大楼(有)多高? <br><br> 這棟大樓(有)五十英呎高。 <br> 这栋大楼(有)五十英尺高。 | How tall is the building? <br><br> This building is 50 feet tall. |
| How far? | (有)多遠? <br> (有)多远? | 這兒離飛機場(有)多遠? <br> 这儿离飞机场(有)多远? <br><br> 這兒離飛機場有十英哩。 <br> 这儿离飞机场有十英里。 | How far is it from here to the airport? <br><br> It is 10 miles from here to the airport. |
| How fast? | (有)多快? <br> (有)多快? | 他開車開得(有)多快? <br> 他开车开得(有)多快? <br><br> 他開時速八十五英哩。 <br> 他开时速八十五英里。 <br><br> – 時速(时速) [shísù]: speed per hour | How fast does he drive? <br><br> He drives 85 miles per hour. |
| How heavy? | (有)多重? <br> (有)多重? | 這個包裹(有)多重? <br> 这个包裹(有)多重? <br><br> 這個包裹(有)三十磅。 <br> 这个包裹(有)三十磅。 <br><br> – 包裹 [bāoguǒ]: package | How heavy is this package? <br><br> This package weighs 30 pounds. |
| How big? | (有)多大? <br> (有)多大? | 你的車(有)多大? <br> 你的车(有)多大? <br><br> 我的車可以坐七個人。 <br> 我的车可以坐七个人。 | How big is your car? <br><br> My car can carry seven people. |

*Note:* 多 pronounced as [duō] may function as an adjective meaning "many." In the pattern of (有)多 + Adj. (How + Adj.?) 多 can be pronounced as either [duó] or [duō].

---

> **»Try it!**   **With a partner, ask and answer the following questions.**

1. 你來這兒有多久了?
   你来这儿有多久了?

2. 你(有)多高?
   你(有)多高?

3. 你的房間(有)多大?
   你的房间(有)多大?

## II. Ask for and Give Directions: 往/向 + Direction/location + V.

The common expressions for asking and giving directions are as follows:

| 往/向 + | Direction/location | + | V. |
|---|---|---|---|
| | (e.g.東，前，右/市中心，飛機場，那棟大樓) | | (e.g.拐，轉，走，跑，開) |
| | (e.g.东，前，右/市中心，飞机场，那栋大楼) | | (e.g.拐，转，走，跑，开) |

*Examples:*  i) A: 請問，到火車站去怎麼走?
             请问，到火车站去怎么走?

          B: 你從這兒往前走，再向左拐就到了。
             你从这儿往前走，再向左拐就到了。

       ii) A: 請問，假日旅館在哪兒?
             请问，假日旅馆在哪儿?

          B: 你往市中心方向開二十分鐘就到了。
             你往市中心方向开二十分钟就到了。

             – 市中心(市中心) [shìzhōngxīn]: downtown
             – 方向(方向) [fāngxiàng]: direction

*Notes:*
– 往 can be pronounced as either [wǎng] or [wàng]
– 往 and 向 used as prepositions both mean "in the direction of."
  – For most of the directional words, such as 東邊(东边), and 右邊(右边), the suffix 邊(边) is usually omitted when the directional word occurs after 往 or 向.

---

**»Try it!** | With a partner, ask and answer the following questions.

1. 從這兒怎麼到圖書館?
   从这儿怎么到图书馆?

2. 從宿舍怎麼到書店?
   从宿舍怎么到书店?

3. 從這兒怎麼到餐廳?
   从这儿怎么到餐厅?

---

## III. V. + 起來 (看起來, 聽起來; 想起來; 說起來容易, 做起來難) [V. + 起来 (看起来, 听起来; 想起来; 说起来容易, 做起来难)]

V. + 起來(起来) is a compound DC. It combines with certain verbs to give a sense of an action beginning unexpectedly, or a gradual change. It is also used in a few idiomatic expressions.

1. An action that begins unexpectedly

   *Examples:* i) 我們才遲到一分鐘, 他就生起氣來了。
   我们才迟到一分钟, 他就生起气来了。
   We were just one minute late and he started to get angry.

   – 遲到(迟到) [chídào]: to be late
   – 生氣(生气) [shēngqì]: to get angry

   ii) 他又看起電視來了。
   他又看起电视来了。
   He has started to watch the movie.

   *Note:* the verb is placed between 起 and 來(来) in the pattern V. + 起 + Object + 來(来).

2. A gradual change

*Examples:*

i) 他開始胖起來了。
他开始胖起来了。
He is getting chubby.

– 胖(胖) [pàng]: chubby, fat

ii) 春天就要來了，天氣暖和起來了。
春天就要来了，天气暖和起来了。
Spring is coming, the weather is getting warmer.

3. Idiomatic expressions

i) 想起來(想起来): to recall

*Example:*

我想起來了！你是我小學的同學，王大中。
我想起来了！你是我小学的同学，王大中。
I remember! You are my elementary school classmate, Dazhong Wang.

ii) 想不起來(想不起来): cannot recall

*Example:*

對不起，我真的想不起來在哪兒見過你。
对不起，我真的想不起来在哪儿见过你。
Sorry! I really cannot recall where I have seen you before.

iii) 看起來(看起来): to look

*Example:*

你今天看起來很累。
你今天看起来很累。
You look very tired today.

iv) 聽起來(听起来): to sound

*Example:*

這首歌聽起來真美。
这首歌听起来真美。
This song sounds beautiful.

– 首 [shǒu]: measure word (classifier) for songs
– 歌 [gē]: song

v) 說起來(说起来): to say
   做起來(做起来): to do

*Example:*

說起來容易，做起來難。
说起来容易，做起来难。
To say it is easy, to do it is hard.

> **» Try it!**  **With a partner, ask and answer the following questions.**

1. 你常會想不起什麼來?
   你常会想不起什么来?

2. 你覺得什麼是說起來容易，做起來難?
   你觉得什么是说起来容易，做起来难?

# 補充課文 (补充课文) SUPPLEMENTARY PRACTICE

*Read the following passage. Then listen and repeat.*

## At Shanghai Zoo (繁體字 Traditional Character Version)

(在動物園的售票處)

售票員: 歡迎光臨！請問你們要買幾張票?

王先生: 我們全家一共要買四張票。兩張全票，兩張兒童票。謝謝。

售票員: 一共二十塊。這是動物園的地圖，今天有特別的海豚表演，在海洋世界那兒。

王先生: 海洋世界離這兒有多遠?

售票員: 不太遠，你看，這是入口，你們從這兒往前走，走到前面的交叉口，再往右拐，過了獅子大象區，就是海洋世界了。海豚表演每兩個小時一次。

王先生: 聽起來好像很不錯，謝謝。

## 補充課文 (补充课文) SUPPLEMENTARY PRACTICE

*Read the following passage. Then listen and repeat.*

### At Shanghai Zoo (简体字 Simplified Character Version)

(在动物园的售票处)

售票员：欢迎光临！请问你们要买几张票？

王先生：我们全家一共要买四张票。两张全票，两张儿童票。谢谢。

售票员：一共二十块。这是动物园的地图，今天有特别的海豚表演，在海洋世界那儿。

王先生：海洋世界离这儿有多远？

售票员：不太远，你看，这是入口，你们从这儿往前走，走到前面的交叉口，再往右拐，过了狮子大象区，就是海洋世界了。海豚表演每两个小时一次。

王先生：听起来好像很不错，谢谢。

*Notes:*
動物園(动物园) [dòngwùyuán]: zoo
售票處(售票处) [shòupiàochù]: ticket booth
歡迎光臨(欢迎光临) [huānyíng guānglín]: welcome
全票(全票) [quánpiào]: full ticket
兒童(儿童) [értóng]: children
海豚(海豚) [hǎitún]: dolphin
海洋世界(海洋世界) [hǎiyáng shìjiè]: sea world
入口(入口) [rùkǒu]: entrance
獅子(狮子) [shīzi]: lion
大象(大象) [dàxiàng]: elephant
區(区) [qū]: district

動物園地圖指南

← 往左拐        往右拐 →

## Zoo Map and Vocabulary

區域(区域) [qūyù]: area/legend

1. 售票處(售票处) [shòupiàochù]: ticket booth
2. 禮品店(礼品店) [lǐpǐndiàn]: gift shop
3. 兒童遊樂場(儿童游乐场) [értóng yóulèchǎng]: children's playground
4. 洗手間(洗手间) [xǐshǒujiān]: restroom
5. 旅客服務中心(旅客服务中心) [lǚkè fúwù zhōngxīn]: visitor service (information) center
6. 鳥園(鸟园) [niǎoyuán]: aviary
   孔雀(孔雀) [kǒngquè]: peacock
   蝙蝠(蝙蝠) [biānfú]: bat
7. 熊貓(熊猫) [xióngmāo]: panda

8. 獅子(狮子) [shīzi]: lion
   老虎(老虎) [lǎohǔ]: tiger
   豹(豹) [bào]: leopard
   犀牛(犀牛) [xīniú]: rhinoceros
9. 大象(大象) [dàxiàng]: elephant
   斑馬(斑马) [bānmǎ]: zebra
   長頸鹿(长颈鹿) [chángjǐnglù]: giraffe
   袋鼠(袋鼠) [dàishǔ]: kangaroo
10. 蛇(蛇) [shé]: snake
    鱷魚(鳄鱼) [èyú]: crocodile
    熊(熊) [xióng]: bear
    狐狸(狐狸) [húli]: fox
11. 洗手間(洗手间) [xǐshǒujiān]: restroom
12. 海洋世界(海洋世界) [hǎiyáng shìjiè]: sea world
    水族館(水族馆) [shuǐzúguǎn]: aquarium
    魚(鱼) [yú]: fish
    熱帶魚(热带鱼) [rèdàiyú]: tropical fish
    烏龜(乌龟) [wūguī]: turtle
    海馬(海马) [hǎimǎ]: sea horse
    鯊魚(鲨鱼) [shāyú]: shark
    海豚(海豚) [hǎitún]: dolphin
    海獅(海狮) [hǎishī]: sea lion
    企鵝(企鹅) [qǐ'é]: penguin
13. 販賣部(贩卖部) [fànmàibù]: snack bars
    休息區(休息区) [xiūxiqū]: rest area
    冰淇淋(冰淇淋) [bīngqílín]: ice cream
14. 熱帶雨林區(热带雨林区) [rèdài yǔlínqū]: tropical forest district
    猴子(猴子) [hóuzi]: monkey
    猩猩(猩猩) [xīngxing]: gorilla
    狒狒(狒狒) [fèifei]: baboon

## Exercises: work with a partner or in small groups

1. 小王在兒童遊樂場，他想去看熊貓，要怎麼走呢?
   小王在儿童游乐场，他想去看熊猫，要怎么走呢?
2. 看了獅子老虎以後，他想吃冰淇淋，怎麼去呢?
   看了狮子老虎以后，他想吃冰淇淋，怎么去呢?
3. 在這個動物園，你最喜歡什麼動物? 你要怎麼走才能看到你要看的動物呢?
   在这个动物园，你最喜欢什么动物? 你要怎么走才能看到你要看的动物呢?

## 成語故事 (成语故事) IDIOM STORY

### 愚公移山 (愚公移山) [Yúgōng yí shān]

*Meaning:*  Yugong (the foolish old man) moves the mountain.

*Usage:*  This implies that a determined effort can help accomplish things. That is to say, "Where there is a will, there is a way."

*Example:* A: 上海變化得太快了，我們已經走了兩個小時，可是還是找不到以前的上海小吃店。

上海变化得太快了，我们已经走了两个小时，可是还是找不到以前的上海小吃店。

B: 沒關係，我們要學 "愚公移山" 的精神，再問問看，說不定上海小吃店就在那個路口。

没关系，我们要学 "愚公移山" 的精神，再问问看，说不定上海小吃店就在那个路口。

Pay attention to the usages of (有)多 + Adj.; 往(向) + Direction/location 拐(轉)[拐(转)]; V. + 起來(起来).

(繁體字 Traditional Character Version)

　　中國從前有一個老人叫愚公，他家前面有兩座大山。每次他們要到對面的村莊去的時候，都要拐很多的彎兒，走了很多天的路才能到，很不方便。有一天，愚公把家人找來，討論要移山的事情：

　　愚公問他的家人：我們已經在這兒住了多久了？

　　大兒子說：我們在這兒住了幾十年了。

　　愚公又問：現在我們要到對面的村莊去，有多遠？

　　大兒子說：本來不太遠，可是我們一定要轉很多彎兒。有時候應該向左拐的時候，拐錯了，向右拐了，常常會迷路，很不方便。

　　愚公問：如果我們把前邊的兩座大山搬走，那麼離對面的村莊會有多近？

　　二兒子說：很近，馬上就可以到了。

　　愚公說：太好了，我們來把這兩座大山移走，怎麼樣？雖然聽起來，好像不可能，可是，俗話說 "有志者，事竟成"。我們有子子孫孫，總有一天我們一定可以把這兩座大山移走，到時候，我們的子孫就可以往前一直走，不用辛苦地拐那麼多的彎了。

最後，他們全家都動起來了。大家一起分工合作，決定要把那兩座大山搬走。後來天帝聽到了，很感動，就命令大神把那兩座山移到別的地方去了。這樣一來，愚公和他家人只要往前一直走，就可以到對面的村莊，方便多了。

(简体字 Simplified Character Version)

中国从前有一个老人叫愚公，他家前面有两座大山。每次他们要到对面的村庄去的时候，都要拐很多的弯儿，走了很多天的路才能到，很不方便。有一天，愚公把家人找来，讨论要移山的事情：

愚公问他的家人：我们已经在这儿住了多久了？

大儿子说：我们在这儿住了几十年了。

愚公又问：现在我们要到对面的村庄去，有多远？

大儿子说：本来不太远，可是我们一定要转很多弯儿。有时候应该向左拐的时候，拐错了，向右拐了，常常会迷路，很不方便。

愚公问：如果我们把前边的两座大山搬走，那么离对面的村庄会有多近？

二儿子说：很近，马上就可以到了。

愚公说：太好了，我们来把这两座大山移走，怎么样？虽然听起来，好像不可能，可是，俗话说"有志者，事竟成"。我们有子子孙孙，总有一天我们一定可以把这两座大山移走，到时候，我们的子孙就可以往前一直走，不用辛苦地拐那么多的弯了。

最后，他们全家都动起来了。大家一起分工合作，决定要把那两座大山搬走。后来天帝听到了，很感动，就命令大神把那两座山移到别的地方去了。这样一来，愚公和他家人只要往前一直走，就可以到对面的村庄，方便多了。

*Notes:*

愚公(愚公) [Yúgōng]: the name of the Foolish Old Man

移(移) [yí]: to move

山(山) [shān]: mountain

座(座) [zuò]: a measure word for mountains

村莊(村庄) [cūnzhuāng]: village

討論(讨论) [tǎolùn]: to discuss, discussion

迷路(迷路) [mílù]: to get lost

有志者，事竟成(有志者，事竟成) [yǒuzhìzhě, shìjìngchéng]: Where there is a will, there is a way.

子孫(子孙) [zǐsūn]: children and grandchildren, descendants

總有一天(总有一天) [zǒngyǒuyìtiān]: there will be one day, eventually

辛苦(辛苦) [xīnkǔ]: painstaking, hardship

天帝(天帝) [Tiāndì]: The Lord of the Heavens

感動(感动) [gǎndòng]: to be moved, inspired

大神(大神) [dàshén]: a main god

## Exercises: work with a partner or in small groups

1. 找出有下面語法的句子：(有)多 + Adj.; 往(向) + Direction/location 拐(轉); V. + 起來

   找出有下面语法的句子：(有)多 + Adj.; 往(向) + Direction/location 拐(转); V. + 起来

2. 用你自己的話說說 "愚公移山" 的故事。
   用你自己的话说说 "愚公移山" 的故事。

3. 請用 "愚公移山" 造一個句子或者說一個愚公移山的例子。
   请用 "愚公移山" 造一个句子或者说一个愚公移山的例子。

4. "愚公移山" 的故事，告訴了我們什麼?
   "愚公移山" 的故事，告诉了我们什么?

# 練習 (练习) ACTIVITIES

## I. Listening Exercises

**3-1** In the blanks provided, write the Pinyin with tones for the words you hear, then check with your partner.

1. 感 ＿＿＿ 您搭 ＿＿＿ 我們的出 ＿＿＿ 汽 ＿＿＿。
   感 ＿＿＿ 您搭 ＿＿＿ 我们的出 ＿＿＿ 汽 ＿＿＿。

2. 飛 ＿＿＿ 就要 ＿＿＿ 落了，＿＿＿ 把安 ＿＿＿ 帶 ＿＿＿ 好。
   飞 ＿＿＿ 就要 ＿＿＿ 落了，＿＿＿ 把安 ＿＿＿ 带 ＿＿＿ 好。

3. 你 ＿＿＿ 這兒 ＿＿＿ 前 ＿＿＿，＿＿＿ 往左 ＿＿＿，就到了。
   你 ＿＿＿ 这儿 ＿＿＿ 前 ＿＿＿，＿＿＿ 往左 ＿＿＿，就到了。

4. 一 ＿＿＿ 十四塊 ＿＿＿，＿＿＿ 你六 ＿＿＿，謝謝。
   一 ＿＿＿ 十四块 ＿＿＿，＿＿＿ 你六 ＿＿＿，谢谢。

**3-2** Listen to the following passages and answer the questions. Then check them with your partner.

*Notes:*
告訴(告诉) [gàosu]: to tell
牌子(牌子) [páizi]: a sign
春捲(春卷) [chūnjuǎn]: spring roll
蘿蔔糕(萝卜糕) [luóbo gāo]: turnip cake

**問題(问题):**

1. 他要告訴我們什麼?
   他要告诉我们什么?

2. 那家店離這兒遠嗎，開車要多久?
   那家店离这儿远吗，开车要多久?

3. 我們要從這兒往哪兒開，過了什麼以後向右轉?
   我们要从这儿往哪儿开，过了什么以后向右转?

4. 那家店的牌子是什麼顏色 ([yánsè]: color) 的? 上面寫著什麼?
   那家店的牌子是什么颜色的? 上面写着什么?

5. 那家店的什麼東西很好吃?
   那家店的什么东西很好吃?

## II. Character Exercises

**3-3**   Work with a partner. Read the following words, phrases, and sentences.

往
往

往右拐
往右拐

到前面的交叉口，再往右拐。
到前面的交叉口，再往右拐。

往東走到前面的交叉口，再往
右拐。
往东走到前面的交叉口，再往
右拐。

搭
搭

搭乘出租汽車
搭乘出租汽车

搭乘出租汽車，有多快?
搭乘出租汽车，有多快?

搭乘出租汽車去旅館會有多快?
搭乘出租汽车去旅馆会有多快?

Now with your partner, try to use the following characters to make words, phrases, and then sentences.

| 1. 降 | 2. 全 | 3. 繫 | 4. 品 | 5. 航 |
| 降 | 全 | 系 | 品 | 航 |

| 6. 棟 | 7. 直 | 8. 變 | 9. 農 | 10. 拐 |
| 栋 | 直 | 变 | 农 | 拐 |

**3-4**   Write down the traditional forms for the following simplified characters, then check your answers with a partner.

1. 系上安全带 ____ ____ ____ ____ ____

2. 后车箱 ____ ____ ____

3. 人民币二十块 ____ ____ ____ ____ ____ ____

4. 农田和马路 ____ ____ ____ ____ ____

5. 在红绿灯那儿往右拐 ____ ____ ____ ____ ____ ____ ____ ____ ____

**3-5**   With a partner or a group, create phrases with the following words (pay attention to the various usages of each word).

> *Example:*   塊：十五塊        一塊鏡子，一塊麵包，一塊蛋糕
> 　　　　　    块：十五块        一块镜子，一块面包，一块蛋糕

1. 租：＿＿＿＿＿＿＿＿　　＿＿＿＿＿＿＿＿＿＿＿＿＿＿＿＿＿＿＿

   租：＿＿＿＿＿＿＿＿　　＿＿＿＿＿＿＿＿＿＿＿＿＿＿＿＿＿＿＿

2. 找：＿＿＿＿＿＿＿＿　　＿＿＿＿＿＿＿＿＿＿＿＿＿＿＿＿＿＿＿

   找：＿＿＿＿＿＿＿＿　　＿＿＿＿＿＿＿＿＿＿＿＿＿＿＿＿＿＿＿

3. 感：＿＿＿＿＿＿＿＿　　＿＿＿＿＿＿＿＿＿＿＿＿＿＿＿＿＿＿＿

   感：＿＿＿＿＿＿＿＿　　＿＿＿＿＿＿＿＿＿＿＿＿＿＿＿＿＿＿＿

4. 起：＿＿＿＿＿＿＿＿　　＿＿＿＿＿＿＿＿＿＿＿＿＿＿＿＿＿＿＿

   起：＿＿＿＿＿＿＿＿　　＿＿＿＿＿＿＿＿＿＿＿＿＿＿＿＿＿＿＿

5. 過：＿＿＿＿＿＿＿＿　　＿＿＿＿＿＿＿＿＿＿＿＿＿＿＿＿＿＿＿

   过：＿＿＿＿＿＿＿＿　　＿＿＿＿＿＿＿＿＿＿＿＿＿＿＿＿＿＿＿

## III. Grammar Exercises

**3-6**   Form pairs to ask/answer the following questions (remember to switch roles).

1. 你家離學校有多遠？
   你家离学校有多远？

2. 你有多久沒回家了？
   你有多久没回家了？

3. 你有多高？
   你有多高？

4. 你有多重？
   你有多重？

5. 你今年多大？
   你今年多大？

6. 你常打字 ([dǎzì]: to type) 吧！你打英文字打得有多快？中文字呢？
   你常打字吧！你打英文字打得有多快？中文字呢？

**3-7**   Translation:

Use the pattern 往/向 + Direction/location + V. to translate the following sentences orally.

The points of the compass.

*Note:*
單行道(单行道) [dānxíngdào]: one-way street

1.  First go south, and then turn left at the second traffic light. You will see the taxi stand.
2.  After crossing the road, turn right. You will arrive at a Chinese restaurant.
3.  Go northeast from here, and then go straight.
4.  This is a one-way street. I cannot turn right here. I have to make a few more turns.
5.  Go north from here, go to that intersection, and then turn left.
6.  Go southwest from that big building, keep going, pass two intersections, and then you will soon see the hotel.

**3-8** In pairs or small groups, fill in the blanks to complete the following dialogues. (Pay attention to the V. + 起來(起来) pattern.)

*Notes:*
剛剛(刚刚) [gānggāng]: just now
累(累) [lèi]: tired
公尺(公尺) [gōngchǐ]: meter
跑步(跑步) [pǎobù]: to run
胖(胖) [pàng]: fat, chubby
減肥(减肥) [jiǎnféi]: to lose weight

**Dialogue (1)**

A: 小姐，_____ (sorry)，我剛剛在這兒買了東西，_____ _____ (you forgot to give me my change)。

小姐，_____ (sorry)，我刚刚在这儿买了东西，_____ _____ (you forgot to give me my change)。

B: 是嗎? 我怎麼 _____ (cannot recall that I have seen you; use "V. + 起來")?

是吗? 我怎么 _____ (cannot recall that I have seen you; use "V. + 起来")?

A: 你再想想，_____ (you will recall; use "V. + 起來")，我剛剛在這兒買了一瓶可樂。

你再想想，_____ (you will recall; use "V. + 起来")，我刚刚在这儿买了一瓶可乐。

B: 對了，_____ (I remember; use "V. + 起來")，你給了我十塊錢，_____ (I should give you $8 change)。

对了，_____ (I remember; use "V. + 起来")，你给了我十块钱，_____ (I should give you $8 change)。

**Dialogue (2)**

A: 你 _____ (You look very
tired; use "V. + 起來")。

你 _____ (You look very
tired; use "V. + 起来")。

B: 是呀！我剛剛跑了五千公尺。
是呀！我刚刚跑了五千公尺。

A: 怎麼現在開始 _____
(start running; use "V. + 起來")?

怎么现在开始 _____
(start running; use "V. + 起来")?

B: 我姐姐說我胖了，我也覺得我開始 _____ (start gaining weight; use
"V. + 起來")，就想跑步，_____ (start losing weight; use "V. + 起來")。

我姐姐说我胖了，我也觉得我开始 _____ (start gaining weight; use
"V. + 起来")，就想跑步，_____ (start losing weight; use "V. + 起来")。

A: 這個主意 _____ (sounds good; use "V. + 起來")。

这个主意 _____ (sounds good; use "V. + 起来")。

B: 是呀！可是很多事情常常是 _____ (to say it is easy,
but to do it is hard; use "V. + 起來")。

是呀！可是很多事情常常是 _____ (to say it is easy,
but to do it is hard; use "V. + 起来")。

## IV. Communicative Activities

問路(问路): Form groups. Look at the map, and then take turns asking and answering the following questions.

出租汽車站

公車站

圖書館

超市

郵局    學校    北京小吃店

南

京

路

中山路    中山路

假日旅館    銀行

紅綠燈

加油站    匹薩店    火車站

中正路    中正路

加油站    大新大樓

你在這兒

問題(问题):

1. 我要去超市 ([chāoshì]: supermarket)，請問怎麼走?
   我要去超市，请问怎么走?

2. 小王的車快沒有油 ([yóu]: gas) 了，請告訴他加油站 ([jiāyóuzhàn]: gas station)，在哪兒? 怎麼走?
   小王的车快没有油了，请告诉他加油站，在哪儿? 怎么走?

3. 我想坐公車去吃匹薩 ([pǐsà]: pizza)，怎麼走?
   我想坐公车去吃匹萨，怎么走?

4. 我想吃小籠包，要去哪兒吃? 怎麼走?
   我想吃小笼包，要去哪儿吃? 怎么走?

5. 請問出租汽車站在哪兒? 怎麼走?
   请问出租汽车站在哪儿? 怎么走?

6. 從火車站到假日旅館遠嗎? 要怎麼走?
   从火车站到假日旅馆远吗? 要怎么走?

7. 圖書館在哪條路上? 從假日旅館去圖書館要怎麼走?
   图书馆在哪条路上? 从假日旅馆去图书馆要怎么走?

8. 中正路上有銀行 ([yínháng]: bank) 嗎? 從郵局 ([yóujú]: post office) 到銀行去怎麼走?
   中正路上有银行吗? 从邮局到银行去怎么走?

9. 我在銀行，要去寄 ([jì]: to send) 一個包裹 ([bāoguǒ]: package)，要去哪兒寄? 從這兒到那兒怎麼走呢?
   我在银行，要去寄一个包裹，要去哪儿寄? 从这儿到那儿怎么走呢?

10. 學校離大新大樓遠嗎? 要怎麼走?
    学校离大新大楼远吗? 要怎么走?

# 文化知識 (文化知识) Culture Link

## 文化點滴 (文化点滴) CULTURE NOTES

### 中國的新經濟開發區 (中国的新经济开发区)
### China's New Economic Development Zones

China's economy is growing and improving rapidly. One of the major features of China's economic growth has been the establishment of new economic development zones.

Since the late 1970s, China has worked to reform its economy, with one of the biggest changes being the opening of its vast economy to foreign countries. During the 1980s, China established economic development zones (also known as special economic zones) to encourage foreign investment. Currently, there are economic development zones in Shenzhen, Zhuhai, and Shantou in Guangdong Province, in Xiamen in Fujian Province, and in the entire province of Hainan. They have flourished and have also stimulated growth in other areas of China.

The new economic development zones receive special treatment under China's economic laws. The government grants these zones special policies and flexible measures. They are especially preferred by foreign investors because they offer significant tax concessions for foreign direct investment during the early stage of a company's operations. They have helped the Chinese economy by bringing jobs, technical knowledge, and future tax revenues to the country.

In addition to the new economic development zones, China has also opened several coastal cities and areas to foreign investment, including the Pudong zone in Shanghai.

These economic development zones are crucial to the development of the Chinese economy. They open up free trade and foreign investment, as well as inspire market-oriented business and an entrepreneurial spirit in China.

> **Do you know...**
>
> - when and why China began establishing economic development zones?
> - what special treatment the new economic development zones receive?
> - how these zones help the Chinese economy?
> - the name of the Shanghai development zone?
>
> **Read and find out!**

Shanghai, a cosmopolitan city with a well-established stock market and many high-rise buildings, has attracted numerous investors locally and globally. What kinds of stocks options does this Chinese man have? Guess!

The athletic-shoe business is one of many foreign enterprises in China's fast growing economy. Which other items that you use on a daily basis are made in China?

問題討論 (问题讨论) *Discuss the following with a partner or in small groups.*

1. 你對現在中國的經濟發展有什麼看法?
   你对现在中国的经济发展有什么看法?
   What do you think of China's current economic development?

2. 如果你去中國，你想去新經濟開發區還是去偏遠([piānyuǎn]: remote)
   地區? 為什麼?
   如果你去中国，你想去新经济开发区还是去偏远地区? 为什么?
   If you visit China, would you rather visit the economic development zones or the more remote areas of China? Why, why not?

# 趣味中文 (趣味中文) FUN WITH CHINESE

拐彎抹角
拐弯抹角

a roundabout way of talking

| guǎi | wān | mò | jiǎo |
|------|-----|-----|------|
| 拐 | 彎 | 抹 | 角 |
| 拐 | 弯 | 抹 | 角 |
| turn | curve | bypass | corner |

**問題討論 (问题讨论)** *Discuss the following with a partner or in small groups.*

1. Do you like people to be straightforward or to use a "roundabout" way of talking? Why?
2. Are there any expressions in your language which are similar to 拐彎抹角(拐弯抹角)?
3. Try to use your own words to explain 拐彎抹角(拐弯抹角) in Chinese.

# 行動吧! (行动吧!) LET'S GO!

## 機場入境須知及流程 (机场入境须知及流程)
## Airport Arrival Guidelines and Procedures

明明 is helping his American friend get ready to teach English in Taipei, Taiwan. Below is the information he found on the CKS International Airport website. Let's help translate the information into English.

(繁體字 Traditional Character Version)

| ✈ 中正國際機場入境須知及流程 |
|---|
| 入境必備證件: (1) 護照<br>(2) 入境旅客申報單<br>(3) 外籍旅客: 簽證，機票，入境登記表 |
| 入境流程:<br>第一步驟: 填寫入境申請表，入境旅客申報單<br>第二步驟: 證照查驗<br>第三步驟: 領取行李<br>第四步驟: 動植物檢疫<br>第五步驟: 海關行李檢查 |
| * 第一航廈(出境，動畫)<br>* 第二航廈(入境，動畫) |

● (简体字 Simplified Character Version)

 **中正国际机场入境须知及流程**

**入境必备证件：** (1) 护照
(2) 入境旅客申报单
(3) 外籍旅客：签证，机票，入境登记表

**入境流程：**
第一步骤：填写入境申请表，入境旅客申报单
第二步骤：证照查验
第三步骤：领取行李
第四步骤：动植物检疫
第五步骤：海关行李检查

* 第一航厦(出境，动画)
* 第二航厦(入境，动画)

Notes:
國際(国际) [uójì]: international
入境(入境) [rùjìng]: arrival
須知(须知) [xūzhī]: guidelines, information
及(及) [jí]: and
流程(流程) [liúchéng]: procedure checklist
必備(必备) [bìbèi]: necessary, require
證件(证件) [zhèngjiàn]: documents
護照(护照) [hùzhào]: passport
旅客(旅客) [lǔkè]: traveler
申報單(申报单) [shēnbàodān]: declaration form
外籍(外籍) [wàijí]: foreign
登記表(登记表) [dēngjìbiǎo]: registration form
步驟(步骤) [bùzhòu]: step
填寫(填写) [tiánxiě]: to fill in
申請表(申请表) [shēnqǐngbiǎo]: application form
證照(证照) [zhèngzhào]: documents
查驗(查验) [cháyàn]: examination, inspection
領取(领取) [lǐngqǔ]: draw, receive, collect
動植物(动植物) [dòngzhíwù]: plants and animals
檢疫(检疫) [jiǎnyì]: quarantine
海關(海关) [hǎiguān]: customs
檢查(检查) [jiǎnchá]: check up
航廈(航厦) [hángshà]: terminal building
動畫(动画) [dònghuà]: animation movie

**Translation Exercise:** Work with your partner to translate the form into English. Fill in the following blanks:

---

✈ ## 中正國際機場入境須知及流程
(CKS International Airport: The Procedures & Regulations for Arrival)

**入境必備證件** (Essential documents for arrival):

(1) (                              )

(2) (                              )

(3) (                              )

---

**入境流程** (Arrival procedures checklist):

Step 1: (                              )

Step 2: (                              )

Step 3: (                              )

Step 4: (                              )

Step 5: (                              )

---

\* 第一航廈(出境，動畫)

Terminal Building I (Departure, Flash animation movie)

\* 第二航廈(入境，動畫)

Terminal Building II (Arrival, Flash animation movie)

---

# 4

# 請客和做客（请客和做客）
# Hospitality

*For the Chinese, it is common for guests to 敬酒 ([jìngjiǔ]: toast) the host with some polite words to show their appreciation.*

## CONNECTIONS AND COMMUNITIES PREVIEW

Discuss the following questions with a partner or your class. What similarities and differences do you think there might be between Chinese culture and your own culture?

1. How do you welcome guests and show hospitality in your culture?

2. Are there any traditional ways to show that you are a polite guest in your culture? What are they?

## 教學目標（教学目标）OBJECTIVES

- Offering gifts properly and being a polite guest
- Receiving guests properly and being a good host
- Mealtime manners and proper etiquette
- Describing similarities and making comparisons

# 生詞 (生词) VOCABULARY

## 核心詞 (核心词) Core Vocabulary

| TRADITIONAL | SIMPLIFIED | PINYIN | | |
|---|---|---|---|---|
| 1. 師母 | 师母 | shīmǔ | N. | (an honorific term used when addressing the teacher's wife) |
| 2. 些 | 些 | xiē | M.W. | some |
| 3. 維生素 | 维生素 | wéishēngsù | N. | vitamin |
| 4. 永遠 | 永远 | yǒngyuǎn | Adv. | forever |
| 5. 健康 | 健康 | jiànkāng | Adj. | healthy |
| 6. 年輕 | 年轻 | niánqīng | Adj. | young |
| 7. 破費 | 破费 | pòfèi | V.O. | (you) spent too much money, went to great expense (a common polite expression used when receiving a gift) |
| 8. 小意思 | 小意思 | xiǎoyìsi | | no big deal |
| 9. 難得 | 难得 | nándé | Adv. | seldom, rarely |
| 10. 特地 | 特地 | tèdì | Adv. | specially |
| 11. 拿手菜 | 拿手菜 | náshǒucài | N. | best cooking |
| 12. 涼 | 凉 | liáng | Adj. | cool, cold |
| 13. 精神 | 精神 | jīngshen | Adj. | energetic, high-spirited |
| 14. 白頭髮 | 白头发 | báitóufa | N. | gray or white hair |
| 15. 眼睛 | 眼睛 | yǎnjīng | N. | eye(s) |
| 16. 花 | 花 | huā | Adj. / N. | blurred eyesight / flower |

| | TRADITIONAL | SIMPLIFIED | PINYIN | | |
|---|---|---|---|---|---|
| 17. | 適應 | 适应 | shìyìng | V. | to get used to |
| 18. | 時差 | 时差 | shíchā | N. | time difference, jetlag |
| 19. | 白天 | 白天 | báitiān | N. | daytime |
| 20. | 睏 | 困 | kùn | Adj. | sleepy, dozy |
| 21. | 睡不著 | 睡不着 | shuìbuzháo | | unable to sleep |
| 22. | 街道 | 街道 | jiēdào | N. | street |
| 23. | 習慣 | 习惯 | xíguàn | V. | to be used to |
| 24. | 長 | 长 | zhǎng | V. | to grow |
| 25. | 年糕 | 年糕 | niángāo | N. | New Year cake, rice cake |
| 26. | 味道 | 味道 | wèidao | N. | taste |
| 27. | 地道 | 地道 | dìdao | Adj. | original, genuine, authentic |
| 28. | 香 | 香 | xiāng | N. Adj. | aroma aromatic |
| 29. | 俱全 | 俱全 | jùquán | | all included, altogether |
| 30. | 飽 | 饱 | bǎo | Adj. | full |
| 31. | 只是 | 只是 | zhǐshì | Adv. | just, simply |
| 32. | 家常便飯 | 家常便饭 | jiāchángbiànfàn | N. | homemade meal |
| 33. | 相聚 | 相聚 | xiāngjù | V. | to be together, get together |
| 34. | 乾杯 | 干杯 | gānbēi | V.O. | to toast, cheers |
| 35. | 有朋自遠方來，不亦樂乎？ | 有朋自远方来，不亦乐乎？ | Yǒu péng zì yuǎnfāng lái, bú yì yuè hū? | | Isn't it pleasant to have friends coming from afar? |

## 專名 (专名) Proper Nouns

| TRADITIONAL | SIMPLIFIED | PINYIN | | |
|---|---|---|---|---|
| 1. 匹兹堡 | 匹兹堡 | Pǐzībǎo | N. | Pittsburgh |

## 語文知識 (语文知识) LANGUAGE LINK

Read and listen to the following sentence patterns. These patterns use vocabulary, expressions, and grammar that you will study in more detail in this lesson. After reading the sentence patterns, read and listen to the Language in Use section that follows.

### 句型 (句型) Sentence Patterns

A: 來了就好，怎麼還帶東西來呢！
來了就好，怎么还带东西来呢！
Lái le jiù hǎo, zěnme hái dài dōngxi lái ne!

讓你破費了。
让你破费了。
Ràng nǐ pòfèi le.

B: 沒什麼，小意思。
没什么，小意思。
Méi shénme, xiǎoyìsi.

**A:** 你們還是跟以前一樣。
你们还是跟以前一样。
Nǐmen háishì gēn yǐqián yíyàng.

**B:** 我們是一天比一天老了，
我们是一天比一天老了，
Wǒmen shì yìtiān bǐ yìtiān lǎo le,

做事也沒有以前那麼快了。
做事也没有以前那么快了。
zuòshì yě méiyǒu yǐqián nàme kuài le.

---

**A:** 你做的飯真好吃。
你做的饭真好吃。
Nǐ zuò de fàn zhēn hǎochī.

**B:** 哪裡，哪裡！只是家常便飯。
哪里，哪里！只是家常便饭。
Nǎli, nǎli! Zhǐshì jiāchángbiànfàn.

**A:** 你太客氣了，好吃極了！色香味俱全。
你太客气了，好吃极了！色香味俱全。
Nǐ tài kèqi le, hǎochī jí le! Sè xiāng wèi jù quán.

## 課文 Language in Use: Visiting a Chinese Family
## (繁體字 Traditional Character Version)

| | |
|---|---|
| 老師： | 歡迎，歡迎，請進！ |
| 關明遠： | 李訪，來，我給你們介紹一下，這是王老師，這是師母。 |
| 李訪： | 你們好。 |
| 關明遠： | 老師，這是一些您喜歡的美國文學書。師母，這些維生素[1]是給您和老師吃的，祝你們永遠健康年輕。 |
| 師母： | 來了就好，怎麼還帶東西來呢！讓你破費了。 |
| 關明遠： | 沒什麼，小意思[2]。 |
| 老師： | 你們難得來上海，師母特地做了一些拿手菜。來，來，快上座[3]，菜都要涼了！ |
| 關明遠： | 老師，師母，你們倆還是跟以前一樣，看起來真精神。 |
| 師母： | 不行了！我們是一天比一天老了，白頭髮比以前多了，眼睛也花了，做事也沒有以前那麼快了。 |
| 老師： | 李訪，第一次來中國，適應[4]嗎? |
| 李訪： | 還可以，現在還有一點兒時差。白天覺得很睏，晚上就睡不著。不過，今天比昨天好多了。 |

**1. 維生素/維他命(维生素/维他命)**

維生素(维生素) means vitamin. In Taiwan, vitamins are referred to as 維他命 (维他命) [wéitāmìng].

**2. 小意思(小意思)**

小意思(小意思) is a polite expression commonly used by guests when offering gifts to the host. It implies that the gift is simply a small token of their appreciation and helps the receiver feel more comfortable when accepting the gift.

**3. 快上座(快上座) and 請上座(请上座)**

快上座(快上座) and 請上座(请上座) are common and polite ways for the host to invite guests to be seated. 上座(上座) means "the seat at the head of the table reserved for the guest of honor." Note that "please sit down; please be seated" can be expressed as 請坐(请坐) but 請上座 (请上座) is more formal and courteous.

**4. 應(应) [yīng, yìng]**

應(应) has two pronunciations. When it means "should" it is pronounced [yīng], as in 應該(应该); when it means "to suit," it is pronounced [yìng], as in 適應(适应).

*Continued on page 102*

## 课文 Language in Use: Visiting a Chinese Family
### (简体字 Simplified Character Version)

老师：　　欢迎，欢迎，请进！

关明远：李访，来，我给你们介绍一下，这是王老师，这是师母。

李访：　　你们好。

关明远：老师，这是一些您喜欢的美国文学书。师母，这些维生素[1]是
　　　　给您和老师吃的，祝你们永远健康年轻。

师母：　　来了就好，怎么还带东西来呢！让你破费了。

关明远：没什么，小意思[2]。

老师：　　你们难得来上海，师母特地做了一些拿手菜。来，来，
　　　　快上座[3]，菜都要凉了！

关明远：老师，师母，你们俩还是跟以前一样，看起来真精神。

师母：　　不行了！我们是一天比一天老了，白头发比以前多了，眼睛也
　　　　花了，做事也没有以前那么快了。

老师：　　李访，第一次来中国，适应[4]吗？

李访：　　还可以，现在还有一点儿时差。白天觉得很困，晚上就睡不
　　　　着。不过，今天比昨天好多了。

*Continued on page 103*

## 課文 Language in Use: Visiting a Chinese Family
### (繁體字 Traditional Character Version) —— 接第一百頁

關明遠： 李訪說這兒的天氣比匹茲堡熱。還有，這兒的人也比匹茲堡多，街道上到處都是人，他還不太習慣。

李訪： 我長5這麼大，第一次看到這麼多人。

師母： 你們倆誰比較大?

關明遠： 我跟李訪一樣大，都是二十四歲。

師母： 對了，不要只說話，忘了吃菜。來，來，來，多吃一點兒。

老師： 這是師母做的年糕，味道很地道6，你們嚐嚐。

......

關明遠： 師母您做的飯真好吃。

李訪： 是啊! 色香味俱全，我吃了很多，現在已經很飽了。

師母： 哪裡，哪裡7! 只是家常便飯。

老師： 難得我們相聚，來，一起來乾一杯。今天真高興，"有朋自遠方來，不亦樂乎!"

老師、師母、關明遠、李訪： 乾杯!

---

**5. 長(长) [zhǎng, cháng]**

The word 長(长) has two different pronunciations and functions: when it is a verb pronounced as [zhǎng], it means "to grow;" as an adjective, it is pronounced as [cháng] and means "long."

**6. 地道/道地(地道/道地)**

地道(地道) means "genuine, authentic." It is also sometimes expressed as 道地 (道地). The expression is commonly used to describe and compliment delicious food.

**7. 哪裡，哪裡(哪里，哪里)**

哪裡，哪裡(哪里，哪里) is a relatively traditional, polite way to reply to compliments. It can be translated as "It's nothing," or "I don't deserve your praise," or "You flatter me."

## 课文 Language in Use: Visiting a Chinese Family
## (简体字 Simplified Character Version) —— 接第一百零一页

关明远： 李访说这儿的天气比匹兹堡热。还有，这儿的人也比匹兹堡多，街道上到处都是人，他还不太习惯。

李访：　 我长[5]这么大，第一次看到这么多人。

师母：　 你们俩谁比较大？

关明远： 我跟李访一样大，都是二十四岁。

师母：　 对了，不要只说话，忘了吃菜。来，来，来，多吃一点儿。

老师：　 这是师母做的年糕，味道很地道[6]，你们尝尝。

......

关明远： 师母您做的饭真好吃。

李访：　 是啊！色香味俱全，我吃了很多，现在已经很饱了。

师母：　 哪里，哪里[7]！只是家常便饭。

老师：　 难得我们相聚，来，一起来干一杯。今天真高兴，"有朋自远方来，不亦乐乎！"

老师、师母、关明远、李访：干杯！

# 語法 (语法) GRAMMAR

## I. 比較 (比较) Comparison (1): Simple Comparison Sentences
## 簡單的比較句 (简单的比较句)

- Indicate similarity or sameness.

| Patterns | Negatives |
|---|---|
| A 像 B (A is like B)<br><br>e.g. 他像他爸爸。<br>He is like his father. | A 不像 B (A is not like B)<br><br>e.g. 他不像他爸爸。<br>He is not like his father. |
|     像<br>A 跟 B 一樣(一样) (A is the same as B)<br>   和<br><br>e.g. 他長得跟他爸爸一樣。<br>     他长得跟他爸爸一样。<br>He looks like his father. | A 跟 B 不一樣(不一样)<br>  和<br>(A is different from B)<br><br>e.g. 他長得跟他爸爸不一樣。<br>     他长得跟他爸爸不一样。<br>He looks different from his father. |

- Compare certain qualities of A and B.

| Patterns | Negatives |
|---|---|
| A 比 B Adj.<br>(A is more [adjective] than B)<br><br>e.g. 這兒比上海暖和。<br>    这儿比上海暖和。<br>It is warmer here than in Shanghai. | A 不比 B Adj.<br>(A is not more [adjective] than B)<br><br>e.g. 這兒不比上海暖和。<br>    这儿不比上海暖和。<br>It is not any warmer here than in Shanghai.<br>(both places are about the same) |

| Patterns | Negatives |
|---|---|
| A 有 B (這麼/那麼) Adj.<br>      (这么/那么)<br>(A is as [adjective] as B)<br><br>e.g. 這兒有上海(那麼)熱嗎?<br>    这儿有上海(那么)热吗?<br>Is it as warm here as it is in Shanghai? | A 沒有 B (這麼/那麼) Adj.<br>       (这么/那么)<br>(A is as not as [adjective] as B)<br><br>e.g. 這兒沒有上海(那麼)熱。<br>    这儿没有上海(那么)热。<br>It is not as warm here as (it is) in Shanghai. |
| *Note:* 這麼/那麼(这么/那么) is optional. It is used for emphasis. 這麼(这么) indicates that B is near the speaker, while 那麼(那么) indicates that B is distant from the speaker. ||

**»Try it!** With a partner, practice the simple comparison sentences. For example,

1. A: 你長得像爸爸還是像媽媽?
      你长得像爸爸还是像妈妈?

   B: 我長得比較像爸爸。
      我长得比较像爸爸。

2. A: 今天比昨天暖和嗎?
      今天比昨天暖和吗?

   B: 是,今天比昨天暖和。
      是,今天比昨天暖和。

## II. Comparison (2): Relative, Superlative, and Emphatic Degree
## 比較 (比较), 最, 更

| Patterns | Examples |
|---|---|
| 比較(比较) + V.<br><br>– indicates the "relative" degree of comparison | 春夏秋冬我比較喜歡秋天。<br>春夏秋冬我比较喜欢秋天。<br>Of spring, summer, autumn, and winter, I prefer autumn. |
| 最(最) [zuì] (the most) + V./Adj. . . . 了<br><br>– indicates the superlative degree in comparisons<br><br>– 了 can occur at the end of a sentence to indicate a sense of finality or strong conviction | 春夏秋冬我最喜歡秋天了。<br>春夏秋冬我最喜欢秋天了。<br>Of spring, summer, autumn, and winter, I like autumn the most. |
| 更(更) [gèng] + V./Adj.<br><br>– indicates "even more so" or "even less so" | 這兒春天很美,秋天更美。<br>这儿春天很美,秋天更美。<br>It is beautiful here in spring. It is even more beautiful in autumn. |

**≫Try it!**  With a partner, practice the relative, superlative, and emphatic degree sentences. For example,

1. A: 春夏秋冬四季，你比較喜歡哪一個？
春夏秋冬四季，你比较喜欢哪一个？

B: 春夏秋冬四季，我比較喜歡夏天。
春夏秋冬四季，我比较喜欢夏天。

2. A: 中國菜，你最喜歡吃什麼？
中国菜，你最喜欢吃什么？

B: 我最喜歡吃餃子。
我最喜欢吃饺子。

## III. Comparison (3): Gradual Change 一天比一天

一天比一天 is an adverbial expression indicating gradual change. 一次比一次 and 一年比一年 are similar expressions.

*Examples:*

我們是一天比一天老了。
我们是一天比一天老了。
We are getting older by the day.

他說得一次比一次好。
他说得一次比一次好。
He speaks better each time.

房租一年比一年貴。
房租一年比一年贵。
The rent is getting more expensive by the year.

>>**Try it!**　As a group, talk about what is getting more difficult or easier. For example,

1. A: 中文考試，怎麼樣？
　　中文考试，怎么样？

　B: 中文考試，一次比一次難。
　　中文考试，一次比一次难。

　C: 中文考試不難，一次比一次容易。
　　中文考试不难，一次比一次容易。

## IV. Comparison (4): With Emphasis 比 + ... 多了

比 comparisons are commonly followed by the complement 多了 for emphasis.

*Examples:*

今天比昨天冷多了。
今天比昨天冷多了。
Today is much colder than yesterday.

他比以前胖多了。
他比以前胖多了。
He is much fatter than before.

她比她姐姐漂亮多了。
她比她姐姐漂亮多了。
She is much more beautiful than her older sister.

>>**Try it!**　With a partner, use the 比 + ... 多了 pattern to provide some comments. For example,

1. 二年級的課文比一年級的課文長多了。
　 二年级的课文比一年级的课文长多了。

2. 他今天比昨天好多了。
　 他今天比昨天好多了。

## 補充課文 (补充课文) SUPPLEMENTARY PRACTICE

*Read the following passage. Then listen and repeat.*

### In China (繁體字 Traditional Character Version)

十月二日　　　星期六

　　這次很高興去拜訪了老師和師母，他們跟以前一樣，非常健康、好客。師母特地做了一些拿手菜請我們吃，她做的菜很道地，色香味俱全，其中我最喜歡的是年糕和餃子，好吃極了！

　　我們還去看了幾個中國朋友，他們都比以前忙多了。他們看到我們都很高興，還帶我們去了一家新開的四川飯館吃飯。聽說那家的四川菜又好吃又便宜，所以生意是一天比一天好。以下是他們的幾個招牌菜：

酸辣湯 [suānlà tāng]: hot and sour soup

❖

擔擔麵 [dàndàn miàn]: spicy noodles

❖

水煮牛 [shuǐzhǔ niú]: hot and spicy beef

❖

麻婆豆腐 [mápó dòufu]: spicy tofu

❖

回鍋肉 [huíguō ròu]: double sautéed sliced pork

❖

宮保雞丁 [gōngbǎo jīdīng]: Gongbao (Kung Po) chicken

　　以上的菜，我們都嚐過了，真不錯！

　　李訪還有一些時差，白天還會覺得很睏，希望他今晚能睡著。已經是十一點十五分了，該上床睡覺了，明天我們還要出去走走呢！晚安！

# 補充課文 (补充课文) SUPPLEMENTARY PRACTICE

*Read the following passage. Then listen and repeat.*

## In China (简体字 Simplified Character Version)

十月二日　　　星期六

　　这次很高兴去拜访了老师和师母，他们跟以前一样，非常健康、好客。师母特地做了一些拿手菜请我们吃，她做的菜很道地，色香味俱全，其中我最喜欢的是年糕和饺子，好吃极了！

　　我们还去看了几个中国朋友，他们都比以前忙多了。他们看到我们都很高兴，还带我们去了一家新开的四川饭馆吃饭。听说那家的四川菜又好吃又便宜，所以生意是一天比一天好。以下是他们的几个招牌菜：

酸辣汤 [suānlà tāng]: hot and sour soup

❖

担担面 [dàndàn miàn]: spicy noodles

❖

水煮牛 [shuǐzhǔ niú]: hot and spicy beef

❖

麻婆豆腐 [mápó dòufu]: spicy tofu

❖

回锅肉 [huíguō ròu]: double sautéed sliced pork

❖

宫保鸡丁 [gōngbǎo jīdīng]: Gongbao (Kung Po) chicken

　　以上的菜，我们都尝过了，真不错！

　　李访还有一些时差，白天还会觉得很困，希望他今晚能睡着。已经是十一点十五分了，该上床睡觉了，明天我们还要出去走走呢！晚安！

*Notes:*

拜訪(拜访) [bàifǎng]: to visit
生意(生意) [shēngyì]: business
以下(以下) [yǐxià]: below
招牌菜(招牌菜) [zhāopái cài]: house specialties
以上(以上) [yǐshàng]: above
睡著(睡着) [shuìzháo]: to fall asleep
晚安(晚安) [wǎn'ān]: good night

## Exercises: work with a partner or in small groups

1. Did the narrator find the teacher and his wife the same as before, or different? Give examples.

2. How does the narrator describe the dishes served by the teacher's wife? Which were the favorites?

3. Who did the narrator visit next? What was different or the same about these friends?

4. Where did everyone go to eat, and why that particular restaurant?

5. What time is it now? How was everyone feeling?

6. 四川飯館有那些招牌菜？
   四川饭馆有那些招牌菜？

7. 找出有下面語法的句子：(比，跟(像)……一樣，最，比 + ……多了)
   找出有下面语法的句子：(比，跟(像)……一样，最，比 + ……多了)

8. 用你的話再說說每一段的內容。
   用你的话再说说每一段的内容。

# 成語故事 (成语故事) IDIOM STORY

## 自相矛盾 (自相矛盾) [zì xiāng máo dùn]

*Meaning:* Inconsistent; self-contradictory.

*Usage:* Used to indicate that someone's words or behavior are contradictory.

*Example:* 你昨天說不知道王先生是誰，現在你說你以前吃過他做的飯，色香味俱全，好吃極了。那不是 "自相矛盾" 嗎？

你昨天说不知道王先生是谁，现在你说你以前吃过他做的饭，色香味俱全，好吃极了。那不是 "自相矛盾" 吗？

Pay special attention to (比，跟(像)......一樣，最，有......那麼，比 + ......多了)
[(比，跟(像)......一样，最，有......那么，比 + ......多了)].

(繁體字 Traditional Character Version)

古時候，有一個人，他賣矛也賣盾。他把他的盾拿起來說：我的盾是世界上最好的盾，跟石頭一樣堅固，世界上沒有任何東西可以把它戳破。

然後，他又把他的矛拿起來說：我的矛非常鋒利，世界上沒有任何東西像它一樣鋒利。它比別的矛鋒利多了，可以刺穿世界上任何的東西。

旁邊的人問他：你的矛和盾真的有你說的那麼好嗎？你說你的矛和盾都是最好的。你的矛可以刺穿任何東西，你的盾可以擋住任何東西。現在你用你的矛來刺你的盾，讓我們看看吧！

那個賣矛和盾的人不知道要怎麼回答。

(简体字 Simplified Character Version)

　　古时候，有一个人，他卖矛也卖盾。他把他的盾拿起来说：我的盾是世界上最好的盾，跟石头一样坚固，世界上没有任何东西可以把它戳破。

　　然后，他又把他的矛拿起来说：我的矛非常锋利，世界上没有任何东西像它一样锋利。它比别的矛锋利多了，可以刺穿世界上任何的东西。

　　旁边的人问他：你的矛和盾真的有你说的那么好吗？你说你的矛和盾都是最好的。你的矛可以刺穿任何东西，你的盾可以挡住任何东西。现在你用你的矛来刺你的盾，让我们看看吧！

　　那个卖矛和盾的人不知道要怎么回答。

*Notes:*

自(自) [zì]: self

相(相) [xiāng]: each other

矛盾(矛盾) [máodùn]: contradiction; 矛(矛) [máo]: a spear; 盾(盾) [dùn]: a shield

古時候(古时候) [gǔshíhòu]: ancient times

賣(卖) [mài]: to sell

世界上(世界上) [shìjièshàng]: in the world

石頭(石头) [shítóu]: stone, rock

堅固(坚固) [jiāngù]: solid, strong

任何(任何) [rènhé]: any

戳破(戳破) [chuōpò]: to be broken by jabbing or poking

鋒利(锋利) [fēnglì]: sharp

刺穿(刺穿) [cìchuān]: to be broken by piercing or stabbing

擋住(挡住) [dǎngzhù]: to block

回答(回答) [huídá]: to reply

## Exercises: work with a partner or in small groups

1. What was the man selling and what kinds of claims did he make about his goods?

2. What did the person standing nearby say?

3. Why couldn't the peddler answer the question?

4. 找出有下面語法的句子：(比，跟(像)……一樣，最，有……那麼，比 + ……多了)。

　　找出有下面语法的句子：(比，跟(像)……一样，最，有……那么，比 + ……多了)。

5. 用你自己的話說說"自相矛盾"的故事。
　　用你自己的话说说"自相矛盾"的故事。

6. 請用 "自相矛盾" 造一個句子或者說一個自相矛盾的例子。
   请用 "自相矛盾" 造一个句子或者说一个自相矛盾的例子。

7. "自相矛盾" 的故事，告訴了我們什麼？
   "自相矛盾" 的故事，告诉了我们什么？

# 練習 (练习) ACTIVITIES

## I. Listening Exercises

**4-1**  In the blanks provided, write the Pinyin with tones for the words you hear.

1. ＿＿ 你們 ＿＿ 遠 ＿＿ 康年 ＿＿。
   ＿＿ 你们 ＿＿ 远 ＿＿ 康年 ＿＿。

2. 師母特地 ＿＿ 了一 ＿＿ 拿手 ＿＿ 給你們嚐 ＿＿。
   师母特地 ＿＿ 了一 ＿＿ 拿手 ＿＿ 给你们尝 ＿＿。

3. 我有一點兒時 ＿＿，白天 ＿＿ 得很 ＿＿，晚上 ＿＿ 睡不 ＿＿。
   我有一点儿时 ＿＿，白天 ＿＿ 得很 ＿＿，晚上 ＿＿ 睡不 ＿＿。

4. 來乾一 ＿＿，今天真高 ＿＿，"有朋 ＿＿ 遠方來，不 ＿＿ 樂乎!"
   来干一 ＿＿，今天真高 ＿＿，"有朋 ＿＿ 远方来，不 ＿＿ 乐乎!"

**4-2**  Listen to the following passages and answer the questions. Then check them with your partner.

*Notes:*
招待(招待) [zhāodài]: to treat, treat
麻煩(麻烦) [máfan]: to trouble
打擾(打扰) [dǎrǎo]: to bother (someone)
做客(做客) [zuòkè]: to be a guest
文化(文化) [wénhuà]: culture
做東(做东) [zuòdōng]: to play the host; to host

問題(问题)：

1. 他是剛到王家，還是要走了？
   他是刚到王家，还是要走了？

2. 他說了哪些感謝的話？
   他说了哪些感谢的话？

3. 他在王家作客學到了什麼？
   他在王家作客学到了什么？

4. 他送王家什麼東西了？
   他送王家什么东西了？

5. 他請王家以後做什麼？
   他请王家以后做什么？

## II. Character Exercises

**4-3**   Work with a partner. Read the following words, phrases, and sentences.

| | |
|---|---|
| 涼<br>凉 | 髮<br>发 |
| 菜涼了<br>菜凉了 | 白頭髮<br>白头发 |
| 菜都要涼了<br>菜都要凉了 | 白頭髮也比以前多了<br>白头发也比以前多了 |
| 來，快上座，菜都要涼了。<br>来，快上座，菜都要凉了。 | 我們是一天比一天老了，白頭髮也比以前多了。<br>我们是一天比一天老了，白头发也比以前多了。 |

Now with your partner, try to use the following characters to make words, phrases, and then sentences.

1. 維　　2. 永　　3. 輕　　4. 精　　5. 眼
   维　　　　永　　　　轻　　　　精　　　　眼

6. 適　　7. 睏　　8. 慣　　9. 糕　　10. 聚
   适　　　　困　　　　惯　　　　糕　　　　　聚

**4-4** Write down the traditional forms for the following simplified characters, then check your answers with a partner.

1. 永远年轻 _____ _____ _____ _____

2. 难得 _____ _____

3. 适应时差 _____ _____ _____ _____

4. 不太习惯 _____ _____ _____ _____

5. 吃饱了 _____ _____ _____

**4-5** With a partner or a group, create phrases with the following words (pay attention to the various usages of each word).

*Example:* 應：應該，適應
应：应该，适应

1. 生：_____
   生：_____

2. 年：_____
   年：_____

3. 道：_____
   道：_____

4. 長：_____
   长：_____

5. 花：_____
   花：_____

## III.  Grammar Exercises

**4-6**  In small groups, provide at least two types of comparison based on the information below.

– Comparison: Simple

A 像 B; A 像/跟/和 B 一樣; A 比 B; A (沒)有 B (這麼/那麼)
A 像 B; A 像/跟/和 B 一样; A 比 B; A (没)有 B (这么/那么)

– Comparison: Relative, Superlative, and Emphatic Degree 比較，最，更
比较，最，更

– 比 + ……多了
比 + ……多了

*Examples:*

日文書四十五元。                 日文書比英文書貴。
日文书四十五元。                 日文书比英文书贵。

英文書四十元。                   中文書沒有日文書那麼貴。
英文书四十元。                   中文书没有日文书那么贵。

中文書 三十元。                 中文書很貴，英文書更貴，日文書最貴。
中文书 三十元。                 中文书很贵，英文书更贵，日文书最贵。

日文書比中文書貴多了。
日文书比中文书贵多了。

我覺得日文書比較貴。
我觉得日文书比较贵。

1. 王先生今年五十二歲。
   王先生今年五十二岁。

   王太太今年五十二歲。
   王太太今年五十二岁。

   張先生今年四十六歲。
   张先生今年四十六岁。

   張太太今年三十六歲。
   张太太今年三十六岁。

2. 紐約今天華氏 63 度。
   纽约今天华氏 63 度。

   洛杉磯今天華氏 72 度。
   洛杉矶今天华氏 72 度。

3. 爸爸一米七三 ([yìmǐ qīsān]: 173 cm in height)。
   爸爸一米七三。

   哥哥一米七八。
   哥哥一米七八。

   弟弟一米八。
   弟弟一米八。

4. 我室友七點起床。
   我室友七点起床。

   我八點半起床。
   我八点半起床。

5. 媽媽一百四十八磅。
   妈妈一百四十八磅。

   姐姐一百三十磅。
   姐姐一百三十磅。

   妹妹一百三十磅。
   妹妹一百三十磅。

4-7  Form groups to talk about the gradual changes in 小李.

(Use the pattern 一 N. 比一 N., e.g.: 一天比一天，一年比一年，一次比一次)

*Example:*

小李看書：星期一看了一本，星期二看了兩本，星期三看了三本。
小李看书：星期一看了一本，星期二看了两本，星期三看了三本。

A: 小李看書看得怎麼樣?
   小李看书看得怎么样?

B: 小李看書看得一天比一天多。
   小李看书看得一天比一天多。

*Notes:*
年齡(年龄) [niánlíng]: age
身高(身高) [shēngāo]: height
體重(体重) [tǐzhòng]: weight
磅(磅) [bàng]: pound
考試(考试) [kǎoshì]: exam
報告(报告) [bàogào]: report
分(分) [fēn]: points

| | |
|---|---|
| 年齡: | 二〇〇〇年(十歲)　二〇〇一年(十一歲)<br>二〇〇二年(十二歲) |
| 年龄: | 二〇〇〇年(十岁)　二〇〇一年(十一岁)<br>二〇〇二年(十二岁) |
| 身高: | 二〇〇九年(一米六三)　二〇一〇年(一米六八)<br>二〇一一年(一米七二) |
| 身高: | 二〇〇九年(一米六三)　二〇一〇年(一米六八)<br>二〇一一年(一米七二) |
| 體重: | 二〇〇九年(一百三十五磅)　二〇一〇年(一百四十磅)<br>二〇一一年(一百四十五磅) |
| 体重: | 二〇〇九年(一百三十五磅)　二〇一〇年(一百四十磅)<br>二〇一一年(一百四十五磅) |
| 考試: | 第一課(八十分)　第二課(八十八分)　第三課(九十三分) |
| 考试: | 第一课(八十分)　第二课(八十八分)　第三课(九十三分) |
| 報告: | 第一次(八十五分)　第二次(九十分)　第三次(九十四分) |
| 报告: | 第一次(八十五分)　第二次(九十分)　第三次(九十四分) |

## IV. Communicative Activities

**4-8**   猜猜他/她是誰? (猜猜他/她是谁? ) (Play "Guess Who?")

Divide the class into groups. Each group secretly chooses a classmate whose identity the other groups will attempt to guess. Each group member provides one or two sentences to describe the person.

*Useful patterns:*

– Comparison: Simple
   A 像 B; A 像/跟/和 B 一樣; A 比 B; A (沒)有 B (這麼/那麼)
   A 像 B; A 像/跟/和 B 一样; A 比 B; A (没)有 B (这么/那么)

– Comparison: Relative, Superlative, and Emphatic Degree 比較，最，更
                                                                              比较，最，更

– 比 + ......多了
   比 + ......多了

*Vocabulary:*

– 穿，戴 ([dài]: to put on, to wear)
   穿，戴

– 猜 ([cāi]: to guess)
   猜

e.g.:  他/她比我高，他沒有我那麼胖
        ([pàng]: fat)，他今天穿一件白襯衫，
        一條黑褲子，戴一頂 ([dǐng]: measure
        word for hats) 黃帽子 ([màozi]: hat)......

        他/她比我高，他没有我那么胖，
        他今天穿一件白衬衫，一条黑裤子，
        戴一顶黄帽子......

        你們猜猜他/她是誰?
        你们猜猜他/她是谁?

**4-9**  You and your roommates are looking for a new apartment. Refer to the information below about apartments to discuss and compare the options.

*Useful patterns:*

– Comparison: Relative, Superlative, and Emphatic Degree 比較，最，更
比较，最，更

– 比 + ......多了
比 + ......多了

| 公寓地址：<br>中國北京<br>北三環中路<br>公寓地址：<br>中国北京<br>北三环中路 | 房租/月<br>房租/月<br>(2011年) | 房租/月<br>房租/月<br>(2012年) | 水電費<br>水电费 | 離學校<br>离学校 | 超市<br>超市 | 公車站<br>公车站 | 車庫<br>车库 | 寵物<br>(貓，狗)<br>宠物<br>(猫，狗) |
|---|---|---|---|---|---|---|---|---|
| A: 三環公寓<br>三环公寓 | $400<br>$400 | $430<br>$430 | $40<br>$40 | 半英哩<br>半英里 | 有<br>有 | 沒有<br>没有 | 沒有<br>没有 | 可以<br>可以 |
| B: 北京公寓<br>北京公寓 | $400<br>$400 | $430<br>$430 | $50<br>$50 | 一英哩<br>一英里 | 有<br>有 | 有<br>有 | 沒有<br>没有 | 不可以<br>不可以 |
| C: 長春公寓<br>长春公寓 | $500<br>$500 | $530<br>$530 | $50<br>$50 | 一英哩<br>一英里 | 有<br>有 | 有<br>有 | 有<br>有 | 可以<br>可以 |

**4-10** You and your roommates cook a lot of Chinese food. You invite your friends over to eat with you. Form two groups: hosts and guests. The hosts group should write an invitation to the guests inviting them to dinner and explaining what will be on the menu. The guests group should write a thank you note describing the occasion in detail.

*Notes:*

| 破費 | 小意思 | 難得 | 特地 | 拿手菜 | 涼 | 地道 | 香 | 味 |
|---|---|---|---|---|---|---|---|---|
| 破费 | 小意思 | 难得 | 特地 | 拿手菜 | 凉 | 地道 | 香 | 味 |

| 俱全 | 飽 | 家常便飯 | 相聚 | 乾杯 | 有朋自遠方來，不亦樂乎 |
|---|---|---|---|---|---|
| 俱全 | 饱 | 家常便饭 | 相聚 | 干杯 | 有朋自远方来，不亦乐乎 |

**4-11** You and your partner take the roles of Chinese host and Western guest. Using Chinese, play out a dinner scene using Chinese manners. Then change roles to Western host and Chinese guest and play out that dinner scene using Western manners. Afterwards discuss the two scenes. Are the traditions the same or different? If they are different, how so? Why is it important to understand customs and traditions from other countries?

# 文化知識 (文化知识) **Culture Link**

## 文化點滴 (文化点滴) CULTURE NOTES

### 中國人的好客, 請客和做客 (中国人的好客, 请客和做客)
### Chinese Hospitality: Being a Good Host and a Polite Guest

In Chinese culture, it is important to be a good host and a polite guest. Not only is this a way to show kindness and appreciation to others, but it is a way to save face 面子 [miànzi] and nurture relationships 關係(关系) [guānxi]. When a friend comes from out of town, for example, a Chinese person would usually offer to host the friend and show them around. Also, a Chinese guest invited to dine at a restaurant will usually make an attempt to treat the host. In fact, it is common to see both parties arguing over who should pick up the check.

A common way for Chinese to show hospitality is to invite someone to their house for lunch or dinner. Chinese like to serve guests the best food available, and often serve a dish that they cook well and are proud of. Regardless of the quality of the food, however, the host will humbly claim that they do not cook well and that it is "ordinary" food, not worthy, in other words, of their esteemed guest. The guest is not expected to agree with such statements, but should insist that the food is delicious!

Instead of passing each dish around as would be common in Western culture, the

**Do you know...**
- the Chinese way to show hospitality?
- how the Chinese toast during a meal?
- some ways to be a polite guest?

*Read and find out!*

Chinese custom is to place the food in the center of the table, with each guest taking from the dishes that are closest. The host shows hospitality to the guest by continually serving more food (especially those dishes that are not within easy reach). Even if a guest has indicated that he/she is full, the host will keep adding food to his/her plate and inviting him/her to eat and drink more. Any protestations of being full will be disregarded and perceived by the Chinese host as the guest simply being polite. It is the host's responsibility to make sure that all guests have more than enough to eat and drink.

Drinking is also an important part of Chinese culture and social occasions. The drinking usually begins after the host offers a short toast to the group. Toasting tends to be done with two hands. The host will lift his cup toward the guests with two hands, say something polite, and then say 乾杯(干杯) [gānbēi], which literally means "dry cup," or "bottoms up." The guests will join in the drinking by raising their cups toward the center of the table, gently touching each other's cups or nodding to acknowledge each other. Then each guest will empty his/her glass or take a small sip. It is a good idea for the guest to return the toast with some polite words later in the evening or after a few more courses have been served. The toasts usually go back and forth from host to guest, guest to host, and guest to guest many times during a meal.

It is the Chinese way to decline gifts two or even three times before accepting them. Would a Chinese person open a gift in front of the giver?

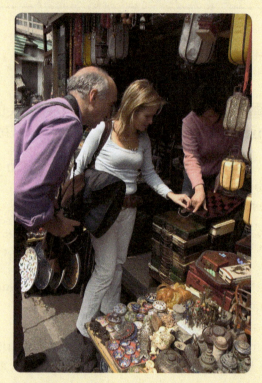

There are many vendors on the streets in China selling souvenirs to tourists. What are some common gifts to take to a Chinese host?

Here are some tips for being a courteous guest:

- At a dinner party, don't begin eating until the host picks up his or her chopsticks.
- It is a Chinese custom to decline gifts two or even three times before accepting them.
- Don't stick your chopsticks upright in your rice. This is considered impolite as it resembles an offering to the dead.
- When you are finished eating, place your chopsticks side by side across your dish or bowl. Bones are often placed directly on the table alongside your dish.
- Guests should sample all of the dishes and leave some food on their plate at the end of the meal. A clean plate indicates that you are still hungry and is a signal that the host should continue to serve you and that they haven't provided you with enough food.
- Refusing food may be considered impolite. If you do not want to eat something, just leave it on the side of your dish.
- Respect elders with acts of kindness like pouring a drink or holding a door open for them.
- Gifts of food are not recommended at dinner parties or other occasions where food is served, since such a gift may imply insufficiency on the part of the hosts. The guests can bring candy, tea, beverages, or fruit to the host as a thank-you gift.
- If possible, it is a good idea for the guests to invite the host to be their guest the next time.

● 問題討論 (问题讨论) **Discuss the following with a partner or in small groups.**

1. 你去過中國人的家做客嗎？說說你的經驗。
   你去过中国人的家做客吗？说说你的经验。
   Have you ever been invited to eat at a Chinese person's house? Share your experience.

2. 你看過哪些電影中(例如《喜宴》)有描述中西文化的差異？
   你看过哪些电影中(例如《喜宴》)有描述中西文化的差异？
   Have you seen any movies, such as "The Wedding Banquet," which show some differences between Chinese and Western culture?

3. What are some examples of Western mealtime manners? How do they differ from Chinese traditions at mealtime?

4. What kinds of misunderstandings could occur if a Chinese or Western guest did not know about the other person's cultural expectations?

## 趣味中文 (趣味中文) FUN WITH CHINESE

人逢喜事精神爽
人逢喜事精神爽
When encountering good news or a joyful occasion,
he/she will be in high spirits and look pleased.

| rén | féng | xǐ | shì | jīng | shén | shuǎng |
|---|---|---|---|---|---|---|
| 人 | 逢 | 喜 | 事 | 精 | 神 | 爽 |
| 人 | 逢 | 喜 | 事 | 精 | 神 | 爽 |
| people | meet | happy | event | spirit | spirit | pleased |

**問題討論 (问题讨论)** *Discuss the following with a partner or in small groups.*

1. What kinds of happy events make you feel pleased? Give some examples in Chinese.
2. Are there any expressions in your language which are similar to, 人逢喜事精神爽 (人逢喜事精神爽)?
3. Try to use your own words to explain 人逢喜事精神爽(人逢喜事精神爽) in Chinese.

# 行動吧! (行动吧!) LET'S GO!

## 機場出境須知及流程 (机场出境须知及流程)
## Airport Departure Guidelines and Procedures

Below is some information from an international airport on departure guidelines and procedures. Let's translate the information into English.

(繁體字 Traditional Character Version)

| ✈ | **出境** |
|---|---|

您必須在起飛前二個小時到機場等候並辦理一些手續。

**出境必備證件：** (1) 護照　(2) 機票　(3) 出境登記表。

**出境流程：**
步驟 1. 辦理報到
步驟 2. 托運行李
步驟 3. 證照查驗
步驟 4. 安全檢查及候機
步驟 5. 登機

(简体字 Simplified Character Version)

| ✈ | **出境** |
|---|---|

| 您必须在起飞前二个小时到机场等候并办理一些手续。 |
|---|
| **出境必备证件**: (1) 护照  (2) 机票  (3) 出境登记表。 |
| **出境流程:**<br>步骤 1. 办理报到<br>步骤 2. 托运行李<br>步骤 3. 证照查验<br>步骤 4. 安全检查及候机<br>步骤 5. 登机 |

*Notes:*
出境(出境) [chūjìng]: departure
起飛(起飞) [qǐfēi]: to take off
等候(等候) [děnghòu]: to wait
辦理(办理) [bànlǐ]: to handle
手續(手续) [shǒuxù]: procedures
報到(报到) [bàodào]: to check in
托運(托运) [tuōyùn]: to transport, ship
安全(安全) [ānquán]: security
登機(登机) [dēngjī]: to board

**Translation Exercise:** With your partner, fill in the blanks below by translating the above airport form into English.

| ✈ | **Departure** |
|---|---|
| (                                                                    ) | |
| (                                          ) | |
| (1) | |
| (2) | |
| (3) | |
| **Departure procedures in order:** | |
| Step 1: (                                    ) | |
| Step 2: (                                    ) | |
| Step 3: (                                    ) | |
| Step 4: (                                    ) | |
| Step 5: (                                    ) | |

# 復習 (复习) **Review**

## LESSON 3 TO LESSON 4

### I. Communicative Activities

Form groups to role-play the following situation.

a. You invite your friends to attend your party held this weekend at your place. Tell them how to get to your place.
b. You are excited. You will attend the party. You would like to ask when and where it takes place, as well as get specific directions.

*Notes:*
你住在哪兒，怎麼走，如果 ([rúguǒ]: if)，週末 ([zhōumò]: weekend)
你住在哪儿，怎么走，如果，周末

(有)多 + Adjective (How + Adj.?)

| 往/向 | + Direction/location | + V. |
|------|----------------------|------|
| 往/向 | +e.g. 東，前，右 / e.g. 市中心，飛機場，那棟大樓 | +e.g. 拐，轉，走，跑，開 |
| 往/向 | +e.g. 东，前，右 / e.g. 市中心，飞机场，那栋大楼 | +e.g. 拐，转，走，跑，开 |

V. + 起來(起来)

### II. Comprehension

Form groups to read aloud the following passage and ask or reply to the questions.

*Situation:* 小英今年二十八歲，可是還沒有男朋友，她的同事給她介紹了三個男孩子。

小英今年二十八岁，可是还没有男朋友，她的同事给她介绍了三个男孩子。

| | 李先生<br>李先生 | 王先生<br>王先生 | 關先生<br>关先生 |
|---|---|---|---|
| | | | |
| 年齡<br>年龄 | 二十八歲<br>二十八岁 | 二十八歲<br>二十八岁 | 三十歲<br>三十岁 |
| 身高<br>身高 | 一米七〇<br>一米七〇 | 一米七〇<br>一米七〇 | 一米七六<br>一米七六 |
| 體重<br>体重 | 一百六十八磅<br>一百六十八磅 | 一百七十八磅<br>一百七十八磅 | 一百七十八磅<br>一百七十八磅 |
| 大學成績<br>大学成绩 | C<br>C | B<br>B | A<br>A |
| 去健身房鍛煉<br>去健身房锻炼 | 一週三次<br>一周三次 | 一週三次<br>一周三次 | 一週三次<br>一周三次 |
| 運動愛好<br>运动爱好 | 游泳，打籃球<br>游泳，打篮球 | 游泳，打籃球<br>游泳，打篮球 | 打籃球，跑步<br>打篮球，跑步 |

*Notes:*
年齡(年龄) [niánlíng]: age
一米七六(一米七六) [yìmǐ qīliù]: 176 cm in height
選(选) [xuǎn]: to choose
當(当) [dāng]: to serve as, to be
如果(如果) [rúguǒ]: if
成績(成绩) [chéngjì]: grades, academic performance
那麼(那么) [nàme]: then
我覺得(我觉得) [wǒ juéde]: I think
帥(帅) [shuài]: handsome
次數(次数) [cìshù]: the number of times
愛好(爱好) [àihào]: hobby
條件(条件) [tiáojiàn]: criteria
適合(适合) [shìhé]: suitable

● Below are 小英's notes. Listen and then answer the questions in Chinese.

1. 我的同事：老李、老王和老關給我介紹了他們的兒子，要我跟他們當
   朋友。我跟他們吃過飯，也看過電影。他們看起來都還不錯。可是我
   不知道要選李先生，王先生還是關先生當我的男朋友。

   我的同事：老李、老王和老关给我介绍了他们的儿子，要我跟他们当
   朋友。我跟他们吃过饭，也看过电影。他们看起来都还不错。可是我
   不知道要选李先生，王先生还是关先生当我的男朋友。

2. 李先生和王先生都跟我一樣大，我們都是二十八歲，關先生三十歲。

   李先生和王先生都跟我一样大，我们都是二十八岁，关先生三十岁。

3. 李先生跟王先生一樣高，可是沒有關先生那麼高，關先生最高。我覺
   得，李先生比王先生帥，也比關先生帥，可是李先生的大學成績最不
   好，王先生還可以，關先生的成績最好。

   李先生跟王先生一样高，可是没有关先生那么高，关先生最高。我觉
   得，李先生比王先生帅，也比关先生帅，可是李先生的大学成绩最不
   好，王先生还可以，关先生的成绩最好。

4. 他們三個都喜歡鍛煉，他們去健身房鍛煉的次數一樣多。李先生游泳
   游得不錯，可是王先生游泳游得更好，關先生不會游泳。他們三個都
   跟我一樣喜歡打籃球，其中關先生籃球打得最好。我的愛好是打籃
   球，看籃球比賽和游泳，可是我不太喜歡跑步。他們三個人的條件都
   不錯，不知道哪一個比較適合我，我很難做最後的決定！

   他们三个都喜欢锻炼，他们去健身房锻炼的次数一样多。李先生游泳
   游得不错，可是王先生游泳游得更好，关先生不会游泳。他们三个都
   跟我一样喜欢打篮球，其中关先生篮球打得最好。我的爱好是打篮
   球，看篮球比赛和游泳，可是我不太喜欢跑步。他们三个人的条件都
   不错，不知道哪一个比较适合我，我很难做最后的决定！

**問題(问题): Answer the following questions with your partner or group.**

1. 小英的問題是什麼?
   小英的问题是什么?

   _____

2. 李先生、王先生和關先生誰最大?
   李先生、王先生和关先生谁最大?

   _____

3. 李先生、王先生和關先生誰比較高?
   李先生、王先生和关先生谁比较高?

   _____

4. 小英覺得誰最帥?
   小英觉得谁最帅?

   _____

5. 他們三個人的大學成績怎麼樣? 誰最好?
   他们三个人的大学成绩怎么样? 谁最好?

   _____

6. 小英的愛好是什麼?
   小英的爱好是什么?

   _____

7. 關先生會不會游泳? 誰游泳游得最好?
   关先生会不会游泳? 谁游泳游得最好?

   _____

8. 如果你是小英, 你會選誰? 為什麼?
   如果你是小英, 你会选谁? 为什么?

   _____

## III.  Picture Description

Form groups to talk about 小李's story. (Be creative!)

*Notes:*

| | | |
|---|---|---|
| 出租汽車(出租汽车) | 變化(变化) | 車費(车费) |
| 人民幣(人民币) | 找(找) | 維生素(维生素) |
| 健康(健康) | 年輕(年轻) | 破費(破费) |
| 小意思(小意思) | 難得(难得) | 特地(特地) |
| 拿手菜(拿手菜) | 精神(精神) | 白頭髮(白头发) |
| 眼睛(眼睛) | 花(花) | 地道(地道) |
| 色香味俱全(色香味俱全) | 吃飽(吃饱) | 家常便飯(家常便饭) |
| 相聚(相聚) | 乾杯(干杯) | |

有朋自遠方來，不亦樂乎(有朋自远方来，不亦乐乎)

(1)　　　　　　(2)　　　　　　(3)　　　　　　(4)

## IV.  寫感謝卡 (写感谢卡) Write thank-you notes

## V. Traditional and Simplified Characters

With your partner, read each character aloud. Write its traditional form, then create a phrase and a sentence using the character.

*Example:* 学 → 學 → 學生 → 我是學生。

L3: 系 ( )    栋 ( )    变 ( )    农 ( )    灯 ( )
转 ( )    弯 ( )    费 ( )    币 ( )

L4: 轻 ( )    发 ( )    适 ( )    困 ( )
味 ( )    俱 ( )    饱 ( )    干 ( )

第五課 (第五课)
# LESSON
# 5

# 我的中國行–復習
# (我的中国行–复习)
# My Trip to China – Review

*A traditional teahouse in Yuyuan 豫園(豫园) [Yùyuán], a famous Chinese garden in Shanghai.*

## CONNECTIONS AND COMMUNITIES PREVIEW

Discuss the following questions with a partner or your class. What similarities and differences do you think there might be between Chinese culture and your own culture?

1. What Chinese cultural experiences have you had? Anything interesting?

2. Have you been anywhere that features both the old and new culture and architecture?

## 教學目標 (教学目标) OBJECTIVES

- Make a report
- Recall memories and past experiences

# 生詞 (生词) VOCABULARY

## 核心詞 (核心词) Core Vocabulary

| | TRADITIONAL | SIMPLIFIED | PINYIN | | |
|---|---|---|---|---|---|
| 1. | 陰 | 阴 | yīn | Adj. | cloudy |
| 2. | 終於 | 终于 | zhōngyú | Adv. | finally, at last |
| 3. | 本來 | 本来 | běnlái | Adv. | originally, at first, initially |
| 4. | 飛行 | 飞行 | fēixíng | N. | flying |
| 5. | 轉機 | 转机 | zhuǎnjī | N. | change planes, transfer |
| 6. | 誤點 | 误点 | wùdiǎn | N. V.O. | delay to delay |
| 7. | 趕上 | 赶上 | gǎnshàng | V.C. | to catch, catch up with |
| 8. | 班機 | 班机 | bānjī | N. | flight |
| 9. | 熱情 | 热情 | rèqíng | Adj. | warm-hearted, enthusiastic |
| 10. | 好客 | 好客 | hàokè | Adj. | hospitable |
| 11. | 津津有味 | 津津有味 | jīnjīnyǒuwèi | | with relish, with keen pleasure |
| 12. | 大開眼界 | 大开眼界 | dàkāiyǎnjiè | | be exposed to many great new things |
| 13. | 團 | 团 | tuán | N. | group |
| 14. | 方向 | 方向 | fāngxiàng | N. | direction |
| 15. | 鬧 | 闹 | nào | V. | to make, cause, induce |
| 16. | 笑話 | 笑话 | xiàohuà | N. | joke |
| 17. | 繁榮 | 繁荣 | fánróng | Adj. | prosperous |
| 18. | 大廈 | 大厦 | dàshà | N. | high-rise building |
| 19. | 雖然 | 虽然 | suīrán | Conj. | although |

| TRADITIONAL | SIMPLIFIED | PINYIN | | |
|---|---|---|---|---|
| 20. 別人 | 别人 | biérén | N. | other people |
| 21. 小吃 | 小吃 | xiǎochī | N. | snack |
| 22. 挺 | 挺 | tǐng | Adv. | very, quite |
| 23. 值得 | 值得 | zhídé | Adj. | worthwhile |

## 語文知識 (语文知识) LANGUAGE LINK

Read and listen to the following sentence patterns. These patterns use vocabulary, expressions, and grammar that you will study in more detail in this lesson. After reading the sentence patterns, read and listen to the Language in Use section that follows.

### 句型 (句型) Sentence Patterns

 這次飛機誤點把我跟李訪累壞了。
这次飞机误点把我跟李访累坏了。
Zhècì fēijī wùdiǎn bǎ wǒ gēn Lǐ Fǎng lèi huài le.

他們看起來都很精神。
他们看起来都很精神。
Tāmen kànqǐlái dōu hěn jīngshen.

他們還是跟以前一樣非常熱情。
他们还是跟以前一样非常热情。
Tāmen háishì gēn yǐqián yíyàng fēicháng rèqíng.

現在的京劇票比以前貴了。
现在的京剧票比以前贵了。
Xiànzài de jīngjù piào bǐ yǐqián guì le.

我們手裡拿著地圖，忙著問路。
我们手里拿着地图，忙着问路。
Wǒmen shǒu lǐ ná zhe dìtú, máng zhe wènlù.

他去過中國，看過京劇。
他去过中国，看过京剧。
Tā qù guo Zhōngguó, kàn guo jīngjù.

## 課文 Language in Use: My Trip to China
### (繁體字 Traditional Character Version)

中國行[1]

十月二十日　　　星期三　　　天氣：陰

我們坐了三十多個小時的飛機，終於回到美國來了。從中國到美國本來十幾個小時就到了，但是在日本轉機的時候，因為我們的飛機誤點了，所以沒趕上我們的班機。我們在機場等了五個小時以後，才坐上了飛機。這次飛機誤點把我跟李訪累壞了。在飛機上，我們一把行李放好，就一直[2]睡覺，睡到飛機降落以後才起來。

不過這次很高興能在上海和老師再次相聚。老師和師母看起來都很精神，他們還是跟以前一樣非常熱情、好客。師母還特地做了幾樣很地道的上海菜，讓我們嚐嚐，其中我最喜歡的是上海年糕。真好吃[3]！

我還帶李訪去看了京劇，我們看得津津有味，他也覺得大開眼界。不過，我聽說現在的京劇劇團比以前少了，所以票也比以前貴了。

上海真的變得很快，有些路都很難找到了。我們手裡拿著地圖，忙著問路、找方向。常常應該向左拐的時候，我們轉錯了，往右拐了，鬧了不少笑話。

中國真的是一天比一天繁榮、進步了。在大城市裡，高樓大廈跟美國的一樣高，到處都能看到外國人。

這次在中國的時間雖然很短，可是我們都玩得很高興。李訪說他現在可以跟別人說他去過中國、看過京劇了。還有，他也嚐了很多中國的小吃，都很棒！

我們倆都覺得這次去中國旅行，挺[4]不錯的，也非常值得。下次有機會，我們還要再去。

---

**1. 中國行(中国行)**

中國行(中国行) is an idiomatic expression meaning "trip to China." 我的中國行(我的中国行) means "My trip to China." 行(行) is a short form of "旅行(旅行)."

---

**2. 一直(一直)**

一直(一直) has two meanings as illustrated below:

i) From beginning to end; always; constantly

*Example:*
我們上飛機以後就一直睡覺。
我们上飞机以后就一直睡觉。
After we boarded the plane, we slept from beginning to end (of the flight).

ii) (to go) straight ahead

*Example:*
從那兒往前一直走。
从那儿往前一直走。
From there, go straight ahead.

---

**3. 好(好) [hǎo, hào]**

好(好) has two pronunciations which have different meanings and functions. When 好(好) is used as an adjective which means "good," as in 好吃(好吃), the pronunciation is [hǎo]; when 好(好) is used as a verb, it is pronounced as [hào] as in 好客(好客).

**课文 Language in Use: My Trip to China**
**(简体字 Simplified Character Version)**

中国行[1]

十月二十日     星期三     天气：阴

　　我们坐了三十多个小时的飞机，终于回到美国来了。从中国到美国本来十几个小时就到了，但是在日本转机的时候，因为我们的飞机误点了，所以没赶上我们的班机。我们在机场等了五个小时以后，才坐上了飞机。这次飞机误点把我跟李访累坏了。在飞机上，我们一把行李放好，就一直[2]睡觉，睡到飞机降落以后才起来。

　　不过这次很高兴能在上海和老师再次相聚。老师和师母看起来都很精神，他们还是跟以前一样非常热情、好客。师母还特地做了几样很地道的上海菜，让我们尝尝，其中我最喜欢的是上海年糕。真好吃[3]！

　　我还带李访去看了京剧，我们看得津津有味，他也觉得大开眼界。不过，我听说现在的京剧剧团比以前少了，所以票也比以前贵了。

　　上海真的变得很快，有些路都很难找到了。我们手里拿着地图，忙着问路、找方向。常常应该向左拐的时候，我们转错了，往右拐了，闹了不少笑话。

　　中国真的是一天比一天繁荣、进步了。在大城市里，高楼大厦跟美国的一样高，到处都能看到外国人。

　　这次在中国的时间虽然很短，可是我们都玩得很高兴。李访说他现在可以跟别人说他去过中国、看过京剧了。还有，他也尝了很多中国的小吃，都很棒！

　　我们俩都觉得这次去中国旅行，挺[4]不错的，也非常值得。下次有机会，我们还要再去。

| 4. 挺(很，非常) [挺(很，非常)] |
| --- |
| 挺(挺) is an adverb meaning "very, quite." It is a more colloquial form than 很(很) "very" and 非常(非常) "extraordinary." |

## 語法復習 (语法复习) GRAMMAR REVIEW

The main grammar points from Lesson 1 to Lesson 4.

### I. 結果補語 (结果补语) Resultative Complement (RC)

The RC indicates the result, extent, or goal of an action.

| V. + Adj. | → RC |
|---|---|
| 看 錯 (wrong) | → 看錯 (seeing it wrong) |
| 看 错 | → 看错 |
| 完 (finish) | → 看完 (finish seeing) |
| 完 | → 看完 |
| 見 (perceive) | → 看見 (see) |
| 见 | → 看见 |

**>>Try it!** With a partner, practice the RC list above and make sentences. For example,

我看見他了。
我看见他了。

### II. 把字句和結果補語的搭配 (把字句和结果补语的搭配) 把 Sentences and the Resultative Complement

Since the RC indicates the result or influence of an action, it is often used with the 把 structure. Note that when the object is definite, the 把 structure is preferred.

| Subject 把 Object + RC | e.g. 看完，收好，找到，放在，穿上，打開，換成 |
|---|---|
| 把 | 看完，收好，找到，放在，穿上，打开，换成 |

*Example:* 我把那本小說看完了。
我把那本小说看完了。

**>>Try it!** With a partner, practice 把 sentences and the RC. For example,

A: 誰把門打開了?　　　　　　　B: 小王把門打開了。
谁把门打开了?　　　　　　　　小王把门打开了。

## III. The Aspects 了, 著 (着), and 過 (过)

- 了 indicates a completed action.

  *Example:* 我吃藥了。
  我吃药了。
  I have taken the medicine.

  When two 了 co-occur, it usually indicates that the action is still ongoing at the moment of speaking.

  *Example:* 她學中文學了三年了。
  她学中文学了三年了。
  She has been studying Chinese for three years.
  (She is still studying Chinese at the moment of speaking.)

- 著(着) describes a state which is continuous or stationary.

  *Example:* 牆上掛著一張照片。
  墙上挂着一张照片。
  There is a picture hanging on the wall.

- 過(过) indicates past experience (ever . . . before).

  *Example:* 我去過長城。
  我去过长城。
  I have been to the Great Wall.

>>**Try it!**  With a partner, practice the aspects 了, 著 (着), and 過 (过) in sentences. For example,

1. A: 你學中文學了多久了?
   你学中文学了多久了?

   B: 我學了兩年了。
   我学了两年了。

2. A: 你包過餃子嗎?
   你包过饺子吗?

   B: 我沒包過餃子。
   我没包过饺子。

## IV. (有) 多 + Adj. (How + Adj.?)

(有)多 + Adj. is a pattern used to ask about the degree of distance, length, speed, size, etc. It is similar to the English pattern "How + Adj." (for example "How far?" or "How fast?").

*Example:* 有多長，多高，多遠，多快，多重，多大 and 多久。
有多长，多高，多远，多快，多重，多大 and 多久。

**»Try it!** With a partner, use the (有) 多 + Adj. pattern to ask and answer questions. For example,

1. 你有多高?
   你有多高?

2. 你開車開得有多快?
   你开车开得有多快?

## V. Ask for and Give Directions

| 往(向) | + Direction/location | + V. |
|---|---|---|

往(向)
| 東(东) | 轉(转) |
| 前(前) | 走(走) |
| 右(右) | 跑(跑) |
| 城裡(城里) | 開(开) |
| 飛機場(飞机场) | 拐(拐) |

*Example:* 從這兒往前走，再向左拐就到了。
从这儿往前走，再向左拐就到了。
Go straight ahead, then turn left, and then it is right there.

**»Try it!** With a partner, practice how to ask for and give directions. For example,

A: 從這兒到圖書館怎麼去?
从这儿到图书馆怎么去?

B: 從這兒往前走，再向右拐就到了。
从这儿往前走，再向右拐就到了。

## VI. 比較 (比较) Comparison (1): Simple Comparison Sentences
### 簡單的比較句 (简单的比较句)

| | |
|---|---|
| A 像(像) B | A is like B |
| A 跟(跟) B 一樣(一样) | A is the same as B |
| A 比(比) B Adj. | A is more [adjective] than B |
| A 有(有) B (這麼(这么)/那麼(那么)) Adj. | A is as [adjective] as B |

**>>Try it!** With a partner, practice the simple comparison sentences. For example,

A: 你有他那麼高嗎?
你有他那么高吗?

B: 是的，我跟他一樣高。
是的，我跟他一样高。

## VII. Comparison (2): Relative, Superlative, and Emphatic Degree
### 比較 (比较), 最, 更

比較(比较): indicates the "relative" degree of comparison
最(最): the superlative degree of comparisons
更(更): even more so

**>>Try it!** With a partner, use the relative, superlative, and emphatic degree to make some sentences. For example,

1. 他很高，我比他更高。
   他很高，我比他更高。

2. 小王是班上最高的學生。
   小王是班上最高的学生。

## 補充課文 (补充课文) SUPPLEMENTARY PRACTICE

*Read the following passage. Then listen and repeat.*

### Travel Diary (繁體字 Traditional Character Version)

關明遠：高飛，你看，我的旅行日記《我的中國行》在校報上登出來了，上面還登了幾張我在中國照的照片呢！

高飛：是嗎？快讓我看看！……嗯，你的文章寫得真不錯，快講講，你這次到中國旅行，去了哪些地方？

關明遠：我們先從美國坐飛機到上海去看了老師和師母，然後從上海坐船沿著長江往西走，一路上看了幾個城市，然後坐飛機到北京，最後從北京飛回美國。

高飛：聽起來你們好像玩得很開心。

關明遠：是的，我們這次真的是大開眼界，挺不錯的。

高飛：這張照片是在上海吧！真漂亮！

關明遠：沒錯，上海是一個很國際化的大城市。現在國際上有一些有名的大公司都把它們的分公司設在上海，他們還要把他們的工廠搬到中國去呢。來，你看，這張照片上的兩個人就是王老師和師母。

高飛：他們看起來真精神。

關明遠：他們每天都去公園鍛煉，比我們年輕人還健康呢。

關明遠：對了，這張照片是我在北京的王府井大街前面照的。去過王府井大街的人都說那兒以前是一條很窄的老街，現在是一條寬敞的商業街了。

高飛：嗯，聽起來很有意思，有機會我也要去中國看看。

關明遠：我的數碼相機裡還有一百多張照片呢。你想不想看？我明天把這些照片都帶過來給你看看。

高飛：太好了！我們一言為定！

## 補充課文 (补充课文) SUPPLEMENTARY PRACTICE

*Read the following passage. Then listen and repeat.*

### Travel Diary (简体字 Simplified Character Version)

关明远： 高飞，你看，我的旅行日记《我的中国行》在校报上登出来了，上面还登了几张我在中国照的照片呢！

高飞： 是吗？快让我看看！……嗯，你的文章写得真不错，快讲讲，你这次到中国旅行，去了哪些地方？

关明远： 我们先从美国坐飞机到上海去看了老师和师母，然后从上海坐船沿着长江往西走，一路上看了几个城市，然后坐飞机到北京，最后从北京飞回美国。

高飞： 听起来你们好像玩得很开心。

关明远： 是的，我们这次真的是大开眼界，挺不错的。

高飞： 这张照片是在上海吧！真漂亮！

关明远： 没错，上海是一个很国际化的大城市。现在国际上有一些有名的大公司都把它们的分公司设在上海，他们还要把他们的工厂搬到中国去呢。来，你看，这张照片上的两个人就是王老师和师母。

高飞： 他们看起来真精神。

关明远： 他们每天都去公园锻炼，比我们年轻人还健康呢。

关明远： 对了，这张照片是我在北京的王府井大街前面照的。去过王府井大街的人都说那儿以前是一条很窄的老街，现在是一条宽敞的商业街了。

高飞： 嗯，听起来很有意思，有机会我也要去中国看看。

关明远： 我的数码相机里还有一百多张照片呢。你想不想看？我明天把这些照片都带过来给你看看。

高飞： 太好了！我们一言为定！

*Notes:*

旅行日記(旅行日记) [lǚxíng rìjì]: travel diary

校報(校报) [xiàobào]: school newspaper

登(登) [dēng]: to publish

講(讲) [jiǎng]: to tell, narrate

長江(长江) [Chángjiāng]: the Yangtze River

國際化(国际化) [guójìhuà]: internationalized

分公司(分公司) [fēn gōngsī]: branch company

設(设) [shè]: to establish

王府井(王府井) [Wángfǔjǐng]: Wang Fu Jing (a shopping street in Beijing)

窄(窄) [zhǎi]: narrow

寬敞(宽敞) [kuānchǎng]: spacious

商業(商业) [shāngyè]: business

數碼相機(数码相机) [shùmǎ xiàngjī]: digital camera. 數位相機(数位相机) [shùwèi xiàngjī] is used in Taiwan

**Exercises: work with a partner or in small groups**

1. 關明遠在中國玩了哪些地方?
   关明远在中国玩了哪些地方?

2. 為什麼上海是一個國際化的大城市?
   为什么上海是一个国际化的大城市?

3. 關明遠看到了中國有哪些變化?
   关明远看到了中国有哪些变化?

## 成語故事 (成语故事) IDIOM STORY

### 守株待兔 (守株待兔) [shōuzhū dàitù]

*Meaning:* Waiting for hares by the tree.

*Usage:* Indicates that someone is stupid and unimaginative about doing things or that someone puts their faith in chance and windfalls.

*Example:* 明天就要考試了，你不努力，只想 "守株待兔"，以為考試會很簡單。

明天就要考试了，你不努力，只想 "守株待兔"，以为考试会很简单。

Pay attention to the usages of 著(着); 過(过); 把......; 往(向) + Direction/location 拐(轉)[拐(转)].

### (繁體字 Traditional Character Version)

　　從前，宋國有一個農夫，他每天去田裡工作。從他的農田走出來向左拐，有一棵大樹。有一天，他在田裡工作的時候，有一隻兔子往農田這邊跑了過來，可是那隻兔子跑得太快，撞到大樹，死了。農夫從來沒有見過這樣的事，就把兔子帶回去煮了，高高興興地把兔子肉吃了。

　　農夫沒做什麼就有兔子肉吃，就想：要是每天有兔子跑過來撞到大樹，那該多好呀，這樣他就不用每天在田裡工作了。

　　這麼想著，他再也不去田裡工作了。他每天都在大樹旁邊坐著，等著有兔子向大樹撞過來。可是一天一天過去了，還是沒有兔子跑過來。

　　人們覺得他想不勞而獲，就把他的故事拿來教育年輕人。

(简体字 Simplified Character Version)

　　从前，宋国有一个农夫，他每天去田里工作。从他的农田走出来向左拐，有一棵大树。有一天，他在田里工作的时候，有一只兔子往农田这边跑了过来，可是那只兔子跑得太快，撞到大树，死了。农夫从来没有见过这样的事，就把兔子带回去煮了，高高兴兴地把兔子肉吃了。

　　农夫没做什么就有兔子肉吃，就想：要是每天有兔子跑过来撞到大树，那该多好呀，这样他就不用每天在田里工作了。

　　这么想着，他再也不去田里工作了。他每天都在大树旁边坐着，等着有兔子向大树撞过来。可是一天一天过去了，还是没有兔子跑过来。

　　人们觉得他想不劳而获，就把他的故事拿来教育年轻人。

*Notes:*
從前(从前) [cóngqián]: once upon a time
宋國(宋国) [Sòngguó]: the State of Song
農夫(农夫) [nóngfū]: peasant, farmer
農田(农田) [nóngtián]: crop field
兔子(兔子) [tùzi]: rabbit
煮(煮) [zhǔ]: to cook
肉(肉) [ròu]: meat
不勞而獲(不劳而获) [bùláo'érhuò]: reap without sowing; profit from other people's work
教育(教育) [jiàoyù]: to educate, education

## Exercises: work with a partner or in small groups

1. 找出有下面語法的句子：著；過；把......；往(向) + Direction/location
   拐(轉)

   找出有下面语法的句子：着；过；把......；往(向) + Direction/location
   拐(转)

2. 用你自己的話說說 "守株待兔" 的故事。
   用你自己的话说说 "守株待兔" 的故事。

3. 請用 "守株待兔" 造一個句子或者說一個守株待兔的例子。
   请用 "守株待兔" 造一个句子或者说一个守株待兔的例子。

4. "守株待兔" 的故事，告訴了我們什麼?

   "守株待兔" 的故事，告诉了我们什么?

## 練習 (练习) ACTIVITIES

### I. Listening Exercises

5-1　In the blanks provided, write the Pinyin with tones for the words you hear. Then check them with your partner.

1. _____ 忘了要在媽媽回來以前 _____ 作業 _____ _____ , _____ 衣服 _____ _____ , _____ 門窗 _____ _____ 。

   _____ 忘了要在妈妈回来以前 _____ 作业 _____ _____ , _____ 衣服 _____ _____ , _____ 门窗 _____ _____ 。

2. 你有沒有去 _____ 中國店 _____ _____ _____ ?

   你有没有去 _____ 中国店 _____ _____ _____ ?

3. 他等公共汽車 _____ _____ _____ _____ _____ ?

   他等公共汽车 _____ _____ _____ _____ ?

4. 沿 ([yán]: along) _____ 這條街道 _____ _____ _____ _____ _____ 走，過三個 _____ _____ _____ 右 _____ ，你就能到圖書館了。

   沿 _____ 这条街道 _____ _____ _____ 走，过三个 _____ _____ _____ 右 _____ ，你就能到图书馆了。

5. 這輛車 _____ 那輛車 _____ _____ 貴，開 _____ _____ _____ 那輛車 _____ ，可是看 _____ _____ 沒有那輛車 _____ 。

   这辆车 _____ 那辆车 _____ _____ 贵，开 _____ _____ _____ 那辆车 _____ ，可是看 _____ _____ 没有那辆车 _____ 。

5-2　Listen to the following passage, then answer the questions orally.

*Notes:*

猜(猜) [cāi]: to guess
字謎(字谜) [zìmí]: riddle of a Chinese character
提醒(提醒) [tíxǐng]: to remind
聰明(聪明) [cōngming]: smart, clever
剩下來(剩下来) [shèngxiàlái]: remaining
答案(答案) [dá'àn]: answer

(繁體字 Traditional Character Version)

　　大中沒有猜過字謎，小美就給大中一個字謎讓他猜猜。小美的字謎是："水池的中間沒有水，土地的上面沒有土。"大中看著字謎想了很久，可是還是猜不出來是什麼字。小美提醒大中，"水池的中間沒有水"就是把"池"這個字的三點水拿走，"土地的上面沒有土"就是把"地"這個字裡面的土拿走。大中說他知道了，把池字裡面的水拿走，把地字裡面的土拿走，剩下來的字就一樣了。這個字謎的答案是"也"字。大中也給小美一個字謎："我沒有，他有；天沒有，地有"。小美說這個字謎的答案跟第一個字謎的答案一樣。你知道為什麼嗎？

(简体字 Simplified Character Version)

　　大中没有猜过字谜，小美就给大中一个字谜让他猜猜。小美的字谜是："水池的中间没有水，土地的上面没有土。"大中看着字谜想了很久，可是还是猜不出来是什么字。小美提醒大中，"水池的中间没有水"就是把"池"这个字的三点水拿走，"土地的上面没有土"就是把"地"这个字里面的土拿走。大中说他知道了，把池字里面的水拿走，把地字里面的土拿走，剩下来的字就一样了。这个字谜的答案是"也"字。大中也给小美一个字谜："我没有，他有；天没有，地有"。小美说这个字谜的答案跟第一个字谜的答案一样。你知道为什么吗？

**問題(问题):**

1. 小美跟大中一起做什麼了？
　 小美跟大中一起做什么了？

2. 小美的字謎是什麼？為什麼是這個答案？
　 小美的字谜是什么？为什么是这个答案？

3. 大中的字謎是什麼？答案是什麼？應該怎麼猜大中的字謎？
　 大中的字谜是什么？答案是什么？应该怎么猜大中的字谜？

## II. Character Exercises

**5-3**    Work with a partner. Read the following words, phrases, and sentences.

| | |
|---|---|
| 趕 | 鬧 |
| 赶 | 闹 |
| | |
| 趕上 | 鬧笑話 |
| 赶上 | 闹笑话 |
| | |
| 終於趕上了 | 鬧了笑話 |
| 终于赶上了 | 闹了笑话 |
| | |
| 他們終於趕上飛機了。 | 鬧了不少笑話 |
| 他们终于赶上飞机了。 | 闹了不少笑话 |
| | |
| 他們終於趕上飛往北京的飛機了。 | 他們在中國鬧了不少笑話。 |
| 他们终于赶上飞往北京的飞机了。 | 他们在中国闹了不少笑话。 |

Now with your partner, try to use the following characters to make words, phrases, and then sentences.

| | | | | |
|---|---|---|---|---|
| 1. 陰 | 2. 終 | 3. 誤 | 4. 情 | 5. 津 |
|    阴 |    终 |    误 |    情 |    津 |
| 6. 界 | 7. 團 | 8. 笑 | 9. 繁 | 10. 挺 |
|    界 |    团 |    笑 |    繁 |     挺 |

**5-4**    With a partner or a group, create phrases with the following words (pay attention to the various usages of each word).

*Example:*    樣：怎麼樣，幾樣菜，跟以前一樣
　　　　　　　样：怎么样，几样菜，跟以前一样

1. 點：＿＿＿＿＿＿＿＿＿＿＿＿＿＿＿＿＿

　　点：＿＿＿＿＿＿＿＿＿＿＿＿＿＿＿＿＿

2. 上：＿＿＿＿＿＿＿＿＿＿＿＿＿＿＿＿＿

　　上：＿＿＿＿＿＿＿＿＿＿＿＿＿＿＿＿＿

3. 本： _____

   本： _____

4. 班： _____

   班： _____

5. 再： _____

   再： _____

6. 熱： _____

   热： _____

7. 味： _____

   味： _____

8. 開： _____

   开： _____

## III. Grammar Exercises

**5-5**  Read aloud the passage with your instructor and fill in the blanks, then answer the questions orally.

*Notes:*
王府井大街(王府井大街) [Wángfǔjǐng dàjiē]: (name of a renowned commercial street in Beijing)
秀水街(秀水街) [Xiùshuǐjiē]: (name of a famous commercial street in Beijing)
禮物(礼物) [lǐwù]: a gift
有名(有名) [yǒumíng]: renowned, famous
商業街(商业街) [shāngyèjiē]: commercial street
天安門廣場(天安门广场) [Tiān'ānmén guǎngchǎng]: Tiananmen Square
茶葉(茶叶) [cháyè]: tea
文物(文物) [wénwù]: antique; artefact
步行街(步行街) [bùxíngjiē]: pedestrianized street
小商品(小商品) [xiǎo shāngpǐn]: small commodity
飾品(饰品) [shìpǐn]: accessory
紀念品(纪念品) [jìniànpǐn]: souvenir

1. 我這次去北京旅遊，給美國的朋友們買了一些中國的禮物帶回去。聽北京的朋友們說，王府井大街和秀水街都是買東西的好地方，所以我去這兩個地方走了走，_____ _____ 眼界，也 _____ _____ (to buy) 不少東西。

   我这次去北京旅游，给美国的朋友们买了一些中国的礼物带回去。听北京的朋友们说，王府井大街和秀水街都是买东西的好地方，所以我去这两个地方走了走，_____ _____ 眼界，也 _____ _____ (to buy) 不少东西。

2. 聽說王府井大街是北京 _____ (the most) 有名的商業街。大街 _____ 天安門廣場很近。從天安門廣場前面 _____ 東走，經過兩條大街 _____ 北 _____ 就是王府井大街了。王府井大街有很多商店。

   听说王府井大街是北京 _____ (the most) 有名的商业街。大街 _____ 天安门广场很近。从天安门广场前面 _____ 东走，经过两条大街 _____ 北 _____ 就是王府井大街了。王府井大街有很多商店。

3. 這裡有全國 _____ 大的 (the biggest) 書店和照相館，有很多餐館，還有不少商店，比如藥店、茶葉店和文物店等等。王府井是步行街，沒有車能開 _____ _____ (to enter)。我走著走著，還 _____ 我的照相機拿 _____ _____ (use 把) (to take out)，_____ 漂亮的王府井大街照了下來 (use 把)。

   这里有全国 _____ 大的 (the biggest) 书店和照相馆，有很多餐馆，还有不少商店，比如药店、茶叶店和文物店等等。王府井是步行街，没有车能开 _____ _____ (to enter)。我走着走着，还 _____ 我的照相机拿 _____ _____ (use 把) (to take out)，_____ 漂亮的王府井大街照了下来 (use 把)。

4. 從王府井大街走出來 _____ 東走，經過三條大街再 _____ 北 _____ (to turn north) 就到秀水街了。秀水街 _____ 王府井大街短 (shorter)，也 _____ _____ 王府井大街那麼大 (not so . . . as . . .)，但是街上的人跟王府井大街 _____ _____ 多 (the same as)。

   从王府井大街走出来 _____ 东走，经过三条大街再 _____ 北 _____ (to turn north) 就到秀水街了。秀水街 _____ 王府井大街短 (shorter)，也 _____ _____ 王府井大街那么大 (not so . . . as . . .)，但是街上的人跟王府井大街 _____ _____ 多 (the same as)。

5. 不 _____ (like) 王府井大街，秀水街上賣的大多是小商品，從穿的衣服，到飾品、小紀念品等都有。你能在那兒買到很便宜的小東西。

不 _____ (like) 王府井大街，秀水街上卖的大多是小商品，从穿的衣服，到饰品、小纪念品等都有。你能在那儿买到很便宜的小东西。

6. 我在王府井大街和秀水街，給爸爸、媽媽、還有朋友們買了很多禮物。下次我一定還要到這兒來。

我在王府井大街和秀水街，给爸爸、妈妈、还有朋友们买了很多礼物。下次我一定还要到这儿来。

問題(问题):

1. 王府井大街和秀水街為什麼這麼有名？
   王府井大街和秀水街为什么这么有名？

2. 從天安門廣場到王府井應該怎麼走？
   从天安门广场到王府井应该怎么走？

3. 王府井大街上有些什麼？
   王府井大街上有些什么？

4. 從王府井大街到秀水街應該怎麼走？
   从王府井大街到秀水街应该怎么走？

5. 秀水街跟王府井大街有什麼不一樣的嗎？
   秀水街跟王府井大街有什么不一样的吗？

6. 從上面的故事中找出這一課的主要語法 (e.g. 結果補語 RC;
把 sentences; the aspects 了，著，and 過；有(多) + Adj.; ask and give
directions; 比較 comparison: 比較，最，更)。

从上面的故事中找出这一课的主要语法 (e.g. 结果补语 RC;
把 sentences; the aspects 了，着，and 过；有(多) + Adj.; ask and give
directions; 比较 comparison: 比较，最，更)。

## IV. Communicative Activities

**5-6**  Read aloud the passage with the instructor. Then answer the questions orally.

*Notes:*
有錢人(有钱人) [yǒuqiánrén]: rich man
瞧不起(瞧不起) [qiáobuqǐ]: to look down on
窮人(穷人) [qióngrén]: poor people
行禮(行礼) [xínglǐ]: to salute
經過(经过) [jīngguò]: to pass
片(片) [piàn]: (measure word/classifier for field)
農夫(农夫) [nóngfū]: farmer, peasant
生氣(生气) [shēngqì]: to get angry

1. 從前有一個有錢人，他瞧不起窮人，
還要窮人在見到他的時候向他行
禮。有一天這個有錢人騎著馬經過
一片農田，他見到有一個農夫正坐
在農田的旁邊休息。農夫看到有錢
人的時候沒有走開，也沒有站起來向有錢人行禮。

从前有一个有钱人，他瞧不起穷人，还要穷人在见到他的时候向
他行礼。有一天这个有钱人骑着马经过一片农田，他见到有一个
农夫正坐在农田的旁边休息。农夫看到有钱人的时候没有走开，
也没有站起来向有钱人行礼。

2. 這個有錢人很生氣，叫人把農夫帶過來，問農夫為什麼不行禮。
農夫問："我為什麼要向你行禮呢？"有錢人說："因為我比你有
錢。"農夫又說："那是你的錢，又不是我的錢。我不用向你行
禮。"有錢人說："那我把我的錢給你一半，你會向我行禮嗎？"
農夫說："那麼我的錢就跟你的錢一樣多了，我為什麼還要向你
行禮呢？"

这个有钱人很生气，叫人把农夫带过来，问农夫为什么不行礼。农夫问："我为什么要向你行礼呢？"有钱人说："因为我比你有钱。"农夫又说："那是你的钱，又不是我的钱。我不用向你行礼。"有钱人说："那我把我的钱给你一半，你会向我行礼吗？"农夫说："那么我的钱就跟你的钱一样多了，我为什么还要向你行礼呢？"

3. 有錢人又說："好吧。我把我的錢全都給你，現在你應該向我行禮了吧。"農夫最後說："那麼我的錢就比你的錢多了，我是有錢人，你是窮人，我就更不用向你行禮了！"有錢人不知道說什麼好，只好騎著馬生氣地走了。

　　有钱人又说："好吧。我把我的钱全都给你，现在你应该向我行礼了吧。"农夫最后说："那么我的钱就比你的钱多了，我是有钱人，你是穷人，我就更不用向你行礼了！"有钱人不知道说什么好，只好骑着马生气地走了。

**問題(问题):**

1. 有錢人要窮人見到他的時候做什麼？
   有钱人要穷人见到他的时候做什么？

2. 有錢人是在哪兒見到農夫的？
   有钱人是在哪儿见到农夫的？

3. 有錢人第一次要把多少錢給農夫？農夫會向有錢人行禮嗎？為什麼？
   有钱人第一次要把多少钱给农夫？农夫会向有钱人行礼吗？为什么？

4. 有錢人又要把多少錢給農夫？農夫有沒有向有錢人行禮？為什麼？
   有钱人又要把多少钱给农夫？农夫有没有向有钱人行礼？为什么？

5. 最後有錢人怎麼樣了？
   最后有钱人怎么样了？

6. 從上面的故事中找出這一課的主要語法。
   从上面的故事中找出这一课的主要语法。

# 文化知識 (文化知识) Culture Link

## 文化點滴 (文化点滴) CULTURE NOTES

### 在中國旅行 (在中国旅行) Traveling in China

The most popular times for travel in China are the two majors holidays, 春節(春节) [chūnjié] Spring Festival (Chinese New Year) and 國慶節(国庆节) [guóqìngjié] China's National Day, October 1. Many companies arrange holiday tours for employees in appreciation of their hard work, and some families choose to travel together during the traditional Chinese festivals instead of having reunions at home. Chinese people are also traveling abroad in greater numbers and can now be seen at tourist destinations all over the world.

People from other nations are also enthusiastic about visiting China. The number of foreign tourists has been increasing by millions each year. Many people know about 兵馬俑(兵马俑) [Bīngmǎyǒng] (the Terracotta Warriors) in Xi'an, 紫禁城 [Zǐjìnchéng] (the Forbidden City), 天安門(天安门) [Tiān'ānmén] (the Tiananmen Square), and 長城 [Chángchéng] (the Great Wall) in Beijing, and the lovely and precious 熊貓(熊猫)

> **Do you know…**
> - the most popular seasons for travel in China?
> - the most popular tourist sites in China?
>
> ***Read and find out!***

[xióngmāo] (panda), and 絲綢之路(丝绸之路) [Sīchóuzhīlù] (the Silk Road). But these are only a few of the vast natural and cultural resources of China. As the longest continuous civilization on the planet with a recorded history of over 4,000 years, China has a tremendously rich cultural heritage. A meaningful visit to China would not be limited to these well-known tourist sites, but would also include sampling the many delicious cuisines, visiting ancient remote villages, listening to the unique Beijing Opera, and appreciating the elegant traditional arts of China.

Tourism in China is booming and is one of the country's most successful industries. Good transportation, ample accommodation, and recreation and catering services are all available at reasonable prices. In many cities, such as Beijing, Shanghai, Guangzhou, and Hong Kong, a foreigner can easily communicate in English. Of course, one can always amaze the Chinese by trying out even a few Chinese words.

A statue of a bronze lion with the traditional architecture of the Forbidden City, Beijing, in the background. If you visit Beijing, would you like to see the cultural attractions or sample the delicious Chinese cuisine?

A camel caravan crosses sand dunes at sunset on the Silk Road in Dunhuang, Gansu Province, China. Which places in China do you want to visit most? Why?

## 問題討論 (问题讨论) *Discuss the following with a partner or in small groups.*

1. Have you ever been to China?
2. If so, where did you go? Share your experience with the class (something fun, or different, or that made a lasting impression).
3. If not, do you plan to go? Say something about your plans.
4. Which places in China do you want to visit most? Why?
5. 在你的國家，有哪些有名的旅遊地點？請與中國的做一個比較。
   在你的国家，有哪些有名的旅游地点？请与中国的做一个比较。
   What are the famous scenic spots in your country? Compare them to some scenic spots in China.

# 趣味中文 (趣味中文) FUN WITH CHINESE

趕鴨子上架
赶鸭子上架
To hurry the duck onto the racks
This indicates that someone is pushed by force to get things done fast.

| găn | yāzi | shàng | jià |
|------|------|-------|------|
| 趕 | 鴨子 | 上 | 架 |
| 赶 | 鸭子 | 上 | 架 |
| hurry | duck | up | racks |

**問題討論 (问题讨论)** *Discuss the following with a partner or in small groups.*

1. Have you ever encountered any situations like 趕鴨子上架(赶鸭子上架)? Describe them to your classmates.
2. Make a sentence using 趕鴨子上架(赶鸭子上架).

## ● 行動吧! (行动吧!) LET'S GO!

### 旅館賓客調查表 (旅馆宾客调查表) Hotel Guest Satisfaction Survey

When 方小文 traveled to China during the summer vacation, he stayed at a hotel in Beijing. On the hotel desk, there was a note asking guests to comment on the hotel's service. Let's read the note and help 方小文 figure out how to provide feedback to the hotel.

| ☺ ☺ ☹ 北京旅馆宾客调查表 ☺ ☺ ☹ | 满意 | 一般 | 不满意 |
|---|---|---|---|
| 1. 我们的旅馆服务 | | | |
| 2. 请告诉我们您对以下服务项目的评价： | 满意 | 一般 | 不满意 |
|    A. 入住服务 | | | |
|    B. 离店服务 | | | |
|    C. 清洁 | | | |
|    D. 餐饮 | | | |
| 您对酒店的意见或建议： | | | |
| 您的姓名： | | | |

*Notes:*

賓客(宾客) [bīnkè]: guests
調查表(调查表) [diàochábiǎo]: survey sheet
滿意(满意) [mǎnyì]: satisfied
一般(一般) [yìbān]: neutral, OK
不滿(不满) [bùmǎn]: dissatisfied
告訴(告诉) [gàosu]: to tell
以下(以下) [yǐxià]: below; the following
項目(项目) [xiàngmù]: item; project
評價(评价) [píngjià]: to evaluate
清潔(清洁) [qīngjié]: to clean
餐飲(餐饮) [cānyǐn]: food and beverages
意見(意见) [yìjiàn]: opinion; suggestion
建議(建议) [jiànyì]: recommendation

## 問題討論 (问题讨论) *Discuss the following with a partner or in small groups.*

1. Translate the form into English.
2. Fill in the following blanks: if you are satisfied with the hotel's services but are not content with the lighting and food facilities, what would you write on the form?

# 開銀行帳戶 (开银行账户)
# Opening a Bank Account

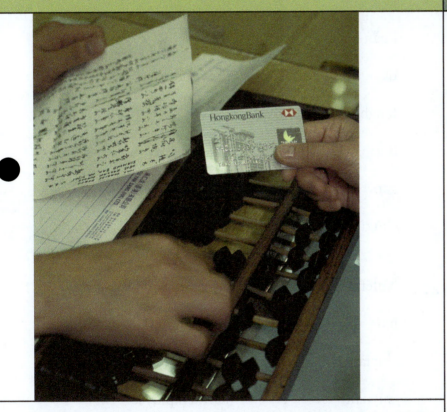

*The abacus has been used as a calculation tool in China for more than 5,000 years.*

## CONNECTIONS AND COMMUNITIES PREVIEW

**Discuss the following questions with a partner or your class. What similarities and differences do you think there might be between Chinese culture and your own culture?**

1. Personal checks are not available in China. Are they available in your country?

2. How do you open a bank account in your country? Can you do it online?

## 教學目標 (教学目标) OBJECTIVES

- Open a bank account
- Describe interest and exchange rates

# 生詞 (生词) VOCABULARY

## 核心詞 (核心词) Core Vocabulary

| | TRADITIONAL | SIMPLIFIED | PINYIN | | |
|---|---|---|---|---|---|
| 1. | 銀行 | 银行 | yínháng | N. | bank |
| 2. | 開 | 开 | kāi | V. | to open |
| 3. | 帳戶 | 账户 | zhànghù | N. | account |
| 4. | 存 | 存 | cún | V. | to deposit |
| 5. | 款 | 款 | kuǎn | N. | money |
| 6. | 取 | 取 | qǔ | V. | to withdraw |
| 7. | 方便 | 方便 | fāngbiàn | Adj. | convenient |
| 8. | 利率 | 利率 | lìlǜ | N. | interest rate |
| 9. | 高 | 高 | gāo | Adj. | high |
| 10. | 儲蓄 | 储蓄 | chǔxù | N.<br>V. | savings<br>to save (money) |
| 11. | 百分之…… | 百分之…… | bǎifēnzhi … | Num. | … percent (%) |
| 12. | 利息 | 利息 | lìxi | N. | interest |
| 13. | 支票 | 支票 | zhīpiào | N. | check |
| 14. | 職員 | 职员 | zhíyuán | N. | staff, employee |
| 15. | 低 | 低 | dī | Adj. | low |
| 16. | 種 | 种 | zhǒng | M.W. | kind |
| 17. | 差不多 | 差不多 | chàbuduō | | similar, about the same |
| 18. | 夠 | 够 | gòu | Adj. | enough |

| TRADITIONAL | SIMPLIFIED | PINYIN | | |
|---|---|---|---|---|
| 19. 單子 | 单子 | dānzi | N. | form |
| 20. 填 | 填 | tián | V. | to fill in/up |
| 21. 千 | 千 | qiān | Num. | thousand |
| 22. 元 | 元 | yuán | M.W. | dollar |
| 23. 寄 | 寄 | jì | V. | to mail |
| 24. 簿 | 簿 | bù | N. | (check) book |
| 25. 拿 | 拿 | ná | V. | to take, fetch; to use |
| 26. 取款卡 | 取款卡 | qǔkuǎnkǎ | N. | ATM card |
| 27. 自動 | 自动 | zìdòng | Adj. | automatic |
| 28. 取款機 | 取款机 | qǔkuǎnjī | N. | banking machine, ATM |
| 29. 現金 | 现金 | xiànjīn | N. | cash |
| 30. 申請 | 申请 | shēnqǐng | N. / V. | application / to apply |
| 31. 信用卡 | 信用卡 | xìnyòngkǎ | N. | credit card |
| 32. 當然 | 当然 | dāngrán | Adv. | of course |
| 33. 表 | 表 | biǎo | N. | form |
| 34. 換 | 换 | huàn | V. | to change |
| 35. 匯率 | 汇率 | huìlǜ | N. | exchange rate |
| 36. 兌換 | 兑换 | duìhuàn | N. / V. | exchange / to exchange |
| 37. 外幣 | 外币 | wàibì | N. | foreign currency |
| 38. 櫃台 | 柜台 | guìtái | N. | counter |

## 專名 (专名) Proper Nouns

| TRADITIONAL | SIMPLIFIED | PINYIN | | |
|---|---|---|---|---|
| 1. 關京華 | 关京华 | Guān Jīnghuá | N. | (name) Jinghua Guan |
| 2. 方小琴 | 方小琴 | Fāng Xiǎoqín | N. | (name) Xiaoqin Fang |
| 3. 美金 | 美金 | Měijīn | N. | US dollar |

## 語文知識 (语文知识) LANGUAGE LINK

Read and listen to the following sentence patterns. These patterns use vocabulary, expressions, and grammar that you will study in more detail in this lesson. After reading the sentence patterns, read and listen to the Language in Use section that follows.

### 句型 (句型) Sentence Patterns

A: 我要開一個支票帳戶。
我要开一个支票账户。
Wǒ yào kāi yíge zhīpiào zhànghù.

B: 好，這是開帳戶的單子，請你填一下。
好，这是开账户的单子，请你填一下。
Hǎo, zhè shì kāi zhànghù de dānzi, qǐng nǐ tián yíxià.

A: 今天的利率是多少?
今天的利率是多少?
Jīntiān de lìlǜ shì duōshǎo?

B: 百分之二點五。
百分之二点五。
Bǎi fēn zhi èr diǎn wǔ.

A: 美元换人民幣的匯率呢?
美元换人民币的汇率呢?
Měiyuán huàn Rénmínbì de huìlǜ ne?

B: 一比六點五三。
一比六点五三。
Yì bǐ liù diǎn wǔ sān.

---

 A: 兑换外幣的地方在哪兒?
兑换外币的地方在哪儿?
Duìhuàn wàibì de dìfang zài nǎr?

B: 在左邊的櫃台那兒。
在左边的柜台那儿。
Zài zuǒbiān de guìtái nàr.

🔊 **課文 Language in Use: Opening a Bank Account
(繁體字 Traditional Character Version)**

**Scene 1:** 在路上

關京華： 小琴，我要去銀行¹開²一個
帳³戶，這樣我存款、取款就
方便多了。你知道哪家銀行
比較好嗎?

方小琴： 我常常去大華銀行存款、取
款。那兒的服務不錯，利率也
比較高，現在儲蓄帳戶的利
率是百分之三點二。

關京華： 那⁴我就去大華銀行吧。

> **1. 行(行)**
>
> When used in "銀行(银行)," 行(行) is pronounced [háng]. When used as a noun in 旅行(旅行), and an adjective to mean "OK" or "good," it is pronounced [xíng].

> **2. 開(开)**
>
> 開(开) means "to open." It is used when opening a bank account 開銀行帳戶 (开银行账户), writing a check 開支票 (开支票), and writing an invoice 開發票 (开发票) [kāifāpiào]

**Scene 2:** 在銀行

關京華： 先生，我想開一個有利息的支票帳戶。請問，有利息的支票帳
戶利率是多少?

職員： 最近利率都比較低，今天是百分之二點六。

關京華： 怎麼這麼低呀? 我聽說是百分之三點二呢。

職員： 那是儲蓄帳戶，儲蓄帳戶的利率
高一點兒，是百分之三點二。這
種帳戶每個月可以開三張支票。
您想開哪一種?

關京華： 我想一個月開三張支票差不多夠
了。我就開一個儲蓄帳戶吧。

職員： 好，請把這張開帳戶的單子填一
下，謝謝。請問您今天想存多少
錢?

*Continued on page 172*

## 课文 Language in Use: Opening a Bank Account
## (简体字 Simplified Character Version)

### Scene 1: 在路上

关京华： 小琴，我要去银行[1]开[2]一个
账[3]户，这样我存款、取款就
方便多了。你知道哪家银行
比较好吗？

方小琴： 我常常去大华银行存款、取
款。那儿的服务不错，利率也
比较高，现在储蓄账户的利
率是百分之三点二。

关京华： 那[4]我就去大华银行吧。

---

**3. 帐(帐) [账(账)]**

Referring to "account," both 帐 and 账 can be used in traditional character texts, i.e. 帐户 or 账户. However, only 账 is used in simplified character texts, i.e. 账户.

---

**4. 那(那)**

那(那) means "then" or "in that case." It is often used in conversations to connect sentences.

---

### Scene 2: 在银行

关京华： 先生，我想开一个有利息的支票账户。请问，有利息的支票账
户利率是多少？

职员： 最近利率都比较低，今天是百分之二点六。

关京华： 怎么这么低呀？我听说是百分之三点二呢。

职员： 那是储蓄账户，储蓄账户的利率高一点儿，是百分之三点二。
这种账户每个月可以开三张支票。您想开哪一种？

关京华： 我想一个月开三张支票差不多够了。我就开一个储蓄账户吧。

职员： 好，请把这张开账户的单子填一下，谢谢。请问您今天想存多
少钱？

*Continued on page 173*

### 課文 Language in Use: Opening a Bank Account
### (繁體字 Traditional Character Version) —— 接第一百七十頁

關京華： 我這兒是三千元美金。

職員： 好⋯⋯一個星期以後，您會收
到我們給您寄去的支票簿和
取款卡5。您可以拿取款卡在
自動取款機6那兒取現金。

關京華： 我可以在你們這兒申請一張
信用卡嗎?

職員： 當然可以。請把這張申請信
用卡的表填一下。

關京華： 下個月我要去中國，要換一
些人民幣。請問美金換人民
幣的匯率7是多少?

職員： 今天的匯率是一比六點五
三。

關京華： 兌換外幣的地方在哪兒?

職員： 就在左邊的櫃台那兒。

關京華： 謝謝。再見。

---

**5. 取款卡/提款卡/借記卡**
**(取款卡/提款卡/借记卡)**

取款卡(取款卡), 提款卡(提款卡), and
借記卡(借记卡) all refer to bank cards.
取款卡(取款卡) and 提款卡(提款卡)
are ATM cards, and 借記卡(借记卡) is a
debit card. Note that 提款卡(提款卡) is
more commonly used in Taiwan.

---

**6. 取款機/提款機(取款机/提款机)**

Both 取款機(取款机) and 提款機
(提款机) mean ATM (automated teller
machine). 取款機(取款机) is used in
mainland China, while 提款機(提款机)
is commonly used in Taiwan. Another term
is 櫃員機(柜员机).

## 课文 Language in Use: Opening a Bank Account
### (简体字 Simplified Character Version) —— 接第一百七十一页

关京华： 我这儿是三千元美金。

职员： 好......一个星期以后，您会收到我们给您寄去的支票簿和取款卡⁵。您可以拿取款卡在自动取款机⁶那儿取现金。

关京华： 我可以在你们这儿申请一张信用卡吗?

职员： 当然可以。请把这张申请信用卡的表填一下。

关京华： 下个月我要去中国，要换一些人民币。请问美金换人民币的汇率⁷是多少?

职员： 今天的汇率是一比六点五三。

> **7. 匯率/兑换率(汇率/兑换率)**
> Both 匯率(汇率) and 兑换率(兑换率) are used in mainland China to mean "exchange rate." In Taiwan, 匯率(汇率) is more commonly used.

关京华： 兑换外币的地方在哪儿?

职员： 就在左边的柜台那儿。

关京华： 谢谢。再见。

# 語法 (语法) GRAMMAR

## I. Various Kinds of Phrases

A phrase is a combination of words that are grammatically related. There are more than 10 kinds of phrases in Chinese which can be used as different parts of a sentence. The major types are juxtaposed phrases, endocentric phrases, Subject + V. phrases, and V. + Object phrases.

### A. Juxtaposed 並列 (并列) [bìngliè] phrase:

This construction is formed by two or more words that are of the same quality and that may be connected by a conjunction (such as 和, 又……又) or a Chinese comma "、", or neither.

*Examples:*

爸爸、媽媽 — 爸爸媽媽
爸爸、妈妈 — 爸爸妈妈

存款、取款 — 存款取款
存款、取款 — 存款取款

洗好、掛好 — 洗好掛好
洗好、挂好 — 洗好挂好

又拉又吹，又唱又跳，又睏又累
又拉又吹，又唱又跳，又困又累

認真地、努力地 — 認真(地)努力地
认真地、努力地 — 认真(地)努力地

*Notes:*

- A juxtaposed construction can be used basically as any part of a sentence, depending on the category of the words.
- The order of the words can be reversed without affecting the meaning. However, some constructions have a fixed order, e.g. 父親母親(父亲母亲) (Chinese seldom use 母親父親(母亲父亲)).

**»Try it!** With a partner, give as many examples of juxtaposed constructions as you can. Make sure they include all the different kinds of juxtaposed construction. For example,

A: 小王，你去哪兒？
　　小王，你去哪儿？

B: 我去銀行<u>存款取款</u>。
　　我去银行<u>存款取款</u>。

**B. Endocentric** 偏正(偏正) [piānzhèng] **phrase:**

An endocentric construction is composed of a modifier 偏(偏) and the modified 正 (focus).

*Examples:*

| Modifier | the Modified |
|---|---|
| 支票<br>支票 | 帳戶<br>账户 |
| 今天的<br>今天的 | 匯率<br>汇率 |
| 自動<br>自动 | 取款機<br>取款机 |
| 認真地<br>认真地 | 學習<br>学习 |

*Notes:*

- The order of words in an endocentric construction cannot be reversed because it indicates a fixed modifying relationship between the words.
- Similar to a compound phrase, an endocentric phrase can be used as any part of a sentence.

**≫Try it!** With a partner, practice asking and answering questions about things you do at a bank. Make sure you use endocentric constructions. For example,

A: 請問，您要開什麽樣的帳戶？
　请问，您要开什么样的账户？

B: 我要開一個<u>支票帳戶</u>。
　我要开一个<u>支票账户</u>。

## C. Subject + V. 主謂 (主谓) [zhǔwèi] *phrase:*

This kind of phrase is one in which the relationship between the components is like that between a subject and a verbal predicate.

*Examples:*

| | Subject    +    V. | | |
|---|---|---|---|
| | <u>我們</u><br><u>我们</u> | 寄去<br>寄去 | 的支票簿<br>的支票簿 |
| | <u>你</u><br><u>你</u> | 會做飯<br>会做饭 | 太好了<br>太好了 |
| 這件衣服<br>这件衣服 | <u>顏色</u><br><u>颜色</u> | <u>太深</u><br><u>太深</u> | |
| 我覺得<br>我觉得 | <u>這兒的服務</u><br><u>这儿的服务</u> | <u>又快又好</u><br><u>又快又好</u> | |

*Notes:*

- The order of a Subject + V. construction is fixed. The Subject always precedes the verbal predicate.
- A Subject + V. phrase can function as any part of a sentence.

**>>Try it!** With a partner, practice discussing what you do at a bank. Make sure that you use the Subject + V. construction in your dialogue. For example,

A: 今天人民幣兌換美元的利率是多少?
今天人民币兑换美元的利率是多少?

B: 今天人民幣兌換美元的利率是六點五三比一。
今天人民币兑换美元的利率是六点五三比一。

**D. V. + Object phrase:**

A V. + Object phrase is formed by a transitive verb and a noun that serves as its object.

*Examples:*

| V.  +  | Object |  |
|--------|--------|--------|
| 有 | 利息 | 的支票帳戶 |
| 有 | 利息 | 的支票账户 |
| 開 | 帳戶 | 的單子 |
| 开 | 账户 | 的单子 |
| 申請 | 信用卡 | 的表 |
| 申请 | 信用卡 | 的表 |
| 兌換 | 外幣 | 的地方 |
| 兑换 | 外币 | 的地方 |

*Notes:*

- The order of a V. + Object phrase is fixed and cannot be changed.
- No conjunction should be used between the verb and its object.
- A particle 的 must be used after V. + Object

**>>Try it!** With your partner, practice opening a bank account. Make sure that you use as many V. + Object phrases as possible. For example,

A: 請問，你們銀行有沒有有利息的帳戶?
请问，你们银行有没有有利息的账户?

B: 有。
有。

## II. Ways to Express Percentages and Proportion

The way to express percentages in Chinese is to use 百分之 plus the percentage figure.

*Examples:*

　1% = 百分之一(百分之一)
　15% = 百分之十五(百分之十五)
　80% = 百分之八十 (百分之八十)
100% = 百分之百/百分之一百(百分之百/百分之一百)

……分之…… also applies to other fractions, such as one-third and three-fourths. The number before it is the denominator and the one after it is the numerator.

*Examples:*

$\frac{1}{3}$ = 三分之一(三分之一)　　　　$\frac{3}{4}$ = 四分之三(四分之三)

---

**»Try it!** | With your partner, talk about the numbers of students and teachers in your university, department, and class. Make sure that you use percentages and fractions for comparison. For example,

A: 你們系的女生有多少?
　你们系的女生有多少?

B: 我們系的女生有五十二個，是全系學生的<u>三分之一</u>。
　我们系的女生有五十二个，是全系学生的<u>三分之一</u>。

## III. Decimals

A decimal number in Chinese is expressed by "A + 點(点) + B." Here A indicates the integer and B, the decimal.

*Examples:*

　2.5 = 二點五(二点五)
　1.8 = 一點八(一点八)
17.9 = 十七點九(十七点九)
26.9 = 二十六點九(二十六点九)

>>**Try it!** With your partner, practice converting the following percentages and fractions into decimals.

四分之一，十分之七，百分之三十，百分之七十五

## IV. N./Pron. + 這兒/那兒 (这儿/那儿)

When a N. or a Pron. is used to indicate a location, it is often followed by 這兒(这儿) or 那兒(那儿), depending on where the speaker is. If it is with or close to the speaker, 這兒(这儿) is used; otherwise, 那兒(那儿) should be used.

*Examples:*

我們這兒 (here with us)　　　　　　他們那兒 (there with them)
我们这儿　　　　　　　　　　　　他们那儿

櫃台這兒 (here at the counter)　　自動取款機那兒 (there at the ATM)
柜台这儿　　　　　　　　　　　　自动取款机那儿

*Examples:*

你的支票在我這兒。
你的支票在我这儿。
Your checks are here with me.

兌換外幣在櫃台那兒。
兑换外币在柜台那儿。
Go to the counter there to convert foreign exchange.

>>**Try it!** With your partner, practice questions and answers using the pattern "N./Pron. + 這兒/那兒 (这儿/那儿). For example,

A: 請問，自動取款機在哪兒?
　　请问，自动取款机在哪儿?

B: 在門那兒。
　　在门那儿。

# 補充課文（补充课文）SUPPLEMENTARY PRACTICE

*Read the following passage. Then listen and repeat.*

## Paying Taxes in the US (繁體字 Traditional Character Version)

小華：

你好！

時間過得真快，我來美國已經三個月了。我在這兒開了銀行帳戶，還申請了信用卡。美國的很多事情對我來說都很新鮮，其中我最感興趣的是這兒的稅收制度。

美國的稅收制度跟中國的很不一樣。在日常生活中，無論是吃飯、買東西，還是銀行的存款利息、打工的收入等等都得交稅。怪不得人們把美國叫做"萬稅之國"呢。

在美國生活一定要了解美國的稅收制度。聯邦稅的稅率每個地方都是一樣的，可是各個地方的稅率就不一樣了，最高的差不多是百分之十點三。非常高。

每年的四月十五號以前，人們都要忙著報稅。現在很多人通過網絡報稅，也可以用信用卡或者銀行帳戶付稅，方便極了。對那些收入低的人，政府還會給他們退稅。

我覺得在這兒要學習的東西還很多，所以我得多看、多聽、多問、多想，這樣才能進步。好，下次再聊。

祝

好

小明
十一月三日

Notes:

信用卡(信用卡) [xìnyòngkǎ]: credit card
對……來說(对……来说) [duì . . . láishuō]: as to . . . ; as for . . .
新鮮(新鲜) [xīnxiān]: novel, fresh
稅收制度(税收制度) [shuìshōu zhìdù]: tax system
無論(无论) [wúlùn]: no matter what
收入(收入) [shōurù]: income
交稅(交税) [jiāoshuì]: to pay tax
怪不得(怪不得) [guàibudé]: no wonder
萬(万) [wàn]: ten thousand
聯邦稅(联邦税) [liánbāngshuì]: federal tax
稅率(税率) [shuìlǜ]: tax rate
報稅(报税) [bàoshuì]: to declare tax
退稅(退税) [tuìshuì]: to refund tax

## 補充課文 (补充课文) SUPPLEMENTARY PRACTICE

*Read the following passage. Then listen and repeat.*

### Paying Taxes in the US (简体字 Simplified Character Version)

小华：

　　你好！

　　时间过得真快，我来美国已经三个月了。我在这儿开了银行账户，还申请了信用卡。美国的很多事情对我来说都很新鲜，其中我最感兴趣的是这儿的税收制度。

　　美国的税收制度跟中国的很不一样。在日常生活中，无论是吃饭、买东西，还是银行的存款利息、打工的收入等等都得交税。怪不得人们把美国叫做"万税之国"呢。

　　在美国生活一定要了解美国的税收制度。联邦税的税率每个地方都是一样的，可是各个地方的税率就不一样了，最高的差不多是百分之十点三。非常高。

　　每年的四月十五号以前，人们都要忙着报税。现在很多人通过网络报税，也可以用信用卡或者银行账户付税，方便极了。对那些收入低的人，政府还会给他们退税。

　　我觉得在这儿要学习的东西还很多，所以我得多看、多听、多问、多想，这样才能进步。好，下次再聊。

祝

　　好

小明
十一月三日

### Exercises: work with a partner or in small groups

1. 到美國以後，小明做了什麼事？
   到美国以后，小明做了什么事？

2. 為什麼人們把美國叫做"萬稅之國"？
   为什么人们把美国叫做"万税之国"？

3. 在美國，稅率怎麼樣？人們怎麼報稅？
   在美国，税率怎么样？人们怎么报税？

## 成語故事 (成语故事) IDIOM STORY

### 井底之蛙 (井底之蛙) [jǐng dǐ zhī wā]

*Meaning:* A frog in a well.

*Usage:* A person with a very limited outlook.

*Example:* 你真是一個 "井底之蛙"，不知道現在中國那兒已經有很多人使用信用卡了。

你真是一个 "井底之蛙"，不知道现在中国那儿已经有很多人使用信用卡了。

Pay attention to the usages of various phrases, expression of percentages, portions, decimals, and 這兒(这儿), 那兒(那儿).

(繁體字 Traditional Character Version)

　　從前，一個井裡住著一隻青蛙。有一天，青蛙在井邊碰到了一隻從大海裡來的海龜。青蛙就對海龜說：
　　"你看，我住在這裡多快樂！高興的時候，就在井邊玩兒；累了的時候，就在井裡睡覺。你們誰也比不上我。我是這兒的主人，在這個井裡舒服極了。你要不要到井裡玩兒玩兒呢？"
　　海龜問青蛙："你見過大海嗎？"青蛙說："我沒見過大海，不過我這兒一定比大海那兒舒服。"海龜笑了笑，說："你這個井的大小還不及大海的百萬分之一。大海可以大到幾千里，深到幾千丈。無論是下大雨還是天旱，大海都不受影響。住在那樣的大海裡，才是真的快樂呢！"
　　青蛙聽了海龜的話以後，吃驚地什麼也說不出來了。

(简体字 Simplified Character Version)

　　从前，一个井里住着一只青蛙。有一天，青蛙在井边碰到了一只从大海里来的海龟。青蛙就对海龟说：

　　"你看，我住在这里多快乐！高兴的时候，就在井边玩儿；累了的时候，就在井里睡觉。你们谁也比不上我。我是这儿的主人，在这个井里舒服极了。你要不要到井里玩儿玩儿呢？"

　　海龟问青蛙："你见过大海吗？"青蛙说："我没见过大海，不过我这儿一定比大海那儿舒服。"海龟笑了笑，说："你这个井的大小还不及大海的百万分之一。大海可以大到几千里，深到几千丈。无论是下大雨还是天旱，大海都不受影响。住在那样的大海里，才是真的快乐呢！"

　　青蛙听了海龟的话以后，吃惊地什么也说不出来了。

*Notes:*
井(井) [jǐng]: well
青蛙(青蛙) [qīngwā]: frog
海龜(海龟) [hǎiguī]: turtle
主人(主人) [zhǔrén]: master
百萬(百万) [bǎiwàn]: million
旱(旱) [hàn]: drought
受……影響(受……影响) [shòu . . . yǐngxiǎng]: to be affected by . . .
吃驚(吃惊) [chījīng]: to be startled

## Exercises: work with a partner or in small groups

1. 從上面的課文中，找出有下面語法點的句子：various phrases, expression of percentage, portions, decimals, and 這兒，那兒

   从上面的课文中，找出有下面语法点的句子：various phrases, expression of percentage, portions, decimals, and 这儿，那儿

2. 用你自己的話說說 "井底之蛙" 的故事。
   用你自己的话说说 "井底之蛙" 的故事。

3. 請用 "井底之蛙" 造一個句子或者說一個井底之蛙的例子。
   请用 "井底之蛙" 造一个句子或者说一个井底之蛙的例子。

4. "井底之蛙" 的故事，告訴了我們什麼？
   "井底之蛙" 的故事，告诉了我们什么？

## 練習 (练习) ACTIVITIES

### I. Listening Exercises

**6-1** 關京華(关京华) went to the bank yesterday. Today in class, he is sharing his experience. Listen, then mark the correct statements with a "✓"and the incorrect statements with a "✗". Then check them with your partner.

1. \_\_\_\_ 關京華去銀行開了一個支票帳戶和一個儲蓄帳戶。
   \_\_\_\_ 关京华去银行开了一个支票账户和一个储蓄账户。

2. \_\_\_\_ 美華銀行的服務不太好。
   \_\_\_\_ 美华银行的服务不太好。

3. \_\_\_\_ 儲蓄帳戶沒有利息。
   \_\_\_\_ 储蓄账户没有利息。

4. \_\_\_\_ 現在支票帳戶的利率是百分之二點八。
   \_\_\_\_ 现在支票账户的利率是百分之二点八。

5. \_\_\_\_ 下個星期關京華就能收到取款卡了。
   \_\_\_\_ 下个星期关京华就能收到取款卡了。

6. \_\_\_\_ 美華銀行可以換人民幣。
   \_\_\_\_ 美华银行可以换人民币。

**6-2** Listen and complete the following sentences in Pinyin.

1. 因為關京華要 \_\_\_\_ \_\_\_\_ 、\_\_\_\_ \_\_\_\_，所以他去銀行開了帳戶。
   因为关京华要 \_\_\_\_ \_\_\_\_ 、\_\_\_\_ \_\_\_\_，所以他去银行开了账户。

2. 小琴覺得美華銀行的 \_\_\_\_ \_\_\_\_ 很好。
   小琴觉得美华银行的 \_\_\_\_ \_\_\_\_ 很好。

3. 最近的 \_\_\_\_ \_\_\_\_ 很低。
   最近的 \_\_\_\_ \_\_\_\_ 很低。

4. 關京華還在銀行 \_\_\_\_ \_\_\_\_ 了信用卡。
   关京华还在银行 \_\_\_\_ \_\_\_\_ 了信用卡。

5. 有了取款卡，他就可以在 ＿＿＿ ＿＿＿ ＿＿＿ ＿＿＿ 那兒存款、
取款了。

有了取款卡，他就可以在 ＿＿＿ ＿＿＿ ＿＿＿ ＿＿＿ 那儿存款、
取款了。

## II. Character Exercises

**6-3**   Work with a partner. Read the following words, phrases, and sentences.

| | |
|---|---|
| 開 | 換 |
| 开 | 换 |
| | |
| 開支票 | 換人民幣 |
| 开支票 | 换人民币 |
| | |
| 開支票帳戶 | 美元換人民幣 |
| 开支票账户 | 美元换人民币 |
| | |
| 開一個支票帳戶 | 美元換人民幣的匯率 |
| 开一个支票账户 | 美元换人民币的汇率 |
| | |
| 開一個有利息的支票帳戶 | 美元換人民幣的匯率是多少 |
| 开一个有利息的支票账户 | 美元换人民币的汇率是多少 |
| | |
| 開一個有利息的支票帳戶很方便 | 美元換人民幣的匯率是一比 |
| 开一个有利息的支票账户很方便 | 六點五三 |
| | 美元换人民币的汇率是一比 |
| | 六点五三 |

Now with your partner, try to use the following characters to make words, phrases,
and then sentences.

| 1. 存 | 2. 取 | 3. 利 | 4. 儲 | 5. 之 |
|---|---|---|---|---|
| 存 | 取 | 利 | 储 | 之 |

| 6. 低 | 7. 種 | 8. 填 | 9. 簿 | 10. 兌 |
|---|---|---|---|---|
| 低 | 种 | 填 | 簿 | 兑 |

**6-4**   In pairs, complete the following sentences with the help of the pictures provided.

*Notes:*
百分之......，帳戶，支票，取款機，開，取款卡，填
百分之......，账户，支票，取款机，开，取款卡，填

1. A: 我可以去哪兒取款?
   我可以去哪儿取款?

   B: 你可以拿 ____ ____ ____ 在自動 ____
   ____ ____ 那兒取款。

   你可以拿 ____ ____ ____ 在自动 ____
   ____ ____ 那儿取款。

2. A: 這個帳戶怎麼用?
   这个账户怎么用?

   B: 這個帳戶每個月可以 ____ 三張 ____
   ____ 。

   这个账户每个月可以 ____ 三张 ____
   ____ 。

3. A: 請問，現在利率是多少?
   请问，现在利率是多少?

   B: 這種帳戶的 ____ ____ 是 ____ ____ ____
   二點九 (2.9%)。

   这种账户的 ____ ____ 是 ____ ____ ____
   二点九 (2.9%)。

4. A: 我想申請信用卡。
   我想申请信用卡。

   B: 好，你把這張表 ____ 一下。
   好，你把这张表 ____ 一下。

**6-5**  京華(京华) wrote a note to 小琴 about his bank account. He cannot write traditional characters so he wrote the note in simplified form. 小琴 has not studied simplified characters. Can you help her? With your partner, circle all the simplified characters in this note and then write out the traditional forms.

学校旁边有一个大华银行。我在那儿开了一个储蓄账户、一个支票账户。大华银行离学校很近，我去存款、取款比较方便。我还有一张取款卡，可以在自动取款机那儿取款。我还申请了信用卡，下个星期就可以拿到了。因为我可能要去中国，所以今天我还在外币柜台那儿换了人民币。

1. _____    2. _____    3. _____    4. _____    5. _____

6. _____    7. _____    8. _____    9. _____    10. _____

11. _____    12. _____    13. _____    14. _____    15. _____

16. _____    17. _____    18. _____    19. _____    20. _____

21. _____

## III. Grammar Exercises

**6-6**  The following underlined parts are different kinds of phrases. With a partner, identify each type of phrase and then write the phrase's number in the appropriate blank below.

1. 我搬來了<u>床、書桌和電腦</u>
   我搬来了<u>床、书桌和电脑</u>

2. 他有很多<u>電子用品</u>
   他有很多<u>电子用品</u>

3. <u>姐姐寄給我</u>的照片
   <u>姐姐寄给我</u>的照片

4. <u>轉飛機</u>的時候
   <u>转飞机</u>的时候

5. 我去拜訪以前的老師
   我去拜访以前的老师

6. 上海的小吃真棒！
   上海的小吃真棒！

7. 這是出租汽車站
   这是出租汽车站

8. 你喜歡的文學書
   你喜欢的文学书

9. 別忘了吃菜
   别忘了吃菜

10. 我沒有去過北京和長城
    我没有去过北京和长城

Juxtaposed phrase: _____

Endocentric phrase: _____

Subject + V. phrase: _____

V. + Object phrase: _____

**6-7**  With a partner, try to say the following in Chinese.

1. 15%  _____

2. 1:2.5  _____

3. 28.3%  _____

4. 9:47  _____

5. 34.6%  _____

6. 1:3.8  _____

**6-8** Work in pairs or small groups and fill in the table below with data describing the students in your class.

| | | 人數<br>人数 | 全班學生數的%<br>全班学生数的% |
|---|---|---|---|
| 全班學生人數<br>全班学生人数<br>[quánbān xuésheng rénshù]<br>Number of students in the class | 男生人數(男生人数) | | |
| | 女生人數(女生人数) | | |
| | 男生：女生(男生：女生) | | |
| | 華裔(华裔) [Huáyì]<br>(Chinese origin) | | |
| | 其他亞裔(其他亚裔) [qítā Yàyì]<br>(other Asians) | | |
| | 歐洲裔(欧洲裔) [Ōuzhōuyì]<br>(European origin) | | |
| | 非洲裔(非洲裔) [Fēizhōuyì]<br>(African origin) | | |
| | 華裔：其他亞裔：歐洲裔：<br>非洲裔 (华裔：其他亚裔：<br>欧洲裔：非洲裔) | | |
| | 一年級學生(一年级学生) | | |
| | 二年級學生(二年级学生) | | |
| | 三年級學生(三年级学生) | | |
| | 四年級學生(四年级学生) | | |
| | 一年級學生：二年級學生<br>三年級學生：四年級學生<br>(一年级学生：二年级学生<br>三年级学生：四年级学生) | | |

**6-9** Look at the diagram below and form groups to answer the questions. Then check them with your partner.

*Notes:*
亞洲(亚洲) [Yàzhōu]: Asia
非洲(非洲) [Fēizhōu]: Africa
大洋洲(大洋洲) [Dàyángzhōu]: Oceania
北美洲(北美洲) [Běiměizhōu]: North America
中東(中东) [Zhōngdōng]: Middle East
拉丁美洲(拉丁美洲) [Lādīngměizhōu]: Latin America
歐洲(欧洲) [Ōuzhōu]: Europe

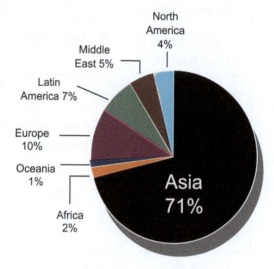

問題(问题):

1. 這個學校有百分之幾的非洲學生?
   这个学校有百分之几的非洲学生?

2. 學校有百分之幾的中東學生? 大洋洲學生呢?
   学校有百分之几的中东学生? 大洋洲学生呢?

3. 歐洲學生和亞洲學生的比例 ([bǐlì]: ratio) 是多少?
   欧洲学生和亚洲学生的比例是多少?

4. 拉丁美洲學生和亞洲學生的比例是多少?
   拉丁美洲学生和亚洲学生的比例是多少?

## IV.  Communicative Activities

**6-10** Work in pairs. Make up a dialogue between a customer and a bank clerk. The following may serve as clues.

1.  Various kinds of bank accounts (e.g., 儲蓄帳戶，支票帳戶(储蓄账户，支票账户)).

2.  Different interest rates (percentage) (e.g., 利率，利息(利率，利息)).

3.  Depositing and withdrawing money (amount) (e.g., 存款，取款(存款，取款)).

4.  Credit card, service (e.g., 信用卡，服務(信用卡，服务)).

5.  Exchange rate between $US and another currency (ratio) (e.g., 換，美金，匯率 (换，美金，汇率)).

**6-11** Form pairs and describe the information shown in the chart below.

*Notes:*
千(千) [qiān]: thousand
萬(万) [wàn]: ten thousand
億(亿) [yì]: hundred million
兆(兆) [zhào]: trillion
國家(国家) [guójiā]: country
面積(面积) [miànjī]: area
平方公里(平方公里) [píngfāng gōnglǐ]: square kilometer
人口(人口) [rénkǒu]: population
貨幣(货币) [huòbì]: currency
首都(首都) [shǒudū]: capital
華盛頓特區(华盛顿特区) [Huáshèngdùn tèqū]: Washington, DC
渥太華(渥太华) [Wòtàihuá]: Ottawa
多倫多(多伦多) [Duōlúnduō]: Toronto
倫敦(伦敦) [Lúndūn]: London
巴黎(巴黎) [Bālí]: Paris
東京(东京) [Dōngjīng]: Tokyo
加元(加元) [Jiāyuán]: Canadian dollar
歐元(欧元) [Ōuyuán]: Euro
日元(日元) [Rìyuán]: Japanese yen

*Useful grammar patterns:*
左右，百分之......，比，最，第......位，M 換 N 的匯率是
左右，百分之......，比，最，第......位，M 换 N 的汇率是

| 國家<br>(国家) | 中國<br>(中国) | 美國<br>(美国) | 加拿大<br>(加拿大) | 英國<br>(英国) | 法國<br>(法国) | 日本<br>(日本) |
|---|---|---|---|---|---|---|
| | | | | | |  |
| 首都<br><br>首都 | 北京<br><br>北京 | 華盛頓<br>特區<br>华盛顿<br>特区 | 渥太華<br><br>渥太华 | 倫敦<br><br>伦敦 | 巴黎<br><br>巴黎 | 東京<br><br>东京 |
| 最大的<br>城市<br>最大的<br>城市 | 上海<br><br>上海 | 紐約<br><br>纽约 | 多倫多<br><br>多伦多 | 倫敦<br><br>伦敦 | 巴黎<br><br>巴黎 | 東京<br><br>东京 |
| 面積/<br>平方公里<br>面积/<br>平方公里 | 九百六<br>十萬<br>九百六<br>十万<br>(3rd) | 九百三十<br>三萬<br>九百三十<br>三万<br>(4th) | 九百九十<br>八萬<br>九百九十<br>八万<br>(2nd) | 二十四萬<br><br>二十四万<br><br>(77th) | 六十七萬<br><br>六十七万<br><br>(40th) | 三十七萬<br><br>三十七万<br><br>(61th) |
| 人口<br><br>人口 | 十三億<br><br>十三亿<br><br>(1st) | 三億<br><br>三亿<br><br>(3rd) | 三千三<br>百萬<br>三千三<br>百万<br>(35th) | 六千萬<br><br>六千万<br><br>(22nd) | 六千萬<br><br>六千万<br><br>(20th) | 一億三<br>千萬<br>一亿三<br>千万<br>(10th) |
| 貨幣<br>货币 | 人民幣<br>人民币 | 美元<br>美元 | 加元<br>加元 | 歐元<br>欧元 | 歐元<br>欧元 | 日元<br>日元 |
| 兌美元的<br>匯率<br>兑美元的<br>汇率 | 1:6.53 | | 1:1.17 | 1:0.56 | 1:0.56 | 1:115.82 |

# 文化知識 (文化知识) Culture Link

## 文化點滴 (文化点滴) CULTURE NOTES

### 中國的銀行業 (中国的银行业) China's Banking Industry

China's banking industry is regulated by 中國人民銀行 (中国人民银行) [Zhōngguó Rénmín Yínháng] (The People's Bank of China, PBOC), the central bank of the People's Republic of China. This bank has the power to control monetary policy, regulate financial institutions, and determine the foreign exchange and interest rates in mainland China. In Hong Kong, the central bank is 香港金融管理局 [Xiānggǎng Jīnróng Guǎnlǐjú] (The Hong Kong Monetary Authority, HKMA), and policy is directed by the Financial Secretary. In Taiwan, it is the 中央銀行(中央银行) [Zhōngyāng Yínháng] (Central Bank of China) whose role it is to make monetary policy.

Traditionally, China has had only four major state-owned commercial banks. They are 中國銀行(中国银行) [Zhōngguó Yínháng] (the Bank of China, BOC), 中國工商銀行(中国工商银行) [Zhōngguó Gōngshāng Yínháng] (Industrial and Commercial Bank of China, ICBC), 中國農業銀行(中国农业银行) [Zhōngguó Nóngyè Yínháng] (Agricultural Bank of China, ABC), and 中國建設銀行(中国建设银行) [Zhōngguó Jiànshè Yínháng] (China Construction Bank, CCB). But since the 1980s, the number of

> **Do you know...**
> - which bank controls the monetary policy in China and determines the foreign exchange rate?
> - whether state-owned banks are the only banks in China?
> - why the number of home mortgages and credit cards has shown a sharp increase?
>
> *Read and find out!*

commercial banks in China has increased dramatically. At present, there are more than 300 commercial banks operating in China, with approximately 100 foreign banks in Beijing alone. In Hong Kong, there are more than 200 authorized financial institutions operating a comprehensive network of 1,600 local branches, of which an estimated 200 are owned by over 30 countries. No wonder people describe Hong Kong as a place that has more banks than grocery stores!

As for personal finance, home mortgages and credit cards are the fastest-growing banking products in China. With an increasing number of Chinese people buying their own homes, corresponding mortgage-backed securities (MBS) are growing quickly, comprising over 20 percent of total financial securities by the end of 2004. Another fast-growing sector is the credit card business. In contrast to the older generations who preferred a very thrifty lifestyle and put most of their money into savings, the younger generation seems to spend money with the same enthusiasm with which they earn it. Many world-renowned credit card companies have come to China to conduct business. There are also several local credit card companies, usually sub-divisions of major commercial banks. Banks, however, are still very cautious about issuing credit cards because China has yet to establish a national system to keep track of the credit ratings of individuals.

According to WTO agreements, at the end of 2003 China opened its Renminbi market to foreign banks. Moreover, since the end of 2006 when foreigners were authorized to be sole proprietors of their business in China (as opposed to earlier times when foreigners had to co-own businesses with state-owned enterprises), the competition between commercial banks has become more intense. Recent years have already seen the bankruptcies of some financial companies. Mergers, liquidations, acquisitions, and technological innovations are ongoing in the banking field in China. With many banks competing for limited profit, some are taking more risks, resulting in bad loans. As this may be to the disadvantage of consumers, the government has tightened control of banking operations.

The China Construction Bank is one of China's four largest state-owned banks. Are there any state-owned banks in your country?

An electronic board with currency exchange rates. Do you know the currency exchange rate between the RMB and your country's currency?

## 問題討論 (问题讨论) *Discuss the following with a partner or in small groups.*

1. 在你的國家，銀行會為個人提供什麼樣的服務？
   在你的国家，银行会为个人提供什么样的服务？
   What kinds of individual services are provided by the banks in your country?

2. 在你的國家，有哪些外國銀行？他們的服務怎麼樣？
   在你的国家，有哪些外国银行？他们的服务怎么样？
   What are the foreign banks in your country? How is their service?

# ● 趣味中文 (趣味中文) FUN WITH CHINESE

三百六十行，行行出狀元。
三百六十行，行行出状元。

All trades and professions have their cream of the crop. (This proverb is usually
used to encourage people that no matter what kind of job one does,
as long as one works hard one can be successful.)

| sān bǎi liùshí | háng | háng háng | chū | zhuàngyuan |
|---|---|---|---|---|
| 三百六十 | 行 | 行行 | 出 | 狀元 |
| 三百六十 | 行 | 行行 | 出 | 状元 |
| three hundred and sixty | occupations | each occupation | out | elite |

問題討論 (问题讨论) *Discuss the following with a partner or in small groups.*

1. Can you name some occupations in Chinese?
2. Do you know some Chinese people who are among the leaders in their professions?
3. Try to use your own words to explain 三百六十行，行行出狀元
   (三百六十行，行行出状元) in Chinese.

# 行動吧! (行动吧!) LET'S GO!

## 銀行存款單 (银行存款单) Bank Deposit Slip

It's April and 小京 will soon go to study abroad in Beijing. He needs to pay RMB¥198.00 to the university for Chinese textbooks. The money will be withdrawn in May. Since he has never filled in deposit forms in the past, he asks you for help. Can you help him?

*Notes:*

憑條(凭条) [píngtiáo] deposit or withdrawal slip

借(借) [jiè]: debit

貸(贷) [dài]: credit

幣別(币别) [bìbié]: type of currency

金額(金额) [jīn'é]: amount of money

小寫(小写) [xiǎoxiě]: the ordinary form of a Chinese numeral; small letter

存期(存期) [cúnqī]: period of deposit

簽字(签字) [qiānzì]: to sign one's name

回單(回单) [huídān]: bank statement

卡號(卡号) [kǎhào]: card number

戶名(户名) [hùmíng]: account owner's name

## 問題討論 (问题讨论) *Discuss the following with a partner or in small groups.*

1. Fill in the blanks:

   How should 小京 fill in the blanks?

   | | |
   |---|---|
   | 幣別 | _____ |
   | 金額 | _____ |

2. Guess what 存款憑條(存款凭条) and 存款回單(存款回单) are?

# 復習 (复习) Review

## LESSON 5 TO LESSON 6

### I. Retelling a Story

In small groups, listen to the following passage and then briefly retell the story in Chinese.

*Notes:*

南轅北轍(南辕北辙) [nányuán běizhé]: going south by driving the carriage north
從前(从前) [cóngqián]: long, long ago
魏國(魏国) [Wèiguó]: the State of Wei
駕(驾) [jià]: to drive
馬車(马车) [mǎchē]: carriage
楚國(楚国) [Chǔguó]: the State of Chu
雖然(虽然) [suīrán]: although
條件(条件) [tiáojiàn]: condition

## 南轅北轍(南辕北辙)

(繁體字 Traditional Character Version)

從前，魏國有一個人駕著馬車要到楚國去。
楚國在魏國的南邊，可是他卻往北邊走。
有人問他：“楚國在南邊，你為什麼往北
走呢？”這個魏國人說：“我的馬很好，
每天能跑一千里。”那個人說：“雖然你的
馬跑得快，但是你走的路不對啊。”魏國人
說：“我帶的錢很多。”那人又說：“錢多也
沒有用啊！”魏國人很不高興地說：“我很
會駕車。”雖然那個魏國人去楚國的條件都
很好，但是他卻離楚國越來越遠了。

(简体字 Simplified Character Version)

从前，魏国有一个人驾着马车要到楚国去。楚国在魏国的南边，可是
他却往北边走。有人问他：“楚国在南边，你为什么往北走呢？”这个魏
国人说：“我的马很好，每天能跑一千里。”那个人说：“虽然你的马跑
得快，但是你走的路不对啊。”魏国人说：“我带的钱很多。”那人又
说：“钱多也没有用啊！”魏国人很不高兴地说：“我很会驾车。”虽然
那个魏国人去楚国的条件都很好，但是他却离楚国越来越远了。

## II. Paragraph Completion

With a partner, fill in the blanks in the following passage with the help of the clues provided. Then read the whole passage.

*Note:*
大概(大概) [dàgài]: about

(繁體字 Traditional Character Version)

小文：

　　你好！我從匹兹堡搬到波士頓來已經一個星期了。這個星期我做了很多事兒：我把房子整理 ＿＿ 了(clean)，＿(open)了銀行賬戶，＿＿ (apply)了信用卡，還買了汽車保險和健康保險。波士頓的很多東西都 ＿ 匹兹堡 ＿ (more expensive than)，比如房租，在匹兹堡一房一廳的房子每個月的房租只要大概六百美元，在波士頓＿＿＿＿(the same) 房子要一千一百美元，差不多是匹兹堡的 ＿ 倍 (two times)。還有買東西，

在匹兹堡買衣服不用交稅，可是在波士頓要交 ＿＿＿＿＿ (7%) 的稅。還有汽車保險，我以前覺得匹兹堡的汽車保險很貴，每年要八百美元，可是即使這樣，匹兹堡的汽車保險也只有波士頓的 ＿ 分 ＿ 一 (one third)。但是波士頓的中國菜卻 ＿ 匹兹堡的 ＿＿ (cheaper than)。波士頓的中國飯館 ＿ 匹兹堡的 ＿ (more than)，中國菜也 ＿ 匹兹堡的飯館 ＿＿ (more authentic than)。所以在波士頓我要多吃一點兒中國菜。

　　好了，就說到這兒。下次再聊。

　　　　　　　　　　　　　　　　小明
　　　　　　　　　　　　　　　　10月31日

（简体字 Simplified Character Version）

小文：

你好！我从匹兹堡搬到波士顿来已经一个星期了。这个星期我做了很多事儿：我把房子整理 ___ ___ 了(clean)，___ (open)了银行账户，___ ___ (apply)了信用卡，还买了汽车保险和健康保险。波士顿的很多东西都 ___ 匹兹堡 ___ (more expensive than)，比如房租，在匹兹堡一房一厅的房子每个月的房租只要大概六百美元，在波士顿 ___ ___ ___ (the same) 房子要一千一百美元，差不多是匹兹堡的 ___ 倍 (two times)。还有买东西，在匹兹堡买衣服不用交税，可是在波士顿要交 ___ ___ ___ ___ ___ (7%) 的税。还有汽车保险，我以前觉得匹兹堡的汽车保险很贵，每年要八百美元，可是即使这样，匹兹堡的汽车保险也只有波士顿的 ___ 分 ___ 一 (one third)。但是波士顿的中国菜却 ___ 匹兹堡的 ___ ___ (cheaper than)。波士顿的中国饭馆 ___ 匹兹堡的 ___ (more than)，中国菜也 ___ 匹兹堡的饭馆 ___ ___ (more authentic than)。所以在波士顿我要多吃一点儿中国菜。

好了，就说到这儿。下次再聊。

小明
10月31日

## III. Activity

Moving Furniture:

There was a big soccer game in Europe recently. As a soccer fan, in order to watch the game at midnight 小文 moved his TV from the living room to his bedroom. He also adjusted the position of the other furniture in both the living room and bedroom. Please look at the pictures below and use "把" sentences to describe how the furniture was moved.

**(before)**

**(after)**

## IV. Picture Description

Work in small groups to tell a story based on the pictures below. Try to apply 把, 了, 著(着), 過(过), 往, ……起來(起来), 比…… when creating the story.

*Notes:*

踢球(踢球) [tīqiú]: to play (kick) the ball     追(追) [zhuī]: to chase
滾(滚) [gǔn]: to roll     樹洞(树洞) [shùdòng]: hole in a tree
井(井) [jǐng]: the well     桶(桶) [tǒng]: bucket
倒(倒) [dào]: to pour     浮(浮) [fú]: to float

(1)        (2)        (3)

(4)        (5)        (6)

## V. Word Expansion

With your partner, read each character aloud and create a phrase. Then make a sentence with the phrase.

*Example:* 學 → 學生 → 我是學生(学 → 学生 → 我是学生)

陰(阴)　　飛(飞)　　團(团)　　鬧(闹)

種(种)　　單(单)　　儲(储)　　櫃(柜)

# 旅遊與簽證 (旅游与签证)
# Traveling and Visas

*Tiananmen* 天安門(天安门) *Square in Beijing is the largest public square in the world.*

## **CONNECTIONS AND COMMUNITIES PREVIEW**

**Discuss the following questions with a partner or your class. What similarities and differences do you think there might be between Chinese culture and your own culture?**

1. Have you traveled to other countries? If yes, name the country you like best. If not, which country would you most like to go to?

2. Is your own country multi-ethnic? If so, can you name some of the various groups?

## 教學目標 (教学目标) OBJECTIVES

■ Talk about possibility and feasibility

■ Describe how to get plane tickets and travel visas

# 生詞 (生词) VOCABULARY

## 核心詞 (核心词) Core Vocabulary

| | TRADITIONAL | SIMPLIFIED | PINYIN | | |
|----|----|----|----|----|----|
| 1. | 寒假 | 寒假 | hánjià | N. | winter vacation |
| 2. | 旅遊 | 旅游 | lǚyóu | N. | tour |
| 3. | 旅行社 | 旅行社 | lǚxíngshè | N. | travel agency |
| 4. | 訂 | 订 | dìng | V. | to book, make reservations |
| 5. | 機票 | 机票 | jīpiào | N. | plane ticket |
| 6. | 羨慕 | 羨慕 | xiànmù | V. | to envy |
| 7. | 打算 | 打算 | dǎsuàn | V.<br>N. | to plan<br>plan |
| 8. | 親戚 | 亲戚 | qīnqi | N. | relative |
| 9. | 原來 | 原来 | yuánlái | Adv. | originally |
| 10. | 抽空 | 抽空 | chōukòng | V.O. | to manage to find time |
| 11. | 拜訪 | 拜访 | bàifǎng | V.<br>N. | to visit<br>a visit |
| 12. | 一直 | 一直 | yìzhí | Adv. | always |
| 13. | 查 | 查 | chá | V. | to check |
| 14. | 網站 | 网站 | wǎngzhàn | N. | website |
| 15. | 買不起 | 买不起 | mǎibuqǐ | | cannot afford to buy |
| 16. | 買到 | 买到 | mǎidào | V.C. | to succeed in buying |
| 17. | 找得到 | 找得到 | zhǎodedào | | to be able to find |

| TRADITIONAL | SIMPLIFIED | PINYIN | | |
|---|---|---|---|---|
| 18. 便宜 | 便宜 | piányi | Adj. | inexpensive |
| 19. 其實 | 其实 | qíshí | Adv. | as a matter of fact, actually |
| 20. 要是 | 要是 | yàoshì | Conj. | if |
| 21. 南方 | 南方 | nánfāng | N. | southern part |
| 22. 四季如春 | 四季如春 | sìjìrúchūn | | to be like spring all year round |
| 23. 風景如畫 | 风景如画 | fēngjǐngrúhuà | | with picturesque scenic beauty |
| 24. 少數民族 | 少数民族 | shǎoshùmínzú | N. | minority nationalities |
| 25. 如果 | 如果 | rúguǒ | Conj. | if |
| 26. 簽證 | 签证 | qiānzhèng | N. | visa |
| 27. 辦 | 办 | bàn | V. | to apply, process |
| 28. 大概 | 大概 | dàgài | Adv. | probably |
| 29. 來得及 | 来得及 | láidejí | | to have enough time to |

## 專名 (专名) Proper Nouns

| TRADITIONAL | SIMPLIFIED | PINYIN | | |
|---|---|---|---|---|
| 1. 香港 | 香港 | Xiānggǎng | N. | Hong Kong |
| 2. 雲南 | 云南 | Yúnnán | N. | Yunnan, a province in the southwestern part of China |
| 3. 昆明 | 昆明 | Kūnmíng | N. | Kunming, the capital city of Yunnan Province |

## 語文知識 (语文知识) LANGUAGE LINK

Read and listen to the following sentence patterns. These patterns use vocabulary, expressions, and grammar that you will study in more detail in this lesson. After reading the sentence patterns, read and listen to the Language in Use section that follows.

### 句型 (句型) Sentence Patterns

A: 你買得到去北京的機票嗎?
你买得到去北京的机票吗?
Nǐ mǎidedào qù Běijīng de jīpiào ma?

B: 現在機票很難買，我買不到。
现在机票很难买，我买不到。
Xiànzài jīpiào hěnnán mǎi, wǒ mǎibudào.

A: 坐飛機到得了到不了昆明？
坐飞机到得了到不了昆明？
Zuò fēijī dàodeliǎo dàobuliǎo Kūnmíng?

B: 到得了。
到得了。
Dàodeliǎo.

---

A: 今年寒假你有什麼打算嗎？
今年寒假你有什么打算吗？
Jīnnián hánjià nǐ yǒu shénme dǎsuàn ma?

B: 我打算去北京旅遊。
我打算去北京旅游。
Wǒ dǎsuàn qù Běijīng lǚyóu.

### 課文 Language in Use: Booking Our Trip to China (繁體字 Traditional Character Version)

方小琴：　文華，你在找什麼？

金文華：　我在找一本電話簿，我的電話簿找不到了。

方小琴：　你看看電話旁邊有沒有？

金文華：　好像沒有……啊，我看到了，在桌子下面。今年寒假我和方明要去中國旅遊，我要找一家旅行社的電話號碼，我想訂去中國的機票。

方小琴：　真的嗎？太棒了！我真羨慕你們。你們打算去哪兒玩呢？

金文華：　方明在北京有很多親戚，我們原來想先去北京玩幾天，跟他的親戚聚一聚，然後抽空去拜訪他以前的老師，再去別的地方看看，可是我一直買不到去北京的機票。

方小琴：　你們上網查了嗎？

金文華：　查了，我們查了好幾家航空公司的網站[1]，可是都訂不到機票。有的機票太貴了，我們買不起。我想問問這家旅行社，看看他們那兒訂得到訂不到比較便[2]宜的機票。

方小琴：　其實，要是真的買不到去北京的機票，你們可以先去南方[3]的城市，比如上海或者香港，然後去雲南的昆明，再從昆明坐飛機去北京。

---

**1. 網站/網址/網頁(网站/网址/网页)**

網站(网站) [wǎngzhàn]: website

網址(网址) [wǎngzhǐ]: URL

網頁(网页) [wǎngyè]: webpage

---

**2. 便(便) [pián, biàn]**

Note that the word 便(便) has two different pronunciations. It is pronounced as [pián] in 便宜(便宜) (cheap), but is pronounced as [biàn] in 方便(方便) (convenient).

---

**3. 南方/南部(南方/南部)**

南方(南方) is generally used to indicate both a direction and an area while 南部 (南部) generally refers to an area or territory.

---

*Continued on page 208*

## 课文 Language in Use: Booking Our Trip to China
## (简体字 Simplified Character Version)

方小琴： 文华，你在找什么？

金文华： 我在找一本电话簿，我的电话簿找不到了。

方小琴： 你看看电话旁边有没有？

金文华： 好像没有……啊，我看到了，在桌子下面。今年寒假我和方明要去中国旅游，我要找一家旅行社的电话号码，我想订去中国的机票。

方小琴： 真的吗？太棒了！我真羡慕你们。你们打算去哪儿玩呢？

金文华： 方明在北京有很多亲戚，我们原来想先去北京玩几天，跟他的亲戚聚一聚，然后抽空去拜访他以前的老师，再去别的地方看看，可是我一直买不到去北京的机票。

方小琴： 你们上网查了吗？

金文华： 查了，我们查了好几家航空公司的网站[1]，可是都订不到机票。有的机票太贵了，我们买不起。我想问问这家旅行社，看看他们那儿订得到订不到比较便[2]宜的机票。

方小琴： 其实，要是真的买不到去北京的机票，你们可以先去南方[3]的城市，比如上海或者香港，然后去云南的昆明，再从昆明坐飞机去北京。

*Continued on page 209*

課文 **Language in Use: Booking Our Trip to China**
**(繁體字 Traditional Character Version) —— 接第二百零六頁**

金文華：　這個主意真不錯。我也聽說昆明是一個四季如春、風景如畫
　　　　　的城市，雲南那兒還有很多少數民族，去那兒看看一定會很
　　　　　有意思。可是我在地圖上怎麼找不到昆明呢？

方小琴：　我來幫你看看……啊，在這兒。你看，就在中國的西南邊。

金文華：　是啊！如果[4]我真的想去，坐
　　　　　飛機到得了[5]到不了昆明？

方小琴：　當然到得了！你還可以吃得
　　　　　到少數民族的小吃呢！

金文華：　那我一定要去。

方小琴：　對了，你們的簽證辦好了嗎？

金文華：　方明的簽證已經辦好了。我
　　　　　也已經申請了，可是不知道
　　　　　下個星期拿得到拿不到。不
　　　　　過還有一個多月，大概來得及。

---

**4. 要是/如果(要是/如果)**

Both 要是(要是) and 如果(如果) are used as conjunctions to mean "if," but 要是(要是) is more colloquial and used more in conversations, while 如果(如果) is relatively more formal.

---

**5. 到得了(到得了) [liǎo]**

到得了(到得了) means to be accessible or able to be reached.

---

課文 **Language in Use: Booking Our Trip to China**

### 课文 Language in Use: Booking Our Trip to China
### (简体字 Simplified Character Version) —— 接第二百零七页

金文华：这个主意真不错。我也听说昆明是一个四季如春、风景如画
的城市，云南那儿还有很多少数民族，去那儿看看一定会很
有意思。可是我在地图上怎么找不到昆明呢？

方小琴：我来帮你看看……啊，在这儿。你看，就在中国的西南边。

金文华：是啊！如果⁴我真的想去，坐飞机到得了⁵到不了昆明？

方小琴：当然到得了！你还可以吃得到少数民族的小吃呢！

金文华：那我一定要去。

方小琴：对了，你们的签证办好了吗？

金文华：方明的签证已经办好了。我也已经申请了，可是不知道下个
星期拿得到拿不到。不过还有一个多月，大概来得及。

# 語法 (语法) GRAMMAR

## I. 可能補語 (可能补语) Potential Complement (PC)

Sometimes, a verb, an adjective, or a phrase can be used after a verb to indicate the possibility or impossibility of achieving a desired result through an action. Such constructions are called potential complements. A PC usually follows the pattern:

> Major V. + 得 with the DC phrase
> Major V. + 得 with the RC phrase

*Examples:*

DC (Directional complement): 上去 → 我爬得上去。  I am able to climb up there.
　　　　　　　　　　　　　　　我爬不上去。  I am not able to climb up there.

RC (Resultative complement): 找到 → 我找得到他。  I am able to find him.
　　　　　　　　　　　　　　　我找不到他。  I am not able to find him.

*Notes:*

1. The difference between a PC and a RC or DC is mainly in the use of the structural particle 得. When 得 is added, the complement becomes a PC. Compare the following:

| RC | PC |
|---|---|
| 看見(看见)<br>聽清楚(听清楚)<br>買到(买到) | 看得見/看不見(看得见/看不见)<br>聽得清楚/聽不清楚(听得清楚/听不清楚)<br>買得到/買不到(买得到/买不到) |
| **DC** | |
| 搬上來(搬上来)<br>走進去(走进去) | 搬得上來/搬不上來(搬得上来/搬不上来)<br>走得進去/走不進去(走得进去/走不进去) |

2. The A 不 A pattern used in a PC is as follows:

　(V. + 得 + PC)　　　 + (V. + 不 + PC)
　走得到(走得到) + 走不到(走不到)

**»Try it!** With a partner, ask and answer questions with the phrases provided above. Please use the A 不 A pattern. For example,

A: 你找得到找不到那家銀行?
你找得到找不到那家银行?

B: 我一定找得到。
我一定找得到。

3. To make a question, either place the 嗎(吗) or use the "A 不 A" pattern of the PC.

*Examples:*

i) A: 去北京的飛機票買得到嗎?
去北京的飞机票买得到吗?
Are plane tickets to Beijing available now?

B: 買不到。
买不到。
No, they are not available.

ii) A: 飛機票很貴,你買得起嗎?
飞机票很贵,你买得起吗?
The plane tickets are very expensive, can you afford it?

B: 太貴了,我買不起。
太贵了,我买不起。
They are too expensive, and I can't afford it.

iii) A: 飛機到得了到不了昆明?
飞机到得了到不了昆明?
Is Kunming accessible by plane?

B: 到得了。
到得了。
Yes, it is.

iv) A: 這輛車坐得下坐不下六個人?
这辆车坐得下坐不下六个人?
Can this car seat six people?

B: 坐不下。
坐不下。
No, it can't.

>>**Try it!** With a partner, use either the A 不 A pattern or the question word 嗎 (吗) to ask questions with the following phrases: 買得到 (买得到), 看得懂, 聽得見 (听得见), 找得到, 吃得了. For example,

A: 你找得到那家餐廳嗎?
你找得到那家餐厅吗?

B: 我一定找得到。
我一定找得到。

4. 能 or 可以 are sometimes used with a PC to emphasize possibility or ability.

*Example:*

我能搬得動那塊 ([kuài]: measure word for stones) 大石頭 ([shítou]: rock).
我能搬得动那块大石头。
I am able to move that big rock.

>>**Try it!** With a partner, practice questions and answers using the PC. Make sure that you add 能 or 可以 in your answers. For example,

A: 你能搬得動那張桌子嗎?
你能搬得动那张桌子吗?

B: 我想我能搬得動那張桌子。
我想我能搬得动那张桌子。

5. When the verb has an object, the object may be placed after the PC, or at the beginning of the sentence.

*Examples:*

我拿得到簽證。
我拿得到签证。
I am able to get the visa.

簽證我拿得到。
签证我拿得到。
As for the visa, I am able to get it.

>>**Try it!**　With a partner, practice questions and answers using the PC with the object
of the sentence placed at the beginning of your answer. For example,

A: 那家銀行你找得到嗎？
那家银行你找得到吗？

B: 那家銀行我一定找得到。
那家银行我一定找得到。

6. The following are some adjectives or verbs commonly used as PCs.

到 – indicating the potential of achieving a purpose

e.g., 找得到/找不到　(to be able/not able to find)
找得到/找不到

看得到/看不到　(to be able/not able to see)
看得到/看不到

動(动) – indicating the potential of moving

e.g., 拿得動/拿不動　(to be able/not able to carry)
拿得动/拿不动

下 – indicating potential space capacity

e.g., 吃得下/吃不下　(to be able/not able to finish eating/eat up)
吃得下/吃不下

了 [liǎo] – indicating the potential ability to do something

e.g., 做得了/做不了　(to be able/not able to handle)
做得了/做不了

及 – indicating the potential of having enough time to do something

e.g., 來得及/來不及　(to have/not have enough time to do)
来得及/来不及

>>**Try it!**　With a partner, provide more phrases with the above verbs and adjectives
as PCs.

## II. Questions with Structural Particles 嗎/呢 (吗/呢)

Usually a question in Chinese is formed by using a question word in a sentence such as,

你<u>什麼</u>時候去北京?
你<u>什么</u>时候去北京?

她想去<u>哪兒</u>?
她想去<u>哪儿</u>?

But sometimes these kinds of questions may also have the particle 嗎(吗) or 呢 added at the end. When 嗎(吗) is added, the answer to this kind of question is often either positive or negative, with details optional. When 呢 is added at the end, the emphasis of the question does not change very much but the tone of the question is much softer. Compare the following questions:

1.  i) A: 寒假你有什麼打算?
       寒假你有什么打算?

       (The emphasis is on the specific plan.)

    B: 我想先去南方,再去北京。
       我想先去南方,再去北京。

  ii) A: 寒假你有什麼打算<u>呢</u>?
      寒假你有什么打算<u>呢</u>?

      (The emphasis is still on the specific plan, but the tone is softer.)

    B: 我想先去南方,再去北京。
       我想先去南方,再去北京。

 iii) A: 寒假你有什麼打算<u>嗎</u>?
      寒假你有什么打算<u>吗</u>?

      (The emphasis is on whether you have a plan or not, and the tone is softer.)

    B: 有,我想先去南方,再去北京。
       有,我想先去南方,再去北京。

2. i) 我怎麼沒有想到?
　　　我怎么没有想到?

（Emphasizing 怎麼/how）

ii) 我怎麼沒有想到呢?
　　　我怎么没有想到呢?

（The question is the same, but the tone is much softer.）

>>**Try it!** With a partner, make up a short dialogue about your winter plans. Make sure you use questions with the particle 嗎 (吗) or 呢 at the end.

## 補充課文 (补充课文) SUPPLEMENTARY PRACTICE

*Read the following passage. Then listen and repeat.*

### Winter Break in China (繁體字 Traditional Character Version)

小琴：

　　你好嗎？我和方明到中國已經有一個多星期了。因為到上海的飛機票比較容易買得到，所以我們是先到上海的。

　　上海的變化太大了，方明來過上海，可是很多地方他都已經認不出來了。我們還去了蘇州和南京。這些地方都各有特色，非常有意思。我們還吃到了各種小吃，在上海過了聖誕節，真的很開心。如果時間來得及，本來還打算去杭州。"上有天堂，下有蘇杭"嘛，應該去看看。可是因為時間來不及了，所以我們只好下次再去了。

　　我們是昨天到昆明的。昆明真是一個好地方，山青水秀、風景如畫，漂亮極了。這兒的天氣也很好，四季如春，很舒服。這兒有很多少數民族，他們的風俗習慣跟我們的不太一樣，有意思極了。

　　我們打算後天坐飛機去北京看看方明的親戚，不過還不知道買得到買不到去北京的機票，希望能在元旦以前到得了北京。

　　你的寒假過得怎麼樣？希望你以後也有機會到中國來玩玩，真的非常值得。

祝你

　　寒假愉快！

文華
十二月二十八日

*Notes:*

蘇州(苏州) [Sūzhōu]: Suzhou, a city in the southeastern part of China
南京(南京) [Nánjīng]: Nanjing, a city in the southeastern part of China
各有特色(各有特色) [gèyǒutèsè]: each has its own special features
聖誕節(圣诞节) [Shèngdànjié]: Christmas
杭州(杭州) [Hángzhōu]: Hangzhou, a city in the southeastern part of China
天堂(天堂) [tiāntáng]: paradise; heaven
山青水秀(山青水秀) [shānqīng shuǐxiù]: green mountains and clear waters
風俗(风俗) [fēngsú]: custom
習慣(习惯) [xíguàn]: habit
元旦(元旦) [Yuándàn]: New Year's Day
值得(值得) [zhídé]: worthwhile

# 補充課文 (补充课文) SUPPLEMENTARY PRACTICE

*Read the following passage. Then listen and repeat.*

## Winter Break in China (简体字 Simplified Character Version)

小琴：

　　你好吗？我和方明到中国已经有一个多星期了。因为到上海的飞机票比较容易买得到，所以我们是先到上海的。

　　上海的变化太大了，方明来过上海，可是很多地方他都已经认不出来了。我们还去了苏州和南京。这些地方都各有特色，非常有意思。我们还吃到了各种小吃，在上海过了圣诞节，真的很开心。如果时间来得及，本来还打算去杭州。"上有天堂，下有苏杭"嘛，应该去看看。可是因为时间来不及了，所以我们只好下次再去了。

　　我们是昨天到昆明的。昆明真是一个好地方，山青水秀、风景如画，漂亮极了。这儿的天气也很好，四季如春，很舒服。这儿有很多少数民族，他们的风俗习惯跟我们的不太一样，有意思极了。

　　我们打算后天坐飞机去北京看看方明的亲戚，不过还不知道买得到买不到去北京的机票，希望能在元旦以前到得了北京。

　　你的寒假过得怎么样？希望你以后也有机会到中国来玩玩，真的非常值得。

祝你

　　寒假愉快！

文华
十二月二十八日

## Exercises: work with a partner or in small groups

1. 文華寒假去了中國的哪些地方，他還打算去哪兒？
   文华寒假去了中国的哪些地方，他还打算去哪儿？

2. "上有天堂，下有蘇杭" 是什麼意思？
   "上有天堂，下有苏杭" 是什么意思？

3. 方明的很多親戚都在哪兒？文華和方明打算怎麼去那兒？
   方明的很多亲戚都在哪儿？文华和方明打算怎么去那儿？

## 成語故事 (成语故事) IDIOM STORY

### 掩耳盜鈴 (掩耳盗铃) [yǎn'ěr dàolíng]

*Meaning:* Covering one's ears while stealing a bell.

*Usage:* This implies that someone deceives himself/herself.

*Example:* 我們到現在還買不到去北京的機票，簽證也還沒開始申請。
你還說我們下星期一定去得了中國，那不是"掩耳盜鈴"嗎?

我们到现在还买不到去北京的机票，签证也还没开始申请。
你还说我们下星期一定去得了中国，那不是"掩耳盗铃"吗?

Pay attention to the usages of PCs and questions with 嗎/呢(吗/呢).

(繁體字 Traditional Character Version)

　　從前，有一個小偷看到了一口特別大的鐘。他想：這口鐘這麼大，要是能賣得了，我就可以得到很多錢。所以，他就想把這口鐘偷走。可是這口鐘太大、太重，他試了好幾次，都拿不動，偷不走。後來，他想：如果我把它砸碎，就能偷得走了。所以，他就砸這口鐘。可是砸鐘的聲音非常響，很遠很遠的地方都能聽得到。他就用手把他的耳朵摀起來，這樣他就聽不到了。所以他就一邊摀著自己的耳朵，一邊砸這口鐘。

　　可是他沒有想到，雖然他自己聽不見砸鐘的聲音，但是別人都聽得見。結果很多人都跑過來把他抓住了。

　　"掩耳盜鈴"實際上就是自己騙自己。

(简体字 Simplified Character Version)

　　从前，有一个小偷看到了一口特别大的钟。他想：这口钟这么大，要是能卖得了，我就可以得到很多钱。所以，他就想把这口钟偷走。可是这口钟太大、太重，他试了好几次，都拿不动，偷不走。后来，他想：如果我把它砸碎，就能偷得走了。所以，他就砸这口钟。可是砸钟的声音非常响，很远很远的地方都能听得到。他就用手把他的耳朵捂起来，这样他就听不到了。所以他就一边捂着自己的耳朵，一边砸这口钟。

　　可是他没有想到，虽然他自己听不见砸钟的声音，但是别人都听得见。结果很多人都跑过来把他抓住了。

　　"掩耳盗铃"实际上就是自己骗自己。

*Notes:*

掩(掩) [yǎn]: to cover

耳(朵) 耳(朵) [ěr (duō)]: ear

盗(盗) [dào]: to steal

铃(铃) [líng]: bell

小偷(小偷) [xiǎotōu]: thief

口(口) [kǒu]: measure word for bells

鐘(钟) [zhōng]: bell

偷(偷) [tōu]: to steal

砸碎(砸碎) [zásuì]: to hammer something into bits and pieces

聲音(声音) [shēngyīn]: sound, voice

響(响) [xiǎng]: to ring

捂(捂) [wǔ]: to cover

抓住(抓住) [zhuāzhù]: to grab, to arrest

騙(骗) [piàn]: to deceive, fool

## Exercises: work with a partner or in small groups

1. 找出有 PCs 的句子。
   找出有 PCs 的句子。

2. 用你自己的話說說 "掩耳盗铃" 的故事。
   用你自己的话说说 "掩耳盗铃" 的故事。

3. 請用 "掩耳盗铃" 造一個句子或者說一個掩耳盗铃的例子。
   请用 "掩耳盗铃" 造一个句子或者说一个掩耳盗铃的例子。

4. "掩耳盗铃" 的故事，告訴了我們什麼?
   "掩耳盗铃" 的故事，告诉了我们什么?

# 練習 (練習) ACTIVITIES

## I. Listening Exercises

**7-1**  Listen to the passage, then select the right answer to complete the statements.

1. 昨天我給 _____ 打了電話。
   昨天我给 _____ 打了电话。

   a. 北京的朋友
      北京的朋友

   b. 我的室友
      我的室友

   c. 旅行社
      旅行社

2. 旅行社的工作人員說 _____ 。
   旅行社的工作人员说 _____ 。

   a. 可以買得到去北京的機票
      可以买得到去北京的机票

   b. 去上海的機票很難買
      去上海的机票很难买

   c. 訂不到去北京的機票
      订不到去北京的机票

3. 申請簽證只要 _____ 就可以收到。
   申请签证只要 _____ 就可以收到。

   a. 一個星期
      一个星期

   b. 兩個月
      两个月

   c. 兩個星期
      两个星期

## II. Character Exercises

**7-2** Work with a partner. Read the following words, phrases, and sentences.

| | |
|---|---|
| 算 | 戚 |
| 算 | 戚 |
| 打算 | 親戚 |
| 打算 | 亲戚 |
| 什麼打算 | 我的親戚 |
| 什么打算 | 我的亲戚 |
| 你有什麼打算? | 我的台北親戚 |
| 你有什么打算? | 我的台北亲戚 |
| 寒假你有什麼打算? | 看我的台北親戚。 |
| 寒假你有什么打算? | 看我的台北亲戚。 |
| 今年寒假你有什麼打算呢? | 我去看我的台北親戚。 |
| 今年寒假你有什么打算呢? | 我去看我的台北亲戚。 |

Now with your partner, try to use the following characters to make words, phrases, and then sentences.

| | | | | |
|---|---|---|---|---|
| 1. 查 | 2. 訂 | 3. 方 | 4. 辦 | 5. 便 |
| 查 | 订 | 方 | 办 | 便 |
| 6. 原 | 7. 證 | 8. 及 | 9. 族 | 10. 羡 |
| 原 | 证 | 及 | 族 | 羡 |

**7-3** Write out the radical of each of the following characters and give some examples from the text of characters having the same radical. Then check your answers with a partner.

*Example:* 你 ⟋ 他 俱

1. 社 _____ _____

2. 寒 _____ _____

3. 戚 _____ _____

4. 旅 _____ _____

**7-4**  Character recognition: work with a partner for the following exercises.

1.  The following pairs of characters seem very much alike in appearance. Look carefully at their differences, then for each character write out two expressions.

> a. 北(北) _____ _____
> 比(比) _____ _____
>
> b. 我(我) _____ _____
> 找(找) _____ _____
>
> c. 訂(订) _____ _____
> 計(计) _____ _____
>
> d. 其(其) _____ _____
> 共(共) _____ _____
>
> e. 別(别) _____ _____
> 到(到) _____ _____
>
> f. 季(季) _____ _____
> 李(李) _____ _____

2.  Each of the following pairs of words contains a character which has two different pronunciations. Write down the Pinyin, with tones, for each word.

> a. 便宜(便宜) _____
> 方便(方便) _____
>
> b. 旅行(旅行) _____
> 銀行(银行) _____

## III. Grammar Exercises

**7-5**  With a partner, complete the following sentences using the PC and answer the questions in the affirmative.

1.  A: 昆明很偏遠 ([piānyuǎn]: remote)，飛機到得 _____ 到不 _____?
    昆明很偏远，飞机到得 _____ 到不 _____?

> B: _____ _____ _____ 。
>
> _____ _____ _____ 。

2. A: 你在網上查得 ＿＿＿＿ 飛機票的價錢嗎?
   你在网上查得 ＿＿＿＿ 飞机票的价钱吗?

   B: 當然 ＿＿＿＿ ＿＿＿＿ ＿＿＿＿ 。
   当然 ＿＿＿＿ ＿＿＿＿ ＿＿＿＿ 。

3. A: 這輛車太小，坐得 ＿＿＿＿ 坐不 ＿＿＿＿ 五個人?
   这辆车太小，坐得 ＿＿＿＿ 坐不 ＿＿＿＿ 五个人?

   B: 我看 ＿＿＿＿ ＿＿＿＿ ＿＿＿＿ 。
   我看 ＿＿＿＿ ＿＿＿＿ ＿＿＿＿ 。

4. A: 你的簽證明天收得 ＿＿＿＿ 收不 ＿＿＿＿ ?
   你的签证明天收得 ＿＿＿＿ 收不 ＿＿＿＿ ?

   B: 我不知道。可能 ＿＿＿＿ ＿＿＿＿ ＿＿＿＿ ，我是一個星期以前寄去的。
   我不知道。可能 ＿＿＿＿ ＿＿＿＿ ＿＿＿＿ ，我是一个星期以前寄去的。

5. 去中國的機票不太貴，我想我能 ＿＿＿＿ ＿＿＿＿ ＿＿＿＿ 。
   去中国的机票不太贵，我想我能 ＿＿＿＿ ＿＿＿＿ ＿＿＿＿ 。

**7-6** Work with a partner and rewrite each question using 嗎(吗) or 呢 to switch the emphasis and soften the tone, then answer them accordingly.

*Examples:* 寒假我有計畫。
寒假我有计划。

嗎(吗)

A: 寒假你有什麼計畫嗎?
寒假你有什么计划吗?

B: 有，我想先去南方，再去北京。
有，我想先去南方，再去北京。

呢(呢)

A: 寒假你有什麼計畫 ([jìhuà]: plan) 呢?
寒假你有什么计划呢?

B: 我想去台灣 ([Táiwān]: Taiwan) 玩兒。
我想去台湾玩儿。

1. 你什麼時候去中國?
   你什么时候去中国?

   _____

   _____

2. 我打算在北京住幾天。
   我打算在北京住几天。

   _____

   _____

3. 哪兒可以買得到去上海的機票?
   哪儿可以买得到去上海的机票?

   _____

   _____

4. 有誰認識旅行社的人?
   有谁认识旅行社的人?

   _____

   _____

## IV. Communicative Activities

**7-7**    Discuss in Chinese what Xiaoqin and Wenhua found.

小琴 and 文華(文华) are planning a trip to China this winter break. They checked online or made phone calls to various airlines listed in the table below to find out the price for a plane ticket to either Beijing or Shanghai, or both. Below is the information they gathered. Remember to:

1. Use potential complements where necessary.
2. Try to work out some alternatives for the best deal.

*Notes:*
價格(价格) [jiàgé]: price
比較(比较) [bǐjiào]: comparison
日期(日期) [rìqī]: date
票價(票价) [piàojià]: ticket price
往返票(往返票) [wǎngfǎnpiào]: a round-trip ticket

# 飛機票價格比較(飞机票价格比较)

| 航空公司<br>航空公司 | 旅行日期<br>旅行日期 | | 去上海的票價<br>去上海的票价 | 去北京的票價<br>去北京的票价 |
|---|---|---|---|---|
| | 去(去) | 回(回) | | |
| 達美(达美)<br>[dáměi]: Delta | 12/3 | 12/12 | $850 | $830 |
| 聯合(联合)<br>[liánhé]: United | 12/28 | 01/10 | $900 | $900 |
| 中國(中国)<br>[Zhōngguó]: China | 12/11 | 12/28 | $780 | $775 |
| 新加坡(新加坡)<br>[Xīnjiāpō]: Singapore | 12/28 | 01/28 | $910 | — |
| 美利堅(美利坚)<br>[Měilìjiān]: American | 12/09 | 1/03 | $880 | — |

# 文化知識 (文化知识) Culture Link

## 文化點滴 (文化点滴) CULTURE NOTES

### 中國: 一個多民族的國家 (中国: 一个多民族的国家)
### China: A Multi-Ethnic Country

China is a multi-ethnic country with a population of 1.3 billion people. 中華民族(中华民族) [Zhōnghuá mínzú], the term the Chinese use to refer to themselves, is composed of 56 different ethnic groups, all living on the vast expanse of land known as China.

Among the 56 ethnic groups, the Han is the largest, making up 92 percent of China's total population. The remaining 8 percent comprises the other 55 ethnic groups. Among the various minority ethnic groups there is a great difference in population size. 少數民族(少数民族) (the minority ethnic groups) such as the Zhuang, Hui, Uygur, Yi, Miao, Manchu, Tibetan, Mongolian, Tujia, Bouyei, Korean, Dong, Yao, Bai and Hani each have a population of over a million. The remaining minority groups each have populations of less than one million, some less than 50,000. The smallest ethnic groups are the Hezhen, Gaoshan and Lhoba, with populations of less than 5,000.

China has been a multi-ethnic land for centuries, becoming even more so during the Qing Dynasty (1644–1911) when China's territory extended to cover a vast piece of land across east and central Asia and eastern Europe. The Han people, who speak

> **Do you know...**
> - the term the Chinese use to refer to themselves?
> - how many ethnic groups there are in China and whether they all speak Chinese?
> - where the minority nationalities live in China?
>
> **Read and find out!**

Mandarin (called 漢語 (汉语) [Hànyǔ] in Chinese, literally meaning "Han language"), live mostly in the eastern part of China including the northeast, 黃河(黄河) [Huánghé] (the Yellow River), 長江(长江) [Chángjiāng] (the Yangtze River) and 珠江 [Zhūjiāng] (the Pearl River) valleys, as well as along the coast. They also live in areas inhabited by minority ethnic groups.

The ethnic minorities, although constituting a small percentage of the overall population, live across a wide geographic area in the central and western parts of China. Except for the Hui and the Manchu who mainly speak 漢語(汉语) [Hànyǔ], the minority ethnic groups speak their own languages. A few only have spoken languages, with no written versions. Although the Chinese government has encouraged the national minorities to preserve their mother tongues, they are also required to learn 漢語(汉语) in order to function well in economic and political life.

The Chinese government has adopted various measures to encourage minority groups to preserve their own cultures and traditions. The minority groups are also privileged in various aspects of social and political life. For example, there are 415 representatives from the 55 minorities in the Tenth National People's Congress, which is 14 percent of the total number of representatives, 6 percent higher than their population ratio. Major areas mostly inhabited by minority groups have autonomy in running their own affairs. In China today, there are five autonomous regions, 30 autonomous prefectures, and 120 autonomous counties. Over China's long history, the many ethnic groups have made tremendous contributions to the nation's economic and cultural development.

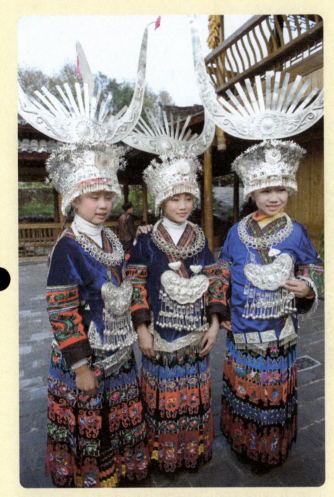

Three Miao girls wearing colorful clothing and elaborate ornamental headdresses. Can you guess where most Miao people live?

Many minority nationalities live in Guilin, a popular tourist destination with unique topographical features. Can you find Guilin on a map of China?

### 問題討論 (问题讨论) *Discuss the following with a partner or in small groups.*

1. 你知道哪些中國的少數民族? 請說出幾個。
   你知道哪些中国的少数民族? 请说出几个。
   Name some of the Chinese minority nationalities.

2. 美國 (or 你自己的國家)有少數民族嗎? 有哪幾個?
   美国 (or 你自己的国家)有少数民族吗? 有哪几个?
   Provide some examples of minority ethnic groups in the United States (or your own country.)

## 趣味中文 (趣味中文) FUN WITH CHINESE

四海之內皆兄弟
四海之内皆兄弟

All people within the four seas can become (as close as)
your older and younger brothers.

| sì | hǎi | zhī | nèi | jiē | xiōngdì |
|------|------|------------|--------|-----|----------|
| 四 | 海 | 之 | 內 | 皆 | 兄弟 |
| 四 | 海 | 之 | 内 | 皆 | 兄弟 |
| four | sea | (particle) | inside | all | brothers |

**問題討論 (问题讨论) Discuss the following with a partner or in small groups.**

1. Use Chinese to name some countries.
2. What does 四海 refer to? Use Chinese to name the 四海.
3. Is there a similar saying in your own culture? Share it with your partner(s).

# 行動吧! (行动吧!) LET'S GO!

### 簽證申請表 (签证申请表) Visa Application Form

小琴 is going to China and needs to apply for a visa. Here is one part of the visa application form. Please take a look at it and help her to fill out the form.

## 中华人民共和国签证申请表 (Q-1)
### Visa Application Form of the People's Republic of China

| | | |
|---|---|---|
| 1. 中文姓名 / Chinese Name (if any) | 2. 曾用名 / Former Name (if any) | 3. 性别 / Sex:<br>□ 男 / M   □ 女 / F |

4. 外文姓名 / Full Name
Last Name:                    First Name:

请将2寸护照
照片粘贴于此
Please affix
one passport photo

| | |
|---|---|
| 5. 出生日期:       年    月    日<br>Date of Birth:    Y    M    D | 7. 国籍 / Nationality |
| 6. 出生地点 (省 / 市):<br>Place (Province/State) of Birth: | 8. 曾有何国籍 / Former Nationality (if any) |

9. 职业:

Occupation:

工作单位:                         工作单位电话 / Office Tel.

Company Name:

10. 家庭住址 / Home Address:            家庭电话 / Home Tel.

| 11. 护照种类:<br>Passport Type: | 普通<br>□ Regular | 外交<br>□ Diplomat | 公务/官员<br>□ Service / Official | 其它证件 (名称)<br>□ Other (Please specify) |
|---|---|---|---|---|

| 12. 护照有效期:       年    月    日<br>Passport Expiration Date:    Y    M    D | 护照号码:<br>Passport No.: | 电子信箱:<br>Email: |
|---|---|---|

*Notes:*

共和國(共和国) [gònghéguó]: republic

曾用(曾用) [céngyòng]: once used

性別(性别) [xìngbié]: gender

護照(护照) [hùzhào]: passport

粘貼(粘贴) [niántiē]: to stick with glue

於(于) [yú]: to be at

此(此) [cǐ]: here

國籍(国籍) [guójí]: citizenship, nationality

單位(单位) [dānwèi]: (work) unit

種類(种类) [zhǒnglèi]: kind, type

普通(普通) [pǔtōng]: ordinary

外交(外交) [wàijiāo]: diplomatic

公務(公务) [gōngwù]: public service

官員(官员) [guānyuán]: official

其他(其他) [qítā]: other

有效期(有效期) [yǒuxiàoqī]: valid period

## 問題討論 (问题讨论) Discuss the following with a partner or in small groups.

1. What is the size of the photo required?
2. How many types of passports are there? Name them.
3. Please translate the following into English.

曾用名 _____

粘貼於此(粘贴于此) _____

護照種類(护照种类) _____

# 中國電影 (中国电影)
# Chinese Movies

*Movie advertisements in Beijing.*

## CONNECTIONS AND COMMUNITIES PREVIEW

Discuss the following questions with a partner or your class. What similarities and differences do you think there might be between Chinese culture and your own culture?

1. China shows many movies imported from other countries. Does your country often show foreign movies? Can you name a few?

2. 張藝謀(张艺谋) [Zhāng Yìmóu] is one of the best-known movie directors in China. Can you name a famous movie director in your country?

## 教學目標 (教学目标) OBJECTIVES

- Talk about movies
- Describe contrasts
- Express personal opinions

# 生詞 (生词) VOCABULARY

## 核心詞 (核心词) Core Vocabulary

| TRADITIONAL | SIMPLIFIED | PINYIN | | |
|---|---|---|---|---|
| 1. 連 | 连 | lián | Prep. | even |
| 2. 影子 | 影子 | yǐngzi | N. | shadow |
| 3. 研究報告 | 研究报告 | yánjiū bàogào | N. | research report |
| 4. 輕鬆 | 轻松 | qīngsōng | Adj. | relieved, relaxed |
| 5. 表妹 | 表妹 | biǎomèi | N. | cousin |
| 6. 強 | 强 | qiáng | Adj. | better than, well off, strong |
| 7. 完 | 完 | wán | V. | to finish |
| 8. 導演 | 导演 | dǎoyǎn | N. | director |
| | | | V. | to direct (a film) |
| 9. 部 | 部 | bù | M.W. | (measure word for films, machines, or cars) |
| 10. 功夫片 | 功夫片 | gōngfupiān | N. | action movie, kung fu movie |
| 11. 主要 | 主要 | zhǔyào | Adj. | major, main |
| 12. 特別 | 特别 | tèbié | Adv. | very, especially |
| 13. 它 | 它 | tā | Pron. | it |
| 14. 場面 | 场面 | chǎngmiàn | N. | scene |
| 15. 情節 | 情节 | qíngjié | N. | story, plot |
| 16. 吸引人 | 吸引人 | xīyǐnrén | Adj. | appealing, attractive |
| 17. 關於 | 关于 | guānyú | Prep. | about, with regard to |
| 18. 古代 | 古代 | gǔdài | Adj. | ancient |

| TRADITIONAL | SIMPLIFIED | PINYIN | | |
|---|---|---|---|---|
| 19. 故事 | 故事 | gùshi | N. | story |
| 20. 不如 | 不如 | bùrú | V. | to be inferior to, to be not as good as |
| 21. 精彩 | 精彩 | jīngcǎi | Adj. | brilliant, wonderful |
| 22. 對 | 对 | duì | Prep. | toward, to |
| 23. 描寫 | 描写 | miáoxiě | N. V. | description, exposition to describe |
| 24. 歷史 | 历史 | lìshǐ | N. | history |
| 25. 同意 | 同意 | tóngyì | V. | to agree |
| 26. 客觀 | 客观 | kèguān | Adj. | factual, objective |
| 27. 感 | 感 | gǎn | V. | to feel, sense |
| 28. 興趣 | 兴趣 | xìngqù | N. | interest |
| 29. 感情 | 感情 | gǎnqíng | N. | emotion |
| 30. 方面 | 方面 | fāngmiàn | N. | aspect |
| 31. 而且 | 而且 | érqiě | Conj. | and also, furthermore |
| 32. 特技 | 特技 | tèjì | N. | special technique |
| 33. 效果 | 效果 | xiàoguǒ | N. | effect |
| 34. 顏色 | 颜色 | yánsè | N. | color |
| 35. 週末 | 周末 | zhōumò | N. | weekend |
| 36. 放 | 放 | fàng | V. | to show (movies), to place |
| 37. 票價 | 票价 | piàojià | N. | ticket price |

## 專名 (专名) Proper Nouns

| TRADITIONAL | SIMPLIFIED | PINYIN | | |
|---|---|---|---|---|
| 1. 季如春 | 季如春 | Jì Rúchūn | N. | (name) Ruchun Ji |
| 2. 方慕華 | 方慕华 | Fāng Mùhuá | N. | (name) Muhua Fang |
| 3. 張藝謀 | 张艺谋 | Zhāng Yìmóu | N. | Yimou Zhang (Chinese film director) |
| 4. 陳道明 | 陈道明 | Chén Dàomíng | N. | Daoming Chen (Chinese movie star) |
| 5. 李連杰 | 李连杰 | Lǐ Liánjié | N. | Jet Li (Chinese kung fu movie star) |
| 6. 張曼玉 | 张曼玉 | Zhāng Mànyù | N. | Maggie Cheung (Chinese movie star) |
| 7. 英雄 | 英雄 | *Yīngxióng* | N. | *Hero* (name of a Chinese martial arts movie directed by Yimou Zhang) |
| 8. 臥虎藏龍 | 卧虎藏龙 | *Wòhǔcánglóng* | N. | *Crouching Tiger, Hidden Dragon* (name of a Chinese martial arts movie directed by Ang Lee 李安) |
| 9. 秦始皇 | 秦始皇 | Qín Shǐhuáng | N. | The first emperor of the Qin Dynasty (221–206 B.C.) |

# 語文知識 (语文知识) LANGUAGE LINK

Read and listen to the following sentence patterns. These patterns use vocabulary, expressions, and grammar that you will study in more detail in this lesson. After reading the sentence patterns, read and listen to the Language in Use section that follows.

## 句型 (句型) Sentence Patterns

 **A:** 最近為什麼連你的影子都看不見？
最近为什么连你的影子都看不见？
Zuìjìn wèishénme lián nǐde yǐngzi dōu kànbújiàn?

**B:** 我最近比以前忙得多，我在寫研究報告。
我最近比以前忙得多，我在写研究报告。
Wǒ zuìjìn bǐ yǐqián máng de duō, wǒ zài xiě yánjiū bàogào.

**A:** 《英雄》這部電影好看嗎？
《英雄》这部电影好看吗？
*Yīngxióng* zhèbù diànyǐng hǎokàn ma?

**B:** 我覺得小說比電影好一些。
我觉得小说比电影好一些。
Wǒ juéde xiǎoshuō bǐ diànyǐng hǎo yìxiē.

**A:** 《英雄》對秦始皇的描寫跟別的
《英雄》对秦始皇的描写跟别的
*Yīngxióng* duì Qín Shǐhuáng de miáoxiě gēn biéde

電影不一樣。
电影不一样。
diànyǐng bù yíyàng.

**B:** 我同意，但是我覺得它的描寫很客觀。
我同意，但是我觉得它的描写很客观。
Wǒ tóngyì, dànshì wǒ juéde tāde miáoxiě hěn kèguān.

## 課文 Language in Use: What's Your Favorite Movie?
### (繁體字 Traditional Character Version)

季如春： 慕華，你好像最近比以前忙得多，是嗎?

方慕華： 沒有啊! 你為什麼覺得我比以前忙得多呢?

季如春： 最近連你的影子[1]都看不見。昨天晚上我給你打電話也找不到你。

方慕華： 昨天上午我把一個大的研究報告交出去了，覺得輕鬆多了，所以我就跟我的表妹[2]去看電影了。

季如春： 你比我強得多，我的報告還沒有寫完呢! 對了，你們看了什麼電影? 好看嗎?

方慕華： 我們看的是《英雄》。

季如春： 是不是張藝謀導演的那部功夫片[3]?

方慕華： 是的。主要演員是陳道明、李連杰和張曼玉。其中我特別喜歡李連杰。

季如春： 有人說它沒有《臥虎藏龍》好看，你覺得怎麼樣?

---

**1. 影子(影子)**

The literal meaning is "shadow," but here it is used in a very idiomatic expression to mean "I haven't seen you at all, not even your shadow."

---

**2. 表妹(表妹)**

表妹(表妹) is a younger female cousin on your mother's side. Chinese make very clear distinctions between relatives on the father's side and the mother's side, and also between older and younger ones.

---

**3. 功夫片(功夫片)**

功夫片(功夫片) means martial arts films. Other kinds of films include:

文藝片(文艺片) [wényìpiān] drama films
喜劇片(喜剧片) [xǐjùpiān] comedy films.
動作片(动作片) [dòngzuòpiān] action films
恐怖片(恐怖片) [kǒngbùpiān] horror films
紀錄片(纪录片) [jìlùpiān] documentary films

*Continued on page 238*

### 课文 Language in Use: What's Your Favorite Movie?
### (简体字 Simplified Character Version)

季如春： 慕华，你好像最近比以前忙得多，是吗？

方慕华： 没有啊！你为什么觉得我比以前忙得多呢？

季如春： 最近连你的影子[1]都看不见。昨天晚上我给你打电话也找不到
你。

方慕华： 昨天上午我把一个大的研究报告交出去了，觉得轻松多了，
所以我就跟我的表妹[2]去看电影了。

季如春： 你比我强得多，我的报告还没有写完呢！对了，你们看了什么
电影？好看吗？

方慕华： 我们看的是《英雄》。

季如春： 是不是张艺谋导演的那部功夫片[3]？

方慕华： 是的。主要演员是陈道明、李连杰和张曼玉。其中我特别喜欢
李连杰。

季如春： 有人说它没有《卧虎藏龙》好看，你觉得怎么样？

*Continued on page 239*

課文 **Language in Use: What's Your Favorite Movie?**
(繁體字 Traditional Character Version) —— 接第二百三十六頁

方慕華： 我覺得這兩部電影差不多[4]。
你呢? 你看過了沒有?

季如春： 我看過《臥虎藏龍》，沒有
看過《英雄》，可是聽說
《英雄》的場面比《臥虎藏
龍》大得多。是真的嗎?

方慕華： 沒錯。《英雄》的場面比
《臥虎藏龍》大一些，
可是我覺得它的情節不像
《臥虎藏龍》那麼吸引人。

季如春： 聽說《英雄》說的是關於
中國古代秦始皇[5]的故事，
那麼，比較起來電影和小說
哪個好?

方慕華： 我覺得電影不如小說精彩。

季如春： 有人說它對秦始皇的描寫跟歷史上的秦始皇不一樣。

方慕華： 我同意，但是我覺得這部電影描寫得比較客觀。

季如春： 我一直對歷史故事很感興趣，所以我很想去看一看這部電影。

方慕華： 你應該去看看。我覺得《英雄》這部電影對感情方面的描寫
比《臥虎藏龍》多一些，而且它的特技效果和顏色都比別的
電影好得多。

季如春： 你知道在哪兒可以看得到《英雄》嗎?

方慕華： 這個週末學校會放[6]這部電
影，票價只要一元，比電影院
的要便宜九元。

季如春： 好，這個週末我就去看。

---

**4. 差(差) [chà, chā]**

差(差) has two different pronunciations: [chà] and [chā]. In 差不多(差不多) (similar), it is pronounced [chà] and in 時差(时差) (time difference, jetlag), it is pronounced [chā].

---

**5. 秦始皇(秦始皇)**

秦始皇(秦始皇) was the first emperor of the Qin Dynasty (221–206 **B.C.**). He unified the country, standardized many things such as the writing system and measurements, and also ordered the building of the Great Wall (at the cost of thousands of lives). His anti-Confucian attitude led him to persecute several hundred Confucian scholars and to burn books on Confucianism and history. Historically he is viewed by many as a tyrant.

---

**6. 放(電影) [放(电影)]**

The word 放(放) in 放電影(放电影) means "to show," and in 放下(放下) it means "to place."

## 课文 Language in Use: What's Your Favorite Movie?
### (简体字 Simplified Character Version) —— 接第二百三十七页

方慕华：我觉得这两部电影差不多[4]。你呢？你看过了没有？

季如春：我看过《卧虎藏龙》，没有看过《英雄》，可是听说《英雄》
的场面比《卧虎藏龙》大得多。是真的吗？

方慕华：没错。《英雄》的场面比《卧虎藏龙》大一些，可是我觉得
它的情节不像《卧虎藏龙》那么吸引人。

季如春：听说《英雄》说的是关于中国古代秦始皇[5]的故事，那么，
比较起来电影和小说哪个好？

方慕华：我觉得电影不如小说精彩。

季如春：有人说它对秦始皇的描写跟历史上的秦始皇不一样。

方慕华：我同意，但是我觉得这部电影描写得比较客观。

季如春：我一直对历史故事很感兴趣，所以我很想去看一看这部电影。

方慕华：你应该去看看。我觉得《英雄》这部电影对感情方面的描写
比《卧虎藏龙》多一些，而且它的特技效果和颜色都比别的
电影好得多。

季如春：你知道在哪儿可以看得到《英雄》吗？

方慕华：这个周末学校会放[6]这部电影，票价只要一元，比电影院的要
便宜九元。

季如春：好，这个周末我就去看。

# 語法 (语法) GRAMMAR

## I. Comparison (2)

### A.  A 比 B + V. + Degree of Complement

- Review of Degree of Complement

  We learned in Lesson 16 of *Chinese Link: Elementary Chinese* that a sentence with a degree of complement is used to describe how an action is performed (such as how fast, how well, how soon, etc.). The pattern is summarized as follows:

> Single V.:  Subject + V. + 得 + Adv. + Adj.

*Example:*

他跑得很快。
他跑得很快。
He runs very fast.

> V.O.:  Subject + V.O. + V. 得 + Adv. + Adj.

*Example:*

他打籃球打得很好。
他打篮球打得很好。
He plays basketball very well.

The object can also be placed at the beginning of a sentence for emphasis:

*Example:*

籃球他打得很好。
篮球他打得很好。

- The degree of complement is commonly used with 比 sentences to indicate the comparison of how an action is performed between A and B.

> *Pattern:*    A 比 B + V. + Degree of Complement

*Examples:*

他比我跑得快。
他比我跑得快。
He runs faster than I do.

我比他寫漢字寫得好。
我比他写汉字写得好。

I write Chinese characters better than he does.

漢字我比他寫得好。
汉字我比他写得好。

(漢字(汉字)) is placed at the beginning of the sentence for emphasis.

我比他吃甜食吃得多。
我比他吃甜食吃得多。

I eat more sweets than he does.

**»Try it!** With a partner, practice questions and answers using the pattern "A 比 B + V. + Degree of Complement." For example,

**A:** 你和他寫漢字誰寫得快?
你和他写汉字谁写得快?

**B:** 我比他寫漢字寫得快。
我比他写汉字写得快。

or

**B:** 我寫漢字寫得比他快。
我写汉字写得比他快。

## B. 比 + Quantifier

*Pattern:* | A 比 B + Adj. + Quantifier |

Quantifiers can be:

1. Definite quantifiers: e.g. a number and a measure word

   *Examples:*

   我比他大三歲。
   我比他大三岁。

   I am three years older than he is.

   這張電影票比那張電影票便宜三塊錢。
   这张电影票比那张电影票便宜三块钱。

   This movie ticket is three dollars cheaper than that one.

2.  Indefinite quantifiers: e.g. 一些, 一點兒(一点儿), 的多

    *Examples:*

    我比他大一點兒。
    我比他大一点儿。
    I am a bit older than he is.

    這張電影票比那張電影票便宜一些。
    这张电影票比那张电影票便宜一些。
    This movie ticket is a bit cheaper than that one.

    我女朋友的錢比我的多的多。
    我女朋友的钱比我的多的多。
    My girlfriend has a lot more money than I do.

3.  Fractions and times: e.g. 一半, 三分之一, 五倍

    *Examples:*

    我們的學費比你們的少一半。
    我们的学费比你们的少一半。
    Our tuition fee is half of yours.

    這兒的中國人比那兒的多兩倍。
    这儿的中国人比那儿的多两倍。
    There are twice as many Chinese people here than there.

    今年的學生比去年的多三分之一。
    今年的学生比去年的多三分之一。
    There are one-third more students this year than last year.

**»Try it!**  With a partner, devise a short dialogue, using the pattern of "A 比 B + Adj. + Quantifier." Make sure you use all three kinds of quantifiers listed above. For example,

A:  這兩部電影，哪一部比較長?
    这两部电影，哪一部比较长?

B:  這部電影比那部電影長三十分鐘。
    这部电影比那部电影长三十分钟。

## II. Emphatic Pattern: 連(连)......都/也......

This is a pattern used for emphasis. The part that is emphasized is usually the subject, the object, or the verb of a sentence.

*Examples:*

這部電影真好看。連<u>我</u>都看了兩次了。
这部电影真好看。连<u>我</u>都看了两次了。
This film is really good. Even I have seen it twice.
(This emphasizes the subject 我 and implies that I don't watch films very often.)

她是在中國出生的，可是她連<u>自己的中文名字</u>都不會寫。
她是在中国出生的，可是她连<u>自己的中文名字</u>都不会写。
She was born in China, but she was not even able to write her own name in Chinese.
(This emphasizes the object 自己的中文名字 and implies that her ability to write Chinese is very poor.)

她男朋友送給她一個音樂 ([yīnyuè]: music) 光碟 ([guāngdié]: disc)，她連<u>聽</u>也沒聽，就把它放在旁邊了。
她男朋友送给她一个音乐光碟，她连<u>听</u>也没听，就把它放在旁边了。
Her boyfriend gave her a music disc. She did not even spend any time listening to it before she put it aside.
(This emphasizes the action 聽(听) and implies that she had no interest in it at all.)

*Notes:*

- The emphasized part is usually placed between 連(连) and 都/也.
- Sometimes, 連(连) can be omitted, but 都/也 can never be omitted.

---

>>**Try it!**  With a partner, practice devising short dialogues with the pattern for emphasis "連(连)......都/也" as explained above. For example,

A: 他的中文怎麼樣?
  他的中文怎么样?

B: 他的中文很不好，連 "你好" 也聽不懂。
  他的中文很不好，连 "你好" 也听不懂。

## III. Preposition 對 (对)

對(对) can be used as a preposition. Together with its object, the 對—phrase (对—phrase) can be used as an adverbial to modify a verb or verb phrase, or as an attributive to modify a noun or a noun phrase. Here are some examples,

A. 對—phrase (对—phrase) as an adverbial modifying a verb or verb phrase:

對......有興趣                      to be interested in . . .
对......有兴趣

對......有幫助 [bāngzhù]           to be helpful to . . .
对......有帮助

對......有用處 [yòngchù]           to be useful to . . .
对......有用处

對......有利    [yǒulì]            to be beneficial to . . .
对......有利

*Examples:*

他對中國文學有興趣。
他对中国文学有兴趣。
He is interested in Chinese literature.

鍛煉對身體有幫助。
锻炼对身体有帮助。
Exercise is good for your health.

游泳對身體有用處。
游泳对身体有用处。
Swimming is good for your health.

學中文對找工作有利。
学中文对找工作有利。
Studying Chinese is beneficial to finding a job.

**>>Try it!** With a partner, practice using all the four phrases with 對(对)...... listed above in short dialogues. For example,

A: 你喜歡打球嗎?
你喜欢打球吗?

B: 我很喜歡。打球對身體很有幫助。
我很喜欢。打球对身体很有帮助。

B. 對—phrase (对—phrase) as an attributive to be followed by 的 + a noun or a noun phrase:

對......的描寫          the description of . . .
对......的描写

對......的幫助          the help to . . .
对......的帮助

對......的介紹          the introduction to . . .
对......的介绍

*Examples:*

這部電影對感情方面的描寫很細膩 ([xìnì]: delicate, detailed) 。
这部电影对感情方面的描写很细腻。
The portrayal of emotion in this movie is very delicate.

他對我們的幫助,我們永遠都忘不了。
他对我们的帮助,我们永远都忘不了。
We will never forget his help to us.

他對中國歷史的介紹,講 ([jiǎng]: to speak) 得很清楚。
他对中国历史的介绍,讲得很清楚。
His introduction to Chinese history was spoken very clearly.

**>>Try it!** With a partner, make up a short dialogue about your opinion of a movie you know. Make sure you use the 對(对)—phrase to be followed by 的 as an attributive to modify a noun or a noun phrase. For example,

A: 你聽得懂她對這部電影的介紹嗎?
你听得懂她对这部电影的介绍吗?

B: 聽得懂。我很喜歡她對這部電影的介紹。
听得懂。我很喜欢她对这部电影的介绍。

# 補充課文 (补充课文) SUPPLEMENTARY PRACTICE

*Read the following passage. Then listen and repeat.*

## Going to the Movies (繁體字 Traditional Character Version)

十一月十五日　　　天氣：晴到多雲

　　今天下午沒有課，我就跟如春一起去大光明電影院看了一場電影。那兒放的電影比別的電影院好。我們看了一場張藝謀導演的功夫片《十面埋伏》。影片的色彩和特技效果都比別的電影好，場面也比《英雄》和《臥虎藏龍》大得多。如春說《十面埋伏》的情節不如《英雄》和《臥虎藏龍》精彩，可是我不同意，我覺得《十面埋伏》比那兩部電影有意思得多。

　　有人說功夫片不像動作片那麼緊張、好看，可是我覺得好的功夫片比動作片精彩多了。我非常喜歡成龍和李連杰這兩個演員，特別是李連杰，演得很不錯。

　　我對張藝謀導演的片子特別有興趣。他導演的很多片子我都看過，連他自己以前演的片子我也看了。我覺得他跟李安導演差不多，都很有創新精神。

　　很多功夫片說的都是歷史故事。我對中國歷史非常感興趣。中國的歷史有五千多年了，比美國歷史要長四千多年。中國的傳統文化也特別豐富多彩。今後有機會，我一定要去中國學習中國歷史、傳統和文化。

*Notes:*

同意(同意) [tóngyì]: to agree
動作片(动作片) [dòngzuòpiān]: action movie
緊張(紧张) [jǐnzhāng]: breathtaking
成龍(成龙) [Chéng Lóng]: Jackie Chan (a Chinese kung fu movie star)
李安(李安) [Lǐ Ān]: Ang Lee (a Chinese film director)
創新(创新) [chuàngxīn]: to be creative
精神(精神) [jīngshén]: spirit
傳統(传统) [chuántǒng]: tradition
文化(文化) [wénhuà]: culture
豐富多彩(丰富多彩) [fēngfùduōcǎi]: rich and colorful
機會(机会) [jīhuì]: opportunity

## 補充課文 (补充课文) SUPPLEMENTARY PRACTICE

*Read the following passage. Then listen and repeat.*

### Going to the Movies (简体字 Simplified Character Version)

十一月十五日　　　　天气：晴到多云

今天下午没有课，我就跟如春一起去大光明电影院看了一场电影。那儿放的电影比别的电影院好。我们看了一场张艺谋导演的功夫片《十面埋伏》。影片的色彩和特技效果都比别的电影好，场面也比《英雄》和《卧虎藏龙》大得多。如春说《十面埋伏》的情节不如《英雄》和《卧虎藏龙》精彩，可是我不同意，我觉得《十面埋伏》比那两部电影有意思得多。

有人说功夫片不像动作片那么紧张、好看，可是我觉得好的功夫片比动作片精彩多了。我非常喜欢成龙和李连杰这两个演员，特别是李连杰，演得很不错。

我对张艺谋导演的片子特别有兴趣。他导演的很多片子我都看过，连他自己以前演的片子我也看了。我觉得他跟李安导演差不多，都很有创新精神。

很多功夫片说的都是历史故事。我对中国历史非常感兴趣。中国的历史有五千多年了，比美国历史要长四千多年。中国的传统文化也特别丰富多彩。今后有机会，我一定要去中国学习中国历史、传统和文化。

### Exercises: work with a partner or in small groups

1. 方慕華覺得《十面埋伏》跟《英雄》和《臥虎藏龍》比起來怎麼樣？
   方慕华觉得《十面埋伏》跟《英雄》和《卧虎藏龙》比起来怎么样？

2. 他為什麼對張藝謀導演的片子特別有興趣？
   他为什么对张艺谋导演的片子特别有兴趣？

3. 中國的歷史和美國的歷史比起來怎麼樣？
   中国的历史和美国的历史比起来怎么样？

# 成語故事 (成语故事) IDIOM STORY

## 得意洋洋 (得意洋洋) [déyìyángyáng]

*Meaning:* Feeling complacent or extremely proud.

*Usage:* This is used to describe someone who is immensely proud or looks triumphant.

*Example:* 他在那部電影裡只出現了一下子，就整天一副"得意洋洋"的樣子。

他在那部电影里只出现了一下子，就整天一副"得意洋洋"的样子。

Pay attention to the usages of grammar points: A 比 B + V. + Degree of Complement, 比 + Quantifier, 對(对) used as a Preposition.

### (繁體字 Traditional Character Version)

　　兩千多年前的春秋戰國時期，有一個宰相名字叫晏子，他的學問比別人多得多，可是他很謙虛，因此大家都很尊敬他。他的馬夫趕馬車趕得也比別的馬夫好得多。可是這個馬夫非常驕傲，覺得別人都不如他，所以每次他趕著馬車出去的時候，都是得意洋洋，看上去比晏子神氣得多。

　　有一次，馬夫的妻子看見了馬夫得意洋洋的樣子，心裡很不高興。馬夫回家時，妻子就說想離開他。馬夫問妻子為什麼，妻子說：你只是一個馬夫，可是你那麼驕傲。趕車的時候那麼得意洋洋，比晏子神氣得多。晏子比你的地位高得多，可是他不像你那麼驕傲、得意洋洋。我對你很失望。我不願意跟你在一起生活了。

　　馬夫覺得妻子說得很對。從那以後，他就比以前謙虛得多了。晏子問他為什麼變了，他說連他的妻子都說他不應該那麼得意洋洋，他怎麼能再驕傲呢！晏子聽了以後覺得馬夫的妻子是一個非常懂道理的女子。後來他就讓馬夫當了官。

　　這個故事告訴我們：一個人應該謙虛，而不應該覺得自己了不起。

(简体字 Simplified Character Version)

两千多年前的春秋战国时期，有一个宰相名字叫晏子，他的学问比别人多得多，可是他很谦虚，因此大家都很尊敬他。他的马夫赶马车赶得也比别的马夫好得多。可是这个马夫非常骄傲，觉得别人都不如他，所以每次他赶着马车出去的时候，都是得意洋洋，看上去比晏子神气得多。

有一次，马夫的妻子看见了马夫得意洋洋的样子，心里很不高兴。马夫回家时，妻子就说想离开他。马夫问妻子为什么，妻子说：你只是一个马夫，可是你那么骄傲。赶车的时候那么得意洋洋，比晏子神气得多。晏子比你的地位高得多，可是他不像你那么骄傲、得意洋洋。我对你很失望。我不愿意跟你在一起生活了。

马夫觉得妻子说得很对。从那以后，他就比以前谦虚得多了。晏子问他为什么变了，他说连他的妻子都说他不应该那么得意洋洋，他怎么能再骄傲呢！晏子听了以后觉得马夫的妻子是一个非常懂道理的女子。后来他就让马夫当了官。

这个故事告诉我们：一个人应该谦虚，而不应该觉得自己了不起。

*Notes:*

得意洋洋(得意洋洋) [déyìyángyáng]: to feel complacent or extremely proud

春秋戰國時期(春秋战国时期) [Chūnqiū Zhànguó shíqī]: Spring & Autumn period (770–476 B.C.) and Warring States (475–221 B.C.) period, two historical periods in China

宰相(宰相) [zǎixiàng]: prime minister

晏子(晏子) [Yànzǐ]: (name of the prime minister of State of Qi)

學問(学问) [xuéwèn]: knowledge

謙虛(谦虚) [qiānxū]: to be modest

尊敬(尊敬) [zūnjìng]: respect; to respect

馬夫(马夫) [mǎfū]: horse-carriage driver

趕馬(赶马) [gǎnmǎ]: to drive a horse

驕傲(骄傲) [jiāo'ào]: arrogant

神氣(神气) [shénqì]: to look cocky

妻子(妻子) [qīzi]: wife

地位(地位) [dìwèi]: (social) status

對......失望(对......失望) [duì . . . shīwàng]: to be disappointed by . . .

懂道理(懂道理) [dǒngdàolǐ]: to be sensible and intelligent, to know the hows and whys

當官(当官) [dāngguān]: to take the position of an official

## Exercises: work with a partner or in small groups

1. 找出有下面語法的句子: A 比 B + V. + Degree of Complement, 比 + Quantifier, 對 used as a Preposition.

   找出有下面语法的句子: A 比 B + V. + Degree of Complement, 比 + Quantifier, 对 used as a Preposition.

2. 用你自己的話說說 "得意洋洋" 的故事。
   用你自己的话说说 "得意洋洋" 的故事。

3. 請用 "得意洋洋" 造一個句子或者說一個得意洋洋的例子。
   请用 "得意洋洋" 造一个句子或者说一个得意洋洋的例子。

4. "得意洋洋" 的故事，告訴了我們什麼?
   "得意洋洋" 的故事，告诉了我们什么?

# 練習 (练习) ACTIVITIES

## I. Listening Exercises

**8-1**  In the blanks provided, write the Pinyin, with tones, for the words you hear.

1. 他們倆 ＿＿ ＿＿ 大，不過哥哥 ＿＿ 弟弟 ＿＿ ＿＿ ＿＿ ＿＿ 。
   他们俩 ＿＿ ＿＿ 大，不过哥哥 ＿＿ 弟弟 ＿＿ ＿＿ ＿＿ ＿＿ 。

2. 這一幢大樓 ＿＿ 那一幢 ＿＿ ＿＿ ＿＿ 。
   这一幢大楼 ＿＿ 那一幢 ＿＿ ＿＿ ＿＿ 。

3. 同學們 ＿＿ 我的 ＿＿ ＿＿ 很大。
   同学们 ＿＿ 我的 ＿＿ ＿＿ 很大。

4. 紐約的房租 ＿＿ 這兒的 ＿＿ ＿＿ ＿＿ 。
   纽约的房租 ＿＿ 这儿的 ＿＿ ＿＿ ＿＿ 。

5. 小說 ＿＿ 電影 ＿＿ ＿＿ ＿＿ 。
   小说 ＿＿ 电影 ＿＿ ＿＿ ＿＿ 。

6. 吃維生素 ＿＿ 健康 ＿＿ ＿＿ 。
   吃维生素 ＿＿ 健康 ＿＿ ＿＿ 。

7. 小琴 ＿＿ 中國書法 ＿＿ ＿＿ ＿＿ 。
   小琴 ＿＿ 中国书法 ＿＿ ＿＿ ＿＿ 。

8. 這部電影太短了，＿＿ 一個小時 ＿＿ ＿＿ ＿＿ 。
   这部电影太短了，＿＿ 一个小时 ＿＿ ＿＿ ＿＿ 。

**8-2**  Listen to the following stories and then answer the questions.

### 第一個故事(第一个故事) [dìyī ge gùshi] Story 1:

*Notes:*
古時候(古时候) [gùshíhòu]: ancient times
孔融(孔融) [Kǒng Róng]: name of a person
梨子(梨子) [lízi]: pear
笑(笑) [xiào]: to smile, laugh

### 第一段問題(第一段问题):

1. 孔融有幾個哥哥? 他是最小的孩子嗎?
   孔融有几个哥哥? 他是最小的孩子吗?

2. 孔融拿的梨子是什麼樣 ([shénmeyàng]:
   what kind of) 的?
   孔融拿的梨子是什么样的?

3. 孔融為什麼拿那個梨子?
   孔融为什么拿那个梨子?

第二個故事(第二个故事) Story 2:

*Notes:*
二手車(二手车) [èrshǒu chē]: used car
決定(决定) [juédìng]: to decide; decision
油(油) [yóu]: gasoline, oil
傷腦筋(伤脑筋) [shāngnǎojīn]: knotty, bothersome
優點(优点) [yōudiǎn]: merit, strong point
缺點(缺点) [quēdiǎn]: weakness

List the traits of the two types of cars in the table below. Then use 比 sentences to make comparisons:

|  | 日本車(日本车) | 德國車(德国车) |
|---|---|---|
| 優點(优点) |  |  |
| 缺點(缺点) |  |  |

## II. Character Exercises

**8-3**    Work with a partner. Read the following words, phrases, and sentences.

| | |
|---|---|
| 關<br>关 | 對<br>对 |
| 關於<br>关于 | 對風景的描寫<br>对风景的描写 |
| 關於歷史<br>关于历史 | 對風景的描寫感興趣<br>对风景的描写感兴趣 |
| 關於中國歷史<br>关于中国历史 | 導演對風景的描寫很感興趣。<br>导演对风景的描写很感兴趣。 |
| 他喜歡關於中國歷史的小說。<br>他喜欢关于中国历史的小说。 | 看起來導演對風景的描寫很感興趣。<br>看起来导演对风景的描写很感兴趣。 |

Now with your partner, try to use the following characters to make words, phrases, and then sentences.

| | | | | |
|---|---|---|---|---|
| 1. 連<br>　 连 | 2. 影<br>　 影 | 3. 強<br>　 强 | 4. 告<br>　 告 | 5. 吸<br>　 吸 |
| 6. 節<br>　 节 | 7. 代<br>　 代 | 8. 它<br>　 它 | 9. 顏<br>　 颜 | 10. 價<br>　 价 |

**8-4** With a partner or a group, create phrases with the following words (pay attention to the various usages of each word).

*Example:* 影：影子，電影
　　　　 影：影子，电影

1. 報：＿＿＿＿＿＿＿＿＿＿＿＿＿＿＿＿＿＿
   报：＿＿＿＿＿＿＿＿＿＿＿＿＿＿＿＿＿＿

2. 輕：＿＿＿＿＿＿＿＿＿＿＿＿＿＿＿＿＿＿
   轻：＿＿＿＿＿＿＿＿＿＿＿＿＿＿＿＿＿＿

3. 別：＿＿＿＿＿＿＿＿＿＿＿＿＿＿＿＿＿＿
   别：＿＿＿＿＿＿＿＿＿＿＿＿＿＿＿＿＿＿

4. 差：＿＿＿＿＿＿＿＿＿＿＿＿＿＿＿＿＿＿
   差：＿＿＿＿＿＿＿＿＿＿＿＿＿＿＿＿＿＿

5. 場：＿＿＿＿＿＿＿＿＿＿＿＿＿＿＿＿＿＿
   场：＿＿＿＿＿＿＿＿＿＿＿＿＿＿＿＿＿＿

6. 趣：＿＿＿＿＿＿＿＿＿＿＿＿＿＿＿＿＿＿
   趣：＿＿＿＿＿＿＿＿＿＿＿＿＿＿＿＿＿＿

7. 情：＿＿＿＿＿＿＿＿＿＿＿＿＿＿＿＿＿＿
   情：＿＿＿＿＿＿＿＿＿＿＿＿＿＿＿＿＿＿

8. 票：＿＿＿＿＿＿＿＿＿＿＿＿＿＿＿＿＿＿
   票：＿＿＿＿＿＿＿＿＿＿＿＿＿＿＿＿＿＿

9. 客：＿＿＿＿＿＿＿＿＿＿＿＿＿＿＿＿

   客：＿＿＿＿＿＿＿＿＿＿＿＿＿＿＿＿

10. 精：＿＿＿＿＿＿＿＿＿＿＿＿＿＿＿＿

   精：＿＿＿＿＿＿＿＿＿＿＿＿＿＿＿＿

## III. Grammar Exercises

**8-5**  The following table lists the collections of several categories of books in a library. Please work in pairs to make comparisons about the book collections. Make at least four comparison sentences for each category.

*Useful comparison patterns:*

A 比 B + Adj.

A 比 B + V. + Degree of Complement

A 比 B + Adj. + Quantifier

*Note:*
商業(商业) [shāngyè]: business

|  | 文學(文学) | 工程(工程) | 商業(商业) |
|---|---|---|---|
| 中文書<br>中文书 | 501本 | 135本 | 356本 |
| 英文書<br>英文书 | 5250本 | 557本 | 1587本 |
| 法文書<br>法文书 | 2138本 | 223本 | 625本 |
| 德文書<br>德文书 | 1253本 | 454本 | 489本 |
| 西班牙文書<br>西班牙文书 | 2517本 | 743本 | 652本 |
| 日文書<br>日文书 | 489本 | 264本 | 422本 |

**8-6**  Fill in the blanks with appropriate words. Then check with your partner.

1. 她的頭髮 ＿＿＿ 他男朋友的頭髮要 ＿＿＿ ＿＿＿ ＿＿＿。

   她的头发 ＿＿＿ 他男朋友的头发要 ＿＿＿ ＿＿＿ ＿＿＿ (much shorter)。

2. 這門課很輕鬆，＿＿＿ 期末考試 ＿＿＿ ＿＿＿ ＿＿＿。

   这门课很轻松，＿＿＿ 期末考试 ＿＿＿ ＿＿＿ ＿＿＿ (even has no final exam)。

3. 她用電腦打中文字 ＿＿＿ 打英文字 ＿＿＿ ＿＿＿ ＿＿＿。

   她用电脑打中文字 ＿＿＿ 打英文字 ＿＿＿ ＿＿＿ ＿＿＿ (much slower than)。

4. 老師和師母 ＿＿＿ 學生們都很 ＿＿＿ ＿＿＿。

   老师和师母 ＿＿＿ 学生们都很 ＿＿＿ ＿＿＿ (warm-hearted towards students)。

5. 早睡早起 ([zǎoshuì zǎoqǐ]: go to bed early, get up early) ＿＿＿ 身體 ＿＿＿ ＿＿＿ ＿＿＿。

   早睡早起 ＿＿＿ 身体 ＿＿＿ ＿＿＿ ＿＿＿ (is beneficial to health)。

6. 我的手錶 ＿＿＿ 你的 ＿＿＿ 五分鐘。

   我的手表 ＿＿＿ 你的 ＿＿＿ 五分钟 (five minutes faster)。

7. 老闆常常忙得連喝水的時間 ＿＿＿ ＿＿＿ ＿＿＿。

   老板常常忙得连喝水的时间 ＿＿＿ ＿＿＿ ＿＿＿ (even has no time to drink water)。

8. 在秀水街 ([Xiùshuǐjiē]: Xiushui Street) 買東西的外國人 ＿＿＿ 中國人 ＿＿＿ ＿＿＿ ＿＿＿。

   在秀水街买东西的外国人 ＿＿＿ 中国人 ＿＿＿ ＿＿＿ ＿＿＿ (twice as many)。

**8-7**    Translate the following Chinese into English orally.

*Notes:*
飲料(饮料) [yǐnliào]: beverage
有效率(有效率) [yǒuxiàolǜ]: efficient
巴西(巴西) [Bāxī]: Brazil
生產(生产) [shēngchǎn]: to produce
國家(国家) [guójiā]: country
茶葉(茶叶) [cháyè]: tea leaves
品種(品种) [pǐnzhǒng]: variety, assortment
加糖(加糖) [jiātáng]: to add sugar
容易(容易) [róngyì]: easy
發胖(发胖) [fāpàng]: to gain weight

# 咖啡和茶(咖啡和茶)

## (繁體字 Traditional Character Version)

咖啡和茶都是人們愛喝的飲料。累的時候喝一點兒咖啡或者茶，都會覺得很有精神，工作效率比沒喝以前要高得多。人們每年喝的咖啡比茶多三倍，可是喝茶的人比喝咖啡的人多得多。巴西是生產咖啡最多的國家。中國是茶葉品種最多的國家。咖啡和茶都很好喝，可是因為很多人喝咖啡的時候都喜歡加糖，所以咖啡喝多了容易發胖。茶葉裡面有很多維生素，所以喝茶對健康很有好處。

## (简体字 Simplified Character Version)

咖啡和茶都是人们爱喝的饮料。累的时候喝一点儿咖啡或者茶，都会觉得很有精神，工作效率比没喝以前要高得多。人们每年喝的咖啡比茶多三倍，可是喝茶的人比喝咖啡的人多得多。巴西是生产咖啡最多的国家。中国是茶叶品种最多的国家。咖啡和茶都很好喝，可是因为很多人喝咖啡的时候都喜欢加糖，所以咖啡喝多了容易发胖。茶叶里面有很多维生素，所以喝茶对健康很有好处。

## IV. Communicative Activities

### Role-playing

Below is a list of items held at the Lost and Found Office. 小英 lost her purse in the airport. Work in pairs, one taking the role of 小英 and the other the role of an employee in the Lost and Found Office. Make comparisons to see whether the item is 小英's.

|  | 時間(时间) | 地點(地点) | 物品(物品) |
|---|---|---|---|
| 2010/7/9 | 下午 02:00 | 美國航空公司服務台<br>美国航空公司服务台 | 照相機<br>照相机 |
| 2010/7/1 | 上午 11:15 | 一樓女洗手間<br>一楼女洗手间 | 外衣<br>外衣 |
| 2010/6/28 | 上午 07:30 | 達美航空公司候機廳<br>达美航空公司候机厅 | 鑰匙<br>钥匙 |
| 2010/6/23 | 晚上 09:40 | 安全檢查通道<br>安全检查通道 | 手錶<br>手表 |
| 2010/6/10 | 下午 03:25 | 咖啡廳<br>咖啡厅 | 錢包<br>钱包 |

*Notes:*
地點(地点) [dìdiǎn]: place
物品(物品) [wùpǐn]: items, things
服務台(服务台) [fúwùtái]: service desk
照相機(照相机) [zhàoxiàngjī]: digital camera
洗手間(洗手间) [xǐshǒujiān]: restroom
候機廳(候机厅) [hòujītīng]: waiting room
安全檢查(安全检查) [ānquán jiǎnchá]: security check
通道(通道) [tōngdào]: passage
手錶(手表) [shǒubiǎo]: watch

*Useful expressions*
*Comparison:*  1. A 比 B + V. + Degree of Complement
　　　　　　　2. A 比 B + Adj. + Quantifier (三倍，一些，一點兒，的多)
　　　　　　　　　　　　　　　　　　(三倍，一些，一点儿，的多)

　　　　　　　　連……都，對……有幫助(有利)
　　　　　　　　连……都，对……有帮助(有利)

# 文化知識 (文化知识) Culture Link

## 文化點滴 (文化点滴) CULTURE NOTES

### 中國的電影事業 (中国的电影事业) The Movie Industry in China

The first film shot in China, about a Beijing Opera performance, was produced in 1905 although China's film industry did not experience its first peak until the 1930s. The second peak came between the 1950s and the mid-1960s. During the Cultural Revolution (1966–1976), however, the film industry suffered and few feature films were made until Chinese films started to flourish again in the early 1980s. Since then, a good number of films produced by the new generation of directors, actors, and actresses have won awards at international film festivals and gained worldwide recognition. Most prominent among them are film directors 張藝謀(张艺谋) [Zhāng Yìmóu] and 陳凱歌(陈凯歌) [Chén Kǎigē], and actresses 鞏俐(巩俐) [Gǒng Lì] and 章子怡 [Zhāng Zǐyí]. In 2005, China celebrated the 100th year of its movie industry which is now capable of producing more than 100 films, 7,000 TV series, and importing more than 1,000 movies and TV programs from overseas each year.

In China today, films fall into four categories: 1) mainstream films, which are generally government-funded and depict political figures and historic events of the Chinese Communist Party; 2) artistic films, which portray the life and thoughts of people in contemporary China; 3) entertainment and commercial films, which started in the late 1980s and consist mainly of comedy New Year celebration films and martial arts films; and 4) new-generation films directed by young artists who received a professional education in the arts and theater and who emphasize a rebellious and avant-garde style.

Along with the globalization of China's economy and its entry into the WTO, China has also instituted reforms in film distribution, release, and marketing. Five companies and three film production centers have been established in China to help its film industry meet international standards.

Foreign investors are now welcomed and encouraged to participate in the construction and renovation of movie theaters as long as they own no more than 49 percent of the shares. The government also encourages film directors, actors, and actresses to "step out of the door of the country" to "face the world" (面向世界 [miànxiàng shìjiè]). As a result, increasing numbers of Chinese films have entered the international community and more Chinese actors and actresses have been invited to participate in foreign films.

> **Do you know...**
> - when the Chinese movie industry made its first film?
> - the major film categories in China?
> - whether China allows foreign movies to be produced in China?
>
> **Read and find out!**

In addition, new laws have been formulated to guard against copyright infringement, protect the lawful rights of all parties concerned, and establish a ratings system to protect young viewers. As the new laws clearly delineate what can and cannot be done, it is now easier for movie-makers to focus on movie-making instead of dealing with the bureaucracy. The implementation of a new law governing movie advertising and distribution has laid the legal foundation for smoother international exchanges. China is playing an increasingly important role in the international movie scene.

Chinese director Li An (Ang Lee) in front of the poster of his award-winning film, *Crouching Tiger, Hidden Dragon* produced in 2000. Do you like martial arts films? Can you name some?

Foreign movies are very popular in China and some have had the best box-office returns. Do people in your country like to watch foreign films more than films from their own countries?

### 問題討論 (问题讨论) *Discuss the following with a partner or in small groups.*

1. 你看過什麼中國電影? 你最喜歡的中國電影是什麼?
   你看过什么中国电影? 你最喜欢的中国电影是什么?
   What Chinese movies have you seen? Which Chinese movie do you like best?

2. 你知道哪些有名的中國演員? 請說說他們為什麼有名?
   你知道哪些有名的中国演员? 请说说他们为什么有名?
   Do you know of any famous Chinese actors or actresses? Why are they famous?

# 趣味中文 (趣味中文) FUN WITH CHINESE

比上不足，比下有餘
比上不足，比下有余
Not as much as those above, but more than those below.

| bǐ | shàng | bù | zú | bǐ | xià | yǒu | yú |
|----|-------|-----|------|----|------|-----|-----|
| 比 | 上 | 不 | 足 | 比 | 下 | 有 | 餘 |
| 比 | 上 | 不 | 足 | 比 | 下 | 有 | 余 |
| to compare | up | not | enough | to compare | down | to have | surplus |

This phrase is usually used to tell someone to "be satisfied."

**問題討論 (问题讨论)** *Discuss the following with a partner or in small groups.*

1. Do you like people who always compare their strengths/weaknesses with others? Why/why not?
2. Are there any expressions in your language which tell you to be satisfied?
3. Try to use your own words to explain 比上不足，比下有餘(比上不足，比下有余) in Chinese.

# 行動吧! (行动吧!) LET'S GO!

## 電影票 (电影票) A movie ticket

When they studied Chinese in China last year, 文美 and 慕華(慕华) went to see a movie. Please read the following movie ticket carefully and answer the questions.

*Notes:*

團體(团体) [tuántǐ]: group

訂(订) [dìng]: to book

折(折) [zhé]: discount

日期(日期) [rìqī]: date

影廳(影厅) [yǐngtīng]: movie theater

座位(座位) [zuòwèi]: seat

類別(类别) [lèibié]: category

哈利波特與火焰杯(哈利波特与火焰杯) [Hālì Bōtè yǔ huǒyàn bēi]: *Harry Potter and the Goblet of Fire*

## 問題討論 (问题讨论) Discuss the following with a partner or in small groups.

1. What movie did 文美 and 慕華(慕华) watch?
2. When did they watch it? At what time?
3. How much was the ticket? How much of a discount did they get?

# 復習 (复习) Review

## LESSON 7 TO LESSON 8

### I. Activities

A. You are making a phone call to a travel agency to book two plane tickets to your home during the Thanksgiving holiday. You need to use *V. + PC* structure and the *patterns for comparison* to cover the following topics in your phone conversation. Work with your partner or in a small group to ask and answer the following questions.

1. 你想買什麼時候的飛機票?
   你想买什么时候的飞机票?

2. 飛機票的價格是多少? 網上的票價
   便宜還是旅行社的票價便宜?
   飞机票的价格是多少? 网上的票价
   便宜还是旅行社的票价便宜?

3. 如果旅行社的人告訴你機票訂不到,
   你願意換時間和航空公司嗎?
   如果旅行社的人告诉你机票订不到,
   你愿意换时间和航空公司吗?

B. You are deciding between 昆明 and 北京 for your winter trip. Your roommate has been to those places. Carry on a conversation with a partner and ask him/her to find out as much information about the two cities as possible. You need to use the following grammatical patterns.

1. Various patterns of comparison
2. Degree of Complement
3. Potential Complement

The following words and expressions should also be used:

差不多(差不多), 棒(棒), 打算(打算), 原來(原来),
其實(其实), 南方(南方), 比如(比如), 風景如畫(风景如画),
連(连)......都(都)......, 網站(网站), 先(先)......, 然後(然后)......,
再(再)......

C. You have just watched a Chinese movie. It was a martial arts movie about Chinese history. You enjoyed it very much. Now you are talking to your roommate about this movie and trying to encourage him/her to go and watch it because you know he/she is very interested in Chinese history. Work with a partner to practice the questions and answers. You should include the following topics.

1. 電影的名字是什麼?
   电影的名字是什么?

2. 你為什麼會去看這部電影?
   你为什么会去看这部电影?

3. 你覺得這部電影怎麼樣? 為什麼?
   你觉得这部电影怎么样? 为什么?

## II. Grammar

A. Work in small groups to fill in the blanks of each sentence with a word as potential complement and then provide a positive answer.

1. 老師上課的時候你聽得 _____ 嗎?
   老师上课的时候你听得 _____ 吗?

   _____ 。

2. 文華找得 _____ 找不 _____ 他的電話簿?
   文华找得 _____ 找不 _____ 他的电话簿?

   _____ 。

3. 文華現在訂不 _____ 去中國的飛機票。你覺得她今年寒假能去得 _____ 中國嗎?

   文华现在订不 _____ 去中国的飞机票。你觉得她今年寒假能去得 _____ 中国吗?

   _____ 。

4. 中國的飛機到得 _____ 到不 _____ 昆明?
   中国的飞机到得 _____ 到不 _____ 昆明?

   _____ 。

B. Work in small groups to compare similarities and differences between China and the US. Use the following patterns of comparison.

1. A 跟 B 一樣 + V. / Adj.
   A 跟 B 一样 + V. / Adj.

2. A 比 B + V. / Adj. + Degree of Complement
   A 比 B + V. / Adj. + Degree of Complement

3. A 不如 B
   A 不如 B

4. A 不像 B (那麼) + V. / Adj.
   A 不像 B (那么) + V. / Adj.

5. A 沒有 B (那麼) + V. / Adj.
   A 没有 B (那么) + V. / Adj.

|  | 中國(中国) | 美國(美国) |
|---|---|---|
| 面積(面积) [miànjī] (area) |  |  |
| 天氣(天气) |  |  |
| 人口(人口) |  |  |
| 歷史(历史) |  |  |
| 變化(变化) |  |  |
| …… |  |  |
| …… |  |  |
| …… |  |  |
| …… |  |  |

C. Use 連(连)……都…… to complete the following sentences, using what is in the brackets as clues.

1. 她的中文真不錯，＿＿＿＿＿＿＿＿＿＿＿＿＿＿＿＿。
   她的中文真不错，＿＿＿＿＿＿＿＿＿＿＿＿＿＿＿＿。
   (she can even understand this Chinese movie)

2. 去中國的飛機票真難買。現在＿＿＿＿＿＿＿＿＿＿＿＿＿。
   去中国的飞机票真难买。现在＿＿＿＿＿＿＿＿＿＿＿＿＿。
   (not even one ticket is available)

3. 我要寫三個大的研究報告，可是 _____ 。

   我要写三个大的研究报告，可是 _____ 。

   (I haven't even finished one yet)

D. The following sentences all have a prepositional phrase with 對(对). Based on the context given, fill in the blanks to complete the sentences. Then check with your partner or the class.

   1. 大明對 _____ 很感興趣，所以他想學中文。

      大明对 _____ 很感兴趣，所以他想学中文。

   2. 我很喜歡這部電影，因為它 _____ 中國歷史的 _____ 很客觀。

      我很喜欢这部电影，因为它 _____ 中国历史的 _____ 很客观。

   3. 我非常感謝我的老師，因為他 _____ 我的 _____ 特別大。

      我非常感谢我的老师，因为他 _____ 我的 _____ 特别大。

## III. Characters

A. Each of the following groups of characters share the same initial and final but their tones might be different. Work with your partner to write out the Pinyin and create a word or phrase by using the characters.

*Example:* 吸(吸) [xī] (吸引人)

  西(西) [xī] (西部)

1. 訂(订) [      ] (            )
   定(定) [      ] (            )

2. 現(现) [      ] (            )
   羨(羨) [      ] (            )

3. 起(起) [      ] (            )
   七(七) [      ] (            )
   戚(戚) [      ] (            )
   其(其) [      ] (            )
   氣(气) [      ] (            )
   汽(汽) [      ] (            )

4. 實(实) [      ] (            )
   時(时) [      ] (            )
   室(室) [      ] (            )
   事(事) [      ] (            )
   試(试) [      ] (            )
   史(史) [      ] (            )

5. 研(研) [        ] (                    )
   言(言) [        ] (                    )
   顏(颜) [        ] (                    )
   演(演) [        ] (                    )

6. 就(就) [        ] (                    )
   究(究) [        ] (                    )
   九(九) [        ] (                    )
   舊(旧) [        ] (                    )

7. 觀(观) [        ] (                    )
   關(关) [        ] (                    )
   館(馆) [        ] (                    )

8. 輕(轻) [        ] (                    )
   請(请) [        ] (                    )
   情(情) [        ] (                    )

B. Match the traditional/simplified form of the following characters.

1. 觀 _____    2. 關 _____    3. 導 _____    4. 興 _____

5. 輕 _____    6. 鬆 _____    7. 歷 _____    8. 場 _____

A. 历   B. 场   C. 松   D. 兴   E. 关   F. 轻   G. 导   H. 观

# IV. Useful Words and Expressions

For 旅遊(旅游):

旅行社(旅行社)，訂(订)，飛機票(飞机票)，聚(聚)，貴(贵)，查(查)，
網站(网站)，地圖(地图)，四季如春(四季如春)，風景如畫(风景如画)，
西南(西南)，買到(买到)，城市(城市)，地方(地方)，辦(办)，簽證(签证)

For 電影(电影):

導演(导演)，演員(演员)，功夫片(功夫片)，好看(好看)，情節(情节)，
場面(场面)，特技(特技)，效果(效果)，顏色(颜色)，票價(票价)，
電影院(电影院)，歷史故事(历史故事)，吸引人(吸引人)，精彩(精彩)，
部(部)

# 健身與健康 (健身与健康)
# Fitness and Health

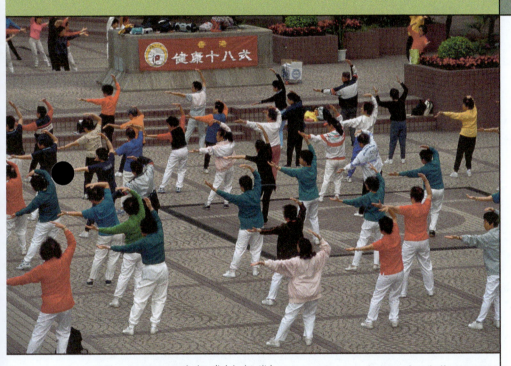

*Taijiquan (Taichi) 太極拳(太极拳) is a popular way for people of all ages in China to stay healthy.*

## CONNECTIONS AND COMMUNITIES PREVIEW

**Discuss the following questions with a partner or your class. What similarities and differences do you think there might be between Chinese culture and your own culture?**

1. What are the most popular ways to stay in shape in your country?

2. What do you think is the most effective way to stay fit and lead a healthy life?

## 教學目標 (教学目标) OBJECTIVES

- Talk about fitness and health
- Make comparisons

# 生詞 (生词) VOCABULARY

## 核心詞 (核心词) Core Vocabulary

| TRADITIONAL | SIMPLIFIED | PINYIN | | |
|---|---|---|---|---|
| 1. 越來越...... | 越来越...... | yuèláiyuè . . . | | more and more . . . |
| 2. 需要 | 需要 | xūyào | V. | to require |
| 3. 鐘頭 | 钟头 | zhōngtóu | N. | hour |
| 4. 瘦 | 瘦 | shòu | Adj. | thin, slim, skinny |
| 5. 減肥 | 减肥 | jiǎnféi | V.O. | to lose weight |
| 6. 堅持 | 坚持 | jiānchí | V. | to persist, persevere |
| 7. 體重 | 体重 | tǐzhòng | N. | body weight |
| 8. 輕 | 轻 | qīng | Adj. | light |
| 9. 磅 | 磅 | bàng | M.W. | pound (weight measurement) |
| 10. 怪不得 | 怪不得 | guàibude | | no wonder |
| 11. 苗條 | 苗条 | miáotiao | Adj. | slim |
| 12. 女孩子 | 女孩子 | nǚháizi | N. | girl |
| 13. 控制 | 控制 | kòngzhì | V. | to control |
| 14. 飲食 | 饮食 | yǐnshí | N. | food and drink, eating |
| 15. 注意 | 注意 | zhùyì | N.<br>V. | attention<br>to pay attention to |
| 16. 甜食 | 甜食 | tiánshí | N. | sweet food |
| 17. 早 | 早 | zǎo | Adv.<br>Adj. | (to emphasize long ago)<br>early |
| 18. 個子 | 个子 | gèzi | N. | height, stature |

| | TRADITIONAL | SIMPLIFIED | PINYIN | | |
|---|---|---|---|---|---|
| 19. | 矮 | 矮 | ǎi | Adj. | short |
| 20. | 呎 | 呎 | chǐ | N. | foot (weight measurement used in the US and UK) |
| 21. | 吋 | 吋 | cùn | N. | inch (length measurement used in the US and UK) |
| 22. | 超過 | 超过 | chāoguò | V. | to surpass |
| 23. | 靈活 | 灵活 | línghuó | Adj. | dexterous, agile, flexible |
| 24. | 總是 | 总是 | zǒngshì | Adv. | always |
| 25. | 重要 | 重要 | zhòngyào | Adj. | important |
| 26. | 更 | 更 | gèng | Adv. | more |

## 專名 (专名) Proper Nouns

| | TRADITIONAL | SIMPLIFIED | PINYIN | | |
|---|---|---|---|---|---|
| 1. | 白思琴 | 白思琴 | Bái Sīqín | N. | (name) Siqin Bai |
| 2. | 胡欣明 | 胡欣明 | Hú Xīnmíng | N. | (name) Xinming Hu |

## 語文知識 (语文知识) LANGUAGE LINK

Read and listen to the following sentence patterns. These patterns use vocabulary, expressions, and grammar that you will study in more detail in this lesson. After reading the sentence patterns, read and listen to the Language in Use section that follows.

### 句型 (句型) Sentence Patterns

A: 最近我很少游泳，每星期都要比以前少游兩、三次。

最近我很少游泳，每星期都要比以前少游两、三次。

Zuìjìn wǒ hěnshǎo yóuyǒng, měi xīngqī dōu yào bǐ yǐqián shǎo yóu liǎng, sān cì.

B: 其實你越忙越需要鍛煉。

其实你越忙越需要锻炼。

Qíshí nǐ yuè máng yuè xūyào duànliàn.

A: 你控制飲食嗎?
你控制饮食吗?
Nǐ kòngzhì yǐnshí ma?

B: 是的。我現在甜食吃得越來越少了。
是的。我现在甜食吃得越来越少了。
Shìde. Wǒ xiànzài tiánshí chī de yuèláiyuè shǎo le.

A: 你比前幾個月還瘦了不少!
你比前几个月还瘦了不少!
Nǐ bǐ qián jǐge yuè hái shòu le bù shǎo!

B: 如果你多運動,身體就會比以前
如果你多运动,身体就会比以前
Rúguǒ nǐ duō yùndòng, shēntǐ jiù huì bǐ yǐqián

更好。
更好。
gèng hǎo.

## 課文 Language in Use: I Have Started to Work Out
## (繁體字 Traditional Character Version)

白思琴： 欣明，你最近常去健身房鍛煉嗎？

胡欣明： 這兩個星期是我最忙的時候，鍛煉得比以前少得多。以前我差不多天天游泳，最近差不多每星期都要比以前少游兩、三次，這個星期一次也沒去過。

白思琴： 那可不好[1]。其實越忙越需要鍛煉。我每天都要去運動一個鐘頭，現在我的精神越來越好了。你看，我比前幾個月還瘦了不少吧！

| 1. 那可不好(那可不好) |
| --- |
| 那可不好(那可不好) means "That is not very good." This is a colloquial expression often used in conversations to express dissatisfaction, disagreement, disappointment, etc. in a mild way. |

胡欣明： 真的，你看上去比上學期瘦了很多。你最近在減肥嗎？

白思琴： 是呀！我已經堅持了三個月了。效果不錯吧！體重比以前輕了十幾磅。

胡欣明： 怪不得[2]你越來越苗條了，差不多是我們女孩子中最苗條的了。你是怎麼減肥的？控制飲食嗎？

| 2. 怪不得(怪不得) |
| --- |
| 怪不得(怪不得) means "no wonder," "so that's why." This is also a colloquial expression often used in conversations to indicate that the speaker has understood the reason for something. |

白思琴： 主要是鍛煉，當然在吃的方面我也比較注意。我以前最喜歡吃甜食，可是現在我吃得越來越少了。

胡欣明： 你怎麼會想到要減肥呢？

白思琴： 我早就想減肥了。我的個子[3]有點兒矮，只有五呎一吋，可是三個月以前我的體重超過了一百五十磅。

| 3. 個子(身高) [个子(身高)], 重量(體重) [重量(体重)] |
| --- |
| 個子(个子)/身高(身高) and 重量(重量)/體重(体重) are expressions used to mean "body height" and "body weight." 個子(个子) and 重量(重量) are more informal and generally used in conversation, while 身高(身高) and 體重(体重) are more formal and used more in written Chinese. |

胡欣明： 那你最重的時候比我還要重呢！

白思琴： 是呀！我要是太重了就會覺得不太靈活，也很不舒服。

胡欣明： 我真應該向你學習，可是我總是覺得功課太多、太忙，沒有時間鍛煉。現在我每天都比別人還要少睡兩、三個鐘頭[4]呢。

白思琴： 其實，最重要的是要多鍛煉、多運動。運動了以後你的身體會比以前更好，你會更有精神，學習的效果可能就會更好了。

## 课文 Language in Use: I Have Started to Work Out
## (简体字 Simplified Character Version)

白思琴：欣明，你最近常去健身房锻炼吗?

胡欣明：这两个星期是我最忙的时候，锻炼得比以前少得多。以前我差不多天天游泳，最近差不多每星期都要比以前少游两、三次，这个星期一次也没去过。

白思琴：那可不好[1]。其实越忙越需要锻炼。我每天都要去运动一个钟头，现在我的精神越来越好了。你看，我比前几个月还瘦了不少吧!

胡欣明：真的，你看上去比上学期瘦了很多。你最近在减肥吗?

白思琴：是呀! 我已经坚持了三个月了。效果不错吧! 体重比以前轻了十几磅。

胡欣明：怪不得[2]你越来越苗条了，差不多是我们女孩子中最苗条的了。你是怎么减肥的? 控制饮食吗?

白思琴：主要是锻炼，当然在吃的方面我也比较注意。我以前最喜欢吃甜食，可是现在我吃得越来越少了。

胡欣明：你怎么会想到要减肥呢?

白思琴：我早就想减肥了。我的个子[3]有点儿矮，只有五呎一吋，可是三个月以前我的体重超过了一百五十磅。

胡欣明：那你最重的时候比我还要重呢!

白思琴：是呀! 我要是太重了就会觉得不太灵活，也很不舒服。

胡欣明：我真应该向你学习，可是我总是觉得功课太多、太忙，没有时间锻炼。现在我每天都比别人还要少睡两、三个钟头[4]呢。

白思琴：其实，最重要的是要多锻炼、多运动。运动了以后你的身体会比以前更好，你会更有精神，学习的效果可能就会更好了。

---

**4. 鐘頭/小時(钟头/小时)**

Both 鐘頭(钟头) and 小時(小时) mean "hour," but 鐘頭(钟头) is generally used in speaking whereas 小時(小时) is a more formal expression used in both conversation and writing.

# 語法 (语法) GRAMMAR

## I. Comparison (3): 比 and the Emphatic Degree 更 (要) [更 (要)], 還 (要) [还 (要)]

*Pattern:*

| A | (compare with) 比 (比) | B | (even more) 更 / 更要 (更 / 更要) 還 / 還要 (还 / 还要) | Adj. |
|---|---|---|---|---|

*Examples:*

她很瘦，可是你比她還(要)瘦。
她很瘦，可是你比她还(要)瘦。

她很瘦，可是你比她更(要)瘦。
她很瘦，可是你比她更(要)瘦。
She is quite thin but you are even thinner than her.

昨天很熱，今天比昨天還(要)熱。
昨天很热，今天比昨天还(要)热。

昨天很熱，今天比昨天更(要)熱。
昨天很热，今天比昨天更(要)热。
It was hot yesterday. Today is even hotter than yesterday.

> **»Try it!** With a partner, practice using the pattern above in sentences. For example,
>
> A: 我很矮。　　B: 他比我更(還)矮。
> 　 我很矮。　　　 他比我更(还)矮。

## II. Progressive Change 越來越 (越来越)......

When we need to express progressive changes in degree, the pattern "越來越(越来越) + V." is used.

*Examples:*

你越來越苗條了。　　　You are getting slimmer and slimmer.
你越来越苗条了。

● 我越來越喜歡功夫片了。　　　　I like kung fu movies more and more.
　我越来越喜欢功夫片了。

　她看上去越來越年輕了。　　　　She looks younger and younger.
　她看上去越来越年轻了。

*Note:*

- 越來越(越来越)…… can only be placed before a verb to function as an adverb. It is never placed before the subject of a sentence.
- The 越來越(越来越)…… phrase is often followed by 了 at the end of the sentence to emphasize the change.

>>**Try it!** With a partner, practice short dialogues, using adjectives and verbs in the pattern 越來越 (越来越)…… to indicate progressive change. For example,

A: 小王最近怎麼樣?　　　　B: 她看上去越來越健康了。
　小王最近怎么样?　　　　　她看上去越来越健康了。

## III. 越……越…… Pattern

The "越……越……" sentence is equivalent to "The more . . . , the more . . ." in English.

*Examples:*

我們越忙越需要鍛煉。
我们越忙越需要锻炼。
The busier we are, the more we need to exercise.

我覺得中文越學越有意思。
我觉得中文越学越有意思。
The more I study Chinese, the more interesting I find it to be.

他越說我越不懂。
他越说我越不懂。
The more he talks, the more confused I am.

>>**Try it!** With a partner, practice using the pattern 越……越…… in short dialogues. For example,

A: 你喜歡中文嗎?　　　　B: 我以前不太喜歡,可是現在越學越喜歡。
　你喜欢中文吗?　　　　　我以前不太喜欢,可是现在越学越喜欢。

# 補充課文 (补充课文) SUPPLEMENTARY PRACTICE

*Read the following passage. Then listen and repeat.*

## My Work Out Plan (繁體字 Traditional Character Version)

三年前我得了一場病，雖然吃了藥以後病好了，可是感覺身體越來越不好。看上去人很胖，還常常會不舒服。醫生說我需要多運動，鍛煉鍛煉。

前天，我的高中同學白思琴來看我，她的變化使我大吃一驚。以前她是班上有名的"小胖子"，是所有女生中最矮、最胖的。可是昨天看到她那麼苗條，那麼有精神，我真不相信自己的眼睛。她告訴我，她堅持鍛煉健身已經三個多月了，效果非常好，不但體重減輕了十多磅，而且精神越來越好，學習的時候精力比以前集中得多，學習成績也就越來越好。

我說我也很想鍛煉，可是功課太多，時間不夠。思琴說其實越忙越需要鍛煉，因為越鍛煉會越有精神，精力越能集中，學習的效果就會越好。我覺得她說得很對，決定聽她的話，訂一個計畫，好好地執行。

思琴說鍛煉身體"重在堅持"，我相信我一定能堅持下去。"有志者，事竟成。"

*Notes:*

場(场) [chǎng]: measure word for illness, games, films, etc.

使(使) [shǐ]: to make

大吃一驚(大吃一惊) [dàchīyìjīng]: to be greatly surprised, amazed, astonished

有名(有名) [yǒumíng]: famous, well-known

相信(相信) [xiāngxìn]: to believe, to be sure

精力(精力) [jīnglì]: energy

集中(集中) [jízhōng]: to concentrate, focus

執行(执行) [zhíxíng]: to execute, to put into action

重在堅持(重在坚持) [zhòng zài jiānchí]: the key lies in persistence

有志者，事竟成(有志者，事竟成) [yǒuzhìzhě, shì jìng chéng]: where there is a will, there is a way.

# 補充課文 (补充课文) SUPPLEMENTARY PRACTICE

*Read the following passage. Then listen and repeat.*

## My Work Out Plan (简体字 Simplified Character Version)

　　三年前我得了一场病，虽然吃了药以后病好了，可是感觉身体越来越不好。看上去人很胖，还常常会不舒服。医生说我需要多运动，锻炼锻炼。

　　前天，我的高中同学白思琴来看我，她的变化使我大吃一惊。以前她是班上有名的"小胖子"，是所有女生中最矮、最胖的。可是昨天看到她那么苗条，那么有精神，我真不相信自己的眼睛。她告诉我，她坚持锻炼健身已经三个多月了，效果非常好，不但体重减轻了十多磅，而且精神越来越好，学习的时候精力比以前集中得多，学习成绩也就越来越好。

　　我说我也很想锻炼，可是功课太多，时间不够。思琴说其实越忙越需要锻炼，因为越锻炼会越有精神，精力越能集中，学习的效果就会越好。我觉得她说得很对，决定听她的话，订一个计划，好好地执行。

　　思琴说锻炼身体"重在坚持"，我相信我一定能坚持下去。"有志者，事竟成。"

## Exercises: work with a partner or in small groups

1. 她為什麼想要訂一個健身計畫呢？
   她为什么想要订一个健身计划呢？

2. 她的同學白思琴有什麼變化？以前怎麼樣？現在又怎麼樣？
   她的同学白思琴有什么变化？以前怎么样？现在又怎么样？

3. 她的健身計畫是怎麼安排的？她覺得自己能堅持下去嗎？
   她的健身计划是怎么安排的？她觉得自己能坚持下去吗？

# 成語故事 (成语故事) IDIOM STORY

## 畫蛇添足 (画蛇添足) [huàshé tiānzú]

*Meaning:* To add feet to a snake while drawing it.

*Usage:* This is used to describe someone who tries to make undesirable or superfluous additions.

*Example:* 你已經很苗條了，又控制飲食，又不吃甜食，還常鍛煉。
你不要再 "畫蛇添足"，買減肥藥了。

你已经很苗条了，又控制饮食，又不吃甜食，还常锻炼。
你不要再 "画蛇添足"，买减肥药了。

Pay attention to the usages of 比 and the emphatic degree 更(要)，還(要)[还(要)]，progressive change 越來越(越来越)……, and the "越……越……" pattern.

### (繁體字 Traditional Character Version)

有一天，一些人得到了一壺酒，他們都想喝。可是一壺酒不夠，想喝酒的人越多，每個人能喝的就越少。怎麼辦呢? 後來有一個人說: "我們來比賽畫蛇。誰畫得最快就給誰喝，你們覺得怎麼樣?" 大家聽了，都覺得這個辦法比別的辦法簡單，所以都同意了。

畫蛇比賽開始了。大家都認真地畫著。有一個人平時做事都比別人快得多，這次畫蛇他畫得更快。他很快就把蛇畫好了，而且他畫的蛇也比別人的好得多。他看到別人都比他畫得慢，就越來越覺得自己比別人強得多。他越想越高興，就說: "你們畫得都比我慢，我再給蛇畫上兩隻腳吧!" 於是，他就給蛇又畫了兩隻腳。可是他在畫腳的時候，另外有一個人把蛇畫好了，然後拿起酒壺，一下子就把酒都喝完了。畫蛇腳的人非常不高興，可是喝酒的人說，"蛇是沒有腳的。你給蛇畫了腳，那就不是蛇了。" 他聽了以後，連一句話也說不出來。雖然他越想越生氣，可是也沒有辦法。

這個故事告訴我們: 花時間做不必要的事是沒有用的。

(简体字 Simplified Character Version)

　　有一天，一些人得到了一壶酒，他们都想喝。可是一壶酒不够，想喝酒的人越多，每个人能喝的就越少。怎么办呢？后来有一个人说："我们来比赛画蛇。谁画得最快就给谁喝，你们觉得怎么样？"大家听了，都觉得这个办法比别的办法简单，所以都同意了。

　　画蛇比赛开始了。大家都认真地画着。有一个人平时做事都比别人快得多，这次画蛇他画得更快。他很快就把蛇画好了，而且他画的蛇也比别人的好得多。他看到别人都比他画得慢，就越来越觉得自己比别人强得多。他越想越高兴，就说："你们画得都比我慢，我再给蛇画上两只脚吧！"于是，他就给蛇又画了两只脚。可是他在画脚的时候，另外有一个人把蛇画好了，然后拿起酒壶，一下子就把酒都喝完了。画蛇脚的人非常不高兴，可是喝酒的人说，"蛇是没有脚的。你给蛇画了脚，那就不是蛇了。"他听了以后，连一句话也说不出来。虽然他越想越生气，可是也没有办法。

　　这个故事告诉我们：花时间做不必要的事是没有用的。

*Notes:*

蛇(蛇) [shé]: snake

添(添) [tiān]: to add

足(足) [zú]: foot

壶(壶) [hú]: pot, and also used as a measure word for pots

比赛(比赛) [bǐsài]: race, competition, contest

简单(简单) [jiǎndān]: simple, easy

同意(同意) [tóngyì]: to agree

开始(开始) [kāishǐ]: to begin

高興(高兴) [gāoxìng]: happy

脚(脚) [jiǎo]: foot (the same as 足, 脚 is more colloquial)

生氣(生气) [shēngqì]: to be angry

告訴(告诉) [gàosù]: to tell

必要(必要) [bìyào]: necessary

## Exercises: work with a partner or in small groups

1. 找出有下面语法的句子：比 and the emphatic degree 更(要)，還(要)，progressive change 越來越……，and the 越……越…… pattern.

   找出有下面语法的句子：比 and the emphatic degree 更(要)，还(要)，progressive change 越来越……，and the 越……越…… pattern.

2. 用你自己的話說說 "畫蛇添足" 的故事。
　　用你自己的话说说 "画蛇添足" 的故事。

3. 請用 "畫蛇添足" 造一個句子或者說一個畫蛇添足的例子。
　　请用 "画蛇添足" 造一个句子或者说一个画蛇添足的例子。

4. "畫蛇添足" 的故事，告訴了我們什麼？
　　"画蛇添足" 的故事，告诉了我们什么？

## 練習 (练习) ACTIVITIES

### I. Listening Exercises

**9-1**　Listen to the following dialogue and then select the correct answer for each question.

1. 最近為什麼白健看不到常明在健身房鍛煉呢？
　　最近为什么白健看不到常明在健身房锻炼呢？

　　a. 因為常明要減肥。
　　　　因为常明要减肥。

　　b. 因為常明要參加比賽。
　　　　因为常明要参加比赛。

　　c. 因為常明去看女朋友了。
　　　　因为常明去看女朋友了。

2. 為什麼白健說常明應該參加游泳比賽？
　　为什么白健说常明应该参加游泳比赛？

　　a. 因為白健是常明的好朋友。
　　　　因为白健是常明的好朋友。

　　b. 因為常明游泳的時候看上去最靈活。
　　　　因为常明游泳的时候看上去最灵活。

　　c. 因為常明游泳游得很快。
　　　　因为常明游泳游得很快。

3. 常明為什麼要減肥?
   常明为什么要减肥?

   a. 因為他的女朋友要他減肥。
   因为他的女朋友要他减肥。

   b. 因為他覺得他不如王華靈活。
   因为他觉得他不如王华灵活。

   c. 因為他覺得他要控制吃甜食。
   因为他觉得他要控制吃甜食。

4. 常明的女朋友為什麼學習成績越來越好?
   常明的女朋友为什么学习成绩越来越好?

   a. 因為她每天睡得很少,學習得很用功。
   因为她每天睡得很少,学习得很用功。

   b. 因為她也在減肥,所以精神很好。
   因为她也在减肥,所以精神很好。

   c. 因為她每天鍛煉,精神很好。
   因为她每天锻炼,精神很好。

**9-2** Based on the short passage you have just heard, complete the following sentences.

1. 常明 _____ 是系裡游泳游得 _____。
   常明 _____ 是系里游泳游得 _____。

2. _____ 王華比常明游泳游得 _____。
   _____ 王华比常明游泳游得 _____。

3. 白健知道常明喜歡吃 _____,他覺得常明應該 _____。
   白健知道常明喜欢吃 _____,他觉得常明应该 _____。

4. 常明的女朋友最近比以前 _____ 多了,因為她也在 _____。
   常明的女朋友最近比以前 _____ 多了,因为她也在 _____。

## II. Character Exercises

**9-3**  Work with a partner. Read the following words, phrases, and sentences.

| | |
|---|---|
| 煉 | 靈 |
| 炼 | 灵 |
| 鍛煉 | 靈活 |
| 锻炼 | 灵活 |
| 要鍛煉 | 更靈活 |
| 要锻炼 | 更灵活 |
| 需要鍛煉 | 會更靈活 |
| 需要锻炼 | 会更灵活 |
| 越需要鍛煉 | 比以前會更靈活 |
| 越需要锻炼 | 比以前会更灵活 |
| 越忙越需要鍛煉 | 運動以後會比以前更靈活 |
| 越忙越需要锻炼 | 运动以后会比以前更灵活 |
| 其實越忙越需要鍛煉 | 你運動以後會比以前更靈活 |
| 其实越忙越需要锻炼 | 你运动以后会比以前更灵活 |

Now with your partner, try to use the following characters to make words, phrases, and then sentences.

| 1. 健 | 2. 光 | 3. 控 | 4. 甜 | 5. 靈 |
|---|---|---|---|---|
| 健 | 光 | 控 | 甜 | 灵 |

| 6. 堅 | 7. 瘦 | 8. 減 | 9. 矮 | 10. 膚 |
|---|---|---|---|---|
| 坚 | 瘦 | 减 | 矮 | 肤 |

**9-4**  Each of the following pairs of characters looks very similar in appearance, but they are actually two very different words. Work with your partner and write out the Pinyin for each character and then create a word or phrase using the characters.

*Example:* 苗(苗)  <u>miáo</u>  <u>苗條(苗条)</u>

1. 輕(轻) _____ _____     2. 瘦(瘦) _____ _____

   經(经) _____ _____        病(病) _____ _____

3. 效(效) _____ _____      4. 飲(饮) _____ _____
   放(放) _____ _____         飯(饭) _____ _____

5. 住(住) _____ _____      6. 害(害) _____ _____
   注(注) _____ _____         宜(宜) _____ _____

**9-5** Match the traditional characters with their simplified forms.

## III. Grammar Exercises

**9-6** With your partner, use A 比 B + 更(更)/更要(更要) + Adj. pattern to describe the
following situations.              還(还)/還要(还要)

1. 印度 [Yìndù] (India) has a big 人口 [rénkǒu] (population); China has the largest
   population in the world.

2. Britain is a 發達國家(发达国家) [fādá guójiā] (developed country); the US is an
   even more developed country.

3. 黃河(黄河) [Huánghé] (the Yellow River) is very long; 長江(长江) [Chángjiāng]
   (the Yangtze River) is even longer.

4. He has been more energetic than before.

**9-7** Sentence-making competition.

Form groups. The instructor will provide stative verbs/adjectives. Each group must
make sentences with the pattern "越來越(越来越)……" as quickly as possible.
The group that makes the most sentences within the time allowed wins the game.

*Note:* The subjects and the verbs used have to be varied from sentence to sentence.
No repetition is allowed.

*Example:* 好：我的中文越來越好。
好：我的中文越来越好。

高：我弟弟越來越高。
高：我弟弟越来越高。

Some suggested adjectives for you to use:

好(好)，高(高)，低(低)，靈活(灵活)，矮(矮)，輕(轻)，光滑(光滑)，
重(重)，苗條(苗条)，甜(甜)，精神(精神)，方便(方便)，不錯(不错)，
棒(棒)，多(多)，貴(贵)，有意思(有意思)，忙(忙)，輕鬆(轻松)，
舒服(舒服)，精彩(精彩)，吸引人(吸引人)，有興趣(有兴趣)，
大(大)，客觀(客观)，便宜(便宜)，健康(健康)，年輕(年轻)，老(老)，
花(花)，熱(热)，地道(地道)，高興(高兴)，好吃(好吃)，快(快)，
熱情(热情)，好客(好客)，不好意思(不好意思)

**9-8**　Work in small groups and combine the following pairs of sentences using the "越……越……" pattern.

1. 她現在經常鍛煉；她比以前苗條了很多。
   她现在经常锻炼；她比以前苗条了很多。

2. 她每次運動以後；學習的效果很好。
   她每次运动以后；学习的效果很好。

3. 她的體重輕了；她覺得輕鬆多了。
   她的体重轻了；她觉得轻松多了。

4. 老師、師母總是非常熱情；我總是覺得不好意思。
   老师、师母总是非常热情；我总是觉得不好意思。

## IV. Communicative Activities

Your friend is a bit overweight and he has been trying various ways to lose weight, but to no avail. He is also becoming less and less focused when studying. You think his major problem is too little exercise. So you are now giving him some suggestions on how to lose weight and keep fit. Work in pairs. Remember to use the following patterns in your sentences.

1. A 比 B + 更(更)/更要(更要) + Adj.
   　　(還(还)/還要(还要))

2. 越來越(越来越)……

3. 越……越……

4. 怪不得

5. 那可不好

6. 不如

# 文化知識 (文化知识) Culture Link

## 文化點滴 (文化点滴) CULTURE NOTES

### 中國的瘦身美容業 (中国的瘦身美容业)
### The Culture of Slimness and Beauty in China

Because of the rapid growth of the Chinese economy, Chinese people now have more money to spend. Finding enough food to eat, a goal for many families in the past, has given way to becoming slim and "beautiful." This does not only apply to the young, but also to middle-aged and even older people.

As Chinese society becomes more and more open, people's concepts about life have also opened up. To love beauty is human nature. With the availability of a higher income and a more relaxed atmosphere in society, more and more people are now spending a great amount of time and money on their appearance. In addition, personal appearance has become a factor that may sway the decision of employers in the more competitive job market. Therefore, a wide variety of 美容護膚品(美容护肤品) [měiróng hùfūpǐn] (beauty and skin-protection products) are becoming very popular.

Following the rise in the standard of living, Chinese people are now facing the problem of being overweight and even, in some cases, obese. By 2004, there were approximately 70,000,000 overweight

**Do you know...**

- what change(s) have taken place in people's life goals in China over the past decades?
- what new problem people in China are facing today?
- why so many people in China feel the pressure to lose weight?

***Read and find out!***

Chinese. As a result, 減肥產品 (减肥产品) [jiǎnféi chǎnpǐn] (weight-loss products) and programs have flourished in China. Recent years have also witnessed a surge in 美容手術 (美容手术) [měiróng shǒushù] (cosmetic surgery).

A great number of middle-aged and older people are taking positive steps to stay fit. They join fitness clubs or do daily exercise, such as walking, jogging, swimming, and dancing. However, there are also growing numbers of people, especially young women, who rely on diet pills, weight-reduction products, or even cosmetic surgery to become slimmer. The culture of slimness—a relatively new phenomenon in China—has begun to affect and control women's attitudes about themselves.

A 2004 survey conducted in Beijing, Shanghai, and Guangzhou shows that overweight people are not the only ones trying to lose weight. So are those whose weight is normal or even below normal, especially some young women and girls. Among those women trying to lose weight, only 44 percent are overweight and 4 percent are actually underweight.

Why, then, are so many women dissatisfied with their weight, even when their weight is normal? It is likely that commercial advertisements have played a large role. Modern ads create cultural ideals of beauty and slimness. Weight-loss companies are chasing profits and preying on women's self-doubts. Their ads promote products to women, claiming they will help them look better.

Today, Chinese people are increasingly concerned about health and beauty. A better understanding of the true sense of the word "beauty," however, would help them to become healthy, as well as beautiful.

Acupuncture is a traditional weight-reduction treatment in China. Do people in your country also use acupuncture?

In today's China, young girls want to be tall and slim. What is the concept of beauty among young people in your own culture?

## 問題討論 (问题讨论) *Discuss the following with a partner or in small groups.*

1. 你想過要瘦身美容嗎? 你用過什麼方法?
   你想过要瘦身美容吗? 你用过什么方法?

   Have you thought about losing weight to become more beautiful? What kinds of methods have you used?

2. 你聽說過中國的針灸 ([zhēnjiǔ]: acupuncture) 美容嗎? 你會想試試看嗎? 為什麼?
   你听说过中国的针灸美容吗? 你会想试试看吗? 为什么?

   Have you heard about the use of Chinese acupuncture to achieve slimness and beauty? Would you like to try it? Why or why not?

# ● 趣味中文 (趣味中文) FUN WITH CHINESE

人不可貌相
人不可貌相

A man's worth cannot be measured by his looks.

| rén | bù | kě | mào | xiàng |
|-----|-----|-----|-----|-----|
| 人 | 不 | 可 | 貌 | 相 |
| 人 | 不 | 可 | 貌 | 相 |
| person | not | can | appearance | to judge |

**問題討論 (问题讨论)** *Discuss the following with a partner or in small groups.*

1. Do you know anyone whose talent surprises you so much that you would describe him/her as 人不可貌相?
2. Are there any expressions in your language which are similar to 人不可貌相?

# 行動吧! (行动吧!) **LET'S GO!**

## 瘦身廣告 (瘦身广告) **Weight-Loss Advertisement**

For some time 思琴 has not been happy about her weight, so she's been interested in weight-loss products. Below is a weight-loss advertisement. Based on what you see in the advertisement, answer the questions below.

*Notes:*

塗(涂) [tú]: to coat with, spread on

纖(纤) [xiān]: slim and delicate

滋潤(滋润) [zīrùn]: to moisturize

霜(霜) [shuāng]: cream

配方(配方) [pèifāng]: formula chemicals or metallurgical products

免費熱線(免费热线) [miǎnfèi rèxiàn]: free hotline

特許(特许) [tèxǔ]: with special permission

## 問題討論 (问题讨论) *Discuss the following with a partner or in small groups.*

1. What is the product? What is its function?
2. What is the name of the manufacturer?
3. What are the English translations of the following?

纖臉(纤脸)

滋潤霜(滋润霜)

# 假期在中國–復習
# (假期在中国–复习)
# A Vacation in China – Review

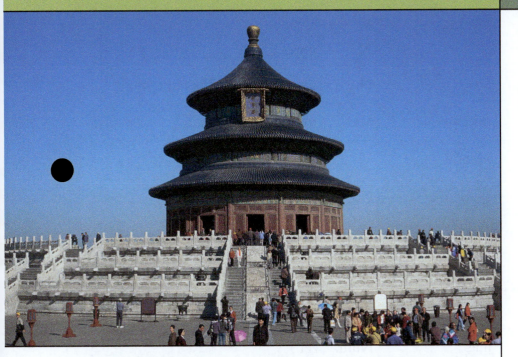

Tian Tan 天壇(天坛), a unique example of traditional architecture in Beijing, attracts visitors from all over the world.

## CONNECTIONS AND COMMUNITIES PREVIEW

Discuss the following questions with a partner or your class. What similarities and differences do you think there might be between Chinese culture and your own culture?

1. Have you visited China before? Where else have you been?

2. What do you plan to do during your next vacation?

## 教學目標 (教学目标) OBJECTIVES

- Make an oral report
- Discuss plans

# 生詞 (生词) VOCABULARY

## 核心詞 (核心词) Core Vocabulary

| TRADITIONAL | SIMPLIFIED | PINYIN | | |
|---|---|---|---|---|
| 1. 計畫 | 计划 | jìhuà | V.<br>N. | to plan<br>plan |
| 2. 最後 | 最后 | zuìhòu | Adv. | finally |
| 3. 說好了 | 说好了 | shuōhǎo le | | to have agreement on, agree |
| 4. 希望 | 希望 | xīwàng | V.<br>N. | to hope<br>hope |
| 5. 旬 | 旬 | xún | N. | a period of 10 days in a month |
| 6. 付款 | 付款 | fùkuǎn | V.O. | to make payment |
| 7. 接受 | 接受 | jiēshòu | V. | to accept |
| 8. 商店 | 商店 | shāngdiàn | N. | store |
| 9. 根據 | 根据 | gēnjù | Prep. | according to, based on |
| 10. 當天 | 当天 | dāngtiān | Adv. | on that day |
| 11. 安全 | 安全 | ānquán | Adj. | safe |
| 12. 零 | 零 | líng | Num. | zero |
| 13. 爬 | 爬 | pá | V. | to climb |
| 14. 頂 | 顶 | dǐng | N. | top |
| 15. 幫助 | 帮助 | bāngzhù | N. | help |
| 16. 非 | 非 | fēi | Adv. | not (used in Classical Chinese) |
| 17. 好漢 | 好汉 | hǎohàn | N. | hero |

| TRADITIONAL | SIMPLIFIED | PINYIN | | |
|---|---|---|---|---|
| 18. 告訴 | 告诉 | gàosu | V. | to tell |
| 19. 壯觀 | 壮观 | zhuàngguān | Adj. | magnificent |
| 20. 曲折 | 曲折 | qūzhé | Adj. | with twists and turns, complicated |
| 21. 滿載而歸 | 满载而归 | mǎnzàiérguī | | to return with tremendous accomplishments |

## 專名 (专名) Proper Nouns

| TRADITIONAL | SIMPLIFIED | PINYIN | | |
|---|---|---|---|---|
| 1. 黃山 | 黄山 | Huángshān | N. | Mt. Huang (Yellow Mountain, a famous tourist attraction in Anhui Province, central China) |
| 2. 十面埋伏 | 十面埋伏 | *Shímiàn máifu* | N. | *House of Flying Daggers* (name of a Chinese martial arts film) |

## 語文知識 (语文知识) LANGUAGE LINK

Read and listen to the following sentence patterns. These patterns use vocabulary, expressions, and grammar that you will study in more detail in this lesson. After reading the sentence patterns, read and listen to the Language in Use section that follows.

### 句型 (句型) Sentence Patterns

現在美元換人民幣的匯率
现在美元换人民币的汇率
Xiànzài Měiyuán huàn Rénmínbì de huìlǜ

是一比六點五三。
是一比六点五三。
shì yī bǐ liù diǎn wǔ sān.

這班飛機到得了到不了北京?
这班飞机到得了到不了北京?
Zhè bān fēijī dàodeliǎo dàobùliǎo Běijīng?

小說比電影好一些。
小说比电影好一些。
Xiǎoshuō bǐ diànyǐng hǎo yìxiē.

你看上去越來越苗條了。
你看上去越来越苗条了。
Nǐ kàn shàngqù yuèláiyuè miáotiao le.

我希望這次中國行會比上次更好，
我希望这次中国行会比上次更好，
Wǒ xīwàng zhècì Zhōngguó xíng huì bǐ shàngcì gèng hǎo,

能滿載而歸，然後可以跟大家報告一下。
能满载而归，然后可以跟大家报告一下。
néng mǎnzàiérguī, ránhòu kěyǐ gēn dàjiā bàogào yíxià.

🔊 **課文 Language in Use: I'll Get to Climb the Great Wall!**
**(繁體字 Traditional Character Version)**

同學們好!

今天，我想把我的寒假計畫[1]跟大家報告一下。

今年是我在大學的最後一個寒假。我已經跟我的男朋友說好了[2]，一起去中國旅遊。我們在北京有很多親戚朋友，我希望這次去北京能見得到他們每個人。

這兩年去中國的人比以前多了很多，所以飛機票也比前兩年難買多了。特別是去北京的機票，更難買得到，我們到現在還沒有訂到票呢。我們打算十二月中旬[3]出發，一月上旬回來。現在已經給好幾家旅行社打了電話，還不知道買得到買不到。我們上個星期已經申請了去中國的簽證，不知道這個星期收得到收不到。不過我們還有不少時間，大概來得及。

我還要去銀行取一些現金，買幾張旅行支票。在中國用信用卡付款不像在美國這麼方便。不過，聽說現在接受信用卡的商店越來越多了，而且在中國銀行還可以取美金，也可以根據當天的匯率換成人民幣，這比帶很多現金要安全得多。最近人民幣換美金的匯率差不多是一比六點五三，比上個月低了零點一個百分點[4]。

---

**1. 計畫(计划)**

計畫(计划) means plan. It can be written as 計劃 in traditional form.

---

**2. 說好了(说好了)**

Here 好(好) is used to indicate a result meaning "being settled successfully."

---

**3. 旬(旬)**

旬(旬) is a period of 10 days. In Chinese tradition, a month can be divided into 3 10-day periods that are labeled 上(上), 中(中), and 下(下). Therefore, the 1st to the 10th of a month is called 上旬(上旬), the 11th to the 20th 中旬(中旬) and the 21st to the end of the month 下旬(下旬). When using 旬(旬), the speaker's emphasis is on the 10-day period in general, not any specific day.

---

**4. 零點一個百分點(零点一个百分点)**

零點一個百分點(零点一个百分点) means 0.1. 百分點(百分点) is an alternative way of expressing percentage, hence 10% can be either "百分之十(百分之十)" or "十個百分點(十个百分点)."

---

*Continued on page 296*

## 课文 Language in Use: I'll Get to Climb the Great Wall! (简体字 Simplified Character Version)

同学们好！

　　今天，我想把我的寒假计划[1]跟大家报告一下。

　　今年是我在大学的最后一个寒假。我已经跟我的男朋友说好了[2]，一起去中国旅游。我们在北京有很多亲戚朋友，我希望这次去北京能见得到他们每个人。

　　这两年去中国的人比以前多了很多，所以飞机票也比前两年难买多了。特别是去北京的机票，更难买得到，我们到现在还没有订到票呢。我们打算十二月中旬[3]出发，一月上旬回来。现在已经给好几家旅行社打了电话，还不知道买得到买不到。我们上个星期已经申请了去中国的签证，不知道这个星期收得到收不到。不过我们还有不少时间，大概来得及。

　　我还要去银行取一些现金，买几张旅行支票。在中国用信用卡付款不像在美国这么方便。不过，听说现在接受信用卡的商店越来越多了，而且在中国银行还可以取美金，也可以根据当天的汇率换成人民币，这比带很多现金要安全得多。最近人民币换美金的汇率差不多是一比六点五三，比上个月低了零点一个百分点[4]。

*Continued on page 297*

## 課文 Language in Use: I'll Get to Climb the Great Wall!
### (繁體字 Traditional Character Version) —— 接第二百九十四頁

　　這次去中國我最想去的地方是長城。聽說爬長城很累，只有百分之五十的人能爬得到長城的頂上。我覺得那是一個很好的鍛煉，還能幫助我減肥呢！而且，中國人不是說"不到長城非好漢"嗎？所以我一定要試一試。我還想去黃山⁵，我的朋友告訴我黃山那兒風景如畫，美極了！

| 5. 黃山(黄山) |
| --- |
| 黃山(黄山) is Yellow Mountain, a mountain in Anhui Province in China. Approximately 350 miles northwest of Shanghai, it is one of the most famous tourist attractions in China and has been acknowledged by the United Nations as one of the geographical heritages of the world. |

　　我還想去看看張藝謀導演的功夫片《十面埋伏》。看過這部電影的人都說它的場面比《英雄》還要壯觀，情節也很曲折。

　　你們看，我今年寒假要做的事多不多？我希望我從中國回來的時候，能滿載而歸。

　　這就是我今天的報告。謝謝大家！

## 课文 Language in Use: I'll Get to Climb the Great Wall!
## (简体字 Simplified Character Version) —— 接第二百九十五页

这次去中国我最想去的地方是长城。听说爬长城很累，只有百分之五十的人能爬得到长城的顶上。我觉得那是一个很好的锻炼，还能帮助我减肥呢！而且，中国人不是说"不到长城非好汉"吗？所以我一定要试一试。我还想去黄山⁵，我的朋友告诉我黄山那儿风景如画，美极了！

我还想去看看张艺谋导演的功夫片《十面埋伏》。看过这部电影的人都说它的场面比《英雄》还要壮观，情节也很曲折。

你们看，我今年寒假要做的事多不多？我希望我从中国回来的时候，能满载而归。

这就是我今天的报告。谢谢大家！

## 語法復習（语法复习）GRAMMAR REVIEW

The main grammar points from Lesson 6 to Lesson 9.

### I. Phrases

The following is a list of different types of phrases in Chinese:

| Name | Definition | Examples |
|---|---|---|
| Juxtaposed Phrases | formed by two or more words with the same features | 存款、取款(存款、取款)<br>學習和工作(学习和工作)<br>又唱又跳(又唱又跳) |
| Endocentric Phrases | composed of a modifier (偏[piān]) and the modified (正[zhèng]) | 儲蓄帳戶(储蓄账户)<br>努力學習(努力学习) |
| Subject + V. Phrases | a phrase in which the relationship between the components is like the relationship between a subject and a verb predicate | <u>我游泳</u>的地方<br><u>我游泳</u>的地方<br><br><u>你們寄來</u>的支票簿<br><u>你们寄来</u>的支票簿<br><br>我覺得這兒的<u>服務又快又好</u>。<br>我觉得这儿的<u>服务又快又好</u>。 |
| V. + Object Phrases | formed by a transitive verb and a noun that serves as its object | <u>換外幣</u>的櫃台<br><u>換外币</u>的柜台<br><br><u>申請信用卡</u>的表<br><u>申请信用卡</u>的表 |

>>**Try it!**    With a partner, practice using all the different types of phrases listed above in sentences. For example,

A: 請問，那兒是什麼櫃台？            (V. + Object phrase)
　　请问，那儿是什么柜台？

B: 那是換外幣的櫃台。
　　那是换外币的柜台。

## II. Percentages and Proportions

| Percentage | 百分之…… | 百分之三十五 | 35% (35 percent) |
| --- | --- | --- | --- |
| | 百分之…… | 百分之三十五 | |
| Proportion | $N_1$ 比 $N_2$ | 五比一 | (5:1) 5 to 1 |
| | $N_1$ 比 $N_2$ | 五比一 | |

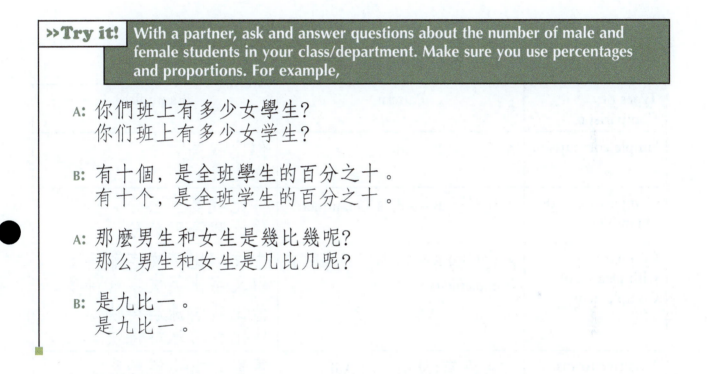

**»Try it!**  With a partner, ask and answer questions about the number of male and female students in your class/department. Make sure you use percentages and proportions. For example,

A: 你們班上有多少女學生?
你们班上有多少女学生?

B: 有十個，是全班學生的百分之十。
有十个，是全班学生的百分之十。

A: 那麼男生和女生是幾比幾呢?
那么男生和女生是几比几呢?

B: 是九比一。
是九比一。

## III. Complements

Potential Complement:

| Name | Definition | Examples |
| --- | --- | --- |
| Potential Complement | a verb, an adjective, or a phrase used after a verb to indicate the potential result of the main verb | 我的電話簿找不到了。<br>我的电话簿找不到了。<br><br>今年寒假你去得了北京嗎?<br>今年寒假你去得了北京吗?<br><br>這輛車坐得下五個人嗎?<br>这辆车坐得下五个人吗? |

>>**Try it!**   With a partner, construct a short dialogue using the PC. For example,

A: 現在還訂得到去北京的機票嗎?
現在还订得到去北京的机票吗?

B: 現在去北京的人太多,機票已經訂不到了。
現在去北京的人太多,机票已经订不到了。

## IV. Comparison

The following chart shows common ways to make comparisons.

| Types of Comparison | Pattern | Examples |
|---|---|---|
| Simple comparison | A 比(比) B + Adj. | 你比我高。<br>你比我高。 |
| Comparison with Quantifier | A 比(比) B + Adj. + Quantifier | 你比我高五公分。<br>你比我高五公分。 |
| Comparison with Degree of Complement | A 比(比) B + Adj./V. + Degree of Complement | 中文字比英文字難得多。<br>中文字比英文字难得多。<br><br>他比我游泳游得快。<br>他比我游泳游得快。 |
| Negative forms | 1. A 沒有(没有) B + Adj.<br><br>2. A 不如(不如) B + Adj.<br><br>3. A 不像(不像) B + 那麼 (那么) + Adj. | 電影沒有小說精彩。<br>电影没有小说精彩。<br><br>電影不如小說精彩。<br>电影不如小说精彩。<br><br>電影不像小說那麼精彩。<br>电影不像小说那么精彩。 |
| Comparison and the Emphatic Degree | A 比(比) B +<br>更(更)/更要(更要) + Adj.<br>還(还)/還要(还要) | 電影比小說更精彩。<br>电影比小说更精彩。 |
| Relative and Superlative Degree | 比較(比较) + Adj./Adv.<br><br>最(最) | 這部電影比較精彩。<br>这部电影比较精彩。<br><br>這部電影最精彩。<br>这部电影最精彩。 |

**»Try it!** With a partner, practice asking and answering questions using patterns of comparison. For example,

A: 小說和電影，哪一個精彩？
小说和电影，哪一个精彩？

B: 小說比電影精彩多了。
小说比电影精彩多了。

## V. Progressive Change 越來越 (越来越)......

她越來越胖了。
她越来越胖了。
She is getting fatter and fatter.

**»Try it!** With a partner, practice asking and answering questions using the pattern 越來越 (越来越)...... to indicate progressive change. For example,

A: 他最近身體怎麼樣？
他最近身体怎么样？

B: 最近他身體是越來越好。
最近他身体是越来越好。

## VI. 越......越...... Pattern

她越胖，我就越喜歡她。
她越胖，我就越喜欢她。
The fatter she is, the more I like her.

**»Try it!** With a partner, practice short dialogues with the pattern 越......越......
For example,

A: 你喜歡看中文小說嗎？
你喜欢看中文小说吗？

B: 喜歡，我越看越喜歡。
喜欢，我越看越喜欢。

## 補充課文 (补充课文) SUPPLEMENTARY PRACTICE

*Read the following passage. Then listen and repeat.*

### Wenhua's Winter Trip to China (繁體字 Traditional Character Version)

李訪： 今天我們聽了五個同學的報告。

謝進學： 他們的報告做得怎麼樣?

李訪： 都很不錯，不過我更喜歡方文華的報告，我覺得她的報告最有意思，她的中文也說得最好。

謝進學： 她的報告是關於什麼的?

李訪： 是關於她的寒假計畫的。她告訴我們今年寒假她打算去中國旅遊，同時也去看看她的親戚朋友。

謝進學： 聽說現在去中國的人越來越多，所以飛機票也越來越難買。她應該要早一點訂票。票訂得越晚，票價越貴，也就越難買得到。

李訪： 是的。文華也說了，去北京的飛機票比去上海和廣州的更難買，現在已經買不到了，所以他們打算先去南方玩玩，再到北京。

謝進學： 他們可以先去昆明，那是一個四季如春、風景如畫的城市，聽說那兒百分之六十的人是少數民族，很值得去看看。

李訪： 是的。文華打算先去廣州，再去昆明，然後到上海，最後從上海再去北京。

謝進學： 哇噻! 寒假這麼短的時間，她去得了這麼多的地方嗎?

李訪： 她打算十二月中旬出發，一月上旬回來。她計畫得很好，應該沒問題。

謝進學： 真希望我也能有這樣的機會!

李訪： 我希望我的報告也能像她的報告那麼精彩。我的寒假計畫比她的簡單得多，也不如她的那麼有趣，不過我想我的寒假也會過得很愉快。

*Notes:*

關於(关于) [guānyú]: about

值得(值得) [zhídé]: to be worthwhile

哇噻(哇噻) [wàsài]: wow (an expression to show amazement)

希望(希望) [xīwàng]: to hope

愉快(愉快) [yúkuài]: to be happy

## 補充課文 (补充课文) SUPPLEMENTARY PRACTICE

*Read the following passage. Then listen and repeat.*

### Wenhua's Winter Trip to China (简体字 Simplified Character Version)

| | |
|---|---|
| 李访: | 今天我们听了五个同学的报告。 |
| 谢进学: | 他们的报告做得怎么样? |
| 李访: | 都很不错,不过我更喜欢方文华的报告,我觉得她的报告最有意思,她的中文也说得最好。 |
| 谢进学: | 她的报告是关于什么的? |
| 李访: | 是关于她的寒假计划的。她告诉我们今年寒假她打算去中国旅游,同时也去看看她的亲戚朋友。 |
| 谢进学: | 听说现在去中国的人越来越多,所以飞机票也越来越难买。她应该要早一点订票。票订得越晚,票价越贵,也就越难买得到。 |
| 李访: | 是的。文华也说了,去北京的飞机票比去上海和广州的更难买,现在已经买不到了,所以他们打算先去南方玩玩,再到北京。 |
| 谢进学: | 他们可以先去昆明,那是一个四季如春、风景如画的城市,听说那儿百分之六十的人是少数民族,很值得去看看。 |
| 李访: | 是的。文华打算先去广州,再去昆明,然后到上海,最后从上海再去北京。 |
| 谢进学: | 哇噻!寒假这么短的时间,她去得了这么多的地方吗? |
| 李访: | 她打算十二月中旬出发,一月上旬回来。她计划得很好,应该没问题。 |
| 谢进学: | 真希望我也能有这样的机会! |
| 李访: | 我希望我的报告也能像她的报告那么精彩。我的寒假计划比她的简单得多,也不如她的那么有趣,不过我想我的寒假也会过得很愉快。 |

### Exercises: work with a partner or in small groups

1. 李訪為什麼喜歡方文華的報告?
   李访为什么喜欢方文华的报告?

2. 李訪說文華應該先買機票到哪兒?然後再怎麼計畫?
   李访说文华应该先买机票到哪儿?然后再怎么计划?

3. 文華旅行的時候還要做什麼?
   文华旅行的时候还要做什么?

## 成語故事 (成语故事) IDIOM STORY

### 夜郎自大 (夜郎自大) [Yèláng zìdà]

*Meaning:* The arrogance of Yelang.

*Usage:* This is used to describe someone who is ignorant and boastful.

*Example:* 小王沒有看過小李的報告，不知道小李的報告好極了，可是
小王卻很"夜郎自大"，覺得他的報告是最好的。

小王没有看过小李的报告，不知道小李的报告好极了，可是
小王却很"夜郎自大"，觉得他的报告是最好的。

Pay attention to the usages of A 比 B.....; A (不)像/(沒)有 [(没)有] B......

(繁體字 Traditional Character Version)

　　古時候，在中國的西南邊，有個夜郎國。夜郎國有很多山，出去
很不方便，所以夜郎國的人很少到別的地方去。夜郎國的國王叫多
同，他也從來沒有到過別的地方，所以他覺得夜郎國比別的國家都
大。

　　有一天，國王帶著一些人出去玩。看到一座高山就說："這座山
多麼高呀！天下沒有一座山像這座山這麼高。你們說對嗎?"那些人
也說："您說得很對，這座山比別的山都高。"他們上了山，看到下邊
的夜郎國，多同驕傲地說："我的夜郎國多麼大呀，你們知道還有哪
一個國家像夜郎國這麼大呢?"那些人都說："沒有，沒有，夜郎國是
天下最大的。"

　　後來，他們又走到了一條小河的旁邊。多同又說："看，這條大
河多麼寬、多麼長，哪個國家有這麼長的大河呢?"那些人也說："這
是天下最長最大的河！"多同聽了高興極了，他也變得一天比一天驕
傲。

　　有一天，一些人經過夜郎國，跟多同介紹了他們的國家，多同聽
了以後很不相信地問："你們的國家真的比我的夜郎國大嗎?"那些人
笑了，說："我們的國家比你的夜郎國大幾十倍呢！"

　　"夜郎自大"這個成語常常用來諷刺那些知道得很少，但是總是
覺得自己特別了不起的人。

(简体字 Simplified Character Version)

　　古时候，在中国的西南边，有个夜郎国。夜郎国有很多山，出去很不方便，所以夜郎国的人很少到别的地方去。夜郎国的国王叫多同，他也从来没有到过别的地方，所以他觉得夜郎国比别的国家都大。

　　有一天，国王带着一些人出去玩。看到一座高山就说："这座山多么高呀！天下没有一座山像这座山这么高。你们说对吗？"那些人也说："您说得很对，这座山比别的山都高。"他们上了山，看到下边的夜郎国，多同骄傲地说："我的夜郎国多么大呀，你们知道还有哪一个国家像夜郎国这么大呢？"那些人都说："没有，没有，夜郎国是天下最大的。"

　　后来，他们又走到了一条小河的旁边。多同又说："看，这条大河多么宽、多么长，哪个国家有这么长的大河呢？"那些人也说："这是天下最长最大的河！"多同听了高兴极了，他也变得一天比一天骄傲。

　　有一天，一些人经过夜郎国，跟多同介绍了他们的国家，多同听了以后很不相信地问："你们的国家真的比我的夜郎国大吗？"那些人笑了，说："我们的国家比你的夜郎国大几十倍呢！"

　　"夜郎自大"这个成语常常用来讽刺那些知道得很少，但是总是觉得自己特别了不起的人。

*Notes:*

從來(从来) [cónglái]: from the beginning (used only in a negative expression)

座(座) [zuò]: (measure word for mountains)

驕傲(骄傲) [jiāo'ào]: arrogant; conceited

河(河) [hé]: river

寬(宽) [kuān]: wide

經過(经过) [jīngguò]: to pass

倍(倍) [bèi]: times

用來(用来) [yònglái]: to be used for

諷刺(讽刺) [fěngcì]: to satirize

了不起(了不起) [liǎobuqǐ]: terrific; extraordinary

## Exercises: work with a partner or in small groups

1. 夜郎國的人常常到別的地方去嗎? 為什麼?
   夜郎国的人常常到别的地方去吗? 为什么?

2. 夜郎國的國王覺得他的國家怎麼樣?
   夜郎国的国王觉得他的国家怎么样?

3. 這個成語告訴了我們什麼? 你能用它造一個句子嗎?
   这个成语告诉了我们什么? 你能用它造一个句子吗?

## 練習 (练习) ACTIVITIES

### I. Listening Exercises

🔊 **10-1** 高友華(高友华) has big plans for her winter vacation. Listen to what she tells us and then do the following.

*Notes:*
秦始皇墓(秦始皇墓) [Qín Shǐhuáng mù]: tomb of the first emperor of the Qin Dynasty (221–206 B.C.)
兵馬俑(兵马俑) [bīngmǎyǒng]: Terracotta Warriors and Horses
商店(商店) [shāngdiàn]: shopping store
個人支票(个人支票) [gèrén zhīpiào]: personal check

1. Work in small groups to ask and answer the following questions.

   a) 她的寒假大計畫是什麼? 為什麼她去年沒有去成?
      她的寒假大计划是什么? 为什么她去年没有去成?

   _____

   b) 哪個城市是她最想去的? 為什麼?
      哪个城市是她最想去的? 为什么?

   _____

   c) 她想在北京做什麼?
      她想在北京做什么?

   _____

d) 西安那兒有什麼？她還想去哪兒？
西安那儿有什么？她还想去哪儿？

_____

e) 中國的銀行現在有什麼服務？
中国的银行现在有什么服务？

_____

2. Use your own words to retell the story in your group.

## II. Character Exercises

10-2 Work with a partner. Read the following words, phrases, and sentences.

| | |
|---|---|
| 發<br>发 | 觀<br>观 |
| 出發<br>出发 | 壯觀<br>壮观 |
| 從紐約出發<br>从纽约出发 | 景色很壯觀<br>景色很壮观 |
| 十二月從紐約出發<br>十二月从纽约出发 | 中國的長城景色很壯觀<br>中国的长城景色很壮观 |
| 十二月上旬從紐約出發<br>十二月上旬从纽约出发 | 中國的長城景色很壯觀<br>中国的长城景色很壮观 |
| 十二月上旬從紐約出發去台北<br>十二月上旬从纽约出发去台北 | 我覺得中國的長城景色很壯觀<br>我觉得中国的长城景色很壮观 |

Now with your partner, try to use the following characters to make words, phrases, and then sentences.

1. 旬<br>旬    2. 畫<br>划    3. 私<br>私    4. 爬<br>爬    5. 折<br>折

6. 據<br>据    7. 零<br>零    8. 頂<br>顶    9. 載<br>载

**10-3** Write the radical for each group of characters, and then check your answer with your partner.

1. _____ 打，接，據，換，折
   _____ 打，接，据，换，折

2. _____ 寒，安，它
   _____ 寒，安，它

3. _____ 計，訂，證，試，訴
   _____ 计，订，证，试，诉

4. _____ 這，還，道，過，近
   _____ 这，还，道，过，近

## III. Grammar Exercises

**10-4** Work in pairs. Use "V. + Resultative Complement 好" in the following sentences.

1. 我的研究報告已經 _____ 了，現在我輕鬆多了。
   我的研究报告已经 _____ 了，现在我轻松多了。

2. 方明的電話 _____ 了沒有? 我想找他去鍛煉。
   方明的电话 _____ 了没有? 我想找他去锻炼。

3. 你的簽證 _____ 了沒有? 沒有多少時間了。
   你的签证 _____ 了没有? 没有多少时间了。

**10-5** Group the underlined phrases based on their structure, then check with your partner.

Juxtaposed phrases (JP)                Endocentric phrases (EP)
"Subject + V." phrases (SVP)           "V. + Object" phrases (VOP)

1. 去北京的機票 _____
   去北京的机票 _____

2. 爬長城很累 _____
   爬长城很累 _____

3. 現金和支票 _____
   现金和支票 _____

4. 張藝謀導演的功夫片 _____
   张艺谋导演的功夫片 _____

5. 看過這部電影的人 _____
   看过这部电影的人 _____

6. 支票帳戶 _____
   支票账户 _____

7. 我最想做的事 _____
   我最想做的事 _____

8. 親戚朋友 _____
   亲戚朋友 _____

**10-6** The following is a list of exchange rates between US dollars and other currencies. Write out the Chinese for the ratio between US$ and each of the following currencies, then practice saying the whole sentence aloud with your partner or in a small group.

| US$ | RMB ¥ | HK$ | NTD | Euro | Japanese ¥ |
|-----|-------|------|-------|------|------------|
| 1 | 6.53 | 7.76 | 32.57 | 0.82 | 107.82 |

*Examples:*  美元：人民幣　　一比六點五三
          美元：人民币　　一比六点五三

          美元匯率：現在美元兌人民幣的匯率是一比六點五三
          美元汇率：现在美元兑人民币的汇率是一比六点五三

美元：港幣 _____
美元：港币 _____

美元：新台幣 _____
美元：新台币 _____

美元：歐元 _____
美元：欧元 _____

美元：日元 _____
美元：日元 _____

**10-7** You are going to open a bank account. There are three banks near your school. Work in a small group to compare interest rates and complete the following paragraph.

| 大華銀行<br>大华银行 | | 民生銀行<br>民生银行 | | 美華銀行<br>美华银行 | |
|---|---|---|---|---|---|
| 支票帳戶<br>支票账户 | 儲蓄帳戶<br>储蓄账户 | 支票帳戶<br>支票账户 | 儲蓄帳戶<br>储蓄账户 | 支票帳戶<br>支票账户 | 儲蓄帳戶<br>储蓄账户 |
| 2.8% | 3.5% | 2.9% | 3.6% | 2.8% | 3.7% |

在三家銀行裡，民生銀行的利息 _____ (to be the highest)，支票帳戶
在三家银行里，民生银行的利息 _____ (to be the highest)，支票账户

和儲蓄帳戶的利率都比大華銀行高 _____ (0.1%)。美華銀行也
和储蓄账户的利率都比大华银行高 _____ (0.1%)。美华银行也

不錯，可是它的支票帳戶的利息 _____ 大華銀行的 _____ (same)，
不错，可是它的支票账户的利息 _____ 大华银行的 _____ (same)，

只有 _____ (2.8%)。不過它的
只有 _____ (2.8%)。不过它的

儲蓄帳戶的利息比較高，比大華銀行
储蓄账户的利息比较高，比大华银行

_____ (0.2% higher)。我決定去
_____ (0.2% higher)。我决定去

美華銀行開帳戶。
美华银行开账户。

## IV. Communicative Activities

**10-8** In the Listening Exercises, 高友華(高友华) shared her plans for her winter vacation. You and your girl/boyfriend are now working on your own plans. Take what 高友華(高友华) said as a reference and discuss what you are going to do.

**10-9** Work in pairs using the "V. + Potential Complement" structure to find out if your friend is able to:

1. afford to buy a plane ticket to Hong Kong
2. understand the movie *Crouching Tiger, Hidden Dragon* in Chinese
3. find the movie theater nearby
4. finish all the homework today
5. find out if their classroom can seat more than 30 people
6. finish 40 dumplings in one meal

*Example:*

A: 你找得到找不到那家銀行?
   你找得到找不到那家银行?

B: 我一定能找得到。
   我一定能找得到。

You may ask more questions by using the same structure. Try to find out as much as you can about your friend.

# 文化知識 (文化知识) Culture Link

## 文化點滴 (文化点滴) CULTURE NOTES

### 中國的長城 (中国的长城) The Great Wall of China

The Great Wall of China, one of the greatest wonders of the world, is probably the most widely acknowledged symbol of China. Wherever you go in the world, you will see pictures of the Great Wall in any place related to China. Like a gigantic dragon, it crawls through 11 provinces in the northern part of the country, stretching nearly 6,700 kilometers (4,163 miles) from the eastern to the western regions. With its unique architectural and historic significance, in 1987 UNESCO identified the Great Wall as a World Heritage landmark, one of the most appealing tourist attractions in the world. The Chinese saying goes "不到長城非好漢(不到长城非好汉)" [bú dào Chángchéng fēi hǎohàn] (You will not be considered a hero unless you have been to the Great Wall.)

The Great Wall was originally several independent walls built separately as defensive fortifications more than 2,500 years ago during 周朝 [Zhōu Cháo] (the Zhou Dynasty) and 春秋戰國時代 (春秋战国时代) [Chūnqiū Zhànguó shídài] (the Spring and Autumn and Warring States periods). After unifying China in 221 B.C., 秦始皇帝 [Qín Shǐ huángdì] (the first emperor of the Qin Dynasty), connected the walls to fend off invasions

> **Do you know...**
> - the length of the Great Wall?
> - when the Great Wall was built and during which dynasty(ies)?
> - how many workers it took to complete the Great Wall?
>
> *Read and find out!*

from the north. Since then, the Great Wall has served as a monument and symbol of the Chinese nation.

The Chinese call the Great Wall the 萬里長城(万里长城) [wànlǐ Chángchéng] which literally means "the ten thousand li long wall." It took more than ten years and over a million laborers to complete the original construction. Traversing mountain ridges and plateau, the unimaginable difficulty of the project cost the lives of hundreds and thousands of workers. Many of them were buried under the wall. The construction materials, primarily stones, earth, and bricks, were mainly drawn from local resources. The result is considered to be a manifestation of the wisdom and tenacity of the Chinese people.

What is known today as the Great Wall is not the portion first built during the Qin Dynasty, but the sections built during 明朝 [Míngcháo] (the Ming Dynasty) more than 1,500 years later. It took nearly 200 years to repair and rebuild the Great Wall, resulting in a wall with a thickness of 4.5 to 8 meters and numerous watch towers. It stretches 6,700 kilometers from the Shanhaiguan Pass in Hebei Province in the east, to the Jiayuguan Pass of Gansu Province in the west.

To protect and preserve this great treasure, in 2002 the China Great Wall Academy conducted a 45-day survey of 101 sections of the Great Wall, finding 70 percent of the wall damaged by natural causes and human negligence. Calling for more effective protection of this important world relic, a campaign was launched to collect donations for repairs and general maintenance. With the support of UNESCO, the Chinese government has also taken similar measures.

The Great Wall of China, one of the seven wonders of the world, is probably the most widely acknowledged symbol of China. What is the main symbol for your country?

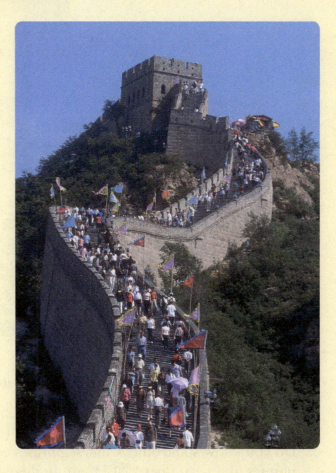

Every day, people from all over the world walk on the Great Wall. What is the best known tourist attraction in your country?

**問題討論 (问题讨论)** *Discuss the following with a partner or in small groups.*

1. 你去過長城嗎？你去中國的時候想去爬長城嗎？為什麼？
   你去过长城吗？你去中国的时候想去爬长城吗？为什么？
   Have you been to the Great Wall? When you go to China, would you like to climb the
   Great Wall? Why or why not?

2. 你知道中國還有什麼有名的地方嗎？請說出幾個。
   你知道中国还有什么有名的地方吗？请说出几个。
   Do you know of any other famous landmarks in China? Provide some examples.

# 趣味中文 (趣味中文) FUN WITH CHINESE

> 滿載而歸
> 满载而归
>
> To return home fully laden with riches, gifts, etc.

| mǎn | zài | ér | guī |
|-----|-----|-----|-----|
| 滿 | 載 | 而 | 歸 |
| 满 | 载 | 而 | 归 |
| full | to carry | and then | to return |

**問題討論 (问题讨论)** *Discuss the following with a partner or in small groups.*

1. In what kinds of situation can you use 滿載而歸(满载而归)? Please describe these
   situations in Chinese by using 滿載而歸(满载而归).
2. Do you know some other Chinese phrases containing the word "而"? What are these
   phrases and what does "而" mean in these phrases?

## 行動吧! (行动吧!) LET'S GO!

**大巴指南 (大巴指南) Bus Guide**

最新机场大巴专线指南

| 1号线：虹桥机场→浦东机场 | 68346912 |
| 2号线：上海航站楼→浦东机场 | 62690022 |
| 3号线：银河宾馆→徐家汇上无四厂→张江→浦东机场 | 68346645 |
| 4号线：东江湾路(虹口公园)→大柏树→五角场→浦东机场 | 68346830 |
| 5号线：上海火车站→浦东东方医院→浦东机场 | 68346830 |
| 6号线：桃浦路→浦东机场 | 68346645 |

夜间订票：62274356

长期有效　敬请保留　以备急用

*Notes:*
大巴(大巴) [dàbā]: big bus
專線(专线) [zhuānxiàn]: special route
指南(指南) [zhǐnán]: guide
浦東(浦东) [Pǔdōng]: Pudong, an area east of the Huangpu River in Shanghai
夜間(夜间) [yèjiān]: night time
訂票(订票) [dìngpiào]: to book tickets
敬請(敬请) [jìngqǐng]: please (formal)
保留(保留) [bǎoliú]: to keep, reserve
以備(以备) [yǐbèi]: to be ready for
急用(急用) [jíyòng]: urgent need, for use in an emergency

**問題討論 (问题讨论)** *Discuss the following with a partner or in small groups.*

1. How many bus routes are there that lead to the Pudong International Airport in Shanghai?
2. Can you book a ticket at night? How?
3. What do the following expressions mean in English?

長期有效(长期有效)
敬請保留(敬请保留)
以備急用(以备急用)

# 復習 (复习) Review

## LESSON 9 TO LESSON 10

### I. Activities

A. Are you satisfied with your weight? Do you have a weight-control/-loss plan? If you do, tell us something about your plan. Work with a partner or in small groups. The following questions are for your reference.

    1. 你原來身體怎麼樣? 體重怎麼樣?
       你原来身体怎么样? 体重怎么样?

    2. 你是怎樣控制你的體重的?
       你是怎样控制你的体重的?

    3. 你控制體重的方法效果好嗎? 為什麼?
       你控制体重的方法效果好吗? 为什么?

Use the following sentence patterns, plus any other sentence patterns of comparison:

    1. 越來越(越来越)...... for progressive comparison
    2. 越......越...... pattern

B. You have not seen your high-school classmate, who used to be overweight, for about two years. When visiting during Thanksgiving, you noticed that he/she seemed to have lost quite a bit of weight and looked much healthier. You were amazed by the change and began to ask questions. With a partner, carry on a conversation of about 10 sentences each between the two of you to chat about the change. Use the following words, expressions, and sentence patterns.

    1. Any sentence patterns of comparison
    2. 最 and 更
    3. Words and expressions such as,

       羨慕(羡慕)，差不多(差不多)，次(次)，瘦/苗條(瘦/苗条)，
       減肥(减肥)，堅持(坚持)，效果(效果)，輕(轻)，精神(精神)，
       控制(控制)，鍛煉(锻炼)，注意(注意)，比(比)，靈活(灵活)，
       磅/公斤(磅/公斤)

C. Make a report on your plan for the winter vacation. Exchange your thoughts with your partner. The following words and expressions must be used.

計畫(计划)，旅遊(旅游)，中文班(中文班)，旬(旬)，
航空公司(航空公司)，旅行社(旅行社)，飛機票(飞机票)，
買(买)，支票(支票)，信用卡(信用卡)，付款(付款)，外幣(外币)，
匯率(汇率)，滿載而歸(满载而归)

## II. Grammar

A. Work in small groups and use 越來越(越来越)...... to complete the following sentences.

1. 去中國的機票 _____。我還沒有買到。
   去中国的机票 _____。我还没有买到。

2. 因為效果很好，我現在 _____ 鍛鍊了。
   因为效果很好，我现在 _____ 锻炼了。

3. 你知道為什麼他的精神 _____ 了嗎？
   你知道为什么他的精神 _____ 了吗？

4. 現在 _____ 的中國人喜歡看美國好萊塢 ([hǎoláiwū]:
   Hollywood) 的電影。
   现在 _____ 的中国人喜欢看美国好莱坞的电影。

B. Use 越......，越...... to combine the following pairs of sentences.

1. 他鍛鍊得很多，他很靈活。
   他锻炼得很多，他很灵活。

2. 去中國的人非常多，機票很難買。
   去中国的人非常多，机票很难买。

3. 他買了很多飛機票，票價很便宜。
   他买了很多飞机票，票价很便宜。

4. 電影的情節很曲折，我非常喜歡。
   电影的情节很曲折，我非常喜欢。

## III. Characters

A. Work in small groups and compare the following pairs of characters to find similarities and differences. Write the Pinyin, with tones, and create a word or phrase.

*Example:* 很(很)  <u>hěn</u>   <u>很好</u>

1. 旬(旬) _____ _____
   句(句) _____ _____

2. 雪(雪) _____ _____
   零(零) _____ _____

3. 超(超) _____ _____
   起(起) _____ _____

4. 精(精) _____ _____
   情(情) _____ _____

5. 跟(跟) _____ _____
   根(根) _____ _____

6. 受(受) _____ _____
   收(收) _____ _____

7. 劇(剧) _____ _____
   據(据) _____ _____

8. 付(付) _____ _____
   什(什) _____ _____

B. With a partner, fill in the blanks with appropriate words from the following words and expressions.

根據，說好了，希望，怪不得，不但……而且……，其實，總是，當然
根据，说好了，希望，怪不得，不但……而且……，其实，总是，当然

1. A: 我要兌換一百元美金。
      我要兑换一百元美金。

   B: _____ 今天的匯率，一百元美金可以換八百二十六元人民幣。
      _____ 今天的汇率，一百元美金可以换八百二十六元人民币。

2. A: 方明，你說什麼是減肥的最好方法？
方明，你说什么是减肥的最好方法？

B: _____ 運動是最好的減肥方法。
_____ 运动是最好的减肥方法。

3. A: 你為什麼 _____ 想去中國？
你为什么 _____ 想去中国？

B: 因為中國是一個非常有意思的國家。
因为中国是一个非常有意思的国家。

4. A: 我在北京有很多親戚。
我在北京有很多亲戚。

B: _____ 你今年冬天想去北京。
_____ 你今年冬天想去北京。

5. 我已經跟我的爸爸媽媽 _____，明年夏天去上海參加暑期中文班學習。

我已经跟我的爸爸妈妈 _____，明年夏天去上海参加暑期中文班学习。

6. A: 這是我認識的一個朋友的電話號碼。他在旅行社工作。
这是我认识的一个朋友的电话号码。他在旅行社工作。

B: _____ 他能幫助我訂到去中國的飛機票。
_____ 他能帮助我订到去中国的飞机票。

7. A: 你喜歡看中國的功夫片嗎？
你喜欢看中国的功夫片吗？

B: _____。我最喜歡看李連杰的電影。
_____。我最喜欢看李连杰的电影。

8. A: 你看過張藝謀導演的電影嗎？
你看过张艺谋导演的电影吗？

B: 我 _____ 看過他最近導演的電影，_____ 還看過他以前自己演的電影。

我 _____ 看过他最近导演的电影，_____ 还看过他以前自己演的电影。

## IV. Report

Last summer, you joined 20 other students on a study-abroad program in Beijing. It was a wonderful experience for you and you had a very good time there. You did a lot of things and took part in many activities, including taking classes, traveling, watching movies and other shows, getting together with Chinese students, learning Taichi, etc. Now write a brief report of your summer experience and share it with your good friend. Encourage him/her to go too. Use as many words and expressions from the lessons as you can. (Write at least 12 sentences.)

# 繁簡體字對照表 (繁简体字对照表)
# TRADITIONAL/SIMPLIFIED CHARACTER TABLE

繁體字(繁体字)： [fán tǐ zì]   traditional character (or complex character)
簡體字(简体字)： [jiǎn tǐ zì]   simplified character

## 第一課 (第一课)  Lesson 1

| 繁： | 樹 | 壞 | 鏡 | 負 | 責 | 裝 | 掃 | 掛 |
|---|---|---|---|---|---|---|---|---|
| 简： | 树 | 坏 | 镜 | 负 | 责 | 装 | 扫 | 挂 |

## 第二課 (第二课)  Lesson 2

| 繁： | 牆 | 著 | 擺 | 種 | 彈 | 齣 | 戲 | 畫 | 臉 | 滿 | 眾 | 長 |
|---|---|---|---|---|---|---|---|---|---|---|---|---|
| 简： | 墙 | 着 | 摆 | 种 | 弹 | 出 | 戏 | 画 | 脸 | 满 | 众 | 长 |

## 第三課 (第三课)  Lesson 3

| 繁： | 全 | 繫 | 計 | 棟 | 變 | 農 | 燈 | 費 | 幣 |
|---|---|---|---|---|---|---|---|---|---|
| 简： | 全 | 系 | 计 | 栋 | 变 | 农 | 灯 | 费 | 币 |

## 第四課 (第四课)  Lesson 4

| 繁： | 維 | 輕 | 涼 | 髮 | 適 | 睏 | 慣 | 飽 | 乾 |
|---|---|---|---|---|---|---|---|---|---|
| 简： | 维 | 轻 | 凉 | 发 | 适 | 困 | 惯 | 饱 | 干 |

## 第五課 (第五课)  Lesson 5

| 繁： | 陰 | 終 | 於 | 誤 | 趕 | 團 | 鬧 | 榮 | 廈 | 雖 |
|---|---|---|---|---|---|---|---|---|---|---|
| 简： | 阴 | 终 | 于 | 误 | 赶 | 团 | 闹 | 荣 | 厦 | 虽 |

## 第六課 (第六课)  Lesson 6

| 繁： | 銀 | 帳 | 戶 | 儲 | 職 | 夠 | 單 | 當 | 換 | 匯 | 櫃 |
|---|---|---|---|---|---|---|---|---|---|---|---|
| 简： | 银 | 账 | 户 | 储 | 职 | 够 | 单 | 当 | 换 | 汇 | 柜 |

## 第七課 (第七课)  Lesson 7

| 繁： | 遊 | 訂 | 羨 | 親 | 訪 | 數 | 簽 | 證 | 辦 |
|---|---|---|---|---|---|---|---|---|---|
| 简： | 游 | 订 | 羡 | 亲 | 访 | 数 | 签 | 证 | 办 |

## 第八課 (第八课)    Lesson 8

| 繁: | 連 | 報 | 鬆 | 強 | 導 | 節 | 歷 | 顏 | 週 | 價 |
|---|---|---|---|---|---|---|---|---|---|---|
| 简: | 连 | 报 | 松 | 强 | 导 | 节 | 历 | 颜 | 周 | 价 |

## 第九課 (第九课)    Lesson 9

| 繁: | 減 | 堅 | 飲 | 靈 | 總 |
|---|---|---|---|---|---|
| 简: | 减 | 坚 | 饮 | 灵 | 总 |

## 第十課 (第十课)    Lesson 10

| 繁: | 據 | 頂 | 漢 | 訴 | 壯 | 載 | 歸 |
|---|---|---|---|---|---|---|---|
| 简: | 据 | 顶 | 汉 | 诉 | 壮 | 载 | 归 |

# 課文英文翻譯 (课文英文翻译)
# ENGLISH TRANSLATIONS OF LANGUAGE IN USE

## Lesson 1    My Friend Helps Me Move

| | |
|---|---|
| Xie Jinxue: | Here we are. Let me park my car on the side. |
| Chang Tian: | Wait a minute. Let me move my car away first, then you drive your car over here. |
| Xia Zhongming: | When you back up, I will check for you. Don't knock down the landlord's tree. |
| Chang Tian: | Right! When we moved in last time, we were not careful enough and broke the landlord's mirror. How embarrassing. |
| Xie Jinxue: | Let's first move the bed and desk upstairs, then we'll divide the tasks. How about that? |
| Xia Zhongming: | Good idea! I'll be responsible for getting the luggage down and putting it away. I'll also install the computer. |
| Xie Jinxue: | OK, I'll sweep the floor, tidy the living room, and then put the books in order. |
| Chang Tian: | I'll wash the dishes, open the boxes, and hang up the clothes. |
| Xie Jinxue: | Thanks for your help. This move is going to tire you out. What would you like to eat for dinner? My treat! |
| Chang Tian: | Great! I'm starving. |
| Xia Zhongming: | There is a pretty good Chinese restaurant nearby, but I've forgotten the address. |
| Chang Tian: | Don't worry. I've got it. Look, I've found it! |
| Xie Jinxue: | Great! Let me close the door and windows first. |
| Xia Zhongming: | Don't forget to put on your jacket. Let's go! |

## Lesson 2    My Sister Enjoys Beijing Opera!

| | |
|---|---|
| Li Fang: | There's a picture hanging on the wall over there. Who's that? I don't think I've seen her before. |
| Guan Mingyuan: | That's a picture taken by my older sister. |
| Li Fang: | Where is she now? |
| Guan Mingyuan: | Right now she is studying abroad in Beijing. She is there learning Chinese, and has been living there for over a year. |
| Li Fang: | How long has she been studying Chinese? |
| Guan Mingyuan: | She has been studying Chinese for three years. |
| Li Fang: | That's a Beijing Opera costume, right? |

| | |
|---|---|
| Guan Mingyuan: | Yes. This is a picture she took when she went to see a Beijing Opera last month. She'd never watched Beijing Opera before and now she's seen it. She's very pleased. |
| Li Fang: | What are those things laid out on the stage? They seem to be different Chinese musical instruments. |
| Guan Mingyuan: | You're right. Look, the opera singers are busy performing. And there are some musicians sitting at the side. Some are beating drums, some playing *erhu* (two-stringed bowed instruments). They are all busy playing their own musical instruments. |
| Li Fang: | What's this opera about? It seems to be pretty interesting. |
| Guan Mingyuan: | It's about Guan Gong. Look, Guan Gong's face is painted red and he's holding a big knife in his hand. Really dignified! |
| Li Fang: | What a crowd! You see, all the seats are occupied. Some people even had to stand. Oh! By the way, have you ever seen Bejing Opera? |
| Guan Mingyuan: | I've seen it twice, both times in Shanghai. |
| Li Fang: | You went to Shanghai when you were in China. Where else did you go in China? |
| Guan Mingyuan: | I only went to Shanghai. At that time, I was busy with my classes every day, so I didn't have a chance to go to Beijing and the Great Wall. |
| Li Fang: | I heard that the mini steamed dumplings in Shanghai are very good. Have you had them? |
| Guan Mingyuan: | I have. I've even learned how to make them! |
| Li Fang: | That's really interesting! I'd love to go to China too. |
| Guan Mingyuan: | I'm going to China next month. Why don't you come with me? We can go see Beijing Opera together. How does that sound? |
| Li Fang: | Good. It's a deal! |

## Lesson 3   Visiting Shanghai

*(Scene 1: On the airplane)*

Hello, passengers. The plane will land in 20 minutes. We will soon arrive at *Pudong* Airport in Shanghai. Please go back to your seats and fasten your seat belts. Also, please turn off your computers and other electronic appliances. Thank you for your cooperation. And thank you again for flying China Airlines.

*(Scene 2: At the airport)*

| | |
|---|---|
| Guan Mingyuan: | We're here. Let's take a cab to the hotel. It will be faster by cab. |
| Li Fang: | How fast is it by cab? |
| Guan Mingyuan: | I think we'll be able to get there in less than 10 minutes. |
| Li Fang: | Good. Let's ask for directions. |
| Guan Mingyuan: | Excuse me, sir, but could you tell me where the taxi stand is? |

| Pedestrian: | The taxi stand is behind that building. Go straight from here, make a left at the crossroad up there, and then walk straight ahead. After you pass two intersections, you will see the taxi stand. |
| Guan Mingyuan: | Thank you. |
| Pedestrian: | You're welcome. |

*(Scene 3: At the taxi station)*

| Driver: | Excuse me, you two gentlemen are looking for a cab, right? |
| Guan Mingyuan: | Yes. We're going to the Holiday Hotel. How far is it from here? |
| Driver: | It's 3 kilometers. Not very far. Please get in. Here, I'll put the luggage in the trunk first. |

. . . . . .

| Li Fang: | China seems to be developing pretty fast. |
| Guan Mingyuan: | Yes! But things have changed fast here too! |
| Driver: | It sounds like you've been to Shanghai before. |
| Guan Mingyuan: | Yes, I came here two years ago, but there are quite a few roads that I don't recognise. |
| Driver: | You're right. Shanghai has changed very fast. Look, it was originally all farmland here, but now everything has changed into big buildings and major streets. |
| Li Fang: | Look! That building is really tall. I don't know how tall it is. |
| Driver: | Oh! That building is new. I heard that it's ninety meters tall. |
| Guan Mingyuan: | Yes, now I remember. That's *Zhongshan* Road. I used to wait at that traffic light to cross the road. After crossing the road, I turned right, walked for another two or three minutes, and there was the Shanghai Snackbar. The food there is really delicious! |
| Driver: | The Holiday Hotel is right ahead. But I can't turn left here. I have to make a few more turns. |
| Li Fang: | OK, no problem. |

. . . . . .

| Driver: | Here we are. |
| Li Fang: | How much is the cab fare? |
| Driver: | Altogether 28 *kuai* RMB. |
| Guan Mingyuan: | Here's 30 *kuai*. |
| Driver: | Here's 2 *kuai* change. Thank you. |

## Lesson 4    Visiting a Chinese Family

| | |
|---|---|
| Professor: | Welcome, welcome. Come in, please. |
| Guan Mingyuan: | Come, Li Fang. Let me introduce you. This is Professor Wang, and this is Mrs. Wang. |
| Li Fang: | Hello. |
| Guan Mingyuan: | Professor, here are some books that I hope you'll like on American literature. Mrs. Wang, these vitamins are for you and Professor Wang. I wish you everlasting health and youth. |
| Mrs. Wang: | It's enough that you could come. You didn't have to bring so many things. You'll spend all your money! |
| Guan Mingyuan: | It's nothing, just a small token (of our appreciation). |
| Professor: | You don't come to Shanghai very often. My wife has cooked some of her favorite dishes specially for you. Come, come, sit down. The meal is getting cold. |
| Guan Mingyuan: | Professor, Mrs. Wang, you two are still the same as ever. You look so energetic! |
| Mrs. Wang: | Not any more! We're getting older by the day. We have more gray hair than before, our vision is getting blurry, and we can't do things as quickly any more. |
| Professor: | Li Fang, this is your first visit to China. Are you adjusting OK? |
| Li Fang: | Not too bad. I still have some jetlag. I feel sleepy during the day, but can't get to sleep at night. But I'm much better today than yesterday. |
| Guan Mingyuan: | Li Fang says that the weather here is warmer than in Pittsburgh, and also, there are more people here. The streets are full of people and he's not quite used to it yet. |
| Li Fang: | This the first time in my life I've ever seen so many people! |
| Mrs. Wang: | Who is older of the two of you? |
| Guan Mingyuan: | I'm the same age as Li Fang. We're both 24. |
| Mrs. Wang: | Come, don't just talk and forget to eat. Come on, have some more. |
| Professor: | This is the rice cake my wife made. It's very authentic. Have a taste. |
| Guan Mingyuan: | Mrs. Wang, your food is really delicious! |
| Li Fang: | Absolutely! The color, the flavor, and the taste are all perfect. I've had so much and am very full now. |
| Mrs. Wang: | Not really, not really. Just some simple, home-made dishes. |
| Professor: | It's such a rare chance for us to get together. Come, let's have a toast. I am so happy today. "Isn't it pleasant to have friends coming from afar?" |
| Professor, Mrs. Wang, Guan, and Li: | Cheers! |

## Lesson 5    My Trip to China

China Trip

Wednesday, Oct. 20  Weather: overcast

After being on the plane for more than 30 hours, we're finally back in the US. It should have taken around 10 hours from China to the US, but when we switched flights in Japan our plane was delayed so we missed our connection. We waited at the airport for 5 hours before we finally got a flight. This flight delay made Li Fang and I so exhausted that as soon as we put our luggage away on the plane, we slept until the plane landed.

Nevertheless, I was very happy that I could go to visit my professor in Shanghai. The professor and his wife both looked very healthy. They were still as warm-hearted and hospitable as before. Mrs. Wang also made some very authentic (Chinese) dishes specially for us to taste. Of them all, I liked the Shanghai rice cake the best. It was really delicious!

I also took Li Fang to the Beijing Opera. We were fascinated. It really opened our eyes. But I hear there are not as many Beijing Opera troupes as before so the tickets are more expensive now.

Shanghai has really changed very fast. Some roads are very hard to find now. We were holding a map in our hand and were busy asking directions. Often when we should have made a left turn, we got it wrong and turned right. We made quite a few stupid mistakes.

China is really becoming more prosperous and developed by the day. In large cities, the skyscrapers are as high as those in the US and foreigners can be seen everywhere.

Although our stay in China this time was short, we had a great time. Li Fang says that he can now tell others that he has been to China and seen Beijing Opera, and has also tasted many kinds of Chinese snacks!

We both feel that it was really worthwhile for us to make this trip to China. We will go again when we get a chance.

## Lesson 6    Opening a Bank Account

*(Scene 1: On the street)*

Guan Jinghua:   Xiaoqin, I'm going to the bank to open an account. Then it will be much more convenient to deposit or withdraw money. Do you know which bank is better?

Fang Xiaoqin:   I often go to the Great China Bank to deposit or withdraw money. Their service is good and their interest rate is also relatively high. For a savings account, the current rate is 3.2 percent.

Guan Jinghua:   Then I'll go to the Great China Bank.

*(Scene 2: At the bank)*

Guan Jinghua:   Sir, I'd like to open a checking account with interest. May I ask what the interest rate is for a checking account with interest?

| | |
|---|---|
| Clerk: | The rate has been pretty low recently. It is 2.6 percent today. |
| Guan Jinhua: | How come it is so low? I heard it was 3.2 percent. |
| Clerk: | That's for the savings account. The rate for the savings account is a little higher, 3.2 percent. That kind of account allows you to write 3 checks a month. Which account would you prefer? |
| Guan Jinhua: | 3 checks a month is about enough. I'll just open a savings account then. |
| Clerk: | Good. Please fill in this application. Thank you. How much would you like to deposit into the account today? |
| Guan Jinghua: | I have $3,000 here. |
| Clerk: | OK . . . . In a week you will receive your checks and ATM card. You may use your ATM card to withdraw cash at the ATM. |
| Guan Jinghua: | May I apply for a credit card here? |
| Clerk: | Of course you may. Please fill in this credit card application form. |
| Guan Jinhua: | I'm going to China next month. I need to buy some Renminbi. May I ask what the exchange rate is from US dollars to Renminbi? |
| Clerk: | Today's exchange rate is 1:6.53. |
| Guan Jinghua: | Where can I exchange foreign currency? |
| Clerk: | Just at the counter to the left. |
| Guan Jinghua: | Thanks. Bye. |

## Lesson 7    Booking Our Trip to China

| | |
|---|---|
| Fang Xiaoqin: | Wenhua, what are you looking for? |
| Jin Wenhua: | I am looking for a phone book. I can't find my phone book. |
| Fang Xiaoqin: | See if it's by the phone. |
| Jin Wenhua: | I see nothing . . . . Oh, I see it. It's under the table. I'm going on a trip to China with Fang Ming this winter break. I need to find the number of a travel agency. I want to book some plane tickets. |
| Fang Xiaoqin: | Really? That's wonderful! I really envy you. Where exactly are you going? |
| Jin Wenhua: | Fang Ming has a lot of relatives in Beijing. Originally we planned to stay in Beijing for a few days, have a get-together with his relatives, take some time to visit his former teachers, and then go to other places to have a look round. But I haven't been able to book any tickets to Beijing. |
| Fang Xiaoqin: | Have you checked on the web yet? |
| Jin Wenhua: | We've checked several airlines' websites, but still haven't been able to book the tickets. Some tickets are too expensive and we can't afford them. I want to check with this travel agency to see whether I can book some cheaper tickets. |
| Fang Xiaoqin: | Actually, if you really can't get plane tickets to Beijing, you could go to a city in the south first, such as Shanghai or Hong Kong, then go to Kunming in Yunnan. After that you can fly to Beijing from Kunming. |

● Jin Wenhua:     That's a good idea. I hear Kunming is a city where it's like spring all year round and the scenery is picturesque. There are also many ethnic minorities there. It would certainly be very interesting to have a look there. But how come I can't find Kunming on the map?

Fang Xiaoqin:     Let me help you . . . . Look, right here, in the southwest of China.

Jin Wenhua:     Oh, yes! If I really want to go, is Kunming accessible by plane?

Fang Xiaoqin:     Of course it is! You will also be able to taste snacks made by the ethnic minorities.

Jin Wenhua:     Then I'll definitely go.

Fang Xiaoqin:     Oh by the way, have you got your visas yet?

Jin Wenhua:     Ming's visa is done already. I have also applied. I don't know whether I'll receive it next week or not, but there is still a month to go. It should be in time.

## Lesson 8    What's Your Favorite Movie?

Ji Ruchun:     Muhua, you seem to be much busier than before recently, right?

Fang Muhua:     Not really! Why do you think I'm much busier than before?

Ji Ruchun:     Recently I haven't seen you at all, not even your shadow. When I called you last night, you weren't in either.

Fang Muhua:     I submitted a major project report yesterday morning and felt much more relaxed, so I went to see a movie with my cousin.

Ji Ruchun:     You are much better than I am. I haven't finished my report yet. By the way, what movie did you watch? Was it good?

Fang Muhua:     We watched *Hero*.

Ji Ruchun:     Is that the one directed by Yimou Zhang?

Fang Muhua:     Yes. The main actors are Daoming Chen, Jet Li, and Maggie Cheung. My favourite is Jet Li.

Ji Ruchun:     Some people say it is not as good as *Crouching Tiger, Hidden Dragon*. What do you think?

Fang Muhua:     I think both movies are about the same. Have you seen them?

Ji Ruchun:     I've seen *Crouching Tiger, Hidden Dragon*, not *Hero*, but I hear that the cinematography in *Hero* is more spectacular than in *Crouching Tiger, Hidden Dragon*. Is that true?

Fang Muhua:     Exactly. Its cinematography is more spectacular, but I don't think the plot is as interesting as *Crouching Tiger, Hidden Dragon*.

Ji Ruchun:     They say that *Hero* is about the first emperor of the Qin Dynasty in ancient China. Comparatively speaking, which one is better, the movie or the novel?

● Fang Muhua:     I don't think the movie is as good as the novel.

Ji Ruchen:     Some say that its description of the first emperor of the Qin Dynasty is not historically accurate.

Fang Muhua:    I agree, but I think the description in the movie is more objective.

Ji Ruchun:     I've always been very interested in historical stories, so I'd very much like to see this movie.

Fang Muhua:    You should go and see it. *Hero* has more love scenes than *Crouching Tiger, Hidden Dragon*, and its special effects and colors are much better than other movies.

Ji Ruchun:     Do you know where I can see *Hero*?

Fang Muhua:    It will be shown on campus this weekend and the tickets are only $1 each. That's 9 dollars cheaper than tickets at the cinema.

Ji Ruchun:     Good. I'll go and see it this weekend then.

## Lesson 9   I Have Started to Work Out

Bai Siqin:     Xinming, have you been going to the gym regularly to exercise recently?

Hu Xinming:    These two weeks have been my busiest time, and I have exercised much less than usual. I used to go swimming almost every day, but now it's two or three times less per week than before. And I haven't been even once this week.

Bai Siqin:     That's not very good. Actually, the busier you are, the more you need to exercise. I exercise for an hour every day. Now I feel more and more energetic. You see, I am much thinner than several months ago!

Hu Xinming:    That's true. You look much slimmer than last semester. Have you been on a diet recently?

Bai Siqin:     Yes. I have kept with it for three months. The result is not bad, huh? I've lost over ten pounds.

Hu Xinming:    No wonder you are getting slimmer and slimmer, almost the slimmest girl among us. How have you managed to lose weight? By controlling your diet?

Bai Siqin:     Mainly by exercising. And of course I do watch my diet as well. I used to love sweet things, but now I eat less and less sweet food.

Hu Xinming:    How did you come to think of losing weight?

Bai Siqin:     I wanted to do it a long time ago. I am a bit short, only 5 feet 1 inch, but my weight was over 150 pounds three months ago.

Hu Xinming:    Then you were even heavier than me when you were the heaviest.

Bai Siqin:     That's right. If I am too heavy, I am not so agile and I don't feel comfortable.

Hu Xinming:    I really should learn from you. But I always feel that I have too much homework, I am too busy, and I don't have time to exercise. Every day I even sleep two or three hours less than everyone else.

Bai Siqin:     Actually, the most important thing is to exercise, and play more sports. After you exercise, your health will be better than before. You will feel more alert, be able to concentrate more, and you will achieve better result in your studies.

## Lesson 10   I'll Get to Climb the Great Wall!

Hello, everyone!

Today, I would like to tell you about my plans for the winter vacation.

This is my last winter vacation at the university. I have talked to my boyfriend and we've decided to go for a trip to China. We have lots of relatives and friends in Beijing. I hope we will be able to meet all of them this time.

During the past two years, many more people have been going to China. As a result, it is getting much harder to buy plane tickets, especially those to Beijing which are more difficult to obtain. We haven't been able to book our tickets yet. We plan to leave in the middle of December and return in early January. We have called quite a few travel agencies and still don't know whether we will be able to get tickets. We sent in our visa applications last week and don't know whether they'll arrive this week. But we still have plenty of time and so will probably get them in time.

I also need to withdraw some cash and buy some traveler's checks from the bank. In China, it is not as convenient as in the US to pay with a credit card, although I have heard that credit cards are accepted at more and more stores. And you may withdraw US dollars at the Bank of China, or exchange for Renminbi based on the exchange rate of that day. This is much safer than carrying a lot of cash. Recently the exchange rate between US dollars and the Renminbi was approximately 1:7.97, 0.1 percent lower than last month.

The place I want to visit most this time in China is the Great Wall. I hear it is very tiring to climb the Great Wall, and only 50 percent of those who try it succeed in getting to the top. I think it is good exercise and will help me lose weight as well. And as the Chinese say: "You will not be a hero unless you have climbed the Great Wall." So, I must give it a try! I also want to go to Mt. Huang. My friends told me that the scenery there is picturesque. Very beautiful!

I also want to go and see the martial arts film *House of the Flying Daggers*, directed by Zhang Yimou. Those who have seen it all say that it has even better cinematography than *Hero*, and its plot is also very complicated.

You see, there are many things that I want to do this winter vacation, aren't there? I hope it will be a very rewarding journey.

That is my report today. Thank you all.

# 課文拼音 (课文拼音)
# LANGUAGE IN USE WITH PINYIN

## Lesson 1    My Friend Helps Me Move

| | |
|---|---|
| 謝進學: | 我們到了，讓我把車停在旁邊。 |
| 谢进学: | 我们到了，让我把车停在旁边。 |
| Xiè Jìnxué: | Wǒmen dào le, ràng wǒ bǎ chē tíng zài pángbiān. |

| | |
|---|---|
| 常天: | 等一會兒，我先把我的車開走，你再把車開過來。 |
| 常天: | 等一会儿，我先把我的车开走，你再把车开过来。 |
| Cháng Tiān: | Děng yíhuèr, wǒ xiān bǎ wǒde chē kāi zǒu, nǐ zài bǎ chē kāi guòlái. |

| | |
|---|---|
| 夏中明: | 你在倒車的時候，我幫你看看，別把房東的樹 |
| 夏中明: | 你在倒车的时候，我帮你看看，别把房东的树 |
| Xià Zhōngmíng: | Nǐ zài dàochē de shíhou, wǒ bāng nǐ kànkan, bié bǎ fángdōng de shù |

撞壞了。

撞坏了。

zhuàng huài le.

| | |
|---|---|
| 常天: | 對呀！上次我們搬進來的時候，不小心把房東的 |
| 常天: | 对呀！上次我们搬进来的时候，不小心把房东的 |
| Cháng Tiān: | Duìya! Shàngcì wǒmen bān jìnlái de shíhou, bù xiǎoxīn bǎ fángdōng de |

鏡子打破了，真不好意思。

镜子打破了，真不好意思。

jìngzi dǎpò le, zhēn bùhǎoyìsi.

| | |
|---|---|
| 謝進學: | 我們先把床和書桌搬到樓上去， |
| 谢进学: | 我们先把床和书桌搬到楼上去， |
| Xiè Jìnxué: | Wǒmen xiān bǎ chuáng hé shūzhuō bān dào lóushàng qù, |

然後再分工合作，怎麼樣？

然后再分工合作，怎么样？

ránhòu zài fēngōnghézuò, zěnmeyàng?

● 夏中明：　　　　好主意，我負責把行李搬下來、放好，我也會把
　　夏中明：　　　　好主意，我负责把行李搬下来、放好，我也会把
　　Xià Zhōngmíng:　Hǎo zhǔyi, wǒ fùzé bǎ xíngli bān xiàlái, fàng hǎo, wǒ yě huì bǎ

　　　　　　　　　　電腦裝好。
　　　　　　　　　　电脑装好。
　　　　　　　　　　diànnǎo zhuāng hǎo.

　　謝進學：　　　　好，我來掃地、整理客廳，再把書放好。
　　谢进学：　　　　好，我来扫地、整理客厅，再把书放好。
　　Xiè Jìnxué:　　　Hǎo, wǒ lái sǎodì, zhěnglǐ kètīng, zài bǎ shū fàng hǎo.

　　常天：　　　　　我來洗碗，把箱子打開，再把衣服掛好。
　　常天：　　　　　我来洗碗，把箱子打开，再把衣服挂好。
　　Cháng Tiān:　　 Wǒ lái xǐwǎn, bǎ xiāngzi dǎkāi, zài bǎ yīfu guàhǎo.

　　謝進學：　　　　謝謝你們幫我的忙，這次搬家把你們累壞了。
　　谢进学：　　　　谢谢你们帮我的忙，这次搬家把你们累坏了。
　　Xiè Jìnxué:　　　Xièxie nǐmen bāng wǒde máng, zhècì bānjiā bǎ nǐmen lèihuài le.

● 　　　　　　　　　今天晚上想吃什麼？我請客！
　　　　　　　　　　今天晚上想吃什么？我请客！
　　　　　　　　　　Jīntiān wǎnshang xiǎng chī shénme? Wǒ qǐngkè!

　　常天：　　　　　好極了！我快餓死了。
　　常天：　　　　　好极了！我快饿死了。
　　Cháng Tiān:　　 Hǎo jí le! Wǒ kuài èsǐ le.

　　夏中明：　　　　這附近有一家很不錯的中國飯館，可是我把
　　夏中明：　　　　这附近有一家很不错的中国饭馆，可是我把
　　Xià Zhōngmíng:　Zhè fùjìn yǒu yìjiā hěn búcuò de Zhōngguó fànguǎn, kěshì wǒ bǎ

　　　　　　　　　　地址忘了。
　　　　　　　　　　地址忘了。
　　　　　　　　　　dìzhǐ wàng le.

　　常天：　　　　　沒關係，我有。你們看，我找到了。
　　常天：　　　　　没关系，我有。你们看，我找到了。
　　Cháng Tiān:　　 Méi guānxi, wǒ yǒu. Nǐmen kàn, wǒ zhǎodào le.

　　謝進學：　　　　太好了，讓我把門窗關上。
● 　　谢进学：　　　　太好了，让我把门窗关上。
　　Xiè Jìnxué:　　　Tài hǎole, ràng wǒ bǎ ménchuāng guānshàng.

夏中明：　　　　別忘了把外套穿上，咱們走吧！
夏中明：　　　　别忘了把外套穿上，咱们走吧！
Xià Zhōngmíng:　Bié wàngle bǎ wàitào chuānshàng, zánmen zǒu ba!

## Lesson 2　My Sister Enjoys Beijing Opera!

李訪：　　　　那邊牆上掛著一張照片。那是誰？
李访：　　　　那边墙上挂着一张照片。那是谁？
Lǐ Fǎng:　　　Nàbiān qiángshàng guàzhe yìzhāng zhàopiàn. Nà shì shéi?

　　　　　　　我好像沒見過。
　　　　　　　我好像没见过。
　　　　　　　Wǒ hǎoxiàng méi jiàn guo.

關明遠：　　　　那是我姐姐照的照片。
关明远：　　　　那是我姐姐照的照片。
Guān Míngyuǎn:　Nà shì wǒ jiějie zhàode zhàopiàn.

李訪：　　　　她現在在哪兒？
李访：　　　　她现在在哪儿？
Lǐ Fǎng:　　　Tā xiànzài zài nǎr?

關明遠：　　　　她現在正在北京留學，她在那兒學中文，
关明远：　　　　她现在正在北京留学，她在那儿学中文，
Guān Míngyuǎn:　Tā xiànzài zhèngzài Běijīng liúxué, tā zài nàr xué Zhōngwén,

　　　　　　　已經在那兒住了一年多了。
　　　　　　　已经在那儿住了一年多了。
　　　　　　　yǐjīng zài nàr zhùle yìnián duō le.

李訪：　　　　她學中文學了多久了？
李访：　　　　她学中文学了多久了？
Lǐ Fǎng:　　　Tā xué Zhōngwén xué le duō jiǔ le?

關明遠：　　　　她學了三年了。
关明远：　　　　她学了三年了。
Guān Míngyuǎn:　Tā xué le sānnián le.

李訪：　　　　那是京劇的服裝吧！
李访：　　　　那是京剧的服装吧！
Lǐ Fǎng:　　　Nà shì Jīngjù de fúzhuāng ba!

關明遠：　是的。這是她上個月去看京劇的時候照的照片。
关明远：　是的。这是她上个月去看京剧的时候照的照片。
Guān Míngyuǎn:　Shìde. Zhè shì tā shàngge yuè qù kàn Jīngjù de shíhou zhàode zhàopiàn.

以前她沒看過京劇，現在看到了，她很高興。
以前她没看过京剧，现在看到了，她很高兴。
Yǐqián tā méi kàn guo Jīngjù, xiànzài kàndào le, tā hěn gāoxìng.

李訪：　舞台上面擺著什麼？好像是中國的各種
李访：　舞台上面摆着什么？好像是中国的各种
Lǐ Fǎng:　Wǔtái shàngmiàn bǎizhe shénme? Hǎoxiàng shì Zhōngguó de gèzhǒng

樂器。
乐器。
yuèqì.

關明遠：　沒錯！你看台上京劇演員，正忙著表演呢。
关明远：　没错！你看台上京剧演员，正忙着表演呢。
Guān Míngyuǎn:　Méicuò! Nǐ kàn táishàng Jīngjù yǎnyuán, zhèng máng zhe biǎoyǎn ne.

旁邊還坐著幾個樂師，有的在打鼓，有的在拉胡琴，
旁边还坐着几个乐师，有的在打鼓，有的在拉胡琴，
Pángbiān hái zuò zhe jǐge yuè shī, yǒude zài dǎgǔ, yǒude zài lā húqín,

他們都忙著彈奏自己的樂器。
他们都忙着弹奏自己的乐器。
tāmen dōu máng zhe tánzòu zìjǐ de yuèqì.

李訪：　這齣戲說的是什麼？好像很不錯。
李访：　这出戏说的是什么？好像很不错。
Lǐ Fǎng:　Zhèchū xì shuōde shì shénme? Hǎoxiàng hěn búcuò.

關明遠：　這齣戲說的是關公。你看關公他畫著紅臉，
关明远：　这出戏说的是关公。你看关公他画着红脸，
Guān Míngyuǎn:　Zhèchū xì shuōde shì Guāngōng. Nǐ kàn Guāngōng tā huà zhe hóngliǎn,

手上拿著一把大刀，真神氣！
手上拿着一把大刀，真神气！
shǒushàng ná zhe yìbǎ dàdāo, zhēn shénqì!

李訪：　　　　　人真不少啊！你看，座位都坐滿了，有的觀眾
李访：　　　　　人真不少啊！你看，座位都坐满了，有的观众
Lǐ Fǎng:　　　　Rén zhēn bùshǎo a! Nǐ kàn, zuòwèi dōu zuòmǎn le, yǒude guānzhòng

　　　　　　　　還得站著。對了，你看過京劇嗎？
　　　　　　　　还得站着。对了，你看过京剧吗？
　　　　　　　　hái děi zhàn zhe. Duìle, nǐ kàn guo Jīngjù ma?

關明遠：　　　　我看過兩次，都是在上海看的。
关明远：　　　　我看过两次，都是在上海看的。
Guān Míngyuǎn:　Wǒ kàn guo liǎngcì, dōushì zài Shànghǎi kàn de.

李訪：　　　　　你在中國的時候去過上海，還去過哪兒？
李访：　　　　　你在中国的时候去过上海，还去过哪儿？
Lǐ Fǎng:　　　　Nǐ zài Zhōngguó de shíhou qù guo Shànghǎi, hái qù guo nǎr?

關明遠：　　　　我只去過上海。那時候，我每天都忙著上課，
关明远：　　　　我只去过上海。那时候，我每天都忙着上课，
Guān Míngyuǎn:　Wǒ zhǐ qù guo Shànghǎi. Nà shíhou, wǒ měitiān dōu máng zhe shàngkè,

　　　　　　　　所以沒有機會去北京和長城。
　　　　　　　　所以没有机会去北京和长城。
　　　　　　　　suǒyǐ méiyou jīhuì qù Běijīng hé Chángchéng.

李訪：　　　　　我聽說上海的小籠包很好吃，你吃過嗎？
李访：　　　　　我听说上海的小笼包很好吃，你吃过吗？
Lǐ Fǎng:　　　　Wǒ tīngshuō Shànghǎi de xiǎolóngbāo hěn hǎochī, nǐ chī guo ma?

關明遠：　　　　吃過，我還學過做小籠包呢！
关明远：　　　　吃过，我还学过做小笼包呢！
Guān Míngyuǎn:　Chī guo, wǒ hái xué guo zuò xiǎolóngbāo ne!

李訪：　　　　　真有意思！我也想去中國看看。
李访：　　　　　真有意思！我也想去中国看看。
Lǐ Fǎng:　　　　Zhēn yǒu yìsi! Wǒ yě xiǎng qù Zhōngguó kànkan.

關明遠：　　　　我下個月要去中國，你跟我去吧！我們可以一起
关明远：　　　　我下个月要去中国，你跟我去吧！我们可以一起
Guān Míngyuǎn:　Wǒ xiàge yuè yào qù Zhōngguó, nǐ gēn wǒ qù ba! Wǒmen kěyi yìqǐ

　　　　　　　　去看京劇，怎麼樣？
　　　　　　　　去看京剧，怎么样？
　　　　　　　　qù kàn Jīngjù, zěnmeyàng?

李訪：        好，一言為定！
李访：        好，一言为定！
Lǐ Fǎng:      Hǎo, yì yán wéi dìng!

## Lesson 3    Visiting Shanghai

Scene 1: 在飛機上
　　　　 在飞机上
　　　　 Zài fēijī shàng

各位旅客，飛機再過二十分鐘就要降落了，
各位旅客，飞机再过二十分钟就要降落了，
Gèwèi lǚkè, fēijī zài guò èrshí fēnzhōng jiùyào jiàngluò le,

我們就要到上海的浦東機場了。請您回到您的座位坐好，
我们就要到上海的浦东机场了。请您回到您的座位坐好，
wǒmen jiùyào dào Shànghǎi de Pǔdōng Jīchǎng le. Qǐng nín huídào nín de zuòwèi zuòhǎo,

把安全帶繫上。請您也把計算機等電子用品關上。
把安全带系上。请您也把计算机等电子用品关上。
bǎ ānquándài jìshàng. Qǐng nín yě bǎ jìsuànjī děng diànzǐ yòngpǐn guānshàng.

謝謝您的合作。再次感謝您搭乘中國航空。
谢谢您的合作。再次感谢您搭乘中国航空。
Xièxie nín de hézuò. Zài cì gǎnxiè nín dāchéng Zhōngguó Hángkōng.

Scene 2: 在機場
　　　　 在机场
　　　　 Zài jīchǎng

關明遠：        我們到了，我們搭出租汽車去旅館吧！搭出租汽車去
关明远：        我们到了，我们搭出租汽车去旅馆吧！搭出租汽车去
Guān Míngyuǎn:  Wǒmen dàole, wǒmen dā chūzū qìchē qù lǚguǎn ba! Dā chūzū qìchē qù

　　　　　　　快多了。
　　　　　　　快多了。
　　　　　　　kuàiduō le.

李訪：        搭出租汽車去有多快？
李访：        搭出租汽车去有多快？
Lǐ Fǎng:      Dā chūzū qìchē qù yǒu duōkuài?

關明遠：　　　　　　我想，不到十分鐘就可以到了。
关明远：　　　　　　我想，不到十分钟就可以到了。
Guān Míngyuǎn:　　Wǒ xiǎng, búdào shí fēnzhōng jiù kěyǐ dào le.

李訪：　　　　　　　好的。我們來問路吧！
李访：　　　　　　　好的。我们来问路吧！
Lǐ Fǎng:　　　　　　Hǎode. Wǒmen lái wènlù ba!

關明遠：　　　　　　先生，對不起，請問，出租汽車站在哪兒？
关明远：　　　　　　先生，对不起，请问，出租汽车站在哪儿？
Guān Míngyuǎn:　　Xiānsheng, duìbuqǐ, qǐngwèn, chūzū qìchē zhàn zài nǎr?

路人：　　　　　　　出租汽車站在那棟樓的後邊。你從這兒往前走，
路人：　　　　　　　出租汽车站在那栋楼的后边。你从这儿往前走，
Lùrén:　　　　　　　Chūzū qìchē zhàn zài nàdòng lóu de hòubiān. Nǐ cóng zhèr wǎng qián zǒu,

　　　　　　　　　　走到前面的交叉口，往左拐。從那兒再往前
　　　　　　　　　　走到前面的交叉口，往左拐。从那儿再往前
　　　　　　　　　　zǒudào qiánmiàn de jiāochākǒu, wǎng zuǒ guǎi. Cóng nàr zài wǎng qián

　　　　　　　　　　一直走，過兩個路口，你就能看到出租汽車站了。
　　　　　　　　　　一直走，过两个路口，你就能看到出租汽车站了。
　　　　　　　　　　yìzhí zǒu, guò liǎngge lùkǒu, nǐ jiù néng kàndào chūzū qìchē zhàn le.

關明遠：　　　　　　謝謝。
关明远：　　　　　　谢谢。
Lǐ Fǎng:　　　　　　Xièxie.

路人：　　　　　　　不客氣。
路人：　　　　　　　不客气。
Lùrén:　　　　　　　Búkèqi.

Scene 3: 在出租汽車站
　　　　　在出租汽车站
　　　　　Zài chūzū qìchē zhàn

司機：　　　　　　　請問，兩位先生要搭車，是嗎？
司机：　　　　　　　请问，两位先生要搭车，是吗？
Sījī:　　　　　　　　Qǐngwèn, liǎngwèi xiānsheng yào dāchē, shìma?

關明遠：　　　　　　是的，我們要去假日旅館，離這兒有多遠？
关明远：　　　　　　是的，我们要去假日旅馆，离这儿有多远？
Guān Míngyuǎn:　　Shìde, wǒmen yào qù jiàrì lǚguǎn, lí zhèr yǒu duō yuǎn?

● 司機:　　　　　有三公里，不太遠，請上車。來，我先把行李
司機:　　　　　有三公里，不太远，请上车。来，我先把行李
Sījī:　　　　　Yǒu sān gōnglǐ, bú tài yuǎn, qǐng shàngchē. Lái, wǒ xiān bǎ xíngli

放到後車箱去。
放到后车箱去。
fàngdào hòuchēxiāng qù.

......

李訪:　　　　　中國看起來發展得很快。
李访:　　　　　中国看起来发展得很快。
Lǐ Fǎng:　　　　Zhōngguó kàn qǐlái fāzhǎn de hěnkuài.

關明遠:　　　　是呀！這兒變得太快了！
关明远:　　　　是呀！这儿变得太快了！
Guān Míngyuǎn:　Shì ya! Zhèr biàn de tài kuài le!

● 司機:　　　　　聽起來你好像來過上海。
司机:　　　　　听起来你好像来过上海。
Sījī:　　　　　Tīng qǐlái nǐ hǎoxiàng lái guo Shànghǎi.

關明遠:　　　　是的。我兩年前來過，可是現在有很多路
关明远:　　　　是的。我两年前来过，可是现在有很多路
Guān Míngyuǎn:　Shì de. Wǒ liǎng nián qián lái guo, kěshì xiànzài yǒu hěnduō lù

我都想不起來了。
我都想不起来了。
wǒ dōu xiǎng bù qǐlái le.

司機:　　　　　沒錯！上海變化得非常快，你看，本來這兒
司机:　　　　　没错！上海变化得非常快，你看，本来这儿
Sījī:　　　　　Méicuò! Shànghǎi biànhuà de fēicháng kuài, nǐ kàn, běnlái zhèr

還都是農田，現在都變成大樓和大馬路了。
还都是农田，现在都变成大楼和大马路了。
hái dōu shì nóngtián, xiànzài dōu biànchéng dàlóu hé dà mǎlù le.

李訪:　　　　　你看，那棟樓真高，不知道有多高?
李访:　　　　　你看，那栋楼真高，不知道有多高?
● Lǐ Fǎng:　　　　Nǐ kàn, nàdòng lóu zhēngāo, bùzhīdào yǒu duō gāo?

司機：　　　　喔！那棟樓是新的，聽說有九十公尺高。
司机：　　　　喔！那栋楼是新的，听说有九十公尺高。
Sījī:　　　　　Ō! Nàdòng lóu shì xīnde, tīngshuō yǒu jiǔ shí gōngchǐ gāo.

關明遠：　　　對了，我想起來了，那條是中山路。以前我常
关明远：　　　对了，我想起来了，那条是中山路。以前我常
Guān Míngyuǎn: Duì le, wǒ xiǎng qǐlái le, nà tiáo shì Zhōngshānlù. Yǐqián wǒ cháng

　　　　　　　在那個紅綠燈等著過馬路，過了馬路以後我就向
　　　　　　　在那个红绿灯等着过马路，过了马路以后我就向
　　　　　　　zài nàge hónglǜdēng děng zhe guò mǎlù, guò le mǎlù yǐhòu wǒ jiù xiàng

　　　　　　　右轉，再走兩三分鐘，就到了上海小吃店。
　　　　　　　右转，再走两三分钟，就到了上海小吃店。
　　　　　　　yòu zhuǎn, zài zǒu liǎng sān fēnzhōng, jiù dào le Shànghǎi xiǎochī diàn.

　　　　　　　那兒的東西好吃極了！
　　　　　　　那儿的东西好吃极了！
　　　　　　　Nàr de dōngxi hǎochī jí le!

司機：　　　　假日旅館就在前面，可是我不能在這兒往左轉，
司机：　　　　假日旅馆就在前面，可是我不能在这儿往左转，
Sījī:　　　　　Jiàrì lǚguǎn jiùzài qiánmiàn, kěshì wǒ bùnéng zài zhèr wǎng zuǒzhuǎn,

　　　　　　　我得多拐幾個彎兒。
　　　　　　　我得多拐几个弯儿。
　　　　　　　wǒ děi duō guǎi jǐge wār.

李訪：　　　　行，沒問題。
李访：　　　　行，没问题。
Lǐ Fǎng:　　　Xíng, méiwèntí.

……

司機：　　　　好，我們到了。
司机：　　　　好，我们到了。
Sījī:　　　　　Hǎo, wǒmen dào le.

李訪：　　　　車費多少錢？
李访：　　　　车费多少钱？
Lǐ Fǎng:　　　Chēfèi duōshǎo qián?

● 司機：　　　　　　一共是二十八塊人民幣。
　司机：　　　　　　一共是二十八块人民币。
　Sījī:　　　　　　　Yígòng shì èr shí bā kuài Rénmínbì.

　關明遠：　　　　　給你三十塊。
　关明远：　　　　　给你三十块。
　Guān Míngyuǎn:　Gěi nǐ sān shí kuài.

　司機：　　　　　　找你兩塊，謝謝！
　司机：　　　　　　找你两块，谢谢！
　Sījī:　　　　　　　Zhǎo nǐ liǎng kuài, xièxie!

## Lesson 4　Visiting a Chinese Family

　老師：　　　　　　歡迎，歡迎，請進！
　老师：　　　　　　欢迎，欢迎，请进！
　Lǎoshī:　　　　　 Huānyíng, huānyíng, qǐngjìn!

　關明遠：　　　　　李訪，來，我給你們介紹一下，這是王老師，
● 关明远：　　　　　李访，来，我给你们介绍一下，这是王老师，
　Guān Míngyuǎn:　Lǐ Fǎng, lái, wǒ gěi nǐmen jièshào yíxià, zhèshì Wáng lǎoshī,

　　　　　　　　　　這是師母。
　　　　　　　　　　这是师母。
　　　　　　　　　　zhèshì shīmǔ.

　李訪：　　　　　　你們好。
　李访：　　　　　　你们好。
　Lǐ Fǎng:　　　　　Nǐmen hǎo.

　關明遠：　　　　　老師，這是一些您喜歡的美國文學書。師母，
　关明远：　　　　　老师，这是一些您喜欢的美国文学书。师母，
　Guān Míngyuǎn:　Lǎoshī, zhèshì yìxiē nín xǐhuān de Měiguó wénxué shū. Shīmǔ,

　　　　　　　　　　這些維生素是給您和老師吃的，祝你們永遠
　　　　　　　　　　这些维生素是给您和老师吃的，祝你们永远
　　　　　　　　　　zhèxiē wéishēngsù shì gěi nín hé lǎoshī chī de, zhù nǐmen yǒngyuǎn

　　　　　　　　　　健康年輕。
　　　　　　　　　　健康年轻。
　　　　　　　　　　jiànkāng niánqīng.

師母：　　　　來了就好，怎麼還帶東西來呢！讓你破費了。
师母：　　　　来了就好，怎么还带东西来呢！让你破费了。
Shīmǔ:　　　Láile jiùhǎo, zěnme hái dài dōngxi lái ne! Ràng nǐ pòfèi le.

關明遠：　　　沒什麼，小意思。
关明远：　　　没什么，小意思。
Guān Míngyuǎn: Méi shénme, xiǎoyìsi.

老師：　　　　你們難得來上海，師母特地做了一些拿手菜。
老师：　　　　你们难得来上海，师母特地做了一些拿手菜。
Lǎoshī:　　　Nǐmen nándé lái Shànghǎi, shīmǔ tèdì zuò le yìxiē náshǒucài.

　　　　　　　來，來，快上座，菜都要涼了！
　　　　　　　来，来，快上座，菜都要凉了！
　　　　　　　Lái, lái, kuài shàngzuò, cài dōuyào liáng le!

關明遠：　　　老師，師母，你們倆還是跟以前一樣，看起來真精神。
关明远：　　　老师，师母，你们俩还是跟以前一样，看起来真精神。
Guān Míngyuǎn: Lǎoshī, shīmǔ, nǐmen liǎ háishì gēn yǐqián yíyàng, kàn qǐlái zhēn jīngshen.

師母：　　　　不行了！我們是一天比一天老了，白頭髮比以前多了，
师母：　　　　不行了！我们是一天比一天老了，白头发比以前多了，
Shīmǔ:　　　Bùxíng le! Wǒmen shì yìtiān bǐ yìtiān lǎo le, bái tóufa bǐ yǐqián duō le,

　　　　　　　眼睛也花了，做事也沒有以前那麼快了。
　　　　　　　眼睛也花了，做事也没有以前那么快了。
　　　　　　　yǎnjīng yě huā le, zuòshì yě méiyou yǐqián nàme kuài le.

老師：　　　　李訪，第一次來中國，適應嗎？
老师：　　　　李访，第一次来中国，适应吗？
Lǎoshī:　　　Lǐ Fǎng, dìyīcì lái Zhōngguó, shìyìng ma?

李訪：　　　　還可以，現在還有一點兒時差。白天覺得很睏，
李访：　　　　还可以，现在还有一点儿时差。白天觉得很困，
Lǐ Fǎng:　　　Hái kěyǐ, xiànzài háiyǒu yìdiǎr shíchā. Báitiān juéde hěn kùn,

　　　　　　　晚上就睡不著。不過，今天比昨天好多了。
　　　　　　　晚上就睡不着。不过，今天比昨天好多了。
　　　　　　　wǎnshang jiù shuìbuzháo. Búguò, jīntiān bǐ zuótiān hǎoduō le.

● 關明遠：　李訪說這兒的天氣比匹茲堡熱。還有，這兒的人
　關明远：　李访说这儿的天气比匹兹堡热。还有，这儿的人
　Guān Míngyuǎn:　Lǐ Fǎng shuō zhèr de tiānqì bǐ Pǐzībǎo rè. Háiyǒu, zhèr de rén

　　　　　　　也比匹茲堡多，街道上到處都是人，他還不太習慣。
　　　　　　　也比匹兹堡多，街道上到处都是人，他还不太习惯。
　　　　　　　yě bǐ Pǐzībǎo duō, jiēdào shàng dàochù dōushì rén, tā hái bú tài xíguàn.

李訪：　我長這麼大，第一次看到這麼多人。
李访：　我长这么大，第一次看到这么多人。
Lǐ Fǎng:　Wǒ zhǎng zhème dà, dìyīcì kàndào zhème duō rén.

師母：　你們倆誰比較大？
师母：　你们俩谁比较大？
Shīmǔ:　Nǐmen liǎ shéi bǐjiào dà?

關明遠：　我跟李訪一樣大，都是二十四歲。
关明远：　我跟李访一样大，都是二十四岁。
Guān Míngyuǎn:　Wǒ gēn Lǐ Fǎng yíyàng dà, dōushì èrshí sì suì.

● 師母：　對了，不要只說話，忘了吃菜。來，來，來，多吃一點兒。
　师母：　对了，不要只说话，忘了吃菜。来，来，来，多吃一点儿。
　Shīmǔ:　Duìle, búyào zhǐ shuōhuà, wàng le chīcài. Lái, lái, lái, duō chī yìdiǎr.

老師：　這是師母做的年糕，味道很地道，你們嚐嚐。
老师：　这是师母做的年糕，味道很地道，你们尝尝。
Lǎoshī:　Zhèshì shīmǔ zuò de niángāo, wèidao hěn dìdao, nǐmen chángchang.

……

關明遠：　師母您做的飯真好吃。
关明远：　师母您做的饭真好吃。
Guān Míngyuǎn:　Shīmǔ nín zuò de fàn zhēn hǎochī.

李訪：　是啊！色香味俱全，我吃了很多，現在已經很飽了。
李访：　是啊！色香味俱全，我吃了很多，现在已经很饱了。
Lǐ Fǎng:　Shì a! Sè xiāng wèi jù quán, wǒ chī le hěnduō, xiànzài yǐjīng hěnbǎo le.

師母：　哪裡，哪裡！只是家常便飯。
师母：　哪里，哪里！只是家常便饭。
● Shīmǔ:　Nǎlǐ, nǎlǐ! Zhǐshì jiācháng biànfàn.

老師：　　　難得我們相聚，來，一起來乾一杯。今天真高興，
老师：　　　难得我们相聚，来，一起来干一杯。今天真高兴，
Lǎoshī:　　Nándé wǒmen xiāngjù, lái, yìqǐ lái gān yìbēi. Jīntiān zhēn gāoxìng,

"有朋自遠方來，不亦樂乎！"
"有朋自远方来，不亦乐乎！"
"yǒu péng zì yuǎnfāng lái, bú yì yuè hū!"

老師、師母、關明遠、李訪：乾杯！
老师、师母、关明远、李访：干杯！
Lǎoshī, Shīmǔ, Guān Míngyuǎn, Lǐ Fǎng: Gānbēi!

# Lesson 5　My Trip to China

中國行
中国行
Zhōngguó xíng

十月二十日　　　星期三　　　天氣：陰
十月二十日　　　星期三　　　天气：阴
Shíyuè èrshí rì　　Xīngqī sān　　Tiānqì: Yīn

我們坐了三十多個小時的飛機，終於回到美國來了。從中國
我们坐了三十多个小时的飞机，终于回到美国来了。从中国
Wǒmen zuòle sānshíduōge xiǎoshí de fēijī, zhōngyú huídào Měiguó láile. Cóng Zhōngguó

到美國本來十幾個小時就到了，但是在日本轉機的時候，因為我們
到美国本来十几个小时就到了，但是在日本转机的时候，因为我们
dào Měiguó běnlái shíjǐge xiǎoshí jiù dào le, dànshì zài Rìběn zhuǎnjī de shíhou, yīnwèi wǒmen

的飛機誤點了，所以沒趕上我們的班機。我們在機場等了五個小時
的飞机误点了，所以没赶上我们的班机。我们在机场等了五个小时
de fēijī wùdiǎn le, suǒyǐ méi gǎnshàng wǒmende bānjī. Wǒmen zài jīchǎng děngle wǔge xiǎoshí

以後，才坐上了飛機。這次飛機誤點把我跟李訪累壞了。在飛機上，
以后，才坐上了飞机。这次飞机误点把我跟李访累坏了。在飞机上，
yǐhòu, cái zuòshàngle fēijī. Zhècì fēijī wùdiǎn bǎ wǒ gēn Lǐ Fǎng lèihuài le. Zài fēijī shàng,

我們一把行李放好，就一直睡覺，睡到飛機降落以後才起來。
我们一把行李放好，就一直睡觉，睡到飞机降落以后才起来。
wǒmen yì bǎ xíngli fànghǎo, jiù yìzhí shuìjiào, shuìdào fēijī jiàngluò yǐhòu cái qǐlái.

不過這次很高興能在上海和老師再次相聚。老師和師母
不过这次很高兴能在上海和老师再次相聚。老师和师母
Búguò zhècì hěn gāoxìng néng zài Shànghǎi hé lǎoshī zàicì xiāngjù. Lǎoshī hé shīmǔ

看起來都很精神，他們還是跟以前一樣非常熱情、好客。師母還
看起来都很精神，他们还是跟以前一样非常热情、好客。师母还
kàn qǐlái dōu hěn jīngshen, tāmen háishì gēn yǐqián yíyàng fēicháng rèqíng, hàokè. Shīmǔ hái

特地做了幾樣很地道的上海菜，讓我們嚐嚐，其中我最喜歡
特地做了几样很地道的上海菜，让我们尝尝，其中我最喜欢
tèdì zuòle jǐyàng hěn dìdao de Shànghǎi cài, ràng wǒmen chángchang, qízhōng wǒ zuì xǐhuān

的是上海年糕。真好吃！
的是上海年糕。真好吃！
de shì Shànghǎi niángāo. Zhēn hǎochī!

我還帶李訪去看了京劇，我們看得津津有味，他也覺得大開眼界。
我还带李访去看了京剧，我们看得津津有味，他也觉得大开眼界。
Wǒ hái dài Lǐ Fǎng qù kànle jīngjù, wǒmen kànde jīnjīnyǒuwèi, tā yě juéde dàkāiyǎnjiè.

不過，我聽說現在的京劇劇團比以前少了，所以票也比以前貴了。
不过，我听说现在的京剧剧团比以前少了，所以票也比以前贵了。
Búguò, wǒ tīngshuō xiànzàide jīngjù jùtuán bǐ yǐqián shǎole, suǒyǐ piào yě bǐ yǐqián guì le.

上海真的變得很快，有些路都很難找到了。我們手裡
上海真的变得很快，有些路都很难找到了。我们手里
Shànghǎi zhēnde biànde hěn kuài, yǒuxiē lù dōu hěn nán zhǎodào le. Wǒmen shǒuli

拿著地圖，忙著問路、找方向。常常應該向左拐的時候，
拿着地图，忙着问路、找方向。常常应该向左拐的时候，
názhe dìtú, mángzhe wènlù, zhǎo fāngxiàng. Chángcháng yīnggāi xiàng zuǒ guǎi de shíhou,

我們轉錯了，往右拐了，鬧了不少笑話。
我们转错了，往右拐了，闹了不少笑话。
wǒmen zhuǎn cuò le, wǎng yòu guǎi le, nàole bùshǎo xiàohua.

中國真的是一天比一天繁榮、進步了。在大城市裡，高樓大廈
中国真的是一天比一天繁荣、进步了。在大城市里，高楼大厦
Zhōngguó zhēnde shì yìtiān bǐ yìtiān fánróng, jìnbù le. Zài dà chéngshì lǐ, gāolóu dàshà

跟美國的一樣高，到處都能看到外國人。
跟美国的一样高，到处都能看到外国人。
gēn Měiguó de yíyàng gāo, dàochù dōu néng kàndào wàiguórén.

這次在中國的時間雖然很短，可是我們都玩得很高興。
这次在中国的时间虽然很短，可是我们都玩得很高兴。
Zhècì zài Zhōngguó de shíjiān suīrán hěn duǎn, kěshì wǒmen dōu wánde hěn gāoxìng.

李訪說他現在可以跟別人說他去過中國、看過京劇了。還有，
李访说他现在可以跟别人说他去过中国、看过京剧了。还有，
Lǐ Fǎng shuō tā xiànzài kěyǐ gēn biérén shuō tā qù guo Zhōngguó, kàn guo jīngjù le. Háiyǒu,

他也嚐了很多中國的小吃，都很棒！
他也尝了很多中国的小吃，都很棒！
tā yě cháng le hěnduō Zhōngguó de xiǎochī, dōu hěn bàng!

我們倆都覺得這次去中國旅行，挺不錯的，也非常值得。
我们俩都觉得这次去中国旅行，挺不错的，也非常值得。
Wǒmen liǎ dōu juéde zhècì qù Zhōngguó lǚxíng, tǐng búcuò de, yě fēicháng zhídé.

下次有機會，我們還要再去。
下次有机会，我们还要再去。
Xiàcì yǒu jīhuì, wǒmen hái yào zài qù.

## Lesson 6    Opening a Bank Account

Scene 1: 在路上
　　　　　在路上
　　　　　Zài lùshàng

| | |
|---|---|
| 關京華： | 小琴，我要去銀行開一個帳戶，這樣我存款、 |
| 关京华： | 小琴，我要去银行开一个账户，这样我存款、 |
| Guān Jīnghuá: | Xiǎoqín, wǒ yào qù yínháng kāi yíge zhàng hù, zhèyàng wǒ cúnkuǎn, |
| | 取款就方便多了。你知道哪家銀行比較好嗎？ |
| | 取款就方便多了。你知道哪家银行比较好吗？ |
| | qǔkuǎn jiù fāngbiàn duō le. Nǐ zhīdào nǎ jiā yínháng bǐjiào hǎo ma? |
| 方小琴： | 我常常去大華銀行存款、取款。那兒的服務不錯， |
| 方小琴： | 我常常去大华银行存款、取款。那儿的服务不错， |
| Fāng Xiǎoqín: | Wǒ chángcháng qù Dàhuá Yínháng cúnkuǎn, qǔkuǎn. Nàr de fúwù búcuò, |
| | 利率也比較高，現在儲蓄帳戶的利率是百分之三點二。 |
| | 利率也比较高，现在储蓄账户的利率是百分之三点二。 |
| | lìlǜ yě bǐjiào gāo, xiànzài chǔxù zhànghù de lìlǜ shì bǎifēn zhī sān diǎn èr. |

關京華:　　　　那我就去大華銀行吧。
关京华:　　　　那我就去大华银行吧。
Guān Jīnghuá:　Nà wǒ jiù qù Dàhuá Yínháng ba.

Scene 2: 在銀行
　　　　　在银行
　　　　　Zài yínháng

關京華:　　　　先生，我想開一個有利息的支票帳戶。請問，
关京华:　　　　先生，我想开一个有利息的支票账户。请问，
Guān Jīnghuá:　Xiānsheng, wǒ xiǎng kāi yíge yǒu lìxi de zhīpiào zhànghù. Qǐngwèn,

　　　　　有利息的支票帳戶利率是多少？
　　　　　有利息的支票账户利率是多少？
　　　　　yǒu lìxi de zhīpiào zhànghù lìlǜ shì duōshǎo?

職員:　　　　最近利率都比較低，今天是百分之二點六。
职员:　　　　最近利率都比较低，今天是百分之二点六。
Zhíyuán:　　Zuìjìn lìlǜ dōu bǐjiào dī, jīntiān shì bǎifēn zhī èr diǎn liù.

關京華:　　　　怎麼這麼低呀？我聽說是百分之三點二呢。
关京华:　　　　怎么这么低呀？我听说是百分之三点二呢。
Guān Jīnghuá:　Zěnme zhème dī ya? Wǒ tīngshuō shì bǎifēn zhī sān diǎn èr ne.

職員:　　　　那是儲蓄帳戶，儲蓄帳戶的利率高一點兒，是百分之
职员:　　　　那是储蓄账户，储蓄账户的利率高一点儿，是百分之
Zhíyuán:　　Nà shì chǔxù zhànghù, chǔxù zhànghù de lìlǜ gāo yìdiǎr, shì bǎifēn zhī

　　　　　三點二。這種帳戶每個月可以開三張支票。
　　　　　三点二。这种账户每个月可以开三张支票。
　　　　　sān diǎn èr. Zhèzhǒng zhànghù měige yuè kěyǐ kāi sānzhāng zhīpiào.

　　　　　您想開哪一種？
　　　　　您想开哪一种？
　　　　　Nín xiǎng kāi nǎyìzhǒng?

關京華:　　　　我想一個月開三張支票差不多夠了。
关京华:　　　　我想一个月开三张支票差不多够了。
Guān Jīnghuá:　Wǒ xiǎng yíge yuè kāi sānzhāng zhīpiào chàbuduō gòu le.

　　　　　我就開一個儲蓄帳戶吧。
　　　　　我就开一个储蓄账户吧。
　　　　　Wǒ jiù kāi yíge chǔxù zhànghù ba.

| 職員: | 好，請把這張開帳戶的單子填一下，謝謝。 |
|---|---|
| 职员: | 好，请把这张开账户的单子填一下，谢谢。 |
| Zhíyuán: | Hǎo, qǐng bǎ zhèzhāng kāi zhànghù de dānzi tián yíxià, xièxie. |

請問您今天想存多少錢？

请问您今天想存多少钱？

Qǐngwèn nín jīntiān xiǎng cún duōshǎo qián?

| 關京華: | 我這兒是三千元美金。 |
|---|---|
| 关京华: | 我这儿是三千元美金。 |
| Guān Jīnghuá: | Wǒ zhèr shì sānqiān yuán Měijīn. |

| 職員: | 好......一個星期以後，您會收到我們給您寄去的 |
|---|---|
| 职员: | 好......一个星期以后，您会收到我们给您寄去的 |
| Zhíyuán: | Hǎo . . . Yíge xīngqī yǐhòu, nín huì shōudào wǒmen gěi nín jìqù de |

支票簿和取款卡。您可以拿取款卡在自動取款機

支票簿和取款卡。您可以拿取款卡在自动取款机

zhīpiàobù hé qǔkuǎnkǎ. Nín kěyǐ ná qǔkuǎnkǎ zài zìdòng qǔkuǎnjī

那兒取現金。

那儿取现金。

nàr qǔ xiànjīn.

| 關京華: | 我可以在你們這兒申請一張信用卡嗎？ |
|---|---|
| 关京华: | 我可以在你们这儿申请一张信用卡吗？ |
| Guān Jīnghuá: | Wǒ kěyǐ zài nǐmen zhèr shēnqǐng yìzhāng xìnyòngkǎ ma? |

| 職員: | 當然可以。請把這張申請信用卡的表填一下。 |
|---|---|
| 职员: | 当然可以。请把这张申请信用卡的表填一下。 |
| Zhíyuán: | Dāngrán kěyi. Qǐng bǎ zhèzhāng shēnqǐng xìnyòngkǎ de biǎo tián yíxià. |

| 關京華: | 下個月我要去中國，要換一些人民幣。 |
|---|---|
| 关京华: | 下个月我要去中国，要换一些人民币。 |
| Guān Jīnghuá: | Xiàge yuè wǒ yào qù Zhōngguó, yào huàn yìxiē Rénmínbì. |

請問美金換人民幣的匯率是多少？

请问美金换人民币的汇率是多少？

Qǐngwèn Měijīn huàn Rénmínbì de huìlǜ shì duōshǎo?

| 職員: | 今天的匯率是一比六點五三。 |
|---|---|
| 职员: | 今天的汇率是一比六点五三。 |
| Zhíyuán: | Jīntiān de huìlǜ shì yī bǐ liù diǎn wǔ sān. |

| 關京華： | 兌換外幣的地方在哪兒？ |
|---|---|
| 关京华： | 兑换外币的地方在哪儿？ |
| Guān Jīnghuá: | Duìhuàn wàibì de dìfang zài nǎr? |

| 職員： | 就在左邊的櫃台那兒。 |
|---|---|
| 职员： | 就在左边的柜台那儿。 |
| Zhíyuán: | Jiù zài zuǒbiān de guìtái nàr. |

| 關京華： | 謝謝。再見。 |
|---|---|
| 关京华： | 谢谢。再见。 |
| Guān Jīnghuá: | Xièxie. Zàijiàn. |

## Lesson 7 · Booking Our Trip to China

| 方小琴： | 文華，你在找什麼？ |
|---|---|
| 方小琴： | 文华，你在找什么？ |
| Fāng Xiǎoqín: | Wénhuá, nǐ zài zhǎo shénme? |

| 金文華： | 我在找一本電話簿，我的電話簿找不到了。 |
|---|---|
| 金文华： | 我在找一本电话簿，我的电话簿找不到了。 |
| Jīn Wénhuá: | Wǒ zài zhǎo yìběn diànhuàbù, wǒde diànhuàbù zhǎobudào le. |

| 方小琴： | 你看看電話旁邊有沒有？ |
|---|---|
| 方小琴： | 你看看电话旁边有没有？ |
| Fāng Xiǎoqín: | Nǐ kànkan diànhuà pángbiān yǒuméiyǒu? |

| 金文華： | 好像沒有……啊，我看到了，在桌子下面。今年寒假 |
|---|---|
| 金文华： | 好像没有……啊，我看到了，在桌子下面。今年寒假 |
| Jīn Wénhuá: | Hǎoxiàng méiyǒu . . . À, wǒ kàndào le, zài zhuōzi xiàmiàn. Jīnnián hánjià |

我和方明要去中國旅遊，我要找一家旅行社
我和方明要去中国旅游，我要找一家旅行社
wǒ hé Fāng Míng yào qù Zhōngguó lǚyóu, wǒ yào zhǎo yì jiā lǚxíngshè

的電話號碼，我想訂去中國的機票。
的电话号码，我想订去中国的机票。
de diànhuà hàomǎ, wǒ xiǎng dìng qù Zhōngguó de jīpiào.

| 方小琴: | 真的嗎? 太棒了! 我真羡慕你們。 |
| 方小琴: | 真的吗? 太棒了! 我真羡慕你们。 |
| Fāng Xiǎoqín: | Zhēnde ma? Tài bàng le! Wǒ zhēn xiànmù nǐmen. |

你們打算去哪兒玩呢?
你们打算去哪儿玩呢?
Nǐmen dǎsuàn qù nǎr wár ne?

| 金文華: | 方明在北京有很多親戚,我們原來想先去 |
| 金文华: | 方明在北京有很多亲戚,我们原来想先去 |
| Jīn Wénhuá: | Fāng Míng zài Běijīng yǒu hěnduō qīnqi, wǒmen yuánlái xiǎng xiān qù |

北京玩幾天,跟他的親戚聚一聚,然後抽空去拜訪
北京玩几天,跟他的亲戚聚一聚,然后抽空去拜访
Běijīng wán jǐ tiān, gēn tāde qīnqi jùyijù, ránhòu chōukòng qù bàifǎng

他以前的老師,再去別的地方看看,可是我一直買不到
他以前的老师,再去别的地方看看,可是我一直买不到
tā yǐqián de lǎoshī, zài qù bié de dìfang kànkan, kěshì wǒ yìzhí mǎibudào

去北京的機票。
去北京的机票。
qù Běijīng de jīpiào.

| 方小琴: | 你們上網查了嗎? |
| 方小琴: | 你们上网查了吗? |
| Fāng Xiǎoqín: | Nǐmen shàngwǎng chá le ma? |

| 金文華: | 查了,我們查了好幾家航空公司的網站, |
| 金文华: | 查了,我们查了好几家航空公司的网站, |
| Jīn Wénhuá: | Chá le, wǒmen chá le hǎo jǐjiā hángkōng gōngsī de wǎngzhàn, |

可是都訂不到機票。有的機票太貴了,我們買不起。
可是都订不到机票。有的机票太贵了,我们买不起。
kěshì dōu dìngbudào jīpiào. Yǒude jīpiào tàiguì le, wǒmen mǎibuqǐ.

我想問問這家旅行社,看看他們那兒訂得到
我想问问这家旅行社,看看他们那儿订得到
Wǒ xiǎng wènwen zhè jiā lǚxíngshè, kànkan tāmēn nàr dìngdedào

訂不到比較便宜的機票。
订不到比较便宜的机票。
dìngbudào bǐjiào piányi de jīpiào.

方小琴：　　　　　其實，要是真的買不到去北京的機票，你們可以先去
方小琴：　　　　　其实，要是真的买不到去北京的机票，你们可以先去
Fāng Xiǎoqín:　　Qíshí, yàoshi zhēnde mǎibudào qù Běijīng de jīpiào, nǐmen kěyǐ xiān qù

南方的城市，比如上海或者香港，然後去雲南
南方的城市，比如上海或者香港，然后去云南
nánfāng de chéngshì, bǐrú Shànghǎi huòzhě Xiānggǎng, ránhòu qù Yúnnán

的昆明，再從昆明坐飛機去北京。
的昆明，再从昆明坐飞机去北京。
de Kūnmíng, zài cóng Kūnmíng zuò fēijī qù Běijīng.

金文華：　　　　　這個主意真不錯。我也聽說昆明是一個四季如春、
金文华：　　　　　这个主意真不错。我也听说昆明是一个四季如春、
Jīn Wénhuá:　　　Zhège zhǔyi zhēn búcuò. Wǒ yě tīngshuō Kūnmíng shì yíge sìjì rúchūn,

風景如畫的城市，雲南那兒還有很多少數民族，
风景如画的城市，云南那儿还有很多少数民族，
fēngjǐng rúhuà de chéngshì, Yúnnán nàr háiyǒu hěnduō shǎoshù mínzú,

去那兒看看一定會很有意思。可是我在地圖上怎麼
去那儿看看一定会很有意思。可是我在地图上怎么
qù nàr kànkan yídìng huì hěnyǒuyìsi. Kěshì wǒ zài dìtú shàng zěnme

找不到昆明呢？
找不到昆明呢？
zhǎobudào Kūnmíng ne?

方小琴：　　　　　我來幫你看看……啊，在這兒。你看，就在中國的西南邊。
方小琴：　　　　　我来帮你看看……啊，在这儿。你看，就在中国的西南边。
Fāng Xiǎoqín:　　Wǒ lái bāng nǐ kànkan . . . À, zài zhèr. Nǐ kàn, jiù zài Zhōngguó de xīnánbiān.

金文華：　　　　　是啊！如果我真的想去，坐飛機到得了到不了昆明？
金文华：　　　　　是啊！如果我真的想去，坐飞机到得了到不了昆明？
Jīn Wénhuá:　　　Shì a! Rúguǒ wǒ zhēnde xiǎng qù, zuò fēijī dàodeliǎo dàobuliǎo Kūnmíng?

方小琴：　　　　　當然到得了！你還可以吃得到少數民族的小吃呢！
方小琴：　　　　　当然到得了！你还可以吃得到少数民族的小吃呢！
Fāng Xiǎoqín:　　Dāngrán dàodeliǎo! Nǐ hái kěyǐ chīdedào shǎoshù mínzú de xiǎochī ne!

金文華：　　　那我一定要去。
金文华：　　　那我一定要去。
Jīn Wénhuá:　Nà wǒ yídìng yào qù.

方小琴：　　　對了，你們的簽證辦好了嗎？
方小琴：　　　对了，你们的签证办好了吗？
Fāng Xiǎoqín:　Duì le, nǐmende qiānzhèng bàn hǎo le ma?

金文華：　　　方明的簽證已經辦好了。我也已經申請了，
金文华：　　　方明的签证已经办好了。我也已经申请了，
Jīn Wénhuá:　Fāng Míng de qiānzhèng yǐjīng bànhǎo le. Wǒ yě yǐjīng shēnqǐng le,

可是不知道下個星期拿得到拿不到。不過還有一個多月，
可是不知道下个星期拿得到拿不到。不过还有一个多月，
kěshì bù zhīdào xiàge xīngqī nádedào nábudào. Búguò hái yǒu yíge duō yuè,

大概來得及。
大概来得及。
dàgài láidejí.

## Lesson 8　What's Your Favorite Movie?

季如春：　　　慕華，你好像最近比以前忙得多，是嗎？
季如春：　　　慕华，你好像最近比以前忙得多，是吗？
Jì Rúchūn:　Mùhuá, nǐ hǎoxiàng zuìjìn bǐ yǐqián mángdeduō, shì ma?

方慕華：　　　沒有啊！你為什麼覺得我比以前忙得多呢？
方慕华：　　　没有啊！你为什么觉得我比以前忙得多呢？
Fāng Mùhuá:　Méiyou ā! Nǐ wèishénme juéde wǒ bǐ yǐqián mángdeduō ne?

季如春：　　　最近連你的影子都看不見。昨天晚上我給你
季如春：　　　最近连你的影子都看不见。昨天晚上我给你
Jì Rúchūn:　Zuìjìn lián nǐde yǐngzi dōu kànbujiàn. Zuótiān wǎnshang wǒ gěi nǐ

打電話也找不到你。
打电话也找不到你。
dǎ diànhuà yě zhǎobudào nǐ.

方慕華：　昨天上午我把一個大的研究報告交出去了，
方慕华：　昨天上午我把一个大的研究报告交出去了，
Fāng Mùhuá:　Zuótiān shàngwǔ wǒ bǎ yíge dàde yánjiū bàogào jiāo chūqù le,

覺得輕鬆多了，所以我就跟我的表妹去看電影了。
觉得轻松多了，所以我就跟我的表妹去看电影了。
juéde qīngsōng duō le, suǒyǐ wǒ jiù gēn wǒde biǎomèi qù kàn diànyǐng le.

季如春：　你比我強得多，我的報告還沒有寫完呢！
季如春：　你比我强得多，我的报告还没有写完呢！
Jì Rúchūn:　Nǐ bǐ wǒ qiáng de duō, wǒde bàogào hái méiyou xiě wán ne!

對了，你們看了什麼電影？好看嗎？
对了，你们看了什么电影？好看吗？
Duìle, nǐmen kàn le shénme diànyǐng? Hǎo kàn ma?

方慕華：　我們看的是《英雄》。
方慕华：　我们看的是《英雄》。
Fāng Mùhuá:　Wǒmen kàn de shì《Yīngxióng》.

季如春：　是不是張藝謀導演的那部功夫片？
季如春：　是不是张艺谋导演的那部功夫片？
Jì Rúchūn:　Shìbushì Zhāng Yìmóu dǎoyǎn de nà bù gōngfūpiān?

方慕華：　是的。主要演員是陳道明、李連杰和張曼玉。
方慕华：　是的。主要演员是陈道明、李连杰和张曼玉。
Fāng Mùhuá:　Shìde. Zhǔyào yǎnyuán shì Chén Dàomíng, Lǐ Liánjié hé Zhāng Mànyù.

其中我特別喜歡李連杰。
其中我特别喜欢李连杰。
Qízhōng wǒ tèbié xǐhuān Lǐ Liánjié.

季如春：　有人說它沒有《臥虎藏龍》好看，你覺得怎麼樣？
季如春：　有人说它没有《卧虎藏龙》好看，你觉得怎么样？
Jì Rúchūn:　Yǒurén shuō tā méiyou《Wòhǔcánglóng》hǎokàn, nǐ juéde zhěnmeyàng?

方慕華：　我覺得這兩部電影差不多。你呢？你看過了沒有？
方慕华：　我觉得这两部电影差不多。你呢？你看过了没有？
Fāng Mùhuá:　Wǒ juéde zhè liǎngbù diànyǐng chàbuduō. Nǐ ne? Nǐ kàn guo le méiyou?

季如春:　　我看過《臥虎藏龍》，沒有看過《英雄》，
季如春:　　我看过《卧虎藏龙》，没有看过《英雄》，
Jì Rúchūn:　Wǒ kàn guo《Wòhǔcánglóng》, méiyou kàn guo《Yīngxióng》,

　　　　　可是聽說《英雄》的場面比《臥虎藏龍》大得多。
　　　　　可是听说《英雄》的场面比《卧虎藏龙》大得多。
　　　　　kěshì tīngshuō《Yīngxióng》de chǎngmiàn bǐ《Wòhǔcánglóng》dàdeduō.

　　　　　是真的嗎?
　　　　　是真的吗?
　　　　　Shì zhēnde ma?

方慕華:　　沒錯。《英雄》的場面比《臥虎藏龍》大一些，
方慕华:　　没错。《英雄》的场面比《卧虎藏龙》大一些，
Fāng Mùhuá:　Méi cuò.《Yīngxióng》de chǎngmiàn bǐ《Wòhǔcánglóng》dà yìxiē,

　　　　　可是我覺得它的情節不像《臥虎藏龍》那麼吸引人。
　　　　　可是我觉得它的情节不像《卧虎藏龙》那么吸引人。
　　　　　kěshì wǒ juéde tāde qíngjié búxiàng《Wòhǔcánglóng》nàme xīyǐnrén.

季如春:　　聽說《英雄》說的是關於中國古代秦始皇的
季如春:　　听说《英雄》说的是关于中国古代秦始皇的
Jì Rúchūn:　Tīngshuō《Yīngxióng》shuōde shì guānyú Zhōngguó gǔdài Qínshǐhuáng de

　　　　　故事，那麼，比較起來電影和小說哪個好?
　　　　　故事，那么，比较起来电影和小说哪个好?
　　　　　gùshi, nàme, bǐjiào qǐlái diànyǐng hé xiǎoshuō nǎge hǎo?

方慕華:　　我覺得電影不如小說精彩。
方慕华:　　我觉得电影不如小说精彩。
Fāng Mùhuá:　Wǒ juéde diànyǐng bùrú xiǎoshuō jīngcǎi.

季如春:　　有人說它對秦始皇的描寫跟歷史上的秦始皇
季如春:　　有人说它对秦始皇的描写跟历史上的秦始皇
Jì Rúchūn:　Yǒurén shuō tā duì Qínshǐhuáng de miáoxiě gēn lìshǐ shàng de Qíshǐhuáng

　　　　　不一樣。
　　　　　不一样。
　　　　　bù yíyàng.

方慕華：　　我同意，但是我覺得這部電影描寫得比較客觀。
方慕华：　　我同意，但是我觉得这部电影描写得比较客观。
Fāng Mùhuá:　Wǒ tóngyì, dànshì wǒ juéde zhè bù diànyǐng miáoxiě de bǐjiào kèguān.

季如春：　　我一直對歷史故事很感興趣，所以我很想去看一看
季如春：　　我一直对历史故事很感兴趣，所以我很想去看一看
Jì Rúchūn:　Wǒ yìzhí duì lìshǐ gùshi hěn gǎn xìngqu, suǒyǐ wǒ hěn xiǎng qù kànyikàn

　　　　　　這部電影。
　　　　　　这部电影。
　　　　　　zhè bù diànyǐng.

方慕華：　　你應該去看看。我覺得《英雄》這部電影對感情
方慕华：　　你应该去看看。我觉得《英雄》这部电影对感情
Fāng Mùhuá:　Nǐ yīnggāi qù kànkan. Wǒ juéde《Yīngxióng》zhè bù diànyǐng duì gǎnqíng

　　　　　　方面的描寫比《臥虎藏龍》多一些，而且它的特技效果
　　　　　　方面的描写比《卧虎藏龙》多一些，而且它的特技效果
　　　　　　fāngmiàn de miánxiě bǐ《Wòhǔcánglóng》duō yìxiē, érqiě tāde tèjì xiàoguǒ

　　　　　　和顏色都比別的電影好得多。
　　　　　　和颜色都比别的电影好得多。
　　　　　　hé yánsè dōu bǐ bié de diànyǐng hǎodeduō.

季如春：　　你知道在哪兒可以看得到《英雄》嗎?
季如春：　　你知道在哪儿可以看得到《英雄》吗?
Jì Rúchūn:　Nǐ zhīdào zài nǎr kěyǐ kàndedào《Yīngxióng》ma?

方慕華：　　這個週末學校會放這部電影，票價只要一元，
方慕华：　　这个周末学校会放这部电影，票价只要一元，
Fāng Mùhuá:　Zhège zhōumò xuéxiào huì fàng zhè bù diànyǐng, piàojià zhǐyào yì Yuán,

　　　　　　比電影院的要便宜九元。
　　　　　　比电影院的要便宜九元。
　　　　　　bǐ diànyǐngyuàn de yào piányi jiǔ Yuán.

季如春：　　好，這個週末我就去看。
季如春：　　好，这个周末我就去看。
Jì Rúchūn:　Hǎo, zhège zhōumò wǒ jiù qù kàn.

## Lesson 9    I Have Started to Work Out

白思琴：　欣明，你最近常去健身房鍛煉嗎？
白思琴：　欣明，你最近常去健身房锻炼吗？
Bái Sīqín:　Xīnmíng, nǐ zuìjìn cháng qù jiànshēnfáng duànliàn ma?

胡欣明：　這兩個星期是我最忙的時候，鍛煉得比以前
胡欣明：　这两个星期是我最忙的时候，锻炼得比以前
Hú Xīnmíng:　Zhè liǎngge xīngqī shì wǒ zuì máng de shíhou, duànliàn de bǐ yǐqián

少得多。以前我差不多天天游泳，最近差不多
少得多。以前我差不多天天游泳，最近差不多
shǎo de duō. Yǐqián wǒ chàbuduō tiāntiān yóuyǒng, zuìjìn chàbuduō

每星期都要比以前少游兩、三次，這個星期一次
每星期都要比以前少游两、三次，这个星期一次
měi xīngqī dōu yào bǐ yǐqián shǎo yóu liǎng, sān cì, zhège xīngqī yícì

也沒去過。
也没去过。
yě méi qù guo.

白思琴：　那可不好。其實越忙越需要鍛煉。我每天都要
白思琴：　那可不好。其实越忙越需要锻炼。我每天都要
Bái Sīqín:　Nà kě bù hǎo. Qíshí yuè máng yuè xūyào duànliàn. Wǒ měitiān dōu yào

去運動一個鐘頭，現在我的精神越來越好了。
去运动一个钟头，现在我的精神越来越好了。
qù yùndòng yíge zhōngtóu, xiànzài wǒde jīngshen yuèláiyuè hǎo le.

你看，我比前幾個月還瘦了不少吧！
你看，我比前几个月还瘦了不少吧！
Nǐ kàn, wǒ bǐ qián jǐge yuè hái shòu le bù shǎo ba!

胡欣明：　真的，你看上去比上學期瘦了很多。
胡欣明：　真的，你看上去比上学期瘦了很多。
Hú Xīnmíng:　Zhēn de, nǐ kànshàngqù bǐ shàng xuéqī shòu le hěn duō.

你最近在減肥嗎？
你最近在减肥吗？
Nǐ zuìjìn zài jiǎnféi ma?

白思琴:　　是呀！我已經堅持了三個月了。效果不錯吧！
白思琴:　　是呀！我已经坚持了三个月了。效果不错吧！
Bái Sīqín:　Shì ya! Wǒ yǐjīng jiānchí le sānge yuè le. Xiàoguǒ búcuò ba!

體重比以前輕了十幾磅。
体重比以前轻了十几磅。
Tǐzhòng bǐ yǐqián qīngle shí jǐ bàng.

胡欣明:　　怪不得你越來越苗條了，差不多是我們女孩子中
胡欣明:　　怪不得你越来越苗条了，差不多是我们女孩子中
Hú Xīnmíng:　Guàibudé nǐ yuèláiyuè miáotiao le, chàbuduō shì wǒmen nǚháizi zhōng

最苗條的了。你是怎麼減肥的？控制飲食嗎？
最苗条的了。你是怎么减肥的？控制饮食吗？
zuì miáotiao de le. Nǐ shì zěnme jiǎnféi de? Kòngzhi yǐnshí ma?

白思琴:　　主要是鍛煉，當然在吃的方面我也比較注意。
白思琴:　　主要是锻炼，当然在吃的方面我也比较注意。
Bái Sīqín:　Zhǔyào shì duànliàn, dāngrán zài chīde fāngmiàn wǒ yě bǐjiào zhùyì.

我以前最喜歡吃甜食，可是現在我吃得越來越少了。
我以前最喜欢吃甜食，可是现在我吃得越来越少了。
Wǒ yǐqián zuì xǐhuān chī tiánshí, kěshì xiànzài wǒ chī de yuèláiyuè shǎo le.

胡欣明:　　你怎麼會想到要減肥呢？
胡欣明:　　你怎么会想到要减肥呢？
Hú Xīnmíng:　Nǐ zěnme huì xiǎng dào yào jiǎnféi ne?

白思琴:　　我早就想減肥了。我的個子有點兒矮，只有五呎一吋，
白思琴:　　我早就想减肥了。我的个子有点儿矮，只有五呎一吋，
Bái Sīqín:　Wǒ zǎo jiù xiǎng jiǎnféi le. Wǒde gèzi yǒudiǎr ǎi, zhǐyǒu wǔ chǐ yí cùn,

可是三個月以前我的體重超過了一百五十磅。
可是三个月以前我的体重超过了一百五十磅。
kěshì sānge yuè yǐqián wǒde tǐzhòng chāoguò le yìbǎi wǔshí bàng.

胡欣明:　　那你最重的時候比我還要重呢！
胡欣明:　　那你最重的时候比我还要重呢！
Hú Xīnmíng:　Nà nǐ zuì zhòng de shíhou bǐ wǒ hái yào zhòng ne!

白思琴:　　是呀！我要是太重了就會覺得不太靈活，也很不舒服。
白思琴:　　是呀！我要是太重了就会觉得不太灵活，也很不舒服。
Bái Sīqín:　Shì ya! Wǒ yàoshì tài zhòng le jiùhuì juéde bù tài línghuó, yě hěn bù shūfu.

胡欣明： 我真應該向你學習，可是我總是覺得功課太多、
胡欣明： 我真应该向你学习，可是我总是觉得功课太多、
Hú Xīnmíng: Wǒ zhēn yīnggāi xiàng nǐ xuéxí, kěshì wǒ zǒngshì juéde gōngkè tài duō,

太忙，沒有時間鍛煉。現在我每天都比別人還要
太忙，没有时间锻炼。现在我每天都比别人还要
tài máng, méiyou shíjiān duànliàn. Xiànzài wǒ měitiān dōu bǐ biérén hái yào

少睡兩、三個鐘頭呢。
少睡两、三个钟头呢。
shǎo shuì liǎng, sān ge zhōngtóu ne.

白思琴： 其實，最重要的是要多鍛煉、多運動。運動了以後
白思琴： 其实，最重要的是要多锻炼、多运动。运动了以后
Bái Sīqín: Qíshí, zuì zhòngyào de shì yào duō duànliàn, duō yùndòng. Yùndòng le yǐhòu

你的身體會比以前更好，你會更有精神，學習的效果
你的身体会比以前更好，你会更有精神，学习的效果
nǐde shēntǐ huì bǐ yǐqián gèng hǎo, nǐ huì gèng yǒu jīngshén, xuéxí de xiàoguǒ

可能就會更好了。
可能就会更好了。
kěnéng jiù huì gèng hǎo le.

## Lesson 10    I'll Get to Climb the Great Wall!

同學們好！
同学们好！
Tóngxuémen hǎo!

今天，我想把我的寒假計畫跟大家報告一下。
今天，我想把我的寒假计划跟大家报告一下。
Jīntiān, wǒ xiǎng bǎ wǒde hánjià jìhuà gēn dàjiā bàogào yíxià.

今年是我在大學的最後一個寒假。我已經跟我的男朋友
今年是我在大学的最后一个寒假。我已经跟我的男朋友
Jīnnián shì wǒ zài dàxué de zuìhòu yíge hánjià. Wǒ yǐjīng gēn wǒde nánpéngyou

說好了，一起去中國旅遊。我們在北京有很多親戚朋友，
说好了，一起去中国旅游。我们在北京有很多亲戚朋友，
shuō hǎo le, yìqǐ qù Zhōngguó lǚyóu. Wǒmen zài Běijīng yǒu hěnduō qīnqì péngyou,

我希望這次去北京能見得到他們每個人。
我希望这次去北京能见得到他们每个人。
wǒ xīwàng zhècì qù Běijīng néng jiàndedào tāmen měige rén.

這兩年去中國的人比以前多了很多，所以飛機票
这两年去中国的人比以前多了很多，所以飞机票
Zhè liǎng nián qù Zhōngguó de rén bǐ yǐqián duō le hěn duō, suǒyǐ fēijīpiào

也比前兩年難買多了。特別是去北京的機票，更難買得到，
也比前两年难买多了。特别是去北京的机票，更难买得到，
yě bǐ qián liǎngnián nán mǎi duō le. Tèbié shì qù Běijīng de jīpiào, gèng nán mǎidedào,

我們到現在還沒有訂到票呢。我們打算十二月中旬出發，
我们到现在还没有订到票呢。我们打算十二月中旬出发，
wǒmen dào xiànzài hái méiyou dìng dào piào ne. Wǒmen dǎsuàn shí èr yuè zhōngxún chūfā,

一月上旬回來。現在已經給好幾家旅行社打了電話，還不知道
一月上旬回来。现在已经给好几家旅行社打了电话，还不知道
yīyuè shàngxún huílai. Xiànzài yǐjīng gěi hǎo jǐ jiā lǚxíngshè dǎ le diànhuà, hái bù zhīdào

買得到買不到。我們上個星期已經申請了去中國的簽證，
买得到买不到。我们上个星期已经申请了去中国的签证，
mǎidedào mǎibudào. Wǒmen shàngge xīngqī yǐjīng shēnqǐng le qù Zhōngguó de qiānzhèng,

不知道這個星期收得到收不到。不過我們還有不少時間，
不知道这个星期收得到收不到。不过我们还有不少时间，
bù zhīdào zhège xīngqī shōudedào shōubudào. Búguò wǒmen háiyou bù shǎo shíjiān,

大概來得及。
大概来得及。
dàgài láidejí.

我還要去銀行取一些現金，買幾張旅行支票。
我还要去银行取一些现金，买几张旅行支票。
Wǒ háiyào qù yínháng qǔ yìxiē xiànjīn, mǎi jǐzhāng lǚxíng zhīpiào.

在中國用信用卡付款不像在美國這麼方便。
在中国用信用卡付款不像在美国这么方便。
Zài Zhōngguó yòng xìnyòngkǎ fùkuǎn búxiàng zài Měiguó zhème fāngbiàn.

不過，聽說現在接受信用卡的商店越來越多了，
不过，听说现在接受信用卡的商店越来越多了，
Búguò, tīngshuō xiànzài jiēshòu xìnyòngkǎ de shāngdiàn yuèláiyuè duō le,

而且在中國銀行還可以取美金，也可以根據當天的匯率換成
而且在中国银行还可以取美金，也可以根据当天的汇率换成
érqiě zài Zhōngguó Yínháng hái kěyǐ qǔ Měijīn, yě kěyǐ gēnjù dāngtiān de huìlǜ huàn chéng

人民幣，這比帶很多現金要安全得多。最近人民幣換美金的
人民币，这比带很多现金要安全得多。最近人民币换美金的
Rénmínbì, zhè bǐ dài hěnduō xiànjīn yào ānquán de duō. Zuìjìn Rénmínbì huàn Měijīn de

匯率差不多是一比六點五三，比上個月低了零點一個百分點。
汇率差不多是一比六点五三，比上个月低了零点一个百分点。
huìlǜ chàbuduō shì yī bǐ liù diǎn wǔ sān, bǐ shàngge yuè dī le líng diǎn yī ge bǎifēndiǎn.

　　這次去中國我最想去的地方是長城。聽說爬
　　这次去中国我最想去的地方是长城。听说爬
　　Zhècì qù Zhōngguó wǒ zuì xiǎng qù de dìfang shì Chángchéng. Tīngshuō pá

長城很累，只有百分之五十的人能爬得到長城的頂上。
长城很累，只有百分之五十的人能爬得到长城的顶上。
Chángchéng hěn lèi, zhǐ yǒu bǎi fēn zhī wǔshí de rén néng pádedào Chángchéng de dǐng shàng.

我覺得那是一個很好的鍛煉，還能幫助我減肥呢！而且，
我觉得那是一个很好的锻炼，还能帮助我减肥呢！而且，
Wǒ juéde nà shì yíge hěnhǎo de duànliàn, hái néng bāngzhù wǒ jiǎnféi ne! Érqiě,

中國人不是說"不到長城非好漢"嗎？所以我一定要試一試。
中国人不是说"不到长城非好汉"吗？所以我一定要试一试。
Zhōngguórén búshì shuō "bú dào Chángchéng fēi hǎohàn" ma? Suǒyǐ wǒ yídìng yào shìyishì.

我還想去黃山，我的朋友告訴我黃山那兒風景如畫，
我还想去黄山，我的朋友告诉我黄山那儿风景如画，
Wǒ hái xiǎng qù Huángshān, wǒde péngyou gàosu wǒ Huángshān nàr fēngjǐngrúhuà,

美極了！
美极了！
měi jí le!

我還想去看看張藝謀導演的功夫片《十面埋伏》。
我还想去看看张艺谋导演的功夫片《十面埋伏》。
Wǒ hái xiǎng qù kànkàn Zhāng Yìmóu dǎoyǎn de gōngfūpiān《Shí Miàn Máifu》.

看過這部電影的人都說它的場面比《英雄》還要
看过这部电影的人都说它的场面比《英雄》还要
Kàn guo zhè bù diànyǐng de rén dōu shuō tā de chǎngmiàn bǐ《Yīngxióng》hái yào

壯觀，情節也很曲折。
壮观，情节也很曲折。
zhuàngguān, qíngjié yě hěn qūzhé.

你們看，我今年寒假要做的事多不多？我希望我從
你们看，我今年寒假要做的事多不多？我希望我从
Nǐmen kàn, wǒ jīnnián hánjià yào zuò de shì duōbuduō? Wǒ xīwàng wǒ cóng

中國回來的時候，能滿載而歸。
中国回来的时候，能满载而归。
Zhōngguó huílai de shíhou, néng mǎnzài'érguī.

這就是我今天的報告。謝謝大家！
这就是我今天的报告。谢谢大家！
Zhè jiù shì wǒ jīntiān de bàogào. Xièxie dàjiā!

# 拼音索引 (拼音索引)   PINYIN GLOSSARY

Each entry lists the Pinyin, traditional character, simplified character, part of speech, English meaning, and lesson number.

## A

| | | | | | |
|---|---|---|---|---|---|
| ǎi | 矮 | 矮 | *Adj.* | short | 9 |
| ānquán | 安全 | 安全 | *Adj.* | safe | 10 |
| ānquándài | 安全帶 | 安全带 | *N.* | seat belt, safety belt | 3 |

## B

| | | | | | |
|---|---|---|---|---|---|
| bǎ | 把 | 把 | *M.W.* | measure word (classifier) for a utensil with a handle | 2 |
| báitiān | 白天 | 白天 | *N.* | daytime | 4 |
| báitóufa | 白頭髮 | 白头发 | *N.* | gray hair | 4 |
| bǎi | 擺 | 摆 | *V.* | to place, put | 2 |
| bǎifēnzhi . . . | 百分之…… | 百分之…… | *Num.* | . . . percent (%) | 6 |
| bàifǎng | 拜訪 | 拜访 | *V.* | to visit | 7 |
| | | | *N.* | visit | |
| bānjī | 班機 | 班机 | *N.* | flight | 5 |
| bàn | 辦 | 办 | *V.* | to apply, process | 7 |
| bāngzhù | 幫助 | 帮助 | *N.* | help | 10 |
| bàng | 磅 | 磅 | *M.W.* | pound (measure word for weight measurement) | 9 |
| bǎo | 飽 | 饱 | *Adj.* | full | 4 |
| Běijīng | 北京 | 北京 | *N.* | Beijing, the capital of China | 2 |
| běnlái | 本來 | 本来 | *Adv.* | originally | 3 |
| biànchéng | 變成 | 变成 | *V.C.* | to become | 3 |
| biànhuà | 變化 | 变化 | *V.* | to change | 3 |
| | | | *N.* | change | |
| biǎo | 表 | 表 | *N.* | form | 6 |
| biǎomèi | 表妹 | 表妹 | *N.* | cousin | 8 |
| biǎoyǎn | 表演 | 表演 | *N.* | performance | 2 |
| | | | *V.* | to perform | |
| bié | 別 | 別 | *Aux.* | don't | 1 |
| biérén | 別人 | 別人 | *N.* | other people | 5 |
| bù | 簿 | 簿 | *N.* | check book | 6 |
| | 部 | 部 | *M.W.* | (measure word for films, machines, or cars) | 8 |
| bùrú | 不如 | 不如 | *V.* | to be inferior to, to be not as good as | 8 |

## C

| chá | 查 | 查 | V. | to check | 7 |
|---|---|---|---|---|---|
| chàbuduō | 差不多 | 差不多 | Adv. | not very different, similar, about the same | 6 |
| Chángchéng | 長城 | 长城 | N. | The Great Wall | 2 |
| chǎngmiàn | 場面 | 场面 | N. | scene | 8 |
| chāoguò | 超過 | 超过 | V. | to surpass | 9 |
| chēfèi | 車費 | 车费 | N. | cab fare | 3 |
| chǐ | 呎 | 呎 | N. | foot (US and UK measurement) | 9 |
| chōukòng | 抽空 | 抽空 | V.O. | to manage to find time | 7 |
| chū | 齣 | 出 | M.W. | measure word (modifier) for Chinese theater performance | 2 |
| chūzū | 出租 | 出租 | V. | to rent | 3 |
| chǔxù | 儲蓄 | 储蓄 | N. | savings | 6 |
|  |  |  | V. | to save (money) |  |
| chuāng | 窗 | 窗 | N. | window | 1 |
| cún | 存 | 存 | V. | to deposit | 6 |
| cùn | 吋 | 吋 | N. | inch (US and UK measurment) | 9 |

## D

| dāchéng | 搭乘 | 搭乘 | V. | to take (a means of transportation) | 3 |
|---|---|---|---|---|---|
| dǎ | 打 | 打 | V. | to play (the drum); to hit | 2 |
| dǎsuàn | 打算 | 打算 | V. | to plan | 7 |
|  |  |  | N. | plan |  |
| dàgài | 大概 | 大概 | Adv. | probably | 7 |
| dàkāiyǎnjiè | 大開眼界 | 大开眼界 |  | be exposed to many great new things | 5 |
| dàshà | 大廈 | 大厦 | N. | high-rise building | 5 |
| dānzi | 單子 | 单子 | N. | form | 6 |
| dāngrán | 當然 | 当然 | Adv. | of course | 6 |
| dāngtiān | 當天 | 当天 | Adv. | on that day | 10 |
| dāo | 刀 | 刀 | N. | knife | 2 |
| dǎoyǎn | 導演 | 导演 | N. | director | 8 |
|  |  |  | V. | to direct (a film) |  |
| dào | 倒 | 倒 | V. | to move backwards | 1 |
| dī | 低 | 低 | Adj. | low | 6 |
| dìdào | 地道 | 地道 | Adj. | original, genuine, authentic | 4 |
| diànzǐ | 電子 | 电子 | N. | electronics | 3 |
| dǐng | 頂 | 顶 | N. | top | 10 |
| dìng | 訂 | 订 | V. | to book, make reservations | 7 |
| dòng | 棟 | 栋 | M.W. | (measure word for buildings) | 3 |
| duì | 對 | 对 | Prep. | toward, to | 8 |

| duìhuàn | 兌換 | 兌换 | N. | exchange | 6 |
|---|---|---|---|---|---|
| | | | V. | to exchange | |

## E

| érqiě | 而且 | 而且 | *Conj.* | and also, furthermore | 8 |

## F

| fāzhǎn | 發展 | 发展 | V. | to develop | 3 |
| | | | N. | development | |
| fánróng | 繁榮 | 繁荣 | *Adj.* | prosperous | 5 |
| fāngbiàn | 方便 | 方便 | *Adj.* | convenient | 6 |
| fāngmiàn | 方面 | 方面 | N. | aspect | 8 |
| fāngxiàng | 方向 | 方向 | N. | direction | 5 |
| fángdōng | 房東 | 房东 | N. | landlord | 1 |
| fàng | 放 | 放 | V. | to place, to put | 1 |
| | 放 | 放 | V. | to show (movies); to place | 8 |
| fēi | 非 | 非 | *Adv.* | not (used in Classical Chinese) | 10 |
| fēixíng | 飛行 | 飞行 | N. | flight; flying | 5 |
| fēngōnghézuò | 分工合作 | 分工合作 | | to collaborate by dividing up the work | 1 |
| fēngjǐngrúhuà | 風景如畫 | 风景如画 | | with picturesque scenic beauty | 7 |
| fúzhuāng | 服裝 | 服装 | N. | clothes, costume | 2 |
| fùjìn | 附近 | 附近 | N. | nearby | 1 |
| fùkuǎn | 付款 | 付款 | V.O. | to make payment | 10 |
| fùzé | 負責 | 负责 | V. | to be responsible for | 1 |

## G

| gānbēi | 乾杯 | 干杯 | V.O. | to toast, cheers | 4 |
| gǎn | 感 | 感 | V. | to feel, sense | 8 |
| gǎnqíng | 感情 | 感情 | N. | emotion | 8 |
| gǎnshàng | 趕上 | 赶上 | V.C. | to catch; catch up with | 5 |
| gāo | 高 | 高 | *Adj.* | high | 6 |
| gàosu | 告訴 | 告诉 | V. | to tell | 10 |
| gèwèi | 各位 | 各位 | *Pron.* | everyone (a term to address an audience) | 3 |
| gèzhǒng | 各種 | 各种 | *Adj.* | various, all kinds of | 2 |
| gèzi | 個子 | 个子 | N. | height, stature | 9 |
| gēnjù | 根據 | 根据 | *Prep.* | according to, based on | 10 |
| gèng | 更 | 更 | *Adv.* | more | 9 |

| | | | | | |
|---|---|---|---|---|---|
| gōngchǐ | 公尺 | 公尺 | N. | meter | 3 |
| gōngfupiān | 功夫片 | 功夫片 | N. | action movie | 8 |
| gōnglǐ | 公里 | 公里 | N. | kilometer | 3 |
| gòu | 夠 | 够 | Adj. | enough | 6 |
| gǔ | 鼓 | 鼓 | N. | drum | 2 |
| gǔdài | 古代 | 古代 | Adj. | ancient times | 8 |
| gùshi | 故事 | 故事 | N. | story | 8 |
| guà | 掛 | 挂 | V. | to hang | 1 |
| guǎi | 拐 | 拐 | V. | to turn | 3 |
| guàibude | 怪不得 | 怪不得 | | no wonder | 9 |
| guānshàng | 關上 | 关上 | V. | to close | 1 |
| guānyú | 關於 | 关于 | Prep. | about, with regard to | 8 |
| guānzhòng | 觀眾 | 观众 | N. | audience | 2 |
| guìtái | 櫃台 | 柜台 | N. | counter | 6 |

## H

| | | | | | |
|---|---|---|---|---|---|
| hánjià | 寒假 | 寒假 | N. | winter vacation | 7 |
| hángkōng | 航空 | 航空 | N. | aviation, airline | 3 |
| hǎohàn | 好漢 | 好汉 | N. | hero | 10 |
| hàokè | 好客 | 好客 | Adj. | hospitable | 5 |
| hónglǜdēng | 紅綠燈 | 红绿灯 | N. | traffic light | 3 |
| hòuchēxiāng | 後車箱 | 后车箱 | N. | trunk (car) | 3 |
| húqín | 胡琴 | 胡琴 | N. | two-stringed, bowed instruments | 2 |
| huā | 花 | 花 | Adj. | blurred eyesight | 4 |
| huà | 畫 | 画 | V. | to paint, draw | 2 |
| | | | N. | painting | |
| huài | 壞 | 坏 | Adj. | bad | 1 |
| huàn | 換 | 换 | V. | to change | 6 |
| Huángshān | 黃山 | 黄山 | N. | Mt. Huang (Yellow Mountain, a famous tourist attraction in Anhui Province, central China) | 10 |
| huìlǜ | 匯率 | 汇率 | N. | exchange rate | 6 |

## J

| | | | | | |
|---|---|---|---|---|---|
| jīpiào | 機票 | 机票 | N. | plane ticket | 7 |
| jì | 寄 | 寄 | V. | to mail | 6 |
| jìhuà | 計畫 | 计划 | V. | to plan | 10 |
| | | | N. | plan | |
| jìshàng | 繫上 | 系上 | V.C. | to tie, fasten, buckle up | 3 |
| jìsuànjī | 計算機 | 计算机 | N. | computer | 3 |

| | | | | | |
|---|---|---|---|---|---|
| jiāchángbiànfàn | 家常便飯 | 家常便饭 | N. | home-made meal | 4 |
| jiàrì | 假日 | 假日 | N. | holiday | 3 |
| jiānchí | 堅持 | 坚持 | V. | to persist, persevere | 9 |
| jiǎnféi | 減肥 | 减肥 | V.O. | to lose weight | 9 |
| jiànkāng | 健康 | 健康 | Adj. | healthy | 4 |
| jiàngluò | 降落 | 降落 | V. | to land, descend | 3 |
| jiāochākǒu | 交叉口 | 交叉口 | N. | intersection | 3 |
| jiēdào | 街道 | 街道 | N. | street | 4 |
| jiēshòu | 接受 | 接受 | V. | to accept | 10 |
| jīnjīnyǒuwèi | 津津有味 | 津津有味 | | with relish, with keen pleasure | 5 |
| jīngcǎi | 精彩 | 精彩 | Adj. | brilliant, wonderful | 8 |
| jīngshen | 精神 | 精神 | Adj. | energetic, high-spirited | 4 |
| jìngzi | 鏡子 | 镜子 | N. | mirror | 1 |
| jùquán | 俱全 | 俱全 | | all included, altogether | 4 |

## K

| | | | | | |
|---|---|---|---|---|---|
| kāi | 開 | 开 | V. | to open | 6 |
| kèguān | 客觀 | 客观 | Adj. | factual, objective | 8 |
| kòngzhì | 控制 | 控制 | V. | to control | 9 |
| kuǎn | 款 | 款 | N. | money | 6 |
| Kūnmíng | 昆明 | 昆明 | N. | Kunming, the capital city of Yunnan Province | 7 |
| kùn | 睏 | 困 | Adj. | sleepy, dozy | 4 |

## L

| | | | | | |
|---|---|---|---|---|---|
| lā | 拉 | 拉 | V. | to play (stringed musical instruments); to pull | 2 |
| láidejí | 來得及 | 来得及 | | to have enough time to | 7 |
| lèi | 累 | 累 | Adj. | tired, get tired of | 1 |
| lìlǜ | 利率 | 利率 | N. | interest rate | 6 |
| lìshǐ | 歷史 | 历史 | N. | history | 8 |
| lìxī | 利息 | 利息 | N. | interest | 6 |
| lián | 連 | 连 | Prep. | even | 8 |
| liǎn | 臉 | 脸 | N. | face | 2 |
| liáng | 涼 | 凉 | Adj. | cool, cold | 4 |
| líng | 零 | 零 | Num. | zero | 10 |
| línghuó | 靈活 | 灵活 | Adj. | dexterous, agile, flexible | 9 |
| lùkǒu | 路口 | 路口 | N. | blocks, diverging point of a road | 3 |
| lùrén | 路人 | 路人 | N. | passer-by | 3 |
| lǚguǎn | 旅館 | 旅馆 | N. | hotel, hostel | 3 |
| lǚkè | 旅客 | 旅客 | N. | traveler, passenger | 3 |

| | | | | | |
|---|---|---|---|---|---|
| lǚxíngshè | 旅行社 | 旅行社 | N. | travel agency | 7 |
| lǚyóu | 旅遊 | 旅游 | N. | tour | 7 |

## M

| | | | | | |
|---|---|---|---|---|---|
| mǎlù | 馬路 | 马路 | N. | road, avenue, street | 3 |
| mǎibuqǐ | 買不起 | 买不起 | | cannot afford to buy | 7 |
| mǎidào | 買到 | 买到 | V.C. | to succeed in buying | 7 |
| mǎn | 滿 | 满 | Adj. | full | 2 |
| mǎnzàiérguī | 滿載而歸 | 满载而归 | | to return with tremendous accomplishment | 10 |
| měijīn | 美金 | 美金 | N. | US dollar | 6 |
| mén | 門 | 门 | N. | door | 1 |
| miáotiao | 苗條 | 苗条 | Adj. | slim | 9 |
| miáoxiě | 描寫 | 描写 | N. | description, exposition | 8 |
| | | | V. | to describe | |

## N

| | | | | | |
|---|---|---|---|---|---|
| ná | 拿 | 拿 | V. | to hold; take | 2 |
| náshǒucài | 拿手菜 | 拿手菜 | N. | best cooking | 4 |
| nándé | 難得 | 难得 | Adv. | seldom, rarely | 4 |
| nánfāng | 南方 | 南方 | N. | southern part | 7 |
| nào | 鬧 | 闹 | V. | to make, cause, induce | 5 |
| niángāo | 年糕 | 年糕 | N. | New Year cake, rice cake | 4 |
| niánqīng | 年輕 | 年轻 | Adj. | young | 4 |
| nóngtián | 農田 | 农田 | N. | farmland; cropland | 3 |
| nǚháizi | 女孩子 | 女孩子 | N. | girl | 9 |

## O

| | | | | | |
|---|---|---|---|---|---|
| ō | 喔 | 喔 | Int. | (used to indicate realization) | 3 |

## P

| | | | | | |
|---|---|---|---|---|---|
| pá | 爬 | 爬 | V. | to climb | 10 |
| piányi | 便宜 | 便宜 | Adj. | inexpensive | 7 |
| piàojià | 票價 | 票价 | N. | ticket price | 8 |
| pò | 破 | 破 | Adj. | broken | 1 |
| pòfèi | 破費 | 破费 | V.O. | (a common courteous expression used by the gift receiver) to spend money; go to such an expense | 4 |

# Q

| qíshí | 其實 | 其实 | Adv. | as a matter of fact, actually | 7 |
| qiān | 千 | 千 | Num. | thousand | 6 |
| qiānzhèng | 簽證 | 签证 | N. | visa | 7 |
| qiáng | 牆 | 墙 | N. | wall | 2 |
| | 強 | 强 | Adj. | better than, well off | 8 |
| qīnqi | 親戚 | 亲戚 | N. | relative | 7 |
| qīng | 輕 | 轻 | Adj. | light | 9 |
| qīngsōng | 輕鬆 | 轻松 | Adj. | relieved, relaxed | 8 |
| qíngjié | 情節 | 情节 | N. | story; plot | 8 |
| qǐngkè | 請客 | 请客 | V. | to act as the host, to treat | 1 |
| qūzhé | 曲折 | 曲折 | Adj. | with twists and turns, complicated | 10 |
| qǔ | 取 | 取 | V. | to withdraw | 6 |
| qǔkuǎnjī | 取款機 | 取款机 | N. | banking machine | 6 |
| qǔkuǎnkǎ | 取款卡 | 取款卡 | N. | ATM card | 6 |

# R

| rèqíng | 熱情 | 热情 | Adj. | warm-hearted, enthusiastic | 5 |
| rénmínbì | 人民幣 | 人民币 | N. | Renminbi, RMB (name of currency used in mainland China) | 3 |
| rúguǒ | 如果 | 如果 | Conj. | if | 7 |

# S

| sǎo | 掃 | 扫 | V. | to clean, sweep | 1 |
| shāngdiàn | 商店 | 商店 | N. | store | 10 |
| shǎoshùmínzú | 少數民族 | 少数民族 | N. | minority nationalities | 7 |
| shēnqǐng | 申請 | 申请 | N. V. | application to apply | 6 |
| shénqì | 神氣 | 神气 | Adj. | energetic; high-spirited; proud | 2 |
| shīmǔ | 師母 | 师母 | N. | (a honorific term used when addressing a teacher's wife) | 4 |
| shíchā | 時差 | 时差 | N. | time difference; jet lag | 4 |
| shìyìng | 適應 | 适应 | V. | to get used to | 4 |
| shòu | 瘦 | 瘦 | Adj. | thin, slim, skinny | 9 |
| shù | 樹 | 树 | N. | tree | 1 |
| shuìbuzháo | 睡不著 | 睡不着 | V. | cannot fall asleep | 4 |
| shuōhǎo le | 說好了 | 说好了 | | to have agreement on | 10 |
| sījī | 司機 | 司机 | N. | driver | 3 |
| sǐ | 死 | 死 | Adj. V. | dead to die | 1 |
| sìjìrúchūn | 四季如春 | 四季如春 | | spring-like all year | 7 |
| suīrán | 雖然 | 虽然 | Conj. | although | 5 |

# T

| | | | | | |
|---|---|---|---|---|---|
| tā | 它 | 它 | *Pron.* | it | 8 |
| tánzòu | 彈奏 | 弹奏 | *V.* | to play, pluck; strike | 2 |
| tèbié | 特別 | 特别 | *Adv.* | very, especially | 8 |
| tèdì | 特地 | 特地 | *Adv.* | specially | 4 |
| tèjì | 特技 | 特技 | *N.* | special technique | 8 |
| tǐzhòng | 體重 | 体重 | *N.* | body weight | 9 |
| tián | 填 | 填 | *V.* | to fill in/up | 6 |
| tiánshí | 甜食 | 甜食 | *N.* | sweet food | 9 |
| tǐng | 挺 | 挺 | *Adv.* | very | 5 |
| tóngyì | 同意 | 同意 | *V.* | to agree | 8 |
| tuán | 團 | 团 | *N.* | group | 5 |

# W

| | | | | | |
|---|---|---|---|---|---|
| wàibì | 外幣 | 外币 | *N.* | foreign currency | 6 |
| wàitào | 外套 | 外套 | *N.* | coat | 1 |
| wán | 完 | 完 | *V.* | to finish | 8 |
| wǎng | 往 | 往 | *Prep.* | toward | 3 |
| wǎngzhàn | 網站 | 网站 | *N.* | website | 7 |
| wàng | 忘 | 忘 | *V.* | to forget | 1 |
| wār | 彎兒 | 弯儿 | *N.* | turn, detour | 3 |
| wéishēngsù | 維生素 | 维生素 | *N.* | vitamin | 4 |
| wèidao | 味道 | 味道 | *N.* | taste | 4 |
| wǔtái | 舞台 | 舞台 | *N.* | stage (performance) | 2 |
| wùdiǎn | 誤點 | 误点 | *N.* | delay | 5 |
| | | | *V.O.* | to delay | |

# X

| | | | | | |
|---|---|---|---|---|---|
| xīwàng | 希望 | 希望 | *V.* | to hope | 10 |
| | | | *N.* | hope | |
| xīyǐnrén | 吸引人 | 吸引人 | *Adj.* | appealing, attractive | 8 |
| xíguàn | 習慣 | 习惯 | *V.* | to be used to | 4 |
| xì | 戲 | 戏 | *N.* | play; drama | 2 |
| xiànjīn | 現金 | 现金 | *N.* | cash | 6 |
| xiànmù | 羨慕 | 羡慕 | *V.* | to envy | 7 |
| xiāng | 香 | 香 | *N.* | aroma | 4 |
| | | | *Adj.* | aromatic | |
| Xiānggǎng | 香港 | 香港 | *N.* | Hong Kong | 7 |
| xiāngjù | 相聚 | 相聚 | *V.* | to be together, get together | 4 |
| xiāngzi | 箱子 | 箱子 | *N.* | box, suitcase | 1 |
| xiàng | 向 | 向 | *Prep.* | toward | 3 |

| xiǎochī | 小吃 | 小吃 | N. | snack | 5 |
| xiǎochīdiàn | 小吃店 | 小吃店 | N. | snack bar | 3 |
| xiǎoxīn | 小心 | 小心 | Adj. | be careful | 1 |
| xiǎoyìsi | 小意思 | 小意思 | | not a big deal | 4 |
| xiàoguǒ | 效果 | 效果 | N. | effect | 8 |
| xiàohua | 笑話 | 笑话 | N. | joke | 5 |
| xiē | 些 | 些 | M.W. | some | 4 |
| xìnyòngkǎ | 信用卡 | 信用卡 | N. | credit card | 6 |
| xíngli | 行李 | 行李 | N. | luggage, baggage | 1 |
| xìngqù | 興趣 | 兴趣 | N. | interest | 8 |
| xūyào | 需要 | 需要 | V. | to require | 9 |
| xún | 旬 | 旬 | N. | a period of 10 days in a month | 10 |

# Y

| ya | 呀 | 呀 | Part. | (used at the end of the sentence to soften the tone) | 1 |
| yánjiū bàogào | 研究報告 | 研究报告 | N. | research report | 8 |
| yánsè | 顏色 | 颜色 | N. | color | 8 |
| yǎnjīng | 眼睛 | 眼睛 | N. | eye | 4 |
| yǎnyuán | 演員 | 演员 | N. | actor or actress; performer | 2 |
| yàoshì | 要是 | 要是 | Conj. | if | 7 |
| yīfu | 衣服 | 衣服 | N. | clothes | 1 |
| yìyánwéidìng | 一言為定 | 一言为定 | | it's a deal | 2 |
| yìzhí | 一直 | 一直 | | straight | 3 |
| | | | Adv. | always | 7 |
| yīn | 陰 | 阴 | Adj. | cloudy | 5 |
| yínháng | 銀行 | 银行 | N. | bank | 6 |
| yǐnshí | 飲食 | 饮食 | N. | food and drink, eating | 9 |
| yǐngzi | 影子 | 影子 | N. | shadow | 8 |
| yǒngyuǎn | 永遠 | 永远 | Adv. | forever | 4 |
| yòngpǐn | 用品 | 用品 | N. | product | 3 |
| yǒu péng zì yuǎnfāng lái, bú yì yuè hu? | 有朋自遠方來,不亦樂乎? | 有朋自远方来,不亦乐乎? | | isn't it pleasant to have friends coming from afar? | 4 |
| yòu | 右 | 右 | Adj. | right side | 3 |
| yuán | 元 | 元 | M.W. | dollar | 6 |
| yuánlái | 原來 | 原来 | Adv. | originally | 7 |
| yuèláiyuè . . . | 越來越...... | 越来越...... | | more and more . . . | 9 |
| yuèqì | 樂器 | 乐器 | N. | musical instrument | 2 |
| yuèshī | 樂師 | 乐师 | N. | musician | 2 |
| Yúnnán | 雲南 | 云南 | N. | Yunnan, a province in southwestern China | 7 |

# Z

| | | | | | |
|---|---|---|---|---|---|
| zánmen | 咱們 | 咱们 | N. | we, us | 1 |
| zǎo | 早 | 早 | Adj. | (to emphasize long ago) | 9 |
| zhàn | 站 | 站 | V. | to stand | 2 |
| zhǎng | 長 | 长 | V. | to grow | 4 |
| zhànghù | 帳戶 | 账户 | N. | account | 6 |
| zhǎo | 找 | 找 | V. | to seek, look for; to give (change) | 3 |
| zhǎodedào | 找得到 | 找得到 | | to be able to find | 7 |
| zhàopiàn | 照片 | 照片 | N. | photograph, picture | 2 |
| zhe | 著 | 着 | Part. | (indicates continuous or stationary status) | 2 |
| zhěnglǐ | 整理 | 整理 | V. | to arrange, sort out | 1 |
| zhīpiào | 支票 | 支票 | N. | check | 6 |
| zhídé | 值得 | 值得 | Adj. | worthwhile | 5 |
| zhíyuán | 職員 | 职员 | N. | staff, employee | 6 |
| zhǐshì | 只是 | 只是 | Adv. | just, simply | 4 |
| zhōngtóu | 鐘頭 | 钟头 | N. | hour | 9 |
| zhōngyú | 終於 | 终于 | Adv. | finally, at last | 5 |
| zhǒng | 種 | 种 | M.W. | kind | 6 |
| zhòngyào | 重要 | 重要 | Adj. | important | 9 |
| zhōumò | 週末 | 周末 | N. | weekend | 8 |
| zhǔyào | 主要 | 主要 | Adj. | main, major | 8 |
| zhǔyi | 主意 | 主意 | N. | idea | 1 |
| zhùyì | 注意 | 注意 | V. | to pay attention to | 9 |
| zhuǎn | 轉 | 转 | V. | to turn | 3 |
| zhuǎnjī | 轉機 | 转机 | N. | change planes; transfer | 5 |
| zhuāng | 裝 | 装 | V. | to install, assemble; load, pack | 1 |
| zhuàng | 撞 | 撞 | V. | to collide with, hit, strike | 1 |
| zhuàngguān | 壯觀 | 壮观 | Adj. | magnificent | 10 |
| zìdòng | 自動 | 自动 | Adj. | automatic | 6 |
| zìjǐ | 自己 | 自己 | N. | self | 2 |
| zǒngshì | 總是 | 总是 | Adv. | always | 9 |
| zuìhòu | 最後 | 最后 | Adv. | finally | 10 |
| zuǒ | 左 | 左 | Adj. | left side | 3 |
| zuòwèi | 座位 | 座位 | N. | seat | 2 |

## 英文索引 (英文索引)   ENGLISH GLOSSARY

Each entry lists the English meanings, traditional character, simplified character, Pinyin, part of speech, and lesson number.

## A

| English | Traditional | Simplified | Pinyin | Part of speech | Lesson |
|---|---|---|---|---|---|
| able to find | 找得到 | 找得到 | zhǎodedào | | 7 |
| about, with regard to | 關於 | 关于 | guānyú | *Prep.* | 8 |
| accept | 接受 | 接受 | jiēshòu | *V.* | 10 |
| according to, based on | 根據 | 根据 | gēnjù | *Prep.* | 10 |
| account | 帳戶 | 账户 | zhànghù | *N.* | 6 |
| action movie | 功夫片 | 功夫片 | gōngfupiān | *N.* | 8 |
| actor or actress, performer | 演員 | 演员 | yǎnyuán | *N.* | 2 |
| agree | 同意 | 同意 | tóngyì | *V.* | 8 |
| agree on | 說好了 | 说好了 | shuōhǎo le | | 10 |
| all included, altogether | 俱全 | 俱全 | jùquán | | 4 |
| all kinds of, various | 各種 | 各种 | gèzhǒng | *Adj.* | 2 |
| although | 雖然 | 虽然 | suīrán | *Conj.* | 5 |
| always | 一直 | 一直 | yìzhí | *Adv.* | 7 |
| always | 總是 | 总是 | zǒngshì | *Adv.* | 9 |
| ancient times | 古代 | 古代 | gǔdài | *Adj.* | 8 |
| appealing, attractive | 吸引人 | 吸引人 | xīyǐnrén | *Adj.* | 8 |
| application | 申請 | 申请 | shēnqǐng | *N.* | 6 |
| apply | 應用 | 应用 | yìngyòng | *V.* | 6 |
| apply, process | 辦 | 办 | bàn | *V.* | 7 |
| aroma | 香 | 香 | xiāng | *N.* | 4 |
| aromatic | 香 | 香 | xiāng | *Adj.* | 4 |
| arrange, sort out | 整理 | 整理 | zhěnglǐ | *V.* | 1 |
| as a matter of fact, actually | 其實 | 其实 | qíshí | *Adv.* | 7 |
| aspect | 方面 | 方面 | fāngmiàn | *N.* | 8 |
| ATM card | 取款卡 | 取款卡 | qǔkuǎnkǎ | *N.* | 6 |
| audience | 觀眾 | 观众 | guānzhòng | *N.* | 2 |
| automatic | 自動 | 自动 | zìdòng | *Adj.* | 6 |
| aviation, airline | 航空 | 航空 | hángkōng | *N.* | 3 |

## B

| English | Traditional | Simplified | Pinyin | Part of speech | Lesson |
|---|---|---|---|---|---|
| bad | 壞 | 坏 | huài | *Adj.* | 1 |
| bank | 銀行 | 银行 | yínháng | *N.* | 6 |
| banking machine | 取款機 | 取款机 | qǔkuǎnjī | *N.* | 6 |

| become | 變成 | 变成 | biànchéng | V.C. | 3 |
| Beijing, the capital of China | 北京 | 北京 | Běijīng | N. | 2 |
| best cooking | 拿手菜 | 拿手菜 | náshǒucài | N. | 4 |
| better than, well off; strong | 強 | 强 | qiáng | Adj. | 8 |
| blocks, diverging point of a road | 路口 | 路口 | lùkǒu | N. | 3 |
| blurred eyesight | 花 | 花 | huā | Adj. | 4 |
| body weight | 體重 | 体重 | tǐzhòng | N. | 9 |
| book, make reservations | 訂 | 订 | dìng | V. | 7 |
| box, suitcase | 箱子 | 箱子 | xiāngzi | N. | 1 |
| brilliant, wonderful | 精彩 | 精彩 | jīngcǎi | Adj. | 8 |
| broken | 破 | 破 | pò | Adj. | 1 |
| buildings (measure word) | 棟 | 栋 | dòng | M.W. | 3 |

## C

| cab fare | 車費 | 车费 | chēfèi | N. | 3 |
| cannot afford to buy | 買不起 | 买不起 | mǎibuqǐ | | 7 |
| cannot fall asleep | 睡不著 | 睡不着 | shuìbuzháo | V. | 4 |
| careful | 小心 | 小心 | xiǎoxīn | Adj. | 1 |
| cars (measure word) | 部 | 部 | bù | M.W. | 8 |
| cash | 現金 | 现金 | xiànjīn | N. | 6 |
| catch, catch up with | 趕上 | 赶上 | gǎnshàng | V.C. | 5 |
| change | 換 | 换 | huàn | V. | 6 |
| change | 變化 | 变化 | biànhuà | V. | 3 |
| change | 變化 | 变化 | biànhuà | N. | 3 |
| change planes, transfer | 轉機 | 转机 | zhuǎnjī | N. | 5 |
| check | 支票 | 支票 | zhīpiào | N. | 6 |
| check | 查 | 查 | chá | V. | 7 |
| check book | 簿 | 簿 | bù | N. | 6 |
| Chinese theater performance (measure word) | 齣 | 出 | chū | M.W. | 2 |
| clean, sweep | 掃 | 扫 | sǎo | V. | 1 |
| climb | 爬 | 爬 | pá | V. | 10 |
| close | 關上 | 关上 | guānshàng | V. | 1 |
| clothes | 衣服 | 衣服 | yīfu | N. | 1 |
| clothes, costume | 服裝 | 服装 | fúzhuāng | N. | 2 |
| cloudy | 陰 | 阴 | yīn | Adj. | 5 |
| coat | 外套 | 外套 | wàitào | N. | 1 |
| collaborate by dividing up the work | 分工合作 | 分工合作 | fēngōnghézuò | | 1 |
| collide with, hit, strike | 撞 | 撞 | zhuàng | V. | 1 |
| color | 顏色 | 颜色 | yánsè | N. | 8 |
| computer | 計算機 | 计算机 | jìsuànjī | N. | 3 |

| continuous or stationary status | 著 | 着 | zhe | *Part.* | 2 |
| control | 控制 | 控制 | kòngzhì | *V.* | 9 |
| convenient | 方便 | 方便 | fāngbiàn | *Adj.* | 6 |
| cool, cold | 涼 | 凉 | liáng | *Adj.* | 4 |
| counter | 櫃檯 | 柜台 | guìtái | *N.* | 6 |
| courteous expression used by the gift receiver: to spend money, go to such expense | 破費 | 破费 | pòfèi | *V.O* | 4 |
| cousin | 表妹 | 表妹 | biǎomèi | *N.* | 8 |
| credit card | 信用卡 | 信用卡 | xìnyòngkǎ | *N.* | 6 |

# D

| daytime | 白天 | 白天 | báitiān | *N.* | 4 |
| dead | 死 | 死 | sǐ | *Adj.* | 1 |
| delay | 誤點 | 误点 | wùdiǎn | *N.* | 5 |
| delay | 誤點 | 误点 | wùdiǎn | *V.O.* | 5 |
| deposit | 存 | 存 | cún | *V.* | 6 |
| describe | 描寫 | 描写 | miáoxiě | *V.* | 8 |
| description, exposition | 描寫 | 描写 | miáoxiě | *N.* | 8 |
| develop | 發展 | 发展 | fāzhǎn | *V.* | 3 |
| development | 發展 | 发展 | fāzhǎn | *N.* | 3 |
| dexterous, agile, flexible | 靈活 | 灵活 | línghuó | *Adj.* | 9 |
| die | 死 | 死 | sǐ | *V.* | 1 |
| direct (a film) | 導演 | 导演 | dǎoyǎn | *V.* | 8 |
| direction | 方向 | 方向 | fāngxiàng | *N.* | 5 |
| director | 導演 | 导演 | dǎoyǎn | *N.* | 8 |
| dollar | 元 | 元 | yuán | *M.W.* | 6 |
| don't | 別 | 别 | bié | *Aux.* | 1 |
| door | 門 | 门 | mén | *N.* | 1 |
| driver | 司機 | 司机 | sījī | *N.* | 3 |
| drum | 鼓 | 鼓 | gǔ | *N.* | 2 |

# E

| effect | 效果 | 效果 | xiàoguǒ | *N.* | 8 |
| electronics | 電子 | 电子 | diànzǐ | *N.* | 3 |
| emotion | 感情 | 感情 | gǎnqíng | *N.* | 8 |
| employee | 職員 | 职员 | zhíyuán | *N.* | 6 |
| energetic, high-spirited | 精神 | 精神 | jīngshen | *Adj.* | 4 |
| energetic, high-spirited, proud | 神氣 | 神气 | shénqì | *Adj.* | 2 |

| | | | | | |
|---|---|---|---|---|---|
| enough | 夠 | 够 | gòu | *Adj.* | 6 |
| envy | 羨慕 | 羨慕 | xiànmù | *V.* | 7 |
| even | 連 | 连 | lián | *Prep.* | 8 |
| everyone (when addressing an audience) | 各位 | 各位 | gèwèi | *Pron.* | 3 |
| exchange | 兌換 | 兌換 | duìhuàn | *N.* | 6 |
| exchange | 兌換 | 兌換 | duìhuàn | *V.* | 6 |
| exchange rate | 匯率 | 汇率 | huìlǜ | *N.* | 6 |
| exposed to many great new things | 大開眼界 | 大开眼界 | dàkāiyǎnjiè | | 5 |
| eye(s) | 眼睛 | 眼睛 | yǎnjīng | *N.* | 4 |

## F

| | | | | | |
|---|---|---|---|---|---|
| face | 臉 | 脸 | liǎn | *N.* | 2 |
| factual, objective | 客觀 | 客观 | kèguān | *Adj.* | 8 |
| farmland, cropland | 農田 | 农田 | nóngtián | *N.* | 3 |
| feel, sense | 感 | 感 | gǎn | *V.* | 8 |
| fill in/up | 填 | 填 | tián | *V.* | 6 |
| films (measure word) | 部 | 部 | bù | *M.W.* | 8 |
| finally, at last | 終於 | 终于 | zhōngyú | *Adv.* | 5 |
| finally, in the end | 最後 | 最后 | zuìhòu | *Adv.* | 10 |
| finish | 完 | 完 | wán | *V.* | 8 |
| flight | 班機 | 班机 | bānjī | *N.* | 5 |
| flight, flying | 飛行 | 飞行 | fēixíng | *N.* | 5 |
| food and drink, eating | 飲食 | 饮食 | yǐnshí | *N.* | 9 |
| foot (US and UK measurement) | 呎 | 呎 | chǐ | *N.* | 9 |
| foreign currency | 外幣 | 外币 | wàibì | *N.* | 6 |
| forever | 永遠 | 永远 | yǒngyuǎn | *Adv.* | 4 |
| forget | 忘 | 忘 | wàng | *V.* | 1 |
| form | 表 | 表 | biǎo | *N.* | 6 |
| form | 單子 | 单子 | dānzi | *N.* | 6 |
| full | 滿 | 满 | mǎn | *Adj.* | 2 |
| full | 飽 | 饱 | bǎo | *Adj.* | 4 |
| furthermore | 而且 | 而且 | érqiě | *Conj.* | 8 |

## G

| | | | | | |
|---|---|---|---|---|---|
| get used to | 適應 | 适应 | shìyìng | *V.* | 4 |
| girl | 女孩子 | 女孩子 | nǚháizi | *N.* | 9 |
| gray hair | 白頭髮 | 白头发 | báitóufa | *N.* | 4 |
| Great Wall, the | 長城 | 长城 | Chángchéng | *N.* | 2 |
| group | 團 | 团 | tuán | *N.* | 5 |
| grow | 長 | 长 | zhǎng | *V.* | 4 |

# H

| hang | 掛 | 挂 | guà | V. | 1 |
|------|-----|-----|------|------|---|
| have enough time to | 來得及 | 来得及 | láidejí | | 7 |
| healthy | 健康 | 健康 | jiànkāng | Adj. | 4 |
| height, stature | 個子 | 个子 | gèzi | N. | 9 |
| help | 幫助 | 帮助 | bāngzhù | N. | 10 |
| hero | 好漢 | 好汉 | hǎohàn | N. | 10 |
| high | 高 | 高 | gāo | Adj. | 6 |
| high-rise building | 大廈 | 大厦 | dàshà | N. | 5 |
| history | 歷史 | 历史 | lìshǐ | N. | 8 |
| hold, take | 拿 | 拿 | ná | V. | 2 |
| holiday | 假日 | 假日 | jiàrì | N. | 3 |
| home-made meal | 家常便飯 | 家常便饭 | jiāchángbiànfàn | N. | 4 |
| Hong Kong | 香港 | 香港 | Xiānggǎng | N. | 7 |
| honorific term used when addressing a teacher's wife | 師母 | 师母 | shīmǔ | N. | 4 |
| hope | 希望 | 希望 | xīwàng | V. | 10 |
| hope | 希望 | 希望 | xīwàng | N. | 10 |
| hospitable | 好客 | 好客 | hàokè | Adj. | 5 |
| host, treat | 請客 | 请客 | qǐngkè | V. | 1 |
| hotel, hostel | 旅館 | 旅馆 | lǚguǎn | N. | 3 |
| hour | 鐘頭 | 钟头 | zhōngtóu | N. | 9 |

# I

| idea | 主意 | 主意 | zhǔyi | N. | 1 |
|------|-----|-----|------|------|---|
| if | 如果 | 如果 | rúguǒ | Conj. | 7 |
| if | 要是 | 要是 | yàoshì | Conj. | 7 |
| important | 重要 | 重要 | zhòngyào | Adj. | 9 |
| inch (US and UK measurment) | 吋 | 吋 | cùn | N. | 9 |
| inexpensive | 便宜 | 便宜 | piányi | Adj. | 7 |
| inferior to, not as good as | 不如 | 不如 | bùrú | V. | 8 |
| install, assemble; load, pack | 裝 | 装 | zhuāng | V. | 1 |
| interest | 利息 | 利息 | lìxī | N. | 6 |
| interest | 興趣 | 兴趣 | xìngqù | N. | 8 |
| interest rate | 利率 | 利率 | lìlǜ | N. | 6 |
| intersection | 交叉口 | 交叉口 | jiāochākǒu | N. | 3 |
| Isn't it pleasant to have friends coming from afar? | 有朋自遠方來，不亦樂乎? | 有朋自远方来，不亦乐乎? | Yǒu péng zì yuǎnfāng lái, bú yì yuè hu? | | 4 |
| it | 它 | 它 | tā | Pron. | 8 |
| it's a deal | 一言為定 | 一言为定 | yìyánwéidìng | | 2 |

# J

| joke | 笑話 | 笑话 | xiàohua | N. | 5 |
| just, simply | 只是 | 只是 | zhǐshì | Adv. | 4 |

# K

| kilometer | 公里 | 公里 | gōnglǐ | N. | 3 |
| kind, type of (measure word) | 種 | 种 | zhǒng | M.W. | 6 |
| knife | 刀 | 刀 | dāo | N. | 2 |
| Kunming, the capital city of Yunnan Province | 昆明 | 昆明 | Kūnmíng | N. | 7 |

# L

| land, descend | 降落 | 降落 | jiàngluò | V. | 3 |
| landlord | 房東 | 房东 | fángdōng | N. | 1 |
| left side | 左 | 左 | zuǒ | Adj. | 3 |
| light | 輕 | 轻 | qīng | Adj. | 9 |
| long ago | 早 | 早 | zǎo | Adj. | 9 |
| lose weight | 減肥 | 减肥 | jiǎnféi | V.O. | 9 |
| low | 低 | 低 | dī | Adj. | 6 |
| luggage, baggage | 行李 | 行李 | xíngli | N. | 1 |

# M

| machines (measure word) | 部 | 部 | bù | M.W. | 8 |
| magnificent | 壯觀 | 壮观 | zhuàngguān | Adj. | 10 |
| mail | 寄 | 寄 | jì | V. | 6 |
| main, major | 主要 | 主要 | zhǔyào | Adj. | 8 |
| make payment | 付款 | 付款 | fùkuǎn | V.O. | 10 |
| make, cause, induce | 鬧 | 闹 | nào | V. | 5 |
| manage to find time | 抽空 | 抽空 | chōukòng | V.O. | 7 |
| meter | 公尺 | 公尺 | gōngchǐ | N. | 3 |
| minority nationalities | 少數民族 | 少数民族 | shǎoshùmínzú | N. | 7 |
| mirror | 鏡子 | 镜子 | jìngzi | N. | 1 |
| money | 款 | 款 | kuǎn | N. | 6 |
| more | 更 | 更 | gèng | Adv. | 9 |
| more and more . . . | 越來越…… | 越来越…… | yuèláiyuè . . . | | 9 |
| move backwards | 倒 | 倒 | dào | V. | 1 |
| Mt. Huang (Yellow Mountain, a famous tourist attraction in Anhui Province, central China) | 黃山 | 黃山 | Huángshān | N. | 10 |

| musical instrument | 樂器 | 乐器 | yuèqì | N. | 2 |
| musician | 樂師 | 乐师 | yuèshī | N. | 2 |

## N

| nearby | 附近 | 附近 | fùjìn | N. | 1 |
| New Year cake, rice cake | 年糕 | 年糕 | niángāo | N. | 4 |
| no wonder | 怪不得 | 怪不得 | guàibude | | 9 |
| not (used in Classical Chinese) | 非 | 非 | fēi | Adv. | 10 |
| not a big deal | 小意思 | 小意思 | xiǎoyìsi | | 4 |
| not very different, similar, about the same | 差不多 | 差不多 | chàbuduō | Adv. | 6 |

## O

| of course | 當然 | 当然 | dāngrán | Adv. | 6 |
| on that day | 當天 | 当天 | dāngtiān | Adv. | 10 |
| open | 開 | 开 | kāi | V. | 6 |
| original, genuine, authentic | 地道 | 地道 | dìdao | Adj. | 4 |
| originally | 本來 | 本来 | běnlái | Adv. | 3 |
| originally | 原來 | 原来 | yuánlái | Adv. | 7 |
| other people | 別人 | 别人 | biérén | N. | 5 |

## P

| paint, draw | 畫 | 画 | huà | V. | 2 |
| painting | 畫 | 画 | huà | N. | 2 |
| passerby | 路人 | 路人 | lùrén | N. | 3 |
| pay attention to | 注意 | 注意 | zhùyì | V. | 9 |
| . . . percent (%) | 百分之…… | 百分之…… | bǎifēnzhi . . . | Num. | 6 |
| perform | 表演 | 表演 | biǎoyǎn | V. | 2 |
| performance | 表演 | 表演 | biǎoyǎn | N. | 2 |
| period of 10 days in a month | 旬 | 旬 | xún | N. | 10 |
| persist, persevere | 堅持 | 坚持 | jiānchí | V. | 9 |
| photograph, picture | 照片 | 照片 | zhàopiàn | N. | 2 |
| picturesque scenic beauty | 風景如畫 | 风景如画 | fēngjǐngrúhuà | | 7 |
| place, put | 擺 | 摆 | bǎi | V. | 2 |
| place, put | 放 | 放 | fàng | V. | 1 |
| plan | 打算 | 打算 | dǎsuàn | V. | 7 |
| plan | 打算 | 打算 | dǎsuàn | N. | 7 |
| plan | 計畫 | 计划 | jìhuà | V. | 10 |
| plan | 計畫 | 计划 | jìhuà | N. | 10 |

| plane ticket | 機票 | 机票 | jīpiào | N. | 7 |
| play, drama | 戲 | 戏 | xì | N. | 2 |
| play (a stringed, musical instrument); to pull | 拉 | 拉 | lā | V. | 2 |
| play (the drum); to hit | 打 | 打 | dǎ | V. | 2 |
| play, pluck; strike | 彈奏 | 弹奏 | tánzòu | V. | 2 |
| pound (measure word for weight measurement) | 磅 | 磅 | bàng | M.W. | 9 |
| probably | 大概 | 大概 | dàgài | Adv. | 7 |
| process, apply | 辦 | 办 | bàn | V. | 7 |
| product | 用品 | 用品 | yòngpǐn | N. | 3 |
| prosperous | 繁榮 | 繁荣 | fánróng | Adj. | 5 |

## R

| realization (at end of sentence) | 喔 | 喔 | ō | Int. | 3 |
| relative | 親戚 | 亲戚 | qīnqi | N. | 7 |
| relieved, relaxed | 輕鬆 | 轻松 | qīngsōng | Adj. | 8 |
| relish, with keen pleasure | 津津有味 | 津津有味 | jīnjīnyǒuwèi | | 5 |
| Renminbi, RMB (name of currency used in mainland China) | 人民幣 | 人民币 | Rénmínbì | N. | 3 |
| rent | 出租 | 出租 | chūzū | V. | 3 |
| require | 需要 | 需要 | xūyào | V. | 9 |
| research report | 研究報告 | 研究报告 | yánjiū bàogào | N. | 8 |
| responsible for | 負責 | 负责 | fùzé | V. | 1 |
| return with tremendous accomplishment | 滿載而歸 | 满载而归 | mǎnzàiérguī | | 10 |
| right side | 右 | 右 | yòu | Adj. | 3 |
| road, avenue, street | 馬路 | 马路 | mǎlù | N. | 3 |

## S

| safe | 安全 | 安全 | ānquán | Adj. | 10 |
| save (money) | 儲蓄 | 储蓄 | chǔxù | V. | |
| savings | 儲蓄 | 储蓄 | chǔxù | N. | 6 |
| scene | 場面 | 场面 | chǎngmiàn | N. | 8 |
| seat | 座位 | 座位 | zuòwèi | N. | 2 |
| seat belt, safety belt | 安全帶 | 安全带 | ānquándài | N. | 3 |
| seek, look for; give change | 找 | 找 | zhǎo | V. | 3 |
| seldom, rarely | 難得 | 难得 | nándé | Adv. | 4 |
| self | 自己 | 自己 | zìjǐ | N. | 2 |
| shadow | 影子 | 影子 | yǐngzi | N. | 8 |

| short | 矮 | 矮 | ǎi | *Adj.* | 9 |
|---|---|---|---|---|---|
| show (movies); to place | 放 | 放 | fàng | *V.* | 8 |
| sleepy, dozy | 睏 | 困 | kùn | *Adj.* | 4 |
| slim | 苗條 | 苗条 | miáotiao | *Adj.* | 9 |
| snack | 小吃 | 小吃 | xiǎochī | *N.* | 5 |
| snack bar | 小吃店 | 小吃店 | xiǎochīdiàn | *N.* | 3 |
| some (measure word) | 些 | 些 | xiē | *M.W.* | 4 |
| sort out, arrange | 整理 | 整理 | zhěnglǐ | *V.* | 1 |
| southern part | 南方 | 南方 | nánfāng | *N.* | 7 |
| special technique | 特技 | 特技 | tèjì | *N.* | 8 |
| specially | 特地 | 特地 | tèdì | *Adv.* | 4 |
| spring-like all year | 四季如春 | 四季如春 | sìjìrúchūn | | 7 |
| staff, employee | 職員 | 职员 | zhíyuán | *N.* | 6 |
| stage (for performance) | 舞台 | 舞台 | wǔtái | *N.* | 2 |
| stand | 站 | 站 | zhàn | *V.* | 2 |
| store | 商店 | 商店 | shāngdiàn | *N.* | 10 |
| story | 故事 | 故事 | gùshi | *N.* | 8 |
| story, plot | 情節 | 情节 | qíngjié | *N.* | 8 |
| straight | 一直 | 一直 | yìzhí | | 3 |
| street | 街道 | 街道 | jiēdào | *N.* | 4 |
| strong; better than, well off | 強 | 强 | qiáng | *Adj.* | 8 |
| succeed in buying | 買到 | 买到 | mǎidào | *V.C.* | 7 |
| surpass | 超過 | 超过 | chāoguò | *V.* | 9 |
| sweet food | 甜食 | 甜食 | tiánshí | *N.* | 9 |

## T

| take (means of transportation) | 搭乘 | 搭乘 | dāchéng | *V.* | 3 |
|---|---|---|---|---|---|
| taste | 味道 | 味道 | wèidao | *N.* | 4 |
| tell | 告訴 | 告诉 | gàosu | *V.* | 10 |
| thin, slim, skinny | 瘦 | 瘦 | shòu | *Adj.* | 9 |
| thousand | 千 | 千 | qiān | *Num.* | 6 |
| ticket price | 票價 | 票价 | piàojià | *N.* | 8 |
| tie, fasten, buckle up | 繫上 | 系上 | jìshàng | *V.C.* | 3 |
| time difference, jetlag | 時差 | 时差 | shíchā | *N.* | 4 |
| tired, get tired of | 累 | 累 | lèi | *Adj.* | 1 |
| toast, cheers | 乾杯 | 干杯 | gānbēi | *V.O.* | 4 |
| together, get together | 相聚 | 相聚 | xiāngjù | *V.* | 4 |
| tone softener (used at end of sentences) | 呀 | 呀 | ya | *Part.* | 1 |
| top | 頂 | 顶 | dǐng | *N.* | 10 |
| tour | 旅遊 | 旅游 | lǚyóu | *N.* | 7 |
| toward | 往 | 往 | wǎng | *Prep.* | 3 |

| toward | 向 | 向 | xiàng | Prep. | 3 |
| toward, to | 對 | 对 | duì | Prep. | 8 |
| traffic light | 紅綠燈 | 红绿灯 | hónglǜdēng | N. | 3 |
| travel agency | 旅行社 | 旅行社 | lǚxíngshè | N. | 7 |
| traveler, passenger | 旅客 | 旅客 | lǚkè | N. | 3 |
| tree | 樹 | 树 | shù | N. | 1 |
| trunk (car) | 後車箱 | 后车箱 | hòuchēxiāng | N. | 3 |
| turn | 拐 | 拐 | guǎi | V. | 3 |
| turn | 轉 | 转 | zhuǎn | V. | 3 |
| turn, detour | 彎兒 | 弯儿 | wār | N. | 3 |
| twists and turns, complicated | 曲折 | 曲折 | qūzhé | Adj. | 10 |
| two-stringed, bowed instruments | 胡琴 | 胡琴 | húqín | N. | 2 |

## U

| US dollar | 美金 | 美金 | Měijīn | N. | 6 |
| used to | 習慣 | 习惯 | xíguàn | V. | 4 |
| utensil with a handle (measure word) | 把 | 把 | bǎ | M.W. | 2 |

## V

| various, all kinds of | 各種 | 各种 | gèzhǒng | Adj. | 2 |
| very | 挺 | 挺 | tǐng | Adv. | 5 |
| very, especially | 特別 | 特别 | tèbié | Adv. | 8 |
| visa | 簽證 | 签证 | qiānzhèng | N. | 7 |
| visit | 拜訪 | 拜访 | bàifǎng | V. | 7 |
| visit | 拜訪 | 拜访 | bàifǎng | N. | 7 |
| vitamin | 維生素 | 维生素 | wéishēngsù | N. | 4 |

## W

| wall | 牆 | 墙 | qiáng | N. | 2 |
| warm-hearted, enthusiastic | 熱情 | 热情 | rèqíng | Adj. | 5 |
| we, us | 咱們 | 咱们 | zánmen | N. | 1 |
| website | 網站 | 网站 | wǎngzhàn | N. | 7 |
| weekend | 週末 | 周末 | zhōumò | N. | 8 |
| window | 窗 | 窗 | chuāng | N. | 1 |
| winter vacation | 寒假 | 寒假 | hánjià | N. | 7 |
| with regard to, about | 關於 | 关于 | guānyú | Prep. | 8 |
| withdraw | 取 | 取 | qǔ | V. | 6 |
| worthwhile | 值得 | 值得 | zhídé | Adj. | 5 |

## Y

| young | 年輕 | 年轻 | niánqīng | *Adj.* | 4 |
| Yunnan, a province in southwestern China | 雲南 | 云南 | Yúnnán | *N.* | 7 |

## Z

| zero | 零 | 零 | líng | *Num.* | 10 |

## 寫字簿的生字 (写字簿的生字)
# CHARACTERS IN THE CHARACTER BOOK

The following list shows the 260 characters that appear in the Character Book, grouped by the lesson in which they are first introduced. Students are required to memorize how to read and write these key characters to build up their literacy skills. The items and number of new characters introduced in each lesson are carefully selected and controlled, and are provided in the list.

### 繁體字版 Traditional Character Version

**(1) 第一課　搬家** (27 characters)
倒 別 樹 撞 壞 呀 鏡 破 合 主 負 責 李 裝 掃 整 理 箱 衣 掛 累 死 附 忘 窗 套 咱

**(2) 第二課　文藝經驗** (31 characters)
牆 著 照 片 北 台 擺 各 種 器 演 表 鼓 拉 胡 琴 彈 奏 已 齣 戲 畫 臉 拿 刀 神 座 滿 眾 站 長

**(3) 第三課　問路** (36 characters)
往 降 落 全 繫 計 算 品 搭 乘 航 棟 交 叉 口 左 拐 直 里 展 變 化 農 田 成 喔 尺 山 燈 向 右 轉 彎 費 民 幣

**(4) 第四課　請客和做客** (28 characters)
母 維 素 永 康 輕 特 涼 精 髮 眼 睛 花 適 差 睏 街 慣 味 香 俱 飽 便 相 聚 乾 亦 乎

**(5) 第五課　我的中國行－復習** (17 characters)
陰 終 於 誤 趕 情 津 界 團 鬧 笑 繁 榮 廈 雖 挺 值

**(6) 第六課　開銀行帳戶** (28 characters)
銀 帳 戶 存 款 取 利 率 儲 蓄 之 支 職 低 夠 單 填 千 元 金 寄 簿 卡 當 換 匯 兌 櫃

**(7) 第七課　旅遊與簽證** (23 characters)
寒 遊 社 訂 羨 慕 親 戚 原 抽 拜 訪 查 宜 季 數 族 果 簽 證 辦 概 及

**(8) 第八課　中國電影** (27 characters)
連 報 告 鬆 強 完 導 夫 它 節 引 古 代 故 彩 描 歷 史 趣 而 且 技 效 顏 週 末 價

**(9)** 第九課　健身與健康 (25 characters)

越 需 瘦 減 肥 堅 持 磅 怪 苗 孩 控 制 飲 食 注 甜 早 矮 呎 吋 超 靈 總 更

**(10)** 第十課　假期在中國—復習 (18 characters)

希 望 旬 受 商 根 據 零 爬 頂 助 漢 訴 壯 曲 折 載 歸

## 简体字版 Simplified Character Version

**(1)** 第一课　搬家 (27 characters)

倒 别 树 撞 坏 呀 镜 破 合 主 负 责 李 装 扫 整 理 箱 衣 挂 累 死 附 忘 窗
套 咱

**(2)** 第二课　文艺经验 (31 characters)

墙 着 照 片 北 台 摆 各 种 器 演 表 鼓 拉 胡 琴 弹 奏 己 出 戏 画 脸 拿 刀
神 座 满 众 站 长

**(3)** 第三课　问路 (36 characters)

往 降 落 全 系 计 算 品 搭 乘 航 栋 交 叉 口 左 拐 直 里 展 变 化 农 田 成
喔 尺 山 灯 向 右 转 弯 费 民 币

**(4)** 第四课　请客和做客 (28 characters)

母 维 素 永 康 轻 特 凉 精 发 眼 睛 花 适 差 困 街 惯 味 香 俱 饱 便 相 聚
干 亦 乎

**(5)** 第五课　我的中国行—复习 (17 characters)

阴 终 于 误 赶 情 津 界 团 闹 笑 繁 荣 厦 虽 挺 值

**(6)** 第六课　开银行账户 (28 characters)

银 账 户 存 款 取 利 率 储 蓄 之 支 职 低 够 单 填 千 元 金 寄 簿 卡 当 换
汇 兑 柜

**(7)** 第七课　旅游与签证 (23 characters)

寒 游 社 订 羡 慕 亲 戚 原 抽 拜 访 查 宜 季 数 族 果 签 证 办 概 及

**(8)** 第八课　中国电影 (27 characters)

连 报 告 松 强 完 导 夫 它 节 引 古 代 故 彩 描 历 史 趣 而 且 技 效 颜 周
末 价

**(9)** 第九课　健身与健康 (25 characters)

越 需 瘦 减 肥 坚 持 磅 怪 苗 孩 控 制 饮 食 注 甜 早 矮 呎 吋 超 灵 总 更

**(10)** 第十课　假期在中国—复习 (18 characters)

希 望 旬 受 商 根 据 零 爬 顶 助 汉 诉 壮 曲 折 载 归